Fighting for Control

Justice, Power, and Politics

Heather Ann Thompson and Rhonda Y. Williams, *editors*

The Justice, Power, and Politics series publishes new works in history that explore the myriad struggles for justice, battles for power, and shifts in politics that have shaped the United States over time. Through the lenses of justice, power, and politics, the series seeks to broaden scholarly debates about America's past as well as to inform public discussions about its future.

A complete list of books published in Justice, Power, and Politics is available at https://uncpress.org/series/justice-power-politics.

Fighting for Control

Power, Reproductive Care, and Race
in the US-Mexico Borderlands

· ·

LINA-MARIA MURILLO

The University of North Carolina Press Chapel Hill

This book was made possible with generous support from the University of Iowa's Office of the Vice President for Research and College of Liberal Arts and Sciences.

Set in Charis by Westchester Publishing Services
Manufactured in the United States of America

Library of Congress Cataloging-in-Publication Data
Names: Murillo, Lina-Maria, author.
Title: Fighting for control : power, reproductive care, and race in the
    US-Mexico borderlands / Lina-Maria Murillo.
Other titles: Justice, power, and politics.
Description: Chapel Hill : The University of North Carolina Press, 2025. |
    Series: Justice, power, and politics | Includes bibliographical references
    and index.
Identifiers: LCCN 2024035440 | ISBN 9781469682587 (cloth ; alk. paper) |
    ISBN 9781469682594 (pbk. ; alk. paper) | ISBN 9781469682600 (epub) |
    ISBN 9781469682617 (pdf)
Subjects: LCSH: Planned Parenthood Federation of America—Influence. |
    Catholic Church—Mexican-American Border Region—Influence. |
    Reproductive rights—Mexican-American Border Region. | Reproductive
    health services—Mexican-American Border Region. | Women—Mexican-
    American Border Region—Social conditions. | BISAC: SOCIAL SCIENCE /
    Ethnic Studies / Caribbean & Latin American Studies | HISTORY /
    United States / State & Local / Southwest (AZ, NM, OK, TX)
Classification: LCC HQ766 .M83 2025 | DDC 363.9/609721—
    dc23/eng/20240820
LC record available at https://lccn.loc.gov/2024035440

Cover art designed by Christin Apodaca.

This book will be made open access within three years of publication thanks to Path to Open, a program developed in partnership between JSTOR, the American Council of Learned Societies (ACLS), University of Michigan Press, and The University of North Carolina Press to bring about equitable access and impact for the entire scholarly community, including authors, researchers, libraries, and university presses around the world. Learn more at https://about.jstor.org/path-to-open/.

This book is dedicated to my children and everyone in the movement for reproductive liberation. The future belongs to us.

All over the world, women are fighting for control over their lives; they are fighting against those who kill their children and destroy their homes; they are fighting for decent jobs and decent wages; they are fighting for daycare centers and the right to bring up their children in decent conditions. We who fight for free abortions on demand join them in that struggle. We know that we will not be able to take control of our lives until every demand is won.

—Catha Maslow, Jane Pincus, Mary Summers, and Karen Weinstein,
   Abortion and Women's Rights 1970

Before,
When rains came in the night
I dreamed of having babies
Of joy, happy babies,
Well-fed, well-fathered.

The drought endures though.
Babies and ghosts of babies
Cry and cry.

Did you ever wish
Never to have brought
Children into this world
My daughter asked.

So did I she whispered.
The men? They don't understand
Do they?

—Bernice Zamora, "Love, A Mother's" (1992)

Contents

Figures

The Past as Prologue

· ·

I was born and raised on the Eastside of San Jose, California—on the very edge of what some consider the US-Mexico borderlands.[1] The Eastside is a predominantly Latino, mostly Chicano and Mexicano, enclave of the Silicon Valley. My parents are Colombian immigrants, and they were welcomed into this community when they arrived in 1980. Many of my friends were also born and raised on the Eastside, going through elementary school and graduating together at the end of the twentieth century. Although my generation came of age in the late 1980s and 1990s, growing into adolescence in the shadow of the HIV/AIDS epidemic, abortion clinic bombings, and Reaganomics, we feared little, including Y2K. By comparison to today's teenagers, I lived a relatively carefree youth.[2]

My high school, James Lick, was less than a block away from Planned Parenthood—there were several in the city, and given the population on the Eastside, I am not surprised we had one so close. It sat flanked by nondescript stores along Alum Rock Avenue and across from one of the most famous bakeries in the city, Peter's Bakery. It's still known for a delicious burnt almond cake. The Alum Rock Public Library stood guard at the intersection of Alum Rock and White Road—many of us often popped in to grab a book while we waited for the bus to take us downtown. We thought nothing of Planned Parenthood's proximity to St. John Vianney, the Catholic church, a mere four blocks away. All the while, the beautiful rolling Evergreen Foothills perpetually embraced our small corner of the valley. This landscape was our world.

Some of my friends, including myself, were sexually active in high school. We spoke of the need to get checked for sexually transmitted infections, including HIV/AIDS, chlamydia, and herpes. We talked to each other about various kinds of birth control, such as condoms and the Pill. We accompanied one another on appointments to Planned Parenthood and walked across the street to eat cake or bread at the bakery afterward. We grew up listening to Salt-N-Pepa, Lil Kim, Foxy Brown, Selena, and Jennifer Lopez, who sang about sex, love, pleasure, and romance. At fifteen and sixteen, we were still kids, yet we knew we wanted to enjoy our bodies (and fall in love or not) on our own terms.

Did some of my friends and acquaintances get pregnant? Yes. And they paid dearly for it. Remember, this was the time when teen pregnancy was frowned upon. Conservatives lashed out at "ghetto youths" having too many babies, supposedly because these young mothers only sought to rip off the welfare system.[3] Unlike the conservative movement of today, teen pregnancy was highly stigmatized and seen as a scourge among young people of color.[4] I knew several young women who were banished to that *other* school—the one reserved for teen moms. Our high school counselors rarely spoke to us about college admissions or scholarships. We were counseled to *not* get pregnant, *not* do drugs, and *not* go to "juvie" (juvenile detention). The system expected very little of children growing up on San Jose's Eastside.

Early on, I made up my mind to take care of myself and still have fun—most of my friends did the same. We were fortunate to do so. I fully enjoyed my youth and the sexual freedoms I afforded myself. I had boyfriends—some serious, some not—and I made sure to make appointments or come for drop-in hours with Planned Parenthood's clinicians to monitor my sexual health. Before smartphones, we would wait hours in the clinic's lobby, with nothing but Planned Parenthood's informational pamphlets to read. It was there that I gained a greater understanding of contraception, ways to prevent sexually transmitted infections, and even information about healthy relationships, including how young women could protect themselves from intimate partner violence, abuse, and sexual assault.

Most of us were free to do this without our parents' knowledge. At the time, we did not need parental consent to make an appointment at Planned Parenthood, and since the clinic worked on a sliding scale, we paid little for sound care. We could, without shame or judgment, go about our sexual lives, exploring their fullness and complexities with little oversight from the government or our parents. By today's standards, we had relatively good sexual education courses at school and the cultural moment seemed to empower our sense of bodily autonomy. At a very young age, I learned to be responsible for my body. In fact, the only time shame was used among my peers was to prod the few sexually active girls who hesitated when making an appointment at our local clinic.

The issue of abortion came up when needed. We knew Planned Parenthood offered those services. If anyone ever sought to exercise their constitutional right to end a pregnancy, we understood that that was their decision to make, and they could find a safe place to get one.

This was a different time. It is almost unthinkable now even though it was less than thirty years ago. We were the generation that second-wave feminists, reproductive justice activists, and many of our mothers and grandmothers dreamed about. We were here. It wasn't always easy, but it was good. I've tried to explain that moment to my children, but it seems otherworldly to them.

I wrote this book, in part, to capture how the politics of sexual and reproductive liberation, especially for Latinas and women of color, have changed over time. As historians often note, progress is not linear. Culture, law, and society shift the power dynamics that provide brief moments of liberation for us. It is critical to understand under what circumstances we can exercise even small amounts of control over our sexual and reproductive lives. We have always created community spaces of support and care that undergird these periods of liberatory existence. History can provide some instruction on how we can imagine and create more liberatory futures.

Introduction

Reproductive Control and Care in the US-Mexico Borderlands

· ·

El Paso, at the time, had one of the largest maternal and infant death rates
among cities of its size in the United States. Ignorance and superstition
among the poverty stricken was rampant.
—Betty Mary Smith Goetting, 1959

It is generally held throughout the Mexican-American community of South
El Paso that the existing health and social welfare systems are not sensitive
to the community problems and needs. Because of the insensitive methods
used in the delivery of health services, several deterrents to seeking, finding
and receiving adequate health care in South El Paso exist.
—Amelia Castillo, circa 1970

In our business, our main capital is the value, the energy, and commitment
of people. Our main objective is to sell ideas, technology education, health,
love, dreams, and hope to the poorest in Mexico.
—Guadalupe Arizpe de la Vega, 1985

Women dominated the movements for reproductive control and justice in
the El Paso-Ciudad Juárez borderlands during the twentieth century. In the
preceding epigraphs, three of the most important leaders in these movements, Betty Mary Goetting, Amelia Castillo, and Guadalupe Arizpe de la
Vega, describe varying visions for reproductive health care. Their positions
toward reproductive health, justice, and rights reflect the communities they
represent, the history of the region, and how reproductive control and care
shaped the lives of thousands of mostly Mexican-origin women in the borderlands for nearly a century. In the early 1910s, birth control advocates
slowly infused demographic fears with eugenic ideology—an amalgamation
of eighteenth-century economist Thomas Malthus's idea linking population
growth to resource depletion and eugenics, the notion that scientists and
social scientists could socially engineer human beings for the betterment

of society. Bringing population concerns and eugenics together helped ground the justifications for birth control campaigns in the borderlands beginning in the 1930s. By the 1960s and 1970s, more expansive reproductive health demands altered this vision and influenced new directions in the movement for reproductive freedom. Goetting, Castillo, and de la Vega's lives span these changes, and their leadership was integral to how reproductive health movements unfolded in the region.

Fighting for Control examines how Mexican-origin women and powerful interest groups shaped the family planning movement in the borderlands. The latter group sought to manage the Mexican-origin population through intense population control campaigns, as the former vied for self-determination through greater access to health care. Planned Parenthood, the Catholic Church, Mexican-origin women activists, population control advocates, and individuals like Goetting, Castillo, and de la Vega are the actors who form the backbone of this book. Men, especially as race science, religious, and population control ideologues, shape critical aspects of this history, but the more powerful organizing skills of their women counterparts eclipsed their roles. Some women sought to reify and protect white racial supremacy and racial capitalism on the fringes of two nation-states, while others enacted reproductive care and created practices for reproductive liberation. These factions sometimes overlapped as people's actions are not always neatly contained within a particular ideology nor do they follow the prescriptions set by those in the present. The border of the United States and Mexico, where—to paraphrase queer Chicana feminist Gloria Anzaldúa—the first world "grates" against the third world and bleeds, forming a new culture, can tell us much about local drives for population control and movements for reproductive freedom that alter national and transnational histories of these social movements.

Fighting for Control adds to the growing feminist literature on how homegrown and regional movements for reproductive control and justice came to be, how the movement's location informed its purpose, and how local communities interpreted the need for and significance of reproductive control and reproductive freedom.[1] I study the ways campaigns for reproductive control and justice unfolded along the US-Mexico border from 1937, marking the opening of the first birth control clinic in El Paso, Texas, through 2009, the year Planned Parenthood of El Paso shuttered its last clinic in the city.[2]

Women Leaders: Visions for Reproductive Control and Liberation

Betty Mary Goetting's story in El Paso's birth control movement officially began in 1937. She, along with other middle- and upper-class white women advocates, helped establish the first birth control clinic, generically called the Mothers' Health Center, along the US-Mexico border in El Paso, Texas.[3] In the months prior to the clinic's inauguration, Goetting worked tirelessly with her ally and friend, US birth control pioneer Margaret Sanger, setting the groundwork for reproductive control on America's southern border. Birth controllers in the borderlands marketed contraception as a social panacea. According to these reformers, birth control would make unruly populations smaller, end poverty, and thus eradicate all social ills poverty engendered. Goetting blamed the poor's supposed ignorance and superstitions for the squalid living conditions that led to infant and maternal death. Since the turn of the twentieth century, these progressive reformers had admonished the dire health conditions in South El Paso, the main Mexican-origin enclave in El Paso, and attributed the spread of disease, ill health, and death to overpopulation within the Mexican community.

Few pointed to de facto segregated schools; low wages coupled with nonexistent public infrastructure, such as sanitation, roads, and health care; and deplorable housing as the main culprits producing high infant and maternal mortality rates in El Paso's south-side barrios. These mostly Mexican-origin neighborhoods were located south of the train tracks and nearest the physical border with Mexico. Instead of addressing the racism that produced these social inequities, birth control advocates weaponized these issues as justifications for directing racist contraceptive campaigns almost exclusively at Mexican-origin women in the borderlands for nearly seventy years. Their insistence that the cause of Mexican-origin people's poverty and ill health lie in their supposed excessive childbearing bred and maintained a specific kind of gendered anti-Mexican racism in the borderlands. Much of this book addresses why and how birth control activists remained steadfast in their racist beliefs for nearly a century.

Borderland birth controllers' efforts met forceful resistance from the Roman Catholic Church—one of the most consistently anti–birth control organized religious groups—in El Paso. Although some priests reviled the deterioration of traditional roles of women in the family, other El Paso clergy decried the class inequalities that led to a demand for reproductive control in the first place. Although this class-based, anti–birth control position from some of El Paso's Catholic clergy came prior to Vatican II (1962–1965), when the Church opened itself to some clergy's greater concerns for the poor and movements for social justice, other scholars assert that this movement was well underway in the United States beginning in the 1930s.[4] From the start, the Catholic Church called for boycotts of Sanger's speeches and businesses that supported her message. Nationally, this period marked a major religious split in the movement for birth control as "liberal denominational bodies," including the Universalist General Convention, the American Unitarian Association, the New York East Conference of Methodist Episcopal Church, the Central Conference of American Rabbis, and the Anglicans' Lambeth Conference, came out in favor of marital contraception in 1930.[5] The Papacy did the opposite. The Catholic Church issued *Casti Connubii* that same year reaffirming its stance against birth control.[6] In El Paso, these religious factions were reimagined racially. While mostly wealthy, white Protestant and Jewish groups came out in favor of contraception, the Catholic community, most of whom were Mexican-origin or Italian, stood in opposition.

Yet, despite birth control activists' neo-Malthusian and eugenic messaging and Catholic antagonism, reproductive health care was in great demand. A dearth of health care provision in El Paso's surrounding areas, including its sister city Ciudad Juárez, Mexico, led large numbers of Mexican-origin women, most of whom were Catholic, to seek support and receive contraceptive information and birth control devices from the birth control clinic. By 1946, the Mothers' Health Center affiliated with Planned Parenthood Federation of America (PPFA), a strong international voice for family limitation, and changed its name to Planned Parenthood of El Paso (PPEP).[7] This change quickly linked PPEP to broader international movements for family planning and population control in the decades after World War II.

As the Cold War began to reshape mid-century ideologies about population control, Mexican-American and Chicano civil rights movements proliferated across the US Southwest. Deprivation, ill health, lack of educational options, and political marginalization continued to plague the Mexican-origin community in the borderlands. The promise of a contraceptive revolution ending poverty and all that came with it never materialized. Inspired by the Chicana/o movement, Chicana and Chicano professionals joined with local community leaders in South El Paso to address the medical crisis in their barrios. For these activists, health care became a major pillar of self-determination for their communities. After community members, mostly women, banded together, activists opened the Father Rahm Clinic in 1969. Chicana/o activists named the clinic in honor of a beloved Jesuit priest,

Harold Rahm, who had, for most of the previous decade, attempted to address violence and poverty in El Paso's Southside barrios. The Father Rahm Clinic provided family planning and reproductive health exams as cornerstones of its mission to serve the community.

As the epigraph describes, Amelia Castillo, the organization's first director, succinctly captured the frustrations of many Mexican-origin people as they continued facing paltry health care resources in their community. Castillo and others confronted the empty promises made by generations of white reformers in El Paso, including that birth control alone would end poverty and social degradation in the barrio. Despite the lip service of white women birth controllers, easier access to contraception had not uniformly ended Mexican-origin people's social and economic precarity. Even as hundreds of Mexican-origin women used contraception, disgraceful living conditions persisted well into the latter part of the twentieth century. While PPEP's mission continued to focus on curbing population growth to end the so-called social problems of the Mexican-origin community, Chicanas believed a more holistic approach, one premised on health and wellness as part of a larger social justice agenda, was needed in their community.

In 1971, two years after Chicanas and Chicanos mobilized to address the health care desert in their communities, another woman emerged as a leader in the movement for contraception and population control, but this time in Ciudad Juárez, Mexico. Described as a blond bombshell in Mexican newspapers, Guadalupe Arizpe de la Vega quickly became the face of a new borderlands family planning movement. Wife of Federico de la Vega Mathews, a wealthy Ciudad Juárez entrepreneur and godfather of the maquiladora industry in the city, de la Vega had everything population control activists desired. She was Mexican, wealthy, Catholic, and powerful. At the time, her story provided a needed balm against the disastrous tales of abortion mills that engulfed Juárez in the years before *Roe v. Wade*, when thousands of American women crossed the border to access abortion care in Mexico's northern borderlands.[8] Her rise to fame also came at a major turning point in Mexican politics—the need to curtail population growth—which likely facilitated her work. De la Vega partnered with key industrialists on both sides of the border who sought to invest in reproductive control as a critical linchpin to the expansion of the maquiladora system in the region. As noted in her statement in the epigraph, she coded her relationships with wealthy financiers and population control agents to sell "love, dreams, and hope to the poorest in Mexico."

Mexico's connection to what scholars call reproductive governance—political actors using various social and cultural tools to "monitor and control reproductive behaviors and practices"—emerged in a different way from how birth control campaigns unfolded in the United States.[9] At the same time that Goetting and Sanger launched the borderlands' birth control movement in the late 1930s, the Mexican state took a pronatalist stance, due in part to falling birth rates during the Mexican Revolution.[10] Mexican politicians tied economic growth to population growth for much of the rest of the twentieth century, popularizing the mantra *gobernar es poblar* (to govern is to populate). They also saw their demographic growth as a boost to nationalist claims of a robust, virile, and expanding modern nation. Not until international population control advocates set their gaze on the so-called third world as the source of a worldwide population bomb did Mexico reverse course and embrace family planning as key to combatting overpopulation within its borders.

Mexico was late to join the population control movement. In the 1950s, population control advocates began to mark rapidly growing populations as risks to national and international economic systems as well as to the deterioration of global health and protection of the environment.[11] By the 1970s, Mexico had become a focal point of these anxieties as its population continued to rise, outpacing the United States and other more "developed" countries. Despite some early hesitations, Mexican politicians acquiesced to a national family planning policy. In opening Mexico to the international population control movement, Mexican politicians sought to assuage US border concerns as undocumented immigration began to rise. Concurrently, Mexican capitalists and entrepreneurs, in border cities like Ciudad Juárez, viewed contraceptive campaigns as a plus for labor control. Transnational assembly plants, staffed by mostly women workers, proliferated across the region, producing a new economic upswing for Mexico's economy. De la Vega, a skilled organizer in her own right, took advantage of these critical changes, enlisting financiers and colleagues from Planned Parenthood of El Paso to help establish family planning clinics in northern Mexico. Her enthusiasm for this kind activism stemmed from a conviction that increased capitalist production in Mexico's northern borderlands would be good for the rich with the potential for social mobility and economic opportunity for the poor. While Mexican entrepreneurs maximized profits, poor Mexican women were expected to control their reproduction, preserving their ability for unencumbered labor in these factories.

Broader Themes and Historical Connections

Fighting for Control is the first study to offer a historical analysis of reproductive control and justice in the US-Mexico borderlands. It centers *control, justice,* and *power,* not simply *rights*. There is a difference. While borderland activists acted in the shadows of various waves of women's movements throughout the twentieth century, neither the women of Planned Parenthood, the Chicanas of the Father Rahm clinic, nor Guadalupe Arizpe de la Vega openly fought for the legal right to contraception or abortion. They fought over the significance of reproductive control and justice, but not rights; they struggled over reproductive power in the borderlands. This is not to say they were disinterested in the legality of access, but fighting for legal rights was not their main concern. The birth controllers acted squarely within the law in accordance with medical professionals to educate Mexican-origin people about contraception.[12] Chicanas fought for access to health care as an innate human right—not necessarily a legal one. Guadalupe Arizpe de la Vega was fully enmeshed with the policies of the Mexican government at the time, and her work forwarded the fight for contraception to avoid the proliferation of abortion in the Mexico borderlands. A focus on control, justice, and power, grounded in reproductive justice frameworks, acts as connective tissue to bring this story to life.

Themes of reproductive control build on what historian Johanna Schoen describes as the tensions between "choice and coercion."[13] Reproductive control technologies have been simultaneously sources for liberation and methods to coercively control women's fertility. This was particularly true in El Paso, as the birth control movement sought to manage what was believed to be an out-of-control, economically poor Mexican population. After the 1910 Mexican Revolution and the Great Depression, wealthy and middle-class El Pasoans viewed Mexicans as a tax burden on Anglo citizens, who strove to make their "community a decent fine place in which to rear . . . children."[14] Given the decrepit state of public education and health care for Mexican children, it was clear El Pasoans meant to create a decent, fine place for Anglo children alone to thrive. Anglo residents viewed Mexican-origin families as suspect and a potential drain on American (presumed Anglo or white non-Mexican) citizens' own reproductive capabilities. As anthropologist Leo R. Chávez suggests of discourse concentrated in the latter part of the twentieth century, Latina reproduction has been cast as "irrational, illogical, chaotic, and therefore, threatening."[15] Thus, birth control clinics were created specifically to bestow upon poor Mexican-origin women the miracle of family limitation. In the eyes of wealthy white El Pasoans, family planning would curb poverty, end the spread of disease and death, and minimize Mexicans' use of public funds, providing social stability across the city.

PPEP clinics embraced this mission well into the 1970s. Seemingly tone-deaf to changing social mores and civil unrest throughout the country, Planned Parenthood of El Paso did not openly advance the fight for abortion access in the late 1960s and 1970s. It did little to support Chicana activists as they sought greater access to health care during those same decades. While PPEP led the birth control movement for a large part of the early twentieth century, by the late 1960s Chicana activists and Mexican-origin patients demanded a much more comprehensive family planning agenda than PPEP was willing to provide.

Tensions between coercion and choice underscore the book's second theme that stretches the length of this study: what sociologist Elena Gutiérrez describes as the construction of Mexican and Chicana reproduction as problematic and in need of control.[16] This process relies on the racialization of Mexicans within the United States, turning Mexican-origin people themselves into a social problem. In the nineteenth century, Anglo settlers referred to Mexicans as racial "half-breeds," considering them "incompatible" with the larger "pure white American stock." Fear of so-called racial impurity was deeply rooted in anti-Black and anti-Indigenous racialist sentiments developing as part of the nascent racial sciences of the mid-nineteenth century, in both the United States and Mexico.[17] Although Mexicans were considered *legally* white under the Treaty of Guadalupe Hidalgo ending the US-Mexico War in 1848, legal scholar and sociologist Laura Gómez explains that Mexicans' social status as racially "in between" constructed Mexicans as constant outsiders inside the United States.[18] Placing border cities like El Paso at the center of histories about reproduction and gendered racial formation further explains how Mexican-origin people were constructed as outside the boundaries of proper American citizenship.[19] This racial and gendered marginalization emboldened Anglos to relegate Mexicans to the most derelict housing and exploitative types of work.[20] These social conditions, coupled with de facto segregated education and lack of access to health care, co-constructed Mexican-origin people and their children as inherently "unfit" to reproduce and unworthy of care.

The process of racialization, what sociologists Michael Omi and Howard Winant refer to as racial formation, invigorated Anglos' demand for Mexican labor.[21] At the same time powerful social and legal forces constructed

Mexicans as racially impure, diseased, unfit to reproduce, and racially ineligible for American citizenship, Mexicans also became indispensable laborers for the expansion of American capital. Mexican residents of El Paso were an integral part of the economic boom in the early twentieth century, primarily because Anglos viewed them as inherently exploitable.[22] Some might consider this a uniquely American paradox: Mexicans were both a burgeoning racial threat and an economic necessity, and Mexicans' exclusion from political and social participation played a critical role in ameliorating this tension for Anglos in the Southwest. Racism, as both ideology and practice, became a powerful tool for controlling the Mexican-origin population.[23]

Examining the history of capitalist exploitation and white supremacy highlights another major line of inquiry in my book: the long history of population control *ideology* in the borderlands.[24] This requires disentangling the ideology of population control from its mid-twentieth-century location as a social movement that attempted to curtail population growth, particularly in the Global South, after World War II.[25] While I certainly write about that particular instantiation of population control that was critical to the international dissemination of contraception after 1950, I use the term *population control ideology* to signify how white settlers and their surrogates envisioned political, social, and economic practices meant to exert power over certain racialized groups; how Anglos in the borderlands invested in *ideas* and *beliefs* outlining different methods for the control of nonwhite populations they deemed incapable of self-rule and thus in need of state-sponsored surveillance and management; and how, over time, this ideology produced moral and ethical grounding for continued white settler rule despite white population loss. White Anglo settlers engendered this ideology as a unifying matrix for "border rule" that included both protection from and outright genocide of nonwhite peoples.[26] Population control ideology is expansive and all-encompassing as a means to maintain Anglo settler rule.[27] Since historians have identified the American paradox as part of settler colonial and imperial histories that are the foundation for histories of the US-Mexico border in the twentieth century, settler investments in controlling populations—where Mexicans live and work, how many children they should have and with whom, where they can go to school and shop—become critical sites for population control ideology to reinvent and reassert itself across time and space.[28] Mexican-origin people certainly did not experience the violence of population control ideology in a vacuum. Their histories of racialized exclusion in this region, combined with coercive labor regimes and dispossession of land, overlap with the histories of other racialized groups, including the histories of Native, Black, and Asian people.[29]

Fighting for Control tugs at the loose threads of established narratives of colonial violence, dispossession, capitalist extraction, and coercive labor regimes. The belief by Anglos that they should and could "manage" Mexicans as a *population* throughout the twentieth century is part of European settler colonial logics and regimes that systematized various kinds of population controls—including labor and human reproduction—for economic and social gain.

Reproductive justice scholars have bound population control efforts to twentieth-century eugenic laws, immigration restrictions, sterilization abuses, targeted family planning, welfare, and incarceration.[30] However, the drive to control populations that white settlers deemed incapable of political sovereignty and bodily autonomy, but considered crucial for economic expansion, precedes wars for independence, revolutions, and declarations of independence. Population control, the use of physical, psychological, spiritual, and emotional force to make a state-formed community of people bend to the political, social, cultural, and economic will of white settlers, was baked into their capitalist project. Population control ideology, the near divinely ordained *belief* that white settlers must manage and control nonwhite populations for the betterment of all, is intertwined in the history of conquest, colonization, empire, nationalism, and modernity that has helped preserve Anglo rule in the region for centuries.[31]

By the 1930s, population control ideology in El Paso had a simple purpose: to preserve white wealth and power in the borderlands and Texas writ large, as democratic ideals had the potential to tie population numbers to political power. Continued immigration and the seemingly high rates of fertility within the Mexican-origin community threatened this delicate equation. Would the Mexican-origin population outnumber whites in El Paso? Would Anglos lose political power if they became the minority? Could the loss of political power hasten the end of Anglos' economic control? Did Anglos have any recourse in averting this demographic disaster for their city and, likely, the country? These questions animated the work of birth control activists in the borderlands. As one early supporter of the clinic noted, "The location of El Paso on the border makes it [a birth control clinic] essential."[32] Birth control, like the border patrol and quarantine stations established in the decades before, became another tool amid growing border enforcement mechanisms developed to curb and potentially stop the proliferation of the Mexican-origin population within the United States and along its border.[33]

Even so, extreme reproductive coercion was not on the table in Texas. Despite several attempts by eugenicists across the country, El Paso leaders and other birth control activists across Texas refused to implement state-sanctioned coercive sterilization programs. Birth controllers struggled for decades to make contraception a part of public health campaigns and mandatory for women with tuberculosis and other signs of ill health. They implemented door-to-door campaigns offering contraceptives to women in the barrio as a model for state-run public health family planning programs. In the early days, public health officials in Texas rebuffed requests to join birth control organizations. Further still, unlike California, Texas lawmakers never passed a sterilization law.[34] El Paso birth controllers believed it was in the city's best interest to simply constrain reproduction through nonpermanent contraception due in part to fear that campaigns for forced sterilization might scare off potential laborers, particularly domestic and factory workers.[35] Nevertheless, intensive contraceptive campaigns produced what anthropologists call *stratified reproduction*: "The power relations by which some categories of people are empowered to nurture and reproduce, while others are disempowered."[36] In the borderlands, racist labor regimes constructed Mexican-origin women's reproduction as inherently inferior and threatening to Anglo women's reproduction.[37] As the de facto domestic labor force in the region, Mexican-origin women were to be silent, childless providers of maternal and household care for many of the same Anglo women who were determined to restrict Mexican-origin reproduction.

Because birth control advocates could not rely on coercive sterilization programs, despite the many who supported those measures in the movement, including Sanger herself, their reproductive educational curricula, in line with other Americanization programs at the time, relied on stigmatization of Mexican-origin women as irresponsible, uneducated, ignorant, and superstitious. To help Mexican-origin women overcome these socially problematic behaviors, birth control activists modified their educational model with a philosophy of reproductive discipline. According to sociologist Adele Clark, "the term *disciplining* becomes inflected with connotations of exercising *control over* participating individuals and groups . . . Disciplining thus can involve policing and enforcing particular perspectives."[38] Reproductive discipline, surveillance, coercion, and control came not in the form of forced sterilizations but in educational campaigns that directly tied Mexican-origin women's supposed racially reproductive "backwardness" to the deterioration of their communities. These campaigns extended beyond access to contraception into the realms of sex, marriage, and motherhood. Birth control advocates depended on social pressures and coercive messaging that simultaneously racialized Mexican-origin women's reproduction as excessive and as the cause of their own poverty and marginalization.

Fighting for Control addresses how reproductive coercion as a critical site for population control operated beyond compulsory sterilization laws. Thus far, literature focusing on Mexican-origin women's reproduction has often centered these histories; however, eugenicists went beyond coercive sterilization campaigns in their attempts to discipline Mexican-origin women's reproduction.[39] In much of its advertising, Planned Parenthood of El Paso insisted that the use of birth control was *voluntary* and *reversible*. Rather than championing forced sterilizations, birth controllers like Goetting sought to enforce specific patterns of reproduction that were in line with a Depression- and World War II–era vision of frugality, rationing, and "living within one's means." As Goetting explained, "this privilege [birth control] has been withheld from the poor who should share in this above any other form of social security. And they pay in terms of ill health, infant deaths, maternal deaths. They pay for it in slums, child labor, unemployment. These are the victims of America[n] society . . ."[40] Even though women were never forced to use contraception, the rhetoric that accompanied the birth control movement sought to inculcate them on the economic morality of contraception. Mexican-origin women could "choose" not to be victims of American society if they regulated the size of their families. Not only could birth control lift them out of poverty, but it would also release the affluent classes from the burden of supporting "unwanted children." Goetting remarked on the values and mores of the well-educated and economically empowered family who "knows that today the excessively large family is physically and economically undesirable and they have replaced chance fecundity with intelligent control."[41] Simply put, large nonwhite families were bad for capitalist accumulation. They ran counter to the ideal small, modern, white, heteronormative, and "intelligently controlled" American family. Mexican-origin people who refused the power of birth control were, in the minds of birth control activists, *choosing* poverty and chaos.

By the 1980s, when Guadalupe Arizpe de la Vega took control of the population control movement in borderlands, international activists proposed similar rationales for family planning in the Global South. Sterilization was but one weapon in an ever-expanding arsenal of population control measures filtered through family planning campaigns. While women like Goetting focused on the benefits of birth control for the preservation of their American city, de la Vega framed the conversation as a binational effort to control populations for the benefit of transnational capital. According to de la Vega, family planning could mitigate "issues of great significance such as migration, population growth, pollution . . . trade, tourism, education, poverty, and political changes [that] challenge the well-being of our countries . . . Social disorders in Mexico brought about by socioeconomic crisis would trigger distress in the United States."[42]

Though historians have long documented the eugenic and population control rhetoric that accompanied Sanger's birth control crusade nationally and internationally, this study is the first to analyze the phenomenon along the US-Mexico border and within the Mexican-origin community on both sides of the line.[43] *Fighting for Control* traces the "transnational circuits of power" and history of coercive family planning measures beyond the confines of compulsory sterilization campaigns that came to represent but one branch of reproductive injustices in the twentieth-century borderlands.[44]

Throughout the book, I weave together reproductive histories of population control with the many counternarratives for liberation and reproductive freedom that contested these coercive programs. The lived experiences of Mexican-origin women in the borderlands move us beyond paradigms of "choice" and "rights," in the choice-versus-coercion model, to highlight how Mexican-origin women provided each other different types of reproductive *care* while simultaneously building networks of care in their communities. As feminist philosopher Virginia Held states, "Care is both value and practice."[45] Mexican-origin women engaged in reproductive care for economic and social survival as they faced exploitative labor conditions, often as domestic and factory workers providing life-affirming care for Anglo families and a burgeoning economy for Anglo capitalists in El Paso. They did this while also expanding care systems to include health and labor justice for their communities, who collectively suffered the city's and state's imposed poverty and neglect.[46] As the very mainstay of care economies in the borderlands, Mexican-origin women began to demand that the state and its surrogates, including birth control activists, reciprocate with economic and social support. In the 1960s, Chicana activists like Amelia Castillo framed their fight for greater access to health care as one premised on an ethos of justice and care.

My concern for analyzing *care* in reproductive histories stems from my engagement with reproductive justice (RJ) as both praxis and theory.

RJ scholars define the framework using four critical tenets: (1) the right to have children, (2) the right not to have children, (3) the right to parent the children we have in safe and sustainable communities, and (4) the inalienable right to bodily autonomy. As a feminist framework, RJ arose from the work of Black women and women of color scholar-activists who for decades sought primarily to make visible the lives and experiences of women of color as actors and participants in both their own reproductive care and movements for reproductive rights. For instance, Loretta Ross's analysis of African American women's experiences with reproductive control and activism brings to the fore the production of scholarship on these issues: "African American women have a long history in the struggle for reproductive freedom, but racist and sexist assumptions about us, our sexuality and our fertility have disguised our contributions to the birth control and abortion movements in the United States. Distilling facts from the myths is difficult because so many accounts of African American history are written from perspectives that fail to even acknowledge our presence in the reproductive freedom movement."[47] Mexican-origin women, Chicanas, and Latinas rarely appear as active agents in narratives about reproductive rights in the United States. As Elena Gutierrez maintains, "The continual marginalization of women of color in organizing wholly erases the significant roles that Latinas have played in the development of both mainstream reproductive rights efforts and community-based reproductive health and sexuality agendas."[48] What little is known about Mexican-origin women's reproductive lives is told in narratives about compulsory sterilization, and few describe how these women sought out birth control and engaged in reproductive care on their own terms.[49]

We have much theorizing to do within RJ's framework that can and should help us understand the past. Historians are known for shying away from theory, and yet it is critical for understanding and engaging our sources. While we are certainly guided by archival evidence, by what is "there," some feel trepidation taking theoretical leaps into what is "not there;" that is, the archival silences. In the absence of archival materials, theory must not be used to embellish a rendering of "feelings" or "thoughts" people might have had in the past. English and comparative literature scholar Saidiya Hartman reminds us: "How can narrative embody life in words and at the same time respect what we cannot know?"[50] Developing the idea of *reproductive care*, a mode of interpreting and analyzing Mexican-origin women's words and deeds that both acknowledges the structural and systemic boundaries of certain possibilities and honors Mexican-origin women's ability to skillfully maneuver around, over, and through obstacles as a means for community survival, allows for a careful reimagining of their agency.

Pinpointing Mexican-origin women's *agency* is no easy feat, given that many of the sources used in *Fighting for Control* belong to white woman–led institutions and personal collections, such as Planned Parenthood of El Paso and Planned Parenthood Federation of America, as well as the Betty Mary Goetting and Margaret Sanger papers. A thorough reading of these documents, particularly the data collected by clinic staff and doctors, reveals how Mexican-origin women scrutinized, accepted, or rejected various forms of contraception and reproductive information. I gathered data from clinic board meeting minutes representing forty years of clinical trials describing the various technological tools available to women from the late 1930s to the 1970s. Tabulating this information on spreadsheets, adding and subtracting numbers of new patients from returning patients, and aligning funding sources for new contraceptive methods revealed a topography of reproductive health that until now remained unknown. While using the records of white missionary workers in South El Paso, Chicana historian Vicki Ruiz contends that "no set of institutional records can provide substantive answers, but by exploring these documents . . . we place Mexican women at the center of our study, not as victims of poverty and superstition as so often depicted by missionaries, but as women who made choices for themselves and for their families."[51] This kind of reading against the grain, proposed by Chicana scholars, including Vicki Ruiz, Antonia Castañeda, Emma Pérez, Deena González, María Cotera, Miroslava Chávez-García, Monica Perales, Natalie Lira, Celeste Menchaca, Laura Gutierrez, Citlali Sosa, Marisela Chávez, Elizabeth Escobedo, and many others, allows us to reimagine the archives as more than the accumulation of statistics.[52] Beyond bringing visibility to Mexican-origin women's influence on reproductive health and population control programs, each number in this data set is a human decision extended against reproductive control regimes for a modicum of reproductive liberation and community care.

My data sets are composed of PPEP information collected to help pharmaceutical companies profit from new contraceptive devices. Chicanas in the Southwest, like their Puerto Rican counterparts, participated in research studies for new spermicidal foams, jellies, and the contraceptive Pill in the late 1950s and early 1960s.[53] While clinic sources say little about how consent was obtained and understood for these trials, some Mexican-origin women's experiences with these new technologies were recorded. Although their "voices" may not ring out loud and clear in the archive—a testament to the power of white women's ability to keep patients marginalized and silenced—their engagement with these new contraceptives tell a story of reproductive power and attempts at autonomy.

Oral histories also substantiate and complicate much of what is located on paper and ink archives. Digging through older historical texts where use of contraceptives is but an aside, I located the "voices" of Mexican-origin women in the early 1920s, 1930s and 1940s. Their understanding of sexuality and reproductive autonomy runs counter to the more conservative stereotypes of the period. I was also fortunate to interview several Mexican-origin women who came of age in the 1940s and 1950s believing it was their human right to control when and how many children they had. And, again, by reading against the grain and asking questions of archival sources where Mexican-origin women's words are but a whisper, it is possible to hear faint yet decisive answers for their reasons for seeking out reproductive health care.

Indeed, the evidence demonstrates that Mexican-origin women took charge of their reproductive health despite decades of neglect from charitable organizations and the state. Amelia Castillo and other Chicana activists' organizing strategies included carving out their own space for providing health care, distributing contraception, and providing comprehensive reproductive medical exams. As scholars of women's history note, concerns for access to women-centered health care were a major imperative of the second-wave women's movement.[54] Chicanas made access to abortion and contraception, as well as a critique of coercive sterilization campaigns, central to their work in the Chicana/o movement. As feminist scholar Maylei Blackwell observes, for Chicanas, "unplanned pregnancies and lack of access to birth control" were obstacles in their ability to complete college and further life goals.[55] This is to say that Mexican-origin women understood, like their white women counterparts, that reproductive autonomy was paramount in the fight for gender liberation. Activists like Amelia Castillo who were deeply devoted to their Catholic faith nevertheless championed access to reproductive services as fundamental to community care and restoration. Castillo wrote grants to fund the Father Rahm Clinic in El Paso's Segundo Barrio, one of the Southside's primary Mexican neighborhoods. Although population control ideology dominated the early part of the reproductive control movement in the borderlands, by mid-century Chicana activists had altered the linear trajectory of institutions like Planned Parenthood of El Paso.

An emphasis on reproductive justice and care also brings the borderlands region and its inhabitants into greater focus. Chicana scholars have long written about *el ambiente fronterizo*, the region's ability to provide spaces for cultural fusion and resurgence as well as a site with a long legacy of violence and death.[56] Reproductive histories of population control and reproductive justice at the border reinvigorate Gloria Anzaldúa's *fronteriza* philosophies. RJ scholars have been quick to engage the possibilities of an Anzaldúan articulation of reproductive freedom, one that emerges from her visions of a mestiza consciousness born of a *fronteriza* life.[57] In *Radical Reproductive Justice*, the editors write: "Women of color inhabit multiple worlds because of our gender, sexuality, race, spiritual beliefs, class, immigration status, abilities, and other identities, and embody what Anzaldúa called the 'mestiza consciousness' from living in the borderlands, or interstices of rigid boundaries."[58] Living in the in-between of violence and liberation, of freedom and coercion, produced a tenuous but nonetheless tangible space for care.

And yet population control programs directed at Mexican-origin women's reproduction know no bounds; they were never contained by national borders. As I make clear in the pages that follow, concerns about Mexican-origin women's supposed hyper-fertility found fertile ground among Mexican population control activists after nearly forty years of US-based birth controllers' attempts to transmit these ideas across the border. This was due in part to political changes in Mexico and the growing geopolitical power of population control advocacy. Racial tropes of Mexican-origin women having too many babies in hopes of exploiting US-based welfare systems—the trope of the "pregnant pilgrim"—have been weaponized for over a hundred years to keep a racialized, laboring class in its place. As I write these words, Texas has become ground zero for reproductive rights wars in the twenty-first century. Borderland cities, such as El Paso, have become the first casualties of these wars as cities endure loss of access to basic reproductive health care. When viewed through a reproductive justice history of population control, this is no coincidence.

By interweaving various branches of scholarship, I show how a reproductive history of population control and reproductive care in the borderlands complements but also contests well-established narratives. Up to this point, historians have focused on the life of Margaret Sanger and her associates, like Clarence Gamble, and other prominent scientists and doctors involved in the movement's inception, mostly focused on the East Coast.[59] There are numerous studies about the history of reproductive technologies, from early douches to the diaphragm and the creation of the Pill.[60] Histories about the creation of birth control clinics as well as research on Catholicism and contraception line the edges of the historiography.[61] Some fascinating research has captured the troubling history of abortion across the United States, although fewer histories exist about women of color's experiences with abortion, particularly in the 1920s and 1930s.[62] These established histories are replete with the achievements of mostly white, middle- and upper-class women, who for decades dominated reproductive control campaigns. Rather than focus solely on the accomplishments of white birth controllers in the borderlands, *Fighting for Control* foregrounds the fraught relationships between white activists and Mexican-origin people in El Paso and later in Ciudad Juárez throughout the twentieth century.

Chapter Outlines

Readers will notice a change in tone as they move through the book's six chapters and epilogue. In chapter 1, I trace the projects that enabled imagined demographic futures of white loss and political scarcity, grounding fears about miscegenation and overpopulation in the imagined hyper-fertility of nonwhite people generally, and Mexican-origin people specifically. Beginning in the nineteenth century, some Anglo settlers envisioned a world in which their victories over land and people could be easily taken away by a growing nonwhite population. The US-Mexico border became a place from which many Anglo settlers developed and honed their fears of "race suicide" through uncontrolled immigration and racial degeneration as Anglos simultaneously racialized nonwhite populations by extracting their labor and expropriating their land. Population control ideology emerges from these fears of white population decline and sets the stage for white women's activism in the birth control movement in following chapters.

Chapter 2 examines the raison d'être for the birth control movement in the borderlands: to protect a burgeoning American white metropolis from Mexican overpopulation. The chapter relies heavily on archival materials from PPEP, foregrounding the voices of white women at the top of the organization as they gave their rationales for establishing the first birth control clinic along the US-Mexico border and places them within a larger context of the birth control movement in the Southwest, namely Arizona and California. Despite their organizing and financial support, Catholics rallied to oppose the establishment of the clinic. Chapter 2 brings into focus the world white women made and how they sought to define the movement for reproductive control in the borderlands.

In chapters 3 and 4, I develop the idea of reproductive care as a mode for understanding Mexican-origin women's connections to reproductive health and community. While Mexican-origin women labored as domestic, factory, and agricultural workers, they were also agents in their own reproductive care. These two chapters rely on oral histories and PPEP records from 1937 to the mid-1960s, describing the most intimate and painful histories of reproductive loss, as well as moments of reproductive triumph and liberation.

Chapter 4 also examines the troubled and fraught history of contraceptive innovation and experimentation Mexican-origin women endured throughout the 1960s. Despite attempts at coercion, data sets reveal liberatory reverberations as Mexican-origin women demanded changes to clinic services and access to different types of contraceptives. These same years show that PPEP reluctantly opened its organization to Mexican-origin women, who became field workers, clinic staff, and volunteers. Birth control activists took Mexican-origin women's interest in supporting the clinic's mission as a sign that their educational programs were working. However, given Mexican-origin women's continued use of clinic services and their early enthusiasm for access to reproductive health care, birth control activists' conclusions must be scrutinized as further attempts to discredit and marginalize the very women they were purporting to help.

In the late 1960s, Chicana/o activists in El Paso began creating safe and sustainable environments for their communities to live and thrive. Chapter 5 explores the work of Amelia "Amy" Castillo and the activists who helped establish the first Chicano-run health care clinic, originally called the Father Rahm Clinic, in the borderlands. Castillo, who had a master's degree in social work, acquired funding for this new clinic and in the process created the infrastructure for Chicana-centered reproductive care. Women who came to the Father Rahm clinic were offered full physical exams, contraception, support with domestic violence issues, and mental health support for their children as well as perinatal care. Guided by the Chicana/o movement's philosophy of self-determination, Castillo centered community solidarity, healing, and care as a radical political act of resistance and survival.

While Castillo worked toward an all-encompassing vision of community health, international population control activists were catching their second wind as they fixed their gaze on Mexico. Chapter 6 investigates the movement for population control in Mexico's northern borderlands as activists sought to contain immigration and a cheap labor pool from crossing the Rio Grande to El Norte. Guadalupe Arizpe de la Vega became an ideal representative of the cause. Even as her rhetoric seemed to compliment the ideas of people like Castillo—de la Vega often mentioned women's self-determination as critical to reproductive health—her family's wealth, their connections to the maquiladora industry, and her support for population control advocates around the globe tinged her efforts with a less-than-altruistic hue. Her open engagement with the Catholic Church certainly surprised activists in the United States and cemented her as an adept organizer in her community.

In the epilogue, I tie these long histories of population control and reproductive liberation together to explain—as best one can—what is happening today in Texas and Mexico regarding reproductive control, care, and justice. For almost a decade, Texas has emerged as a central figure in the fight against reproductive health care producing innovative policies and legislation that seek to end people's reproductive autonomy. In my estimation, this is due in part to population politics and the rapidly changing racial demographics of the state that have made Anglos a numerical minority in Texas. Mexico's approach to reproductive health is moving in the opposite direction, as its supreme court recently decriminalized abortion in the country. Feminists in Mexico have centered their movement around the epidemic of violence against women, girls, and trans and nonbinary people. They have framed denial of reproductive health care as violence. These most recent legal upheavals have once again—as in the days before and after *Roe v. Wade*—created new migrants in search of reproductive liberation in the borderlands.

Fighting for Control is not a condemnation of organizations like Planned Parenthood, nor is it my intention to merely "add and stir" Mexican-origin women into the narrative of a movement dominated by white, upper-middle-class women. Rather, I suggest that examining reproductive control from the nation's margins, both the United States and Mexico, expands earlier histories and complements new studies that stress how Mexican-origin women defied and contested population control ideology as patients and activists and how their emergence in the movement for reproductive *justice* and *care* challenges myths about their disinterest in or lack of concern for their reproductive health and lives. *Fighting for Control* is an examination of the forces that led to the creation of an oppressive reproductive control system along the US-Mexico border and how Mexican-origin women, at various intervals, fought back to reclaim justice, autonomy, and care for themselves and their communities.

Notes on Language

Racial categorization is constituted via time and space. Unless the subjects have specified themselves or there are other archives revealing their nationality or racial categorization, I will use the term *Mexican-origin* to describe the women who attended clinics along the border and people of Mexican descent residing within the borderlands. While *Mexican-origin* is a broad term that includes a diverse group of people, namely US-born, US-raised, US residents, and migrants, I do my best to make clear class, gender, and racial distinctions when materials or people themselves provide this crucial information. I use the term *nonwhite* to encompass those who have been racialized as not white, including Mexican-origin people. As mentioned previously, one of this book's central claims is that Mexican-origin people have been racialized in the United States and in Mexico. Both countries have constructed different but often complementary racial hierarchies that rely on gender, class, and color to denote proximity to whiteness. As stated previously, racism is not only an ideology but also a practice that is deeply entwined with time and space. The white Anglo-Saxon Protestant population in the El Paso-Ciudad Juárez borderlands remained outnumbered for most of its existence in the region and therefore aligned itself with other Euro-descended communities as a means of demographic survival, including El Paso's Jewish community. Thus, not everyone involved in the birth control movement was Anglo, but they would have all been white. I do my best to note this as I describe and examine the movement in the borderlands throughout the twentieth century. The racial hierarchies between Mexican-origin elites and US whites changed inflection given how useful Mexican elites could be to the movement for population control. Guadalupe Arizpe de la Vega is a perfect example of a white-passing Mexican woman whose financial means and European looks allowed her to be a believable messiah for the international population control movement in the borderlands.

1 Making a White Settler World in the Twentieth-Century Borderlands

· ·

The Spaniards mixed to an extent with the Moors, and the resultant cross emigrated to Mexico and South America, and intermixed with the brown natives, Indians and negro slaves, exhibiting an example of breeding downward on a gigantic scale. . . .

Yet there is a slight exception to the general degeneracy, in a few Castilians, noble people, who through pride of ancestry and race have kept themselves to an extent aloof from, and above the surging brown mass.

—Calvin Smith Babbitt, 1909

Calvin Smith Babbitt was a quintessential American settler. He was born in New York in 1833, becoming a farmer like his father and then setting off west to make his destiny manifest.[1] At the end of the Civil War, Babbitt traveled first to the relatively new US state of California after marrying Indiana-born Lucinda Stark in 1865. Then the couple moved to the US-Mexico borderlands in 1882, buying a tract of land in Ysleta—a town with a large Mexican-origin and Indigenous population miles from present-day El Paso, Texas. El Paso, established as a white settlement in the 1850s, was situated just north of and across the Rio Grande from El Paso del Norte, present-day Ciudad Juárez, Mexico. Eventually the Babbitts purchased a home in El Paso proper. Still, according to records, Babbitt preferred living on his Ysleta farm in direct proximity to the national border. The Babbitts had no children. At the age of seventy-six, Babbitt died on June 24, 1909. His funeral was held inside El Paso's Masonic Lodge, and he was later interred in Concordia Cemetery. Babbitt's obituary memorialized him as one of the "best known residents of the El Paso valley."[2]

The year he died, the El Paso Printing Company published Babbitt's *The Remedy for the Decadence of the Latin Race*, a sixty-six-page manifesto that rooted ideas of white supremacy, fears of racial degeneration, miscegenation, and overpopulation to the US-Mexico border. Babbitt's screed became part of a discursive racialist logic identifying what many at the time had coined the "Mexican problem" in Texas. Babbitt's fears about demographic change and racial degeneration, expressed in the preceding epigraph, helped frame the contours of what would become an obsession for many Anglo settlers in the borderlands: population *quality* and *quantity*. Babbitt drew on colonial histories of conquest and miscegenation, producing a white, Anglo worldview hinging on constant fears of its own demise.

For Anglos, the borderlands were simultaneously full of economic possibility but also nearly always on the verge of engendering white demographic collapse and the end of white racial supremacy. The prospect of white population decline at the very border of the American nation presented a great risk to the nation itself. By the 1930s, this settler worldview had set the intellectual foundations for population control projects, such as immigration regimes, labor hierarchies, and birth control campaigns, that had the potential to ease Anglo fears of overpopulation from the ever-present "surging brown mass" in the borderlands.

Historians have used Babbitt's text as a critical example of eugenic and nativist thinking peddled by scientists, public intellectuals, politicians, and many others during these years.[3] His writings, a seminal example of population control ideology, placed a spotlight on the US-Mexico borderlands; an *imagined white community* where questions about land, labor, immigration, population quality and quantity, and biological reproduction had inflected borderlands politics since white settlers founded El Paso in the years after the United States wrestled the territory from Mexico.

Situating himself within the emerging cannon of xenophobic literatures, Babbitt dedicated his musings in *The Remedy* to David Starr Jordan, an ardent eugenicist, founding president of Stanford University, and author of *The Blood of the Nation* (1901).[4] Jordan would visit El Paso in 1916 amid rising tensions between the United States and Mexico and continue his advocacy as a staunch "antiexpansionist and anti-imperialist." Jordan worried that continued US expansion into nonwhite nations such as Mexico would mean "the defilement and mongrelization of the body politic."[5] It is unclear if Jordan ever read Babbitt's tome, but Babbitt's dedication is prophetic in that many among the nativist eugenicists of the period, including Jordan, regarded the borderlands in general and El Paso in particular as ground zero for the battle against racial decay of the white American nation.

Babbitt was certainly no David Starr Jordan, Madison Grant, Lothrop Stoddard, or Edward Alsworth Ross, all well-known anti-immigrant eugenicists who wrote volumes on the decline of the white race and the demographic threat nonwhite people posed to the American nation in the early decades of the twentieth century. Babbitt's lesser-appreciated perspective nonetheless added to the scholarship calling attention to the Latin (European) race's impending doom—due in large part to its catastrophic "breeding" practices. "The doctor has well shown that by the destruction of the strong and virile in constant warfare, and through the emigration of the best to other lands, leaving the weak and cowardly, the unfit in every way to propagate and become fathers of successive generations, that it has had the effect of lowering the stamina, and physical, if not moral vigor, of all Latin races in particular, and other people who have inherited more or less of their blood."[6] Babbitt's words perfectly echoed Jordan's writings. Jordan had observed that "if a nation sends forth the best it breeds to destruction, the second best will take their vacant places. The weak, the vicious, the unthrifty, will propagate, and in default of better will have the land to themselves."[7] This cohort of early-twentieth-century thinkers produced narratives of a European-descended civilization in decline due in part to bad "breeding practices" but also to massive immigration from non-European nations.

Although some academics in the late nineteenth and early twentieth centuries blamed white women's political activism, their demand for the vote, access to education, and calls for "voluntary motherhood"—the precursor to Margaret Sanger's birth control movement—as potential factors for declines in white fertility rates, others like sociologist Edward Alsworth Ross also blamed immigration.[8] Progressive academics of the era included immigration as a major cause for the precipitous decline in "native-born" white births in proportion to the birth rates of newly arrived immigrants. Low birth rates coupled with rising divorce rates among "native-born" American whites unleashed a wave of racial anxieties. Historian Laura Lovett observes that by the end of the nineteenth century, the white "American family was perceived to be in a state of crisis," and the decline in the white birth rate and the increase in divorce raised doubts about the "survival of the [white] family" and the "American race."[9] A Progressive reformer, Ross was steadfast in vocalizing his disdain for immigration—he was virulently anti-Japanese and believed a return to agrarian life and strict immigration controls would turn the tide of low white birth rates. He famously coined the term *race suicide*, referring to the drop in "native-born" birth rates. Ross believed that in the face of unrestricted immigration of groups "incapable" of integrating into American culture, "the higher race [whites] quietly and unmurmuringly eliminates itself rather than endure individually the bitter competition it has failed to ward off from collective action."[10] Ross asserted that whites meekly refused to procreate as a "natural" response to the more fecund, less civilized immigrant invaders. Birth control activists in the borderlands would later latch on to these arguments as well as those made by Babbitt, anchoring their contraceptive campaigns to logics steeped in the protection of "consciously planned" and racially fit (white) families.

Babbitt's preoccupation with Mexican-origin people, miscegenation, and overpopulation led him to acknowledge a potentially complicated economic quagmire. His writing highlighted the paradoxical position of many Anglos toward Mexican-origin people as nonwhite, immigrant laborers:

> So, one may see that the Mexican peon, who we wish to guard against, although classed as a man, is one like Joseph's coat of many colors, and of divers [sic] races. He is the fellow who is crossing the border in numbers. We don't want him, only his labor in gathering fruit and cotton, and at times to build and repair the railroads, and to whom, if he would leave his wives behind and go back when his work is done, we would cordially say "come on," but he goes back and comes again, bringing his family and relatives.[11]

Babbitt's simultaneous contempt for and investment in the "Mexican peon" as an immigrant worker underscored growing racial tensions between Anglos and Mexican-origin people as Anglos tied their economic prosperity to the exploitation of Mexican labor. How might Anglos continue to exploit Mexican labor without allowing the resettlement of Mexican families within the United States, which would produce children with US citizenship? Babbitt offered a prescient remedy to the labor issue when he wrote: "It seems a treaty with Mexico might be so amended as to admit only males, of this class, and under bond to return when their job was finished. In fact, if their females were not admitted, they would voluntarily return in any event."[12] Harkening back to the 1875 Page Act that denied Chinese women workers entry to the United States for "immoral purposes," Babbitt's labor solution, like an invisible hand, connected past and future to his perceived present.[13] His words foreshadowed the Bracero Program (1942–64), a contract labor program between the United States and Mexico that sought to prevent the very "invasion" Babbitt imagined. Both the Page Act and the Bracero Program sought to keep nonwhite women outside US borders to protect the white family and by extension the white nation from further miscegenation and the expansion of what Babbitt called "the great mass of mongrels."[14]

We could call Babbitt's writings ludicrous, but his thoughts were in line with Jordan's *The Blood of the Nation* (1901) as well as later white supremacists' tomes, such as Grant's *The Passing of the Great Race* (1916) and Stoddard's *The Rising Tide of Color* (1920). These books were what sociologist Michael Rodríguez-Muñiz calls narratives of "demographic imagined futures." Amid Euro-US imperial expansion in the late nineteenth century, these texts ushered in waves of "demographobia," meaning the fear of not only population quality (race) but also quantity (excess) with the capacity to destroy white civilization. Through *demostopic* narratives—"fantastical renderings of 'nonwhite' populations as threats to perpetual white dominance"—Babbitt and his ilk used the long history of colonization and "racial-mixing" to write into existence the necessity for race-based population controls.[15] Critically, for Babbitt and many other Anglo borderland residents, race-based population controls should begin in the womb. Protecting white reproduction from miscegenation and decline via segregation and immigration controls was paramount to imagining a racially secure future.[16] As Rodríguez-Muñiz contends, these "imagined" demographic futures have pasts.[17] The historical underpinnings that gave Babbitt's words heft lie in his analysis of the longue durée history of the borderlands and how various waves of human migration and settlement later threatened Anglo-Saxons in the region. Before and after Babbitt, historians and lay scholars spent decades chronicling the history of the region. Their writings produced a borderlands narrative that at times contested Babbitt's degeneration narrative and in other instances reinforced his conclusions.

While not all these writings can be characterized as *demostopic*, they nonetheless attempted to capture the perils of what it meant to proliferate as a white race at the very edges of the American nation. Simply existing in proximity to Mexico and its people represented a threat to white racial supremacy. Mexico's political instability added to these fears. A response from a concerned local El Paso resident on a survey about the state of Mexican politics and immigration captures their fears succinctly: "Each revolution brings out a horde of Mexicans."[18] As the decades passed and new population control projects emerged, although differing in method, the underlying spirit remained the same: to forestall the fall of white political, cultural, and economic power at the nation's border.

Quality and quantity of population always informed white racial anxieties in the borderlands. Although the counting of human beings became important to thinkers prior to colonization to "consider community in relationship to governance," historian Jennifer L. Morgan reminds us that rooted in the Enlightenment "logic" of enumeration was its capacity for "making up people."[19] Creating and counting categories of people—"producing human collectivities"—spawned gender and racial hierarchies that formed powerful political currents in the borderlands. These currents drove capitalist accumulation for land and labor and defined a population's capacity for self-governance, including control over their own bodies.[20] The colonial production of human collectivities began through reproduction. As sociologist Elena Gutiérrez states, the racialization of "women's procreation has been a subject of political interest from the time of the Spanish colonization of Mexico."[21] An analysis of the politics of demography in the history of the nineteenth century helps unearth the roots of demographic anxieties and its links to racialist fears of nonwhite reproduction, breeding a distinct anti-Mexican gendered racism and the proliferation and enforcement of population controls in the twentieth-century borderlands.[22]

Demography and Land Loss in the Borderlands

By the turn of the nineteenth century, Indigenous people, mestizos (people of mixed Indigenous, Spanish, and African ancestry), *criollos* (people born in the Americas but considered of "pure" Spanish ancestry), and *peninsulares* (people born in Spain) inhabited the borderlands, a multiracial region.[23] Anthropologist Martha Menchaca calculates that by 1800 "Indians and mestizos constituted 72 percent of the population," criollos 18 percent, and Black people 10 percent. *Peninsulares* represented less than 1 percent of the population.[24] The largest portion of those populating the borderlands were a mestizo colonial population who were of "southwestern American Indian descent."[25]

Demographic realities and racist ideologies outlined the boundaries of how Mexicans, Native people, and Anglos confronted settler efforts in the borderlands as the United States encroached on Mexican and Native territories. Borderland regions experienced conquest differently—there were marked variations between the areas of Texas, New Mexico, and California, for instance. Yet the politics of population played a role in the ways people came to understand their significance in the process.[26] In the words of historian Brian DeLay, when discussing the relationship between the Diné and Nuevo Mexicanos in the century before the US war with Mexico, "at its most basic this was a matter of raw demography."[27] As Spain and later Mexico counted its people, Native communities such as the Navajo were at a numeric disadvantage. DeLay estimates there were about 10,000 Diné in 1846, while Nuevo Mexicanos (presumed mestizo) numbered nearly 60,000 on the eve of war with the United States.[28] These figures that captured a mostly nonwhite population would later mean that New Mexico would not be easily incorporated into a white American nation. Its large numbers of mixed-race and Native peoples precluded New Mexico from becoming a state until 1912—nearly sixty-four years after the end of the war against Mexico.

A sparsely populated Texas, on the other hand, attracted Anglo settlers and the United States in the 1820s. Despite migratory waves from central Mexico after 1750, the 1790 census revealed that Texas was one of the "least-inhabited" territories of New Spain. One demographer noted that New Spain's interior provinces "had an average of six inhabitants per square league; Texas and Coahuila showed scarcely two, and only desert Baja California had a lower ratio—one inhabitant per square league."[29] Proportionally, these demographics changed little into the next century, reinforcing Anglo ideas about Texas as a vast "wilderness" in need of a white Christian population to claim the territory for the United States.[30] Anglo immigration to Texas, brought about by the Coahuila-Texas Colonization law in 1824, quickly enlarged the Anglo population, providing grounds for rebellion in 1835.[31] Eight years before the Texas rebellion there were "12,000 US citizens living in Texas and 5,000 Mexicans." By 1836, 20,000 Americans resided in the Texas territory while the Mexican population had stayed the same.[32]

To be clear, Mexican authorities were intentional in their pursuit of Anglo migrants as potential settlers of Texas. For too long a small Tejano (as the Mexican residents of the territory called themselves) population lived an embattled existence on the very periphery of the Spanish frontier—a buffer zone between an encroaching American empire from the east and nations of so-called "barbarous Indians" from the north and west. Politicians and elite residents of San Antonio, for instance, supported immigration to help protect what they believed was their century-long battle to shore up civilization at its very edges.[33] The Mexican colonization law contained three major considerations: settlers must be of good moral character, they must be Catholic, and they must obey Mexican laws. While Mexican officials offered somewhat similar provisions to Native people, as individuals to obtain land grants, many were more honest about their inability to assimilate or conform to Catholicism.[34] Anglo settlers, on the other hand, dishonestly took Mexico's lands without any intention of becoming good Mexican citizens.[35] As historian Ernesto Chávez reminds us, ultimately, "transforming Americans into good Mexicans was virtually impossible, since their identity as Americans was already firmly established."[36] Although there is much to be said about the Texas Revolution and a concerted effort by Anglos, Tejanos, and some Native peoples to fight against what they perceived to be Mexico's incompetence in the Texas territory, demographic data in favor of a white, Anglo majority gave white Americans the upper hand in their push for an independent Texas. The Unites States government took notice.

For many US politicians, annexing Texas in 1845 meant the incorporation of a mostly Anglo population, as the nation continued its expansionist ventures toward the Pacific Ocean. Going to war with Mexico the following year, however, became not only about acquiring new territory but also about wresting this sacred land from "backward Mexicans" and bringing America's superior institutions to settle the so-called wilderness.[37] In the aftermath of the war, as US and Mexican officials negotiated peace, politicians like President James K. Polk put forth the idea of ceding all of Mexico. The possibility of extending US borders into territories less white than Texas caused many to question the imperial war's ultimate goals. The "All Mexico Movement," as Polk's push was called, frightened many politicians. It magnified the possibility of "racial mixing" with what Vermont Senator Solomon Foot called a "semi-barbarian population."[38] Others, such as South Carolina Senator John C. Calhoun, an ardent supporter of slavery, did not mince words when pontificating about the dangers of incorporating Mexico's population on the eve of Mexico's defeat in 1848.

During a now-infamous speech, Calhoun first invoked the United States' treatment of Native people as an example of US segregationist strategies to deal with nonwhite populations—what historian Natalia Molina calls the construction of racial scripts. "We have conquered many of the neighboring tribes of Indians, but we have never thought of holding them in subjection—never of incorporating them into our Union," Calhoun stated. "They have either been left as an independent people amongst us, or been driven into the forests." Then he spoke directly to his main concern: race.

> I know further, sir, that we have never dreamt of incorporating into
> our Union any but the Caucasian race—the free white race. To
> incorporate Mexico, would be the very first instance of the kind
> of incorporating an Indian race; for more than half of the Mexicans
> are Indians, and the other is composed chiefly of mixed tribes. I
> protest against such a union as that! Ours, sir, is the Government of
> a white race. The greatest misfortunes of Spanish America are to be
> traced to the fatal error of placing these colored races on an equality
> with the white race . . . And yet it is professed and talked about to

erect these Mexicans into a Territorial Government, and place them on an equality with the people of the United States. I protest utterly against such a project.[39]

Calhoun's unabashed white supremacy was made clear not only in his defense of slavery and embrace of the country's policy toward Native people but also in his disdain for incorporating vast populations of Mexicans considered nonwhite and "mixed race." Elevating Mexicans to the stature of Anglo-Americans, offering them equal rights, was unthinkable to men like Calhoun. Much like Babbitt's assessment of Mexicans more than fifty years later, Calhoun condemned Spanish America's "fatal error" in supposedly placing the "colored races" on an equal footing with whites—one he blamed for destroying the very "basis of society."[40] His condemnation of the "project" of incorporation also pointed to his understanding, and likely the understanding of other congressmen, that manifest destiny was more than a divine inevitability but one that should be ushered in through purposeful population design.

Some historians have pointed to how "not counting Mexicans" was central to the US war against Mexico. As Carey McWilliams wrote, "People fail to count the nonessential, the things and persons that exist only on sufferance; whose life tenure is easily revocable."[41] Counting, however, can also serve as justification for why you should be concerned about certain populations. For politicians like Calhoun, the notion of democratic and economic scarcity became an ever-present threat to white Americans; thus, the number of Mexicans in Mexico was simply *too much* for a white American nation to absorb. In the end, the United States ceded nearly half but not all of Mexico's territory upon signing the Treaty of Guadalupe Hidalgo in February 1848. With this land came people. Approximately 100,000 Mexican citizens could become American citizens within one year after the treaty's signing.[42] While some returned to Mexico, most people stayed on their land.

The US war with Mexico was, as historian Kelly Lytle Hernández contends, "an apex moment in the making of the United States as a settler society, namely, a white settler society," not only in the total destruction of "sovereign native communities" but also in constructing Mexican-origin people as never-citizens, another racial group within a white supremacist racial universe.[43] Despite guarantees under the Treaty of Guadalupe Hidalgo—protections for land, property, and rights as American citizens—the United States could not, in the words of Calhoun, bring Mexicans to the same level of equality as Anglo settlers. Mexicans were, as Rodolfo Acuña observes, a "class apart from the dominant race."[44] It is critical to underscore the significance of this moment in US, Mexican, and Mexican-origin people's history. Popular notions of Mexicans as so-called "half-breeds" or "mongrels" were prevalent before the war—in fact, these racial categorizations were used as justifications for seizing Mexico's territory—but after the war, these ideologies became codified in social, economic, and legal structures relegating Mexicans to the bottom rungs of America's racial ladder.

Of course, it is important to note the relational ways race and racism were conceived after the US war with Mexico and the Civil War and the legislative changes that marked Black people as not racially eligible for citizenship in different ways from Mexican-origin people.[45] Through inverted cartographies of race-making, Mexicans could, at times, exercise a modicum of legal power if they could prove having one drop of Spanish (white blood), while Black people, depending on the state, could be segregated with the most minimal detection of Black ancestry in their family lineage. Racialized notions of blood quantity and racial purity go further back than the colonial period, and they continued to exercise power during the industrial revolution.[46] Note also the qualifiers in the preceding sentences. Racial mechanisms for inclusion and exclusion varied from state to state; crossing internal borders altered one's access to rights and liberties well into the twentieth century.[47] The variations in legal and social standing further highlight the notion of a constructed, built, assembled racial universe, one in which racial categories were not immutable and relied on the racial classification of a host of racialized *Others*, including those who called themselves white.

White Demographic Change in the Late Nineteenth and Early Twentieth Centuries

In the aftermath of the US-Mexico War and the Civil War, older ideas about race splintered, producing new and revitalized racist refractions. Scientists extended the force of biology, medicine, and nature in support of racial classification, segregation, and continued exploitation. Conceptions about the significance of population quality and quantity were refined starting mid-century due, in part, to massive influxes of immigrants from Europe and Asia. Historian Matthew Frye Jacobson traces this back to the 1790 Naturalization Act that allowed "free white persons" access to American citizenship. In the fifty years after, immigration from Europe surged. The great famine in Ireland caused 1.2 million Irish to flee to the United States from

1846 to 1855. In that same period, nearly a million people from Germany arrived on American shores. Immigration waves continued, and by the 1860s, there were more than four million foreign-born persons—most from Ireland and Germany. Surges in the latter part of the nineteenth century and into the twentieth centuries from Italy and Russia produced a foreign-born population of so-called whites of more than 13.5 million in 1920.[48] Floods of European, but not Anglo-Saxon, so-called whites muddied the American racial schema during the early decades of the twentieth century. As scientists measured skull circumferences, nose widths, and eye shapes, they produced vast typologies of Nordic, Celt, Slav, Alpine, Hebrew, Mediterranean, Iberic, Latin, and Anglo-Saxon races.[49] Mexican-origin people were also part of reconfiguring this racial alchemy, but they fared far worse by the turn of the twentieth century than their European counterparts. Although the 1848 Treaty of Guadalupe Hidalgo guaranteed Mexicans in the captured territories American citizenship, making them de jure white under the 1790 Naturalization Act, Mexicans were never completely folded into the racial category, never enjoying its many privileges the way European immigrants could by the 1920s.

Settlers in the Borderlands

Tracking the history of these racial fault lines brings us closer to understanding the heavy burden population controls placed on racialized people in the US-Mexico borderlands at the dawn of the twentieth century. The process of "making up people" in the El Paso-Ciudad Juárez borderlands encapsulates how population pressures framed the region's history from its inception. Built on a massive tract of land originally owned by wealthy merchant Juan María Ponce de León and later sold to Benjamin Franklin Coons in 1849, El Paso straddled the northern Rio Grande. On the other side, surrounding the Spanish mission Nuestra Señora de Guadalupe built in 1659, sat El Paso del Norte.[50] With the signing of the Treaty of Guadalupe Hidalgo, Anglo settlers quickly made their way farther west and began to populate already established areas of the region.[51] The Mexican towns of Paso del Norte, San Elizario, Ysleta, and Socorro became critical outposts as Anglo migrants traveled west in search of gold and land in California.[52] During this time, Mexican communities, "alarmed at the prospects of a famine," were overwhelmed as white hordes sought provisions on their way west.[53]

Anglos who settled in the area worked swiftly with US officials to expropriate Mexican land. For instance, in 1849, T. Frank White, newly appointed prefect of the area, removed Mexicans north and east of the Rio Bravo, claiming Ysleta, Socorro, and San Elizario as US territory. US armed forces occupied and took possession of ejidos (communal land holdings) and the natural resources that surrounded the towns.[54] Although Mexican officials and residents protested the seizures of their lands and resources, wealthy Anglo settlers backed by US troops claimed these areas as their own, establishing military posts to protect their newly usurped lands from Mexicans still living in these towns.[55] A decade later, the US boundary commissioner tasked with delineating the official line in the sand drew the border between El Paso del Norte south of the Rio Grande and the "American city of Franklin"—renamed El Paso—on the northern banks of the river.[56] While migration to the region swelled in the following decades, Chicano historians remind us that the arrival of the railroad, in 1881, completely transformed El Paso and its relationship to its sister city, Ciudad Juárez.[57] Not only did this borderland crossroads become critical to trade between east and west, north and south, it also galvanized various industries including cattle ranching, agriculture, and most especially mining.[58] Critical to this burgeoning industrial zone were people and their labor.

Even before industrialization fanned the flames of economic expansion, it was clear who would be tasked with providing the human element fueling the fires of industry. As one early twentieth-century El Paso chronicler explained: "Nobody worked; that is nobody, except for Mexicans worked regularly. The 'white men' in the community did practically nothing for the very simple reason there was nothing to do, and the very natural result of this pleasing state of affairs was that Uncle Ben Dowell's saloon sheltered the entire American male population of the town for the greater part of every day and for nearly all of every night."[59] From the city's inception, Mexicans and Native people provided the labor for the Anglo elite, who quickly began to dominate the politics of the region. Migration propelled the engines of industry. Less than ten years after the arrival of the railroads there were 7,846 Anglos, 2,069 Mexicans, 810 "Colored" people, and 344 Chinese—a greater than 1,300 percent increase in total population from 736 residents in 1880.[60] At the turn of the century, these immigrants, mostly from Mexico, became the backbone of the mining and smelter, railroad, and ranching industries.[61] As a massive recession swept Mexico in the early 1900s, compounded by the Mexican Revolution in 1910, numbers of newly arrived Mexicans increased precipitously in El Paso.

Before movements of migrants remade the El Paso-Ciudad Juárez borderlands however, xenophobic concerns for new immigrants in the far west borderlands slammed against the United States' ability to control populations more systematically, generating a deep desire to codify the management of nonwhite immigration to the United States. Although European migration intensified racial questions about whiteness during these years, Anglos sought first to restrict Asian migration to the nation in the years after the Civil War. Fears of an invading Chinese population emerged from the westernmost regions of the United States—newly annexed California. Chinese women initially experienced America's racialist exclusion through its clumsily executed immigration system following passage of the Page Act in 1875.[62] The dramatic limitation of Chinese women immigrants was meant to curtail prostitution and the subsequent spread of venereal diseases among (Anglo) miners and laborers in the Sunshine state. Historians have strongly argued that little was done to measure the impact of the law's stated intentions; rather, the law should be read as a gendered racialist immigration policy with a three-pronged objective: to halt the immigration of Chinese people to the United States, to severely hamper their ability to settle, and to prevent them from establishing families in the United States.[63] The political objective, as observed by ethnic studies scholar Eithne Luibhéid, was to respond to "a constellation of what were believed to be serious threats to 'white' values, lives, and futures."[64]

The imagined threat of Chinese women's reproduction on US soil precipitated the first major immigration law of the nineteenth century in the United States. When it was clear that the Page Act would not halt Chinese migration, Congress passed the Chinese Exclusion Act, outlawing all Chinese immigration in 1882. In passing these race-based immigration laws, timing was critical. The 1875 Page Act came into being a mere seven years after the passage of the Fourteenth Amendment to the US Constitution enshrining birthright citizenship. Black Americans had fought to establish their "unassailable belonging" in the United States; their status as citizens, after the Civil War and the end of slavery, was tethered directly to their very birth on this land.[65] Under the Fourteenth Amendment, US citizenship, including all the rights and privileges granted under its protections, had an equalizing potential in this increasingly multiracial nation. Extending US citizenship and all its bounty to those born on US soil, regardless of race, undoubtedly contradicted notions of a white nation for whites only. Therefore, allowing Chinese women to migrate to the US and have US-born children had the potential of further unsettling an already strained relationship between reproduction, race, and citizenship.

Ushered in by eugenicists and nativists of the period, tighter connections were made between reproduction, immigration, and changing demographics in the United States.[66] Immigration restrictions became an important aspect of systematizing population controls to protect demographic futures. Historian Mae Ngai maintains that "immigration policy is constitutive of Americans' understanding of national membership and citizenship, drawing lines of inclusion and exclusion that articulate a desired composition—imagined if not necessarily realized—of the nation."[67] The power of an imagined white dominant population further grounded Anglo-Americans' dread at their inability to control the "desired composition" of their expanding nation.

The immigration debate encouraged eugenicists, nativists, and race-suicide alarmists to find fertile ground in the birth control movement in the United States, providing justifications for the movement's emergence in the US-Mexico borderlands decades later. *Eugenics*, a term coined by Sir Francis Galton in 1883, defined the "science of the improvement of the human race by better breeding."[68] As a field, eugenics was shaped by scientists, including Charles Davenport, a Harvard-trained biology professor, writing about the significance of heredity in relation to groups exhibiting chronic disease coupled with poverty, illiteracy, and other habits considered morally suspect. These groups were also marked as having high fertility rates.[69] Nativists eagerly extended these claims, blaming immigrants for exacerbating racial degeneration. Immigrants lowered the quality of the "native-born" American stock through miscegenation, were "naturally" predisposed to higher birth rates, and, through sheer magnitude of numbers, shunted the "native-born" white birth rate down.[70] Babbitt's contemporaries, famous academics of the era including Ross, Grant, Stoddard, and Jordan, wrote extensively about what they perceived to be the damaging correlations between the precipitous drop in white birth rates at the end of the nineteenth century and rising birth rates among immigrants. Francis Amasa Walker, director of the US census for 1870 and 1880, had made this direct connection a national issue as early as 1890.[71]

Fear Breeds Violence

The irony, of course, that "native-born" whites feared being demographically surpassed by nonwhite migrants flies in the face of the actual terrorism whites perpetrated against Mexicans in the borderlands during the early twentieth century.[72] In the aftermath of the US-Mexico War, the United

States enabled various mechanisms for population control, including violence—a tried-and-true method since the early days of Spanish colonization. At the turn of the century, people could cross the US-Mexico borderline with little effort, but Texas Rangers and other vigilantes made sure to police racial lines with sheer brutality. Historian Monica Muñoz Martinez calls this "forging borders with violence."[73] Anglos instituted regimes of mass terror via surveillance, extrajudicial beatings, and killings, producing real fear among Mexican-origin residents in the region.[74] In Texas alone, estimates suggest that between 1848 and 1928, vigilantes lynched 232 Mexicans—state-sponsored terror would include many more.[75]

Racist violence could, as Muñoz Martinez argues, be a double-edged sword for Anglos attempting to manage Mexican communities in the state. While violence allowed Anglos to maintain a kind of socio-racial dominance over Mexicans, it also had the potential to interrupt the exploitation of Mexican labor. "Crops needed tending," Muñoz Martinez explains, and "if word spread that Mexican laborers were being routinely mistreated, workers might flee for other opportunities in the South or West."[76] For Anglos, C. S. Babbitt's screed was not unfounded; their desires to exploit Mexican labor collided against Mexicans' potential for racially polluting "American civilization." Neil Foley similarly described how "immigration of Mexicans into Texas . . . raised *fears* [my emphasis] among Texas whites that Mexicans would destroy white civilization." Greedy ranchers and farmers argued the opposite: that "Mexicans were simply too inferior to represent a threat to white America."[77] Racial logics justifying exploitative conditions and mass terror bred a dynamic system for population control. While Anglo-Americans manufactured anxieties over the supposed "browning of America," they built long-lasting mechanisms to promote and protect murderous brutality against Mexican workers in the borderlands.

Public Health and Immigration Controls as Population Management

At the same time that vigilantes and Texas Rangers made public violence into one kind of population management, public health campaigns led population control efforts via medicine and immigration across the border.[78] In cities like Los Angeles, public health officials braced against threats of epidemics among the so-called "ignorant aliens"—mostly Mexican and Japanese populations—in the late 1910s.[79] In Texas, public health officials demarcated brown bodies as unclean and infectious as early as 1916 with inspection areas established for border crossers in Laredo and, in the following year, El Paso.[80] Efforts to confront a supposed influx of typhus from Mexico spurred the US Public Health Service (USPHS) to build a disinfection plant on the Santa Fe international bridge linking El Paso with its sister city, Ciudad Juárez.

By early 1917, Claude C. Pierce, a senior surgeon of the USPHS, had established a full-fledged quarantine of all people entering El Paso from Mexico. Mexican people were inspected, deloused, and catalogued to qualify for admittance into the United States. These inspections continued well into the 1920s as Mexicans coming into El Paso and those residing on the city's south side were viewed as purveyors of disease, even as no new cases of typhus were documented.[81] Moreover, after his time with the USPHS, Pierce became part of larger networks of national and international organizations dedicated to fighting overpopulation, this time through massive birth control campaigns seen as critical to public health. Pierce's career was distinguished by his time as medical director of Planned Parenthood Federation of America in the 1940s.[82] In the meantime, El Paso civic leaders welcomed federal public health efforts as Anglo residents, like C. S. Babbitt, became concerned with the rapidly changing population quality and quantity in their city, especially as migrants were increasingly linked to disease.[83]

Thousands of migrants leaving war-torn Mexico arrived at the largest land border crossing as they sought refuge in the United States. Vicki Ruiz has appropriately called the El Paso-Ciudad Juárez border the Ellis Island of the Southwest.[84] Reports of massive famines and the spread of typhus in cities along Mexico's north, including Saltillo, Monterrey, Piedras Negras, and Torreón, became further evidence of the grim economic conditions facing the country during the war, and encouraged US border controls.[85] US immigration records show that approximately 173,663 Mexican nationals entered the United States through "legal channels" between 1910 and 1919. In 1911, over "23,000 people immigrated to the United States through Juárez alone."[86] These figures, however, exclude undocumented border crossers who likely numbered in the thousands as well.

Mexico's 1910 revolution unleashed a flood of racial animosity harbored against Mexican migrants in the borderlands. Babbitt's anti-Mexican screed (1909) was published the year before the Mexican Revolution erupted across the border, causing mass migration into the United States. By 1900, Mexican-origin people numbered 8,748 in a city of over 15,900 residents.[87] After 1910, the Mexican-origin population expanded rapidly, and in 1920, there were 39,571 Mexican-origin people in a city of 77,560. The following decade, numbers had grown to 68,476 among 102,421 total residents of El Paso.[88]

White migrants arrived, too. Trainloads of Anglo health seekers, mostly men, traveled west to find climatic cures for respiratory diseases like tuberculosis. Late in the nineteenth century, these men helped spread the infectious disease to Mexican locals, passing it via Mexican women domestic laborers who came to care for these white men in their homes. By the 1920s, tuberculosis ran rampant in the mostly Mexican neighborhoods of South El Paso, and white El Paso leaders reimagined tuberculosis as a "Mexican disease."[89] Local politicians sought to address disease in overcrowded and poverty-stricken dwellings in South El Paso, as increasing numbers of people settled in the area. Social and economic issues, like poverty and public health, became linked to the city's changing demographics, threatening Anglo-American dreams of a white border metropolis.

According to city officials, El Paso's mostly Mexican-inhabited south side was a prime example of what Thomas Malthus—the late eighteenth-century English political economist and demographer—would have called overpopulation's disastrous links to economic degradation and social degeneration. First published in 1925, the Kessler Report, a City of El Paso planning document, described south-side neighborhoods like Segundo Barrio and Chihuahuita as "covered with one-story or two-story tenement houses crowded with human beings." The Kessler Report reinforced notions that overpopulation was specific to the Mexican-origin community, stating that "the population [in the tenements] is almost entirely of Spanish speaking antecedents, mainly Mexican born or of Mexican parentage. A large proportion are not citizens." Findings in the report were echoed in studies continuing into the 1930s, as its authors pushed for changes such as building new tenements and bathing facilities for residents. A year before the birth control clinic opened in El Paso, the report's author applied for federal aid to help alleviate the destitution of south-side residents. He concluded that "indecent, unsafe, and unsanitary conditions in the housing of the City as a whole are confined almost entirely to the substandard areas of the south side."[90] As historian Mario Garcia contends, overcrowding in South El Paso had much to do with "racial prejudice" among Anglos residents of El Paso. The segregation of Mexican migrants in these barrios also provided a ready "labor pool" to nearby "railroads, construction firms, downtown retail stories, laundries, and other employers, even American housewives, found needed workers" in El Paso's south side.[91]

Local concerns for overpopulation, poverty, and racial degeneration similarly informed national discussions about immigration. After the Chinese Exclusion Act of 1882, the Immigration Act of 1917 barred most Asian migration, including from India and Japan.[92] The 1917 act affected the movement of people along the southern border as well, as immigration controls sought to manage circular migration from Mexico.[93] The passage of the Johnson-Reed Immigration Act of 1924 and the establishment of the Border Patrol that same year were responses to heightened racial anxieties along the US southern border.[94] As Mexicans dodged cumbersome and humiliating immigration requirements like a head tax, a visa fee, and the odious public health inspection centers at the border crossings in cities like El Paso, border patrol agents began deporting those who had entered the country illegally. In 1929, border patrol sent nearly 15,000 people back across the southern border—an increase of over 750 percent since 1925.[95]

The 1924 Immigration Act quota restrictions created what Ngai termed a *new racial taxonomy*, "distinguish[ing] persons of the 'colored races' from 'white' persons from 'white' countries." The quota system formalized a racial hierarchy within the immigration system, and while migration of European whites was restricted, the "colored races," mostly from the so-called Asiatic countries, were denied even a minimal number of entrants. The national origins quota system reinforced the idea that the United States "should remain a white nation descended from Europe."[96] Controlling human reproduction, then, became the natural extension of guarding against massive racial demographic shifts in the United States. Alterations in immigration laws were intimately connected to producing census data and the analysis of US demographics in the early twentieth century. Joseph A. Hill, a prominent statistician and chief of the Division of Statistical Research at the Bureau of the Census in Washington, DC, was charged with constructing the elaborate quota system for the Immigration Act of 1924. The quota figures were not formalized by Congress until 1929.[97] The following year, the national census made a remarkable change. Hill reported, "The Mexicans, defined as a separate race for the first time in the census of 1930, include all persons who were born in Mexico or who have parents born in Mexico and are not definitely white, Negro, Indian, Chinese, or Japanese."[98] Although Mexicans had been omitted from the 1924 quota system and up to this point had been included as "white" on census tabulations, in 1930 Hill declared Mexicans a new racial category. These changes were supported as the definitions of whiteness—particularly as envisioned under the Immigration Act of 1924—began to narrow.

Hill's demographic research was important not only for immigration quotas and census data but also for activists like Margaret Sanger, leader of the birth control movement, who eagerly tabulated patterns of procreation, providing quantifiable justifications for restricting births among migrants and the poor. Hill's position paper "Composition of the American Population" (1936) became part of Sanger's arsenal of information as her organization fought for the distribution of birth control across the country. The statistician's insights suggested that in the span of seventy-five years, most whites in the United States would be "native born"; however, at that moment there were 25 million white persons born of (white) immigrant parents. According to Hill, they would have a "large influence in shaping the future of the country," and thus it would be pertinent to keep a strict tally of their parents' countries of origin.[99] While Hill's analysis pertained to those who descended from a so-called white lineage, his insights were extended to nonwhite groups as well. The longue durée history of demographic futures past was recast through early twentieth-century demography.

Congress considered the progeny of those outside the spheres of whiteness as its members debated bills H.R. 3673 and H.R. 77, meant to extend birthright citizenship to women with US citizenship whose children were born abroad. Armed with statistics of rising demographics among US-born Chinese and US-born Mexican communities, politicians well versed in "race-based immigration laws" worried that nonwhite second- and third-generation residents not only would claim US citizenship but, "more threateningly, were now poised to exercise the rights of citizenship." Natalia Molina contends that politicians' fixation on Mexican-origin women's supposed excessive fecundity suggested that "not even deportation would be the solution most hoped it would be."[100]

The Great Depression brought tensions over population quality and quantity into stark relief. By the 1930s, deportations of Mexican-origin people, many of them US citizens, had skyrocketed, particularly in the border states of California and Texas. While cities like Los Angeles experienced racial turmoil, the havoc of forced deportations was more pronounced in border cities like El Paso, with its immediate proximity to Ciudad Juárez.[101] Cleofás Calleros, a respected El Paso community member, leader of the lay Catholic organization the Knights of Columbus, and Mexican border representative of the National Catholic Welfare Conference's (NCWC) Bureau of Immigration in El Paso, guided the repatriation process in the city. Calleros was often tasked with providing information about the "Mexican question" to city and state officials, as authorities sought to siphon off economic and social pressures, lack of jobs, and need for charity and relief onto the backs of Mexican-origin people.

In 1934, Calleros convened a group of Mexican-origin leaders across the state of Texas to meet in Austin to discuss the creation of a "Mexican Problems Committee" within the Texas Rehabilitation Commission. He testified before the group, including several Anglo members, that in his capacity as the representative of the NCWC's Bureau of Immigration, he had helped many people from Los Angeles County in the process of repatriation and concluded that "California just wanted to get rid of persons of Mexican descent regardless of their condition in life or anything else." Furthermore, he maintained that most of those who had been paid by California to leave were "American citizens." Texas, he confirmed, was no better than California. "I have had the occasion to travel all over Texas for the past twelve years and I am giving you the benefit of my experience," he stated.[102] Calleros continued:

> There is a very peculiar situation in Texas that has been brought
> on by race prejudice. I think that has a lot to do with the suffering
> of these people . . . Mexican people suffer primarily because they
> are classed by themselves . . . There is always a tendency of
> segregation and separation. There is no such thing as social or
> economic equality. There is always that feeling that prevails in every
> community referring to Mexicans as Mexicans and also referring
> people of another color. I always hear the expression 'We have so
> many cases; so many are "Mexicans" and so many are "White." That
> is the thing that all Mexicans or Mexican descent persons do not like
> that. They resent it.[103]

This brand of racial resentment had existed just below the surface in the borderlands since at least 1848, but the Great Depression reinvigorated racial animosities as state and nonstate officials questioned who were the most "deserving" of charity, welfare, and economic relief.

Concerns regarding charity and welfare that were raised during the forced deportation of thousands of Mexican-origin people, many who were themselves US-born citizens, had a compounding effect when viewed in relation to racist public health campaigns and immigration controls that directly targeted Mexican-origin people. This racist ecosystem set the parameters for future anti-Mexican population management projects, such as the borderlands iteration of the birth control movement in the late 1930s. Middle-class, Mexican-origin Catholic community members—men like

Calleros—were not afraid to call out Anglo hostilities and racism. Yet, even as Calleros provided critical documentation of anti-Mexican racism and exclusion in the greater Southwest, he later sought to restrict access to reproductive health care using religious justifications to champion his cause.

Demostopic Narratives and Reproductive Control during the Great Depression

Concerns about population "quality" certainly informed national conversations about reproductive control. For example, in *Buck v. Bell* (1927), the US Supreme Court decided that states could forcibly sterilize people they deemed "unfit" to reproduce.[104] Individuals considered outside the bounds of white racial citizenship—including poor and disabled whites—were inscribed as economic burdens and potential pollutants to the body politic, allowing states to carry out policies for their reproductive control or outright removal.

Babbitt had long since died, and yet those who inspired his racist machinations continued to write and foment anti-Mexican racism in the United States; reproduction was a central concern. The nationally-recognized David Starr Jordan and Madison Grant had deep ties to eugenicists across the country and had worked alongside Drs. Paul Popenoe, Clarence G. Campbell, Charles Goethe, and Harry H. Laughlin, ardent eugenicists and leaders in public policy, who were enabling sterilization campaigns against the so-called feebleminded and hereditarily "unfit" in California. A high proportion of those sterilized were Mexican-origin people.[105] For decades, these men had written extensively about the perils of unchecked fertility among the rapidly growing Mexican-origin community in the American Southwest.[106] Charles Goethe, founder of the Eugenics Society of Northern California and Jordan's close ally in the struggle against white racial degeneration, wrote in 1935 that "it is the high birthrate that makes Mexican peon immigration such a menace. Peons multiply like rabbits."[107] Hysterics over low birth rates among "native-born" whites and increased birth rates among immigrant populations served as counterpoints to rising militarization, public health, and immigration controls along the southern border during these same decades.[108]

While historians have remarked on Laughlin's work in California, as the head of the Eugenics Record Office and a leader of sterilization campaigns in the state, he also engaged in extensive communication with legislators in Texas interested in passing anti-Mexican immigration legislation in

Congress. He addressed many of his letters to John Calvin Box, Democratic congressman from Texas and another staunch supporter of the 1924 Johnson-Reed Act.[109] In 1930, Laughlin detailed a plan wherein the Departments of Labor and Justice would bring forward a test case to determine whether Mexican immigrants were legally "neither a white person nor a person of African descent . . . [and] such as is the case biologically, then he is definitely, under the present law, ineligible for naturalization, and consequently is also ineligible for admission as an immigrant." This could provide a critical legislative workaround to "effectively solve the Mexican problem without any direct legislation," he surmised.[110] As historian Alexandra Stern explains, Laughlin had "strong opinions about sanguinity" and maintaining racial purity among so-called American men and Mexican-origin women in the borderlands.[111] Laughlin understood that some "unpleasantness" would result from closing the US-Mexico border to the "average Mexican immigrant," but perhaps Congress could pursue efforts to reach a "white standard for immigration and naturalization"—with immigrants from Canada.[112] Despite Laughlin's pleas, Box replied with difficult news. Even as many Congress members agreed that something must be done to address the "Mexican emergency" sweeping the American Southwest, "repeated and ample hearings have been granted those who want cheap and abundant peon labor."[113] The unfortunate tensions between realizing a "white standard for immigration and naturalization" and the need to exploit Mexican-origin people's labor consistently thwarted even the most anti-Mexican proponents.[114]

While these ideas circulated among leading eugenicists in the movement, men with the social and intellectual profile of Madison Grant brought these discussions to a national stage. Meant to rival his 1916 *The Passing of the Great Race*, Grant wrote effusively in his final tome about the racial and cultural degeneration that was sure to befall borderland communities if they did not act on the issue of Mexican immigration and their uncontrolled reproduction. Grant had much to say about Mexicans in the face of the 1930 census when Mexicans officially became a racial group. "Since the sixteen million residents of Mexico are the nearest large body of people in a position to supply immigrants to the United States and ready to do so, a study of their composition is of the highest importance at the present time."[115]

Grant, a lawyer, bulwark of nativist thought, and lobbyist for the Immigration Act of 1924, dedicated the last chapter of his book *The Conquest of a Continent, or The Expansion of Races in America* (1933) to America's most pressing racial menace: Mexican immigration and reproduction. He focused on the need for exploitable labor, stating that "industries accustomed to depend upon cheap, ignorant, and docile workers from Mediterranean or Alpine countries turned to the illiterate Indians on the South as a ready substitute." This reliance on exploitable labor created a "stream of arrivals across the border, more illegal than legal," that saw "more than a million Mexicans" enter the United States. The economic depression of 1929, he maintained, "stemmed this tide and apparently prevented Mexico from re-conquering peacefully, by an immigrant invasion, the territory it had lost by the decision of war in 1848 . . ." Grant's fixation on what happens after the need for exploitable labor was satiated influenced much of the birth control movement's work in the borderlands. His foreshadowing observed that:

> Mexican immigration to the United States, which is made up overwhelmingly of the poorer Indian element, has brought nothing but disadvantages. It has created, particularly in the Southwestern States, an exploited peasant class unconformable with the principles of American civilization. This population, neither physically nor mentally up to the prevailing standards, is producing a large contribution to the future American race, since every one of its numerous children born in the States becomes an American citizen by birth . . . Such studies as have been made in the Southwestern States indicate that the average Mexican family is at least half again as large as the average white family. Thus there is every reason to expect that, without a sharp limitation of such immigration, the Southwest will become more and more *Mexicanized* [my emphasis].[116]

While Grant depicted the Mexicanization of the Southwest as inevitable given the geographic proximity of Mexico and the US's ceaseless need for Mexican labor, birth control activists and other El Paso elites were not ready to give up. Historian Monica Perales explains that despite Anglo leaders' need for Mexican labor as a vital asset to the "city's [economic] growth strategy," Anglos were not going to let El Paso become a "Mexican City."[117] Deploying different strategies to subvert the potential Mexicanization of the US Southwest, El Paso city leaders, including birth control advocates, enacted borderland population controls, ones deeply concerned with protecting the United States at the nation's edge.

Conclusion

In a 1929 letter to Charles Davenport, Harry Laughlin suggested he and Davenport "investigate the more immediate" and "possible long-term effect of the present Mexican immigration on the racial make-up and hereditary quality of the population of those regions of American states which are now receiving Mexican immigrants." Laughlin suggested the two men travel to the US-Mexico border to "study" and "add to the knowledge of the formation of population character due to migration."[118] Mexican repatriation—the largest mass deportation event in all US history—began in earnest the following year. Even as eugenicists studied the long-term effects of so-called racial degeneracy among Mexican-origin people and local and state authorities attempted to force Mexican-origin people out of the country, for many borderland Anglos the "Mexican problem" persisted. By the 1930s, the process of counting people and "making people up," denying nonwhite populations the potential for self-governance and bodily autonomy, also came to determine their human value.

Anglos directed their racial fears, accumulated over centuries of conquest, colonization, and capitalist accumulation, at rapidly growing poor nonwhite populations. What cruel projection. The loss of human property during the Civil War, the supposed forfeiture of white rights during Reconstruction, and an imagined vanishing of territory during the great migrations of Asians, Eastern and Southern Europeans, and Mexicans in the latter part of the nineteenth century produced the early seedlings of white victimization. Falling white birth rates confirmed Anglos' imagined great white loss, the end of Western civilization and the crumbling of the world's greatest white nation.[119] Fear breeds violence. In the US-Mexico borderlands, violence was institutionalized through border militarization and public health regimes. These institutions systematized the act of counting and classification, turning it into a source of terror for racialized populations as white vigilantes publicly brutalized Mexican communities in the region. Nativists and eugenicists resurrected Thomas Malthus's thesis, finding eager supporters among white, middle-class women advancing the claim that contraception would solve the problem of excessive reproduction among the group that most threatened white numeric power: Mexicans.

Instead of leaning into fears of white death, however, birth control activists in the borderlands advanced the cause of reproductive control aimed at the "surging brown mass" to promote white life. Emboldened by their fierce sisters in the decades before, the white women who advocated for their own bodily autonomy through suffrage and voluntary motherhood, the twentieth-century white women birth control activists understood the power of discourse and action in support of population control. Securing their place in the American racial and gender hierarchy, upper-middle-class white women activists sided with patriarchal nativists. They would make it their duty to save the nation from the foreign pollutants propagating "like rabbits." White women birth controllers would do what immigration and public health controls and brutal violence could not. They would fight to control the Mexican origin working class via contraception. They would, as C. S. Babbitt had alluded, attack the problem of overpopulation from the womb. The following chapter examines their story.

2 Fighting for Control

Race, Religion, and the World White Women Made

. . . .

"Should we not examine our consciences?" Ruth Tracht asked during a meeting she had infiltrated of the newly assembled El Paso birth control committee. Tracht, first vice president of the El Paso Diocesan Council of Catholic Women, posed the question to various El Paso birth control advocates and the birth control movement's national leader herself, Margaret Sanger. The birth controllers had gathered the day after Sanger and Betty Mary Goetting, the head of the El Paso birth control contingent, had organized a large lecture in support of contraception in the borderlands. It was early 1937, and Sanger was traveling across the United States advancing the movement for birth control and family planning via small women-run birth control clinics. Tracht, questioning the birth control advocate's intentions of establishing the first clinic in the heart of El Paso's Mexican-origin enclave, continued, "Are we paying a living wage to servants from *that* [my emphasis] section of El Paso?"[1] Goetting replied to Tracht's query first. She conceded that perhaps her peers had "abused the house servant wage question." Nonetheless, Goetting believed that if women in that section of town had fewer children, those children "could have gone through high school and fitted themselves for a higher type of work." Not satisfied with Goetting's answer, Tracht carried on, asking again why birth control committee members were set on establishing a clinic on the south side rather than one on El Paso's north side. She reminded birth control activists that city health officials had documented a rise of "social diseases"—sexually transmitted infections—among residents north of the train tracks. This time Sanger responded, "It seems to me that your South side constitutes a great social problem with high birth rate and low economic status."[2] During Sanger's visit to the border, one of many she made as she mentored Goetting and her colleagues, Tracht had been one of the only white women to openly confront Sanger and Goetting's plan to build a birth control clinic on El Paso's south side. Tracht, a devote Catholic, vehemently opposed the birth control movement's activism in El Paso.

While chapter 1 provided the backdrop for the white settler world Anglo residents created and sought to protect, chapter 2 brings to light the worldmaking of upper-middle-class white women as they sought to help preserve white settler power in the borderlands through birth control. Although several studies exist examining the national and international history of the Planned Parenthood Federation of America (PPFA), not many studies focus on community Planned Parenthoods, with particular attention to local and regional contexts, such as the US-Mexico borderlands.[3] This chapter brings into stark relief the organizational mechanisms and rationales produced through and by the work of birth controllers across the state of Texas and the borderlands. It examines how these borderland organizations confronted the Catholic Church, an institution that supposedly represented a paternalistic rebuke to white women's family planning campaigns. Chapter 2 examines the work and ideologies of those who sought, for different reasons, to fight for control over Mexican-origin women's fertility in the aftermath of the Great Depression and amid the forced deportation of thousands of Mexican-origin people in the United States in the 1930s and 1940s borderlands. Tracht's interactions with the leaders of the birth control movement reveal the tensions that characterized the nearly seventy-year history of the birth control movement's activism in the borderlands.

Outlining Tensions over Birth Control

In the borderlands, white women birth control advocates made their world of social reform about cutting "social problems" off at the root. Tracht's suggestion that birth control advocates "examine [their] consciences" regarding the "servant wage" was revealing. Surely, these upper-middle-class white women could afford to pay domestic workers higher salaries. According to Goetting and Sanger, however, low wages did not necessarily impoverish people; rather, they believed in the racist logic that the problems plaguing El Paso's south side could be boiled down to population *quality* and *quantity*. Correlations between race and overpopulation, expressed by C. S. Babbitt and other race theorists during the first decades of the twentieth century, drew a line connecting nativist, eugenic, and neo-Malthusian philosophies to hyper-fertility and its centrality to social ills.[4] Population control *ideology*, the notion that white settlers must build infrastructures, both material and discursive, to manage, maintain, and discipline nonwhite populations for the good of white settler social, political, and economic power, infused the movement for birth control in the borderlands from the beginning.

Contraceptive campaigns touting the end of poverty had the added advantage of deflecting critiques about exploitative labor conditions, including bad pay, as well as deeply imbedded structural and institutional issues that produced and perpetuated poverty in the years after the Great Depression. Tracht's inquiry about the exploitative "living wage paid to the servants from *that* [my emphasis] area of town" and Sanger and Goetting's response provide a window into population control logics embraced during this time. Even as the economic crash of the era revealed—to some extent—how poverty might be mitigated by the state, birth control activists defined poverty as a personal, moral failure rather than a systemic result of economic exploitation and social neglect. Under the birth control clinic's mantra, "The Charity to End All Charities," hundreds of wealthy El Paso residents gave time and money in their attempts to abscond from any social responsibility for producing the conditions that forced Mexican-origin people into poverty. Middle-class white women campaigning for the use of birth control among El Paso's Mexican-origin community was what scholar E. Cassandra Dame-Griff's calls "benevolent interventionism," controlling the supposed *excessiveness* of the Mexican-origin community for the betterment of white settler society.[5] Birth controllers believed smaller, regulated families would be society's silver bullet, solving the issues of poverty, deplorable health conditions, derelict housing, lack of education, and supposed eugenic maladies brought on by uncontrolled fertility.

Contraception, birth control advocates believed, could also help discipline workers. As Goetting suggested, Mexican-origin children (and presumably their parents as well) might fit themselves for a "higher type of work," if there were only fewer of them. Goetting's answer obscured the centrality of Mexican-origin people's "menial labor," and especially Mexican women's labor, to the growth and proliferation of wealth among Anglos in El Paso. For most of the twentieth century, Mexican-origin women were singularly recruited for domestic labor in the region.[6] Mexican-origin women built what some scholars call "economies of care."[7] They provided essential domestic labor, cleaning and maintaining homes as well as rearing Anglo children. Mexican-origin women's work certainly extended beyond Anglo homes, as they also labored in laundries, as farm workers, and in factories across the US Southwest. Census data from the 1930s suggests that Mexican-origin women in this region were overrepresented in the service and farmworker industries, 38.4 percent and 20.7 percent, respectively.[8] Reproductive discipline evoked concern for overpopulation but also had the potential to be a critical tool for labor control. As Natalie Lira contends, in California, "the expressed purpose of institutionalization and sterilization was to facilitate young working-class Mexican-origin women's entry into low-paid domestic, industrial, and care work."[9] I examine the proliferation of care economies, reproductive care, the significance of social and stratified reproduction, and their connection to Mexican-origin women's labor in the following chapter. But it is critical to underscore that, while upper-middle-class white birth control activists pointed to Mexican-origin women's fertility as an important marker of poverty, without Mexican-origin women's labor in their homes, birth control activists would not have had time to engage in such a project.[10]

As birth control activists envisioned how to combat overpopulation, they also confronted the Catholic Church's hostility toward birth control as "unnatural" and the opinion adopted by some Catholics in El Paso, like Tracht's, that birth control campaigns were unfair attacks against the poor. Although this was a common battle in other parts of the country, in the borderlands Mexican-origin people made up the vast majority of Roman Catholics. Protestant and Jewish people were often considered Anglo or white. Confrontations in El Paso, however, revealed deep anti-Catholic sentiments that wove together race, gender, religion, and class. Most of the early supporters of the birth control movement in El Paso were Protestant or Jewish, white, and wealthy. Aside from a small community of elite Mexican exiles, most Catholics in El Paso were economically poor Mexicans and relegated to Chihuahuita and Segundo Barrio, neighborhoods located *south* of the train tracks.[11] These communities represented the largest congregation of Mexican Catholics from 1900 to 1930 in El Paso.[12] Within the birth control movement in the borderlands, religion served as a proxy for race.

Even before Tracht's questions, hostility toward Sanger's 1937 visit started from the "first mention of her name and first printing of her picture" in local newspapers.[13] Despite calls by the Catholic Church for a boycott of Sanger's appearances, she gave a speech at the Hotel Del Norte in El Paso the night before her confrontation with Tracht. Dr. Will Rogers, the president of the El Paso County Medical Society and chief of staff at the Hotel Dieu, the city's only Catholic hospital, introduced Sanger at the event. In a clear swipe at the Catholic Church, Goetting later exclaimed, "What a triumph that was for us!"[14] Addressing more than seventy-five doctors, their wives, El Paso nurses, and other interested guests, Sanger described a dire situation for humanity if overpopulation remained unchecked.[15] "The advance of Christianity, of charity, or humanitarianism, will not allow the natural order of nature to dispose of the feeble-minded, the diseased, the insane, the old as it should," Sanger said. "Though it may sound cruel," she continued, "they should die, if they live they will, in majority of cases reproduce their kind, which is to throw upon the social order of the world certain types who are illiterate, deformed, and diseased, from birth."[16] Sanger's grotesque assessment about those considered potential social pollutants and her support for their demise advanced key issues in the borderlands. She sought to connect social ills to reproduction and the existence of the so-called diseased and deformed to Catholicism.

Sanger's demand for withholding charity and humanitarianism was a direct attack on the Catholic Church. Social Darwinists suggested that aiding the "unfit" interrupted natural selection, and their contempt for charity was meant to provoke Catholics in particular. Historian Kathleen Tobin observes that "this concern over charity increasingly drew Catholicism into the debate [over birth control] as Catholics were viewed as overly sentimental and unrealistic in giving to the poor."[17] Sanger, never one to shy away from controversy, invited the Catholic Church's antagonism as she chided the sentimentality of those wanting to "save" the unfit. She eagerly embraced the "The Charity to End All Charities" slogan of the birth control advocates in El Paso.[18]

A White Middle-Class Woman's World

Birth control's potential for mitigating some of the most pressing social ills of the early twentieth century animated birth control activists' population control ideologies and the overall trajectory of the movement in the borderlands. Increased poverty and disease, coupled with what nativists and eugenicists believed to be excessive fertility among nonwhite populations, led a group of Protestant and Jewish white women in El Paso to take matters into their own hands. This was not an out-of-the-ordinary response since white middle-class women had a well-established history as social reformers—abolitionists, suffragists, and in the temperance movement— throughout the nineteenth century. Many derived their sense of moral authority from Victorian notions of true womanhood, including piety, purity, domesticity, and the importance of producing a good Christian home.[19]

In the twentieth century, other activists firmly grounded their advocacy in the ideology of maternalism. Historian Molly Ladd-Taylor observes that maternalism "cannot be understood apart from the white protestant alarm over 'race suicide'" as well as the rise of scientific motherhood and changes in white middle-class women's connection to domestic work.[20] These virtues were racialized and classed; they were the exclusive domain of white upper- and middle-class women and defined how they viewed their place in society. As the promoters of American values, Anglo women social reformers derived their belief that it was their "moral and civic responsibility" to instruct immigrants in the social and cultural mores of the "American family."[21] As massive changes engulfed the country at the turn of the twentieth century, the ways industrialization, for instance, mobilized millions of young women into the US labor force, white women continued to see themselves as the "guardians of virtue."[22] Often, these young women workers were immigrants, caught in emerging discourses about women's potential sexual agency and their identities as workers, not wives.[23] Notions of whiteness evolved, and white womanhood's power began to take on a greater salience in the years after the passage of the Nineteenth Amendment. Race became linked to gender and class in critical ways. Those defining the parameters of social reform movements were predominately white women (and sometimes men), who used race as a cudgel to reinforce gendered labor expectations as the working class became less white in some areas of the country.

In turn-of-the-century El Paso, middle- and upper-middle class white women had been at the forefront of maternalist efforts to promote El Paso as a beacon of public health. For instance, the Woman's Charity Association championed a "Save the Babies" campaign in 1910 meant to curb soaring infant mortality rates.[24] As one historian of El Paso observed, "while public health reformers claimed to seek social justice, their efforts often resulted in social control."[25] Even as they sought to end infant death, notions of racial superiority compelled white women's ideas of *progress*. These ideas derived from their white, middle-class, Protestant affirmations in restraint, frugality, and order in a place dangerously close to a country understood to be in constant disorder: Mexico. An extension of their baby-saving work was the establishment of a "School for Mothers," which consisted of white women teaching mostly Mexican-origin women how to hygienically care for their babies, since high infant mortality rates were concentrated among the Mexican-origin community.[26] Although these programs did not last, they did, as one historian noted, "set a precedent" for future Anglo women's work in the borderlands. "Mexican mothers, and future mothers, would be an on-going focus of philanthropic efforts" among white women reformers in El Paso.[27]

The only "consistent source of social services" in El Paso's south side was the Rose Gregory Houchen House established in 1912 by white women missionaries. It was meant to support women wage workers by providing Mexican-origin women a place to sleep and a kindergarten for their children.[28] In the decades that followed, the missionaries subjected Mexican-origin women to a vast array of Americanization programs. While Houchen provided much-needed services in the most poverty-stricken areas of El Paso, especially in the arena of health care, offering relatively inexpensive prenatal classes, pregnancy exams, and immunizations at its adjoining clinic and hospital, it nonetheless fostered a white racial gaze whereby white women became the ultimate arbiters of social reform and progress through attempts at religious conversion.[29] And yet, as Vicki Ruiz concludes, "in the end, Mexican women utilized Houchen's social services; they did not, by and large, adopt its tenets of Christian Americanization."[30] Even as these organizations created spaces for Anglo women to engage in missionary efforts to Anglicize their Mexican-origin workers, Mexican-origin women also learned how to utilize what little resources they were offered without succumbing to powerful Americanization programming. Importantly, the history of organizations like Houchen and its affiliation with Newark Methodist Maternity Hospital decades later produced networks that both Anglo women birth controllers and Mexican-origin women of reproductive age tapped into for different reasons. While Mexican-origin women used the tools provided in these spaces as a means of survival as they navigated social, political, and economic marginalization, white middle-class women used these spaces to further enhance their claims to citizenship as the protectors of the nation.[31]

Eugenic Feminists in the Borderlands

Birth control activists in the borderlands, like Goetting and Sanger, enacted what Asha Nadkarni's calls *eugenic feminism*. Rising anti-immigrant sentiment in the late nineteenth and early twentieth centuries coincided with the expansion of white women's feminist activism as suffragists and, later, birth control advocates.[32] In the borderlands, these ideologies were compounded by anti-Mexican racism and fears about overpopulation, the threat of being overcome by Mexicans. These anxieties animated white women's activism and their efforts to constrain the Mexican-origin population in the service of both local and national aims. Goetting and Sanger's eugenic feminist activism brings this borderlands history into conversations with white US feminists' attempts to work in the service of nationalist aims on a local level.[33]

White women in El Paso took up the call to protect their city and nation in various ways, one of the most pernicious being contraceptive campaigns directly targeting Mexican-origin women's reproduction. One scholar suggests that even as Margaret Sanger had redefined the meaning of eugenic feminism, she had abandoned a full investment in eugenics by the 1930s—specifically eugenic sterilization for women deemed "unfit" due to promiscuity. In turn, the eugenics movement had renounced Sanger's ambitions for making birth control a pillar of eugenic legal efforts. A focus on the borderlands contests this conclusion. Birth control activists in the borderlands embraced eugenic feminist ideals because they elevated their positions in their community as legitimate arbiters of women's roles and needs, especially as they taught women of the lower strata how to properly care for themselves and their families. In the US Southwest, eugenic feminism offered a powerful tool of gendered racial formation, one that made clear that white women defined the meaning of social reform. Margaret Sanger understood this and continued to affirm eugenic feminist logics in the region well past the 1940s.[34]

Devaluing the reproduction of racialized women was the product of benevolent interventionism and the culmination of eugenic feminist activism in the borderlands. Scholars call this devaluation *stratified reproduction*, referring to the systems that condemn and punish nonwhite poor people for having children while simultaneously exalting and encouraging the childbearing of white middle- and upper-class women.[35] Stratified reproduction was most distinguishable when nonwhite poor women worked providing reproductive labor—namely raising other people's children, cleaning, and maintaining domestic order—in white wealthy people's homes.[36] Although the birth controllers in El Paso offered birth control to all those who desired it—including poor white women—their education campaigns were directed at Mexican-origin women for nearly seventy years.

Betty Mary Goetting was one such activist whose engagement in the birth control movement exemplified benevolent interventionism and eugenic feminism in the service of upholding stratified reproduction. She experienced major social changes throughout her formative years, helping shape ideas about overpopulation and birth control, as a young Anglo woman coming of age in the borderlands at the turn of the century. The youngest of five children, Betty Mary Smith Goetting was born in Jefferson, Texas, in 1897. Goetting's father, David Smith, originally from Tennessee, moved to Texas as a child. He began his career as a mercantile operator when the railroads opened the East Texas territory. In 1910, at the age of fifty-seven, Smith moved his family over 800 hundred miles across the state to El Paso.[37] The Mexican Revolution began just on the other side of the Rio Grande that same year, prompting mass migrations of displaced Mexican families from Ciudad Juárez into south El Paso.[38] Goetting was a teenager when they moved. Her son, Kurt Goetting, would later recall that watching the Mexican Revolution unfold on the other side of the river—Betty Mary joined fellow classmates on the roof of El Paso High School to watch the gunslinging along the river—greatly impacted his mother's understanding of the region.[39]

While in high school, Goetting befriended Maud Durlin Sullivan, a well-respected El Paso librarian. Sullivan urged Goetting to complete her education in library sciences at Riverside Library Service School in Irvine, California, in 1917. During her time in the Sunshine State, Goetting volunteered for the Red Cross as World War I erupted across Europe. She then traveled briefly to New York to work at the New York Reference Library, where, supposedly, Goetting first heard Sanger speak. Goetting also lobbied for woman's suffrage in New York.[40] Upon her return to the Sun City, Goetting married Charles A. Goetting, a newly returned World War I veteran (and later an accomplished architect and contractor), in 1919—two years after the dramatic typhus quarantine took hold in El Paso.[41] They had three children together, all boys. However, their first child, Charles Augustus Goetting, succumbed to horrific maladies causing his death only six weeks after birth (see fig. 2.1).[42]

Goetting embraced her role as an early twentieth-century feminist, quickly becoming a part of many notable upper-middle-class women's organizations and clubs in the city. She dabbled as an amateur historian, cofounding the El Paso History Club in 1926, founding the city's first book club, and becoming a charter member of El Paso's Historical Society. Goetting even wrote for and curated the historical society's journal *PASSWORD* for over a decade.[43] Her involvement in various charities and women's organizations, including the El Paso's Woman's Club, Daughters of the Confederacy—she assembled women in the Robert E. Lee chapter of the organization—and the Daughters of the American Revolution, typified white women social reformers of the period.[44] Still, amid all the clubs and organizations Goetting sponsored and facilitated, establishing the Mothers' Health Center of El Paso, the first birth control clinic in the borderlands, and expanding the birth control movement in the region were her most hailed achievements.

Perhaps the combination of a rapid influx of Mexican people to El Paso as the Mexican Revolution wore on and Goetting's own desire to control her

FIGURE 2.1 Betty Mary Goetting with sons Charles and Kurt Goetting, circa 1940. MS 316, Kurt Goetting Folder, Betty Mary Smith Goetting Papers, 1910–1979, C. L. Sonnichsen Special Collections Department, University of Texas at El Paso Library.

fertility after marriage prompted her interest in birth control. During the summer of 1918, Goetting began exchanging birth control advice with a friend via the US postal service. This could have landed the twenty-one-year-old Goetting in jail, since she was in clear violation of the 1873 Comstock Act prohibiting distribution of birth control information through the mail.[45] Margaret Sanger's own attempts to skirt the legislation in 1914 had garnered national attention for her cause as she faced trial for violating US Postal Inspector Anthony Comstock's regulation against lascivious materials after she published information about contraception (and then attempted to distribute it) in her magazine, *The Woman Rebel*.[46]

The year before women gained the right to vote, Goetting sought direct contact with leaders of the birth control movement. In 1919, Goetting received guidance from Mary Ware Dennett, a pioneer in the movement along with Sanger, offering a different vision for the social adoption of contraception. Dennett, who at this point had created a splinter organization by becoming director of the Voluntary Parenthood League and fighting for legislative action, replied to Goetting's inquiries about birth control. Stating that it was illegal to send materials via the postal service, Dennett nonetheless encouraged Goetting's enthusiasm for birth control and provided Goetting with a copy of the Comstock law.[47] Sanger, in contrast, was known for direct action, which later helped establish the first birth control clinic in the country in Brooklyn, New York.[48] During her first exchange with Goetting—most likely linked to the *Birth Control Review*, Sanger's periodical promoting the use of birth control, particularly for the very poor—she sent the knowledge Goetting had long desired.[49] Without explicitly mentioning "birth control" in her response, Sanger declared the information contained in the pamphlet—sent under separate cover—the "greatest need of womankind."[50]

Sanger's pamphlet included the latest intellectual literature on the virtues of population control and reproduction. She attached a list of "Books to Read on Birth Control," ranging in topics from birth control to reproduction to eugenics. Among the works listed were *Uncontrolled Breeding* by Adelyne More (1916), *Limitation of Offspring* by William J. Robinson (1916), and *Parenthood and Race Culture* by C. W. Saleeby (1909).[51] Goetting paid close attention to Sanger's recommendations because among her letters, speeches, and scrapbooks devoted to her activism was a collection of books mirroring the preceding works. Other influential texts Goetting acquired were written by Sanger herself, including *Woman and the New Race* (1920), *The Pivot of Civilization* (1922), and *Motherhood in Bondage* (1928).[52]

This literature provided a crucial intellectual link connecting eugenic ideologies, proposals for population control, immigration policies, and quests to offer birth control in the borderlands.[53] Like the inspection mechanisms set up in the borderlands to control supposed "diseased" bodies from crossing into the United States from Mexico, so too could contraception control these same reproductive bodies from demographically overwhelming and potentially degrading the white American body politic.

Goetting and Sanger enacted eugenic feminism—a fundamentally nationalist project seeking to "purify reproduction as the way to assure a more perfect future"—that was specific to a borderlands context.[54] The US-Mexico border provided a territorial and boundary-bound logic where eugenic feminism became an obvious position for white women from which to solve social problems in the region. The border itself thwarted El Paso elites' visions for a modern, white American city because of its potential to let in "hordes" of nonwhite people, not all of whom had the potential to become obedient workers.[55] As discussed in chapter 1, these ideas and fears were part of a national conversation on the importance of immigration restrictions and eugenic sterilizations—early twentieth-century manifestations of population control ideology—to address the racial demographic threats in the country. Eugenic rationales for securing national borders coincided with the emergence of eugenic rationales in Sanger's movement for birth control. By the 1920s, as Sanger established the American Birth Control League (ABCL) and the Birth Control Research Bureau (BCRB), some prominent eugenicists—overwhelmingly male and white— joined her cause.[56]

Women leaders like Sanger and Goetting became the defenders of nationalist visions of racial purity by expounding the importance of negative eugenics—curtailing the ability of the "unfit" to reproduce.[57] Rather than offer a critique of the "family" as a crucial site of women's subordination, Sanger and Goetting sought to reshape the meaning of reproduction within a framework of white middle-class women's authority over the home and family and, thus, over the nation.[58] Their position, which was not a total affront to white heteropatriarchy, helped activists finance the birth control movement among wealthy eugenicists since the work of lobbying and opening clinics demanded major financial investments.[59] Sanger and Goetting found enthusiastic supporters for eugenic remedies in El Paso and greater Texas. Eugenic feminism was certainly not contained to the border. This ideology was critical to the birth control movement in the Lone Star State and the broader Southwest. Although Texas never passed eugenic sterilization laws, many in the state strove to improve and constrain the changing population within their state's borders.

The Birth Control Movement in Texas
and the Greater Southwest

Texas, like other states without specific legislation prohibiting the use of contraceptives, allowed birth control reformers to open clinics with no legal ramifications. Katie Ripley founded the first Texas clinic in Dallas in 1935, and Agnese Nelms opened the second facility in Houston a year later.[60] Nelms, an adept organizer, established the Texas Birth Control League that same year—only months before El Paso opened its own clinic.[61] The movement in states like Texas was further encouraged by the 1936 ruling *US v. One Package* that struck down federal laws prohibiting the dissemination of birth control information and devices.[62] Between 1935 and 1950, twelve states established birth control leagues, and these organizations soon became vehicles for communication with clinics within their state, creating links between government and public health agencies. They became educational sites for doctors and public health workers interested in contraception and population control, and later these organizations became important brokers for accessing state and federal funding for family planning.[63] By the end of the 1930s, clinics had sprouted across the Lone Star State in Houston, Austin, Waco, Fort Worth, San Angelo, San Antonio, and El Paso.[64] As other cities fought to keep one clinic open, El Paso would remain the only state affiliate with three clinics into the late 1940s.[65]

Although scholars of the birth control movement in Texas rightly suggest that the impetus for the creation of clinics across the state began as a response to damning infant and maternal health statistics, as well as a call for smaller families in the aftermath of the Great Depression, few have discussed the problematic connections between racism, population control, and the dissemination of contraceptive information in poor communities across the state.[66] At a time when the birth rate for white middle-class families was in sharp decline, the movement gained support as it championed the use of birth control for the poor and those considered unfit to reproduce.[67] In 1935, a Dallas sterilization proponent explained the necessity for birth control in the state: "Foreigners coming into this country between 1900–1924 were mostly Southern European which rate a point lower in sociological-biological values than the Southern Negro, and which are multiplying twice as fast as the Nordic stock." According to eugenic logic, compulsory sterilization could mitigate a "rapid increase in foreigners . . . the differential birth rate, the biological effects of war upon the next generation, and the growing mixture of races."[68] While Southern Europeans migrated to the American Northeast, in the Southwest Mexican-origin people were fleeing poverty and their country's revolution by entering the United States through major border cities like El Paso. Newspapers made sure to stress fears of "racial mixing" and the dilution of the so-called Nordic stock as the key reasons for eugenic fertility controls. This signaled to many in the birth control movement the need to educate new immigrant groups on the virtues of contraceptive use.

Learning to work with and among communities of color, Texas activists traded knowledge with those in the national movement. They established important relationships with several prominent population control proponents, including Clarence Gamble, heir to the Procter & Gamble fortune and lifelong population control proponent, and Margaret Sanger. Gamble was especially conversant with the Texas activists in Houston and Dallas, who needed little convincing from him that eugenic logics could restrain Texas's changing demographics. Activists eagerly accepted his help. Gamble, Nelms, and Ripley all favored curtailing birth rates among "habitual criminals and those families continually dependent upon the State . . ." as well as those who threatened to pollute the white racial stock.[69] Katie Ripley, the founder of the first Dallas clinic, sought Gamble's approval in their intentions. Early in the movement, Ripley wrote Gamble, stating: "I thought you might be interested in the item published in our Dallas Sunday paper in regard to the birth rate. As a matter of fact, our work is wholly with the indigents. We make no charge for any services or supplies . . . I am told that a perceptible decrease in the birth rate among indigents is now taking place, which I feel is an indorsement [sic] of the Clinic [in Dallas] and proof of the effectiveness of the methods prescribed."[70] As the young Texas league expanded, Gamble maintained tight communication with many of the leaders in the movement, Katie Ripley and Agnes Nelms in particular.

While Gamble had a more limited connection to the El Paso group, he nonetheless collaborated with Margaret Sanger on her work establishing clinics in high Spanish-speaking areas of the Southwest. According to historian Mary Melcher, Sanger had been part of the health-seeker movement of the early twentieth century as she relocated to Tucson, Arizona, in 1934, believing the dry, arid climate would help mitigate her son's respiratory ailments.[71] Once there, Sanger established Tucson's first birth control clinic in the city's "oldest barrio." She used the tactics that went on to define so much of her clinic-centered organizing: she "looked for women with social standing, political connections, and the ability to provide economic support for the new clinic."[72]

As Sanger lobbied important community members, she deployed critical knowledge of the Mexican-origin community in the Southwest. Comparing population control measures in California, she stated that "in the 11 Los Angeles clinics . . . the largest percentage asking [for] aid are Mexican women." Sanger celebrated their extreme measures, noting that "as the result of California's 14 clinics the state has sterilized 18,000 in public supported institutions for the insane, diseased, and habitually criminal."[73] She refined her knowledge of the Mexican-origin community at the Tucson clinic. Tucson's patients, in this small desert town of 33,000 people, were overwhelmingly Mexican-origin and Catholic, while the clinic's board was exclusively Anglo.[74] Melcher recovered a photograph from the clinic's early days showing Margaret Sanger sitting with over fifty patients, their children, clinic workers, and several dozen men and women dressed in *trajes típicos*— men likely wearing common dress from Jalisco and women in China poblana attire. Sitting beside her greatest Southwest advocate, N. Bess Prather, Sanger is flanked by mothers and babies, most of whom are of Mexican descent.[75]

While much of Sanger's history in the movement is tied to her work in New York and later the international stage in India and Japan, less attention has been paid to her work among communities of color in the US Southwest.[76] After founding the clinic in Tucson, she went on to push for clinics in New Mexico and, of course, El Paso. Prather, former president of the Arizona Federation of Women's Clubs, accompanied Sanger to El Paso as they laid the groundwork for the first border clinic in 1937.[77] Although Sanger had arrived in El Paso in 1934, on an earlier visit, she polished her eugenic discourse in cities like Tucson and could deploy generic eugenic ideas about poverty, disease, criminality, and illiteracy that she knew would serve as clear euphemisms for a plurality of the Mexican-origin community disproportionately represented among the most marginalized in the Southwest. Sanger gathered information from the borderlands region and attentively conferred it to Gamble as he monitored the establishment of clinics across Texas.

It is unclear why Gamble held such little sway over the activists in El Paso—not much communication exists between them—yet he still took careful stock of their clinical methods, offered regular monetary contributions to Planned Parenthood of El Paso well into the 1950s, and documented the expansion of their work in the borderlands. Though Goetting relied

Race Building in an Empire

Help Texas Mothers and Children to a Fuller Life

And Preserve for Future Generations of Texas Their Heritage
of Independence and Achievement.

FIGURE 2.2 "Race Building in an Empire," pamphlet from Texas Birth Control
League. H MS c23, folder 685, box 42, Clarence Gamble Papers, 1920–1970s, Center
for the History of Medicine, Countway Library of Medicine, Boston, Massachusetts.

almost exclusively on Sanger's guidance, Gamble's files suggest an interest
in El Paso's work among the Spanish-speaking community as the movement
spread across Texas. He sponsored the movement's mission in Texas to safe-
guard the cornucopia of freedoms at the nation's edge (see fig. 2.2). Gamble
was a dedicated philanthropist and clinical researcher committed to all
forms of birth control for the purposes of population control. He devoted
"his considerable wealth, energy, and intelligence to search for better contraceptives." Importantly, Gamble participated "in almost every important
experiment in population control, and he initiated, organized, or financed a
considerable number of them."[78] By the 1930s and 1940s, Sanger had much
stronger ties to scientists championing birth control as a tool for population
control than any other social cause; Gamble was her steadfast collaborator
in this campaign as they pushed an agenda that would make birth control
an important instrument of public health departments across the nation.

Gamble supported the work of Texas birth control activists in several
ways, including as a lobbyist for access to birth control through public health

offices. He corresponded with the director of the Texas Department of Health, Dr. George W. Cox, offering Cox a variety of financial incentives to test different kinds of population control measures in the Lone Star State. In missives to Cox, Gamble expressed his desire to make Texas into "an experiment in the field of public health and preventative medicine."[79] Gamble then offered Cox $1,750 for supplies and a nurse to distribute birth control in the state. Sanger, meanwhile, recommended a Southwestern Birth Control Conference to bring together Ripley, Nelms, and Goetting as well as other birth controllers in New Mexico and Arizona. She sought to draw the region closer "to our major objective—the inclusion of Birth Control in the public health programs of the various states."[80]

While Sanger and Goetting teamed up, Gamble wrote Nelms in Houston pressing the issue of contraceptives as critical to public health. "I am hoping Dr. Cox may install the work under the State Board of Health," Gamble said. "If there is any way in which you could give this a push, won't you do so?"[81] Gamble made sure to use North Carolina, one of his most prized experiments, as a constant example of the possibilities available to Texas if only activists in the state could persuade the medical community and public health officials to join in. North Carolina had a "marvelous program," Gamble mused. He explained that the "County Nurse, working under direction of the County Health Officer, is now equipped to give contraceptive advice in thirty of their one hundred counties."[82] As Johanna Schoen explains, North Carolina's public health and reproductive access history was mired in eugenic laws that enforced compulsory sterilizations from 1929 to 1975 as well as welcoming men like Gamble to support experimental birth control technologies on poor women in the state.[83] Furthermore, Gamble viewed these communities of color and poor rural areas as spaces in need of birth control. His focus on places like North Carolina, Puerto Rico (which he traveled to in 1938 to survey the birth control movement there), and Texas suggest attempts to capture the attention of regions where birth control could be sold as a proper solution for overpopulation and curbing racial degeneration.[84]

Sanger was not left totally alone in organizing birth control activists in El Paso—Gamble remained engaged behind the scenes. He worked closely with Martha Mumford, the field representative for birth control in Texas, as his primary informant. Mumford synthesized her interactions with the El Paso group in her correspondence with Gamble. Early on, she characterized El Paso as a "lone-wolf operation" and unlike the other clinics in Texas.[85] She reported that El Paso's isolation protected it from squabbling between the founders of the original two clinics in Houston and Dallas. However, she confirmed to Gamble that overall "Texas has great possibilities, the people are interested, the need is great, and the state is not as poverty stricken as most of the south. In fact, it is the only state I have seen, north, east, south or west, which seems pretty much untouched by depression or recession."[86] Indeed, Houston had seen oil booms in the 1930s and 1940s that had largely insulated it from the Great Depression, and El Paso's wealth was growing as trade and refining became prominent staples of the economy, but affluence was concentrated at the top.[87] Poverty became inextricably linked to the racialized and marginalized, namely the Mexican-origin community, as racism excluded them from access to education and better-paying jobs well into the 1960s.[88] Texas's economic stability made the "need" for birth control all the more justified as birth control activists attributed poverty to induval, moral failures rather than systemic inequality.

While Gamble was asked to step down as the director for the Southern Region by 1939, he nonetheless continued his interest in Texas, specifically the clinic in El Paso.[89] Mumford personally inspected the progress of the border clinic and reported back to Gamble and the federation.[90] She listed twelve goals accomplished during her trip to the border. Among them, she cited her contact with public health officials in El Paso as she reasserted the birth control movement's interest in their collaboration. She also had a meeting with Sheriff Fox in which she made him promise to refer all "transients and wives of lawbreakers to the clinic" and tuberculosis and venereal patients—the so-called infected mothers—to the birth control clinic as well.[91]

Mumford's report, and perhaps his recent trip to Puerto Rico, further piqued Gamble's interest in the El Paso clinics. In early 1940, Gamble wrote the El Paso Mothers' Health Center directly to ask for its Spanish-language pamphlets. It replied, sending various advertisements for the clinic, including discussions about the importance of birth control for poor families, particularly those on relief, as well as advice promoting the health of the mother and child (see fig. 2.3). Moreover, the clinic attached instructions on the use and cleaning of diaphragms. Surely Gamble marveled at the detail of all the documents neatly translated into Spanish and at his disposal.[92]

The following decade, Gamble continued to monitor the Texas clinics, including in El Paso, and to receive "progress reports" that provided a rare look into the inner workings of the clinic and the progression of eugenic feminist organizing in the borderlands. A 1942 communiqué described El Paso's Planned Parenthood as "an excellent clinic," informing Gamble that the "work [was] chiefly among Mexicans."[93] These accounts also noted

Instrucciones a los Pacientes

•

BIRTH CONTROL CLINIC of EL PASO

1820 East Rio Grande Street

Telephone Main 7576

El Paso, Texas

•

HORAS DE CLINICA:

Martes a las............12:30 p. m.

Jueves a las............12:30 p. m.

Viernes a las............6:30 p. m.

Es benéfico aún para los niños, no tenerlos seguidos uno despues del otro, con pequeños intervalos entre los nacimientos. Usted misma ha visto nenes recien nacidos, morir en hogares que carecen aún de alimentos para los hijos ya formando la familia donde la pobre madre no tiene ni tiempo ni dinero para alimentarse debidamente.

EL CONTROL DE LA NATALIDAD no es una operación.

CONTROLAR LA NATALIDAD no es hacer abortar.

CONTROL DE LA NATALIDAD es solamente evitar la concepción, posponiendo el nacimiento de un niño hasta en tanto se cuente con los medios necesarios para recibirlo debidamente.

El METODO para el CONTROL DE LA NATALIDAD solo requiere un poco de sentido común, pero es realmente simple y puede ser aprendido por quien lo desee con solo tener un poco de paciencia y cuidado.

El uso del CONTROL DE LA NATALIDAD es altamente MORAL, cuando el fin que se persigue es dilatar el lapso entre nacimientos, asegurando así la salud de la madre y por la felicidad del hogar.

La mujer verdaderamente religiosa es acertada y moral cuando exclama, "Yo quiero tener tantos hijos como podámos mantener y educar debidamente, pero no más."

Tenga presente que el CONTROL DE LA NATALIDAD, no impide a ninguna mujer el tener más hijos. Solamente le permite tenerlos cuando buenamente los quiera. El uso de este METODO del CONTROL DE LA NATALIDAD es ABSOLUTAMENTE VOLUNTARIO.

¡Muchos Niños!

Si quiere usted limitar el número de niños en su familia, ocurra a la

Birth Control Clinic of El Paso

(Clínica del Control de Partos)

1820 Rio Grande al Este—Main 7576

Una enfermera de habla inglés y español tendrá gusto en darle informes acerca del control de partos.

Ud. siempre encontrará un Doctor presente en cada una de las Clínicas.

Horas de clinica
Martes y Jueves 12:30 p. m.
Viernes 6:30 p. m.

FIGURE 2.3 "Instrucciones a Los Pacientes" (a two-page pamphlet giving patients instructions on how to clean their diaphragm) and "¡Muchos Niños!" (a flyer asking parents to visit the clinic if they want to learn about family planning). H MS c23, folder 685, box 42, 1940s Correspondence, Clarence James Gamble Papers, 1920–1970s, Center for the History of Medicine, Countway Library of Medicine, Boston, Massachusetts.

that there were slight deviations from the standard clinical practice, for instance, when fitting patients for diaphragms. "Due to the fact that all clinicians are male, no instruct[tion] by clinician is done," the report explained. Unlike other Texas clinics, no women doctors assisted in the El Paso branches, and the supposed "traditional shyness of the Mexican woman would not allow her [the patient] to be taught the method by a man." Thus, doctors would leave the fitting ring in its place and then have a nurse come in and instruct the patient in placing and removing the diaphragm.[94] El Paso clinic records rarely mentioned doctor-patient protocols, so the reports Gamble received were instructive in this regard. They also contained information about illnesses, such as tuberculosis and sexually transmitted infections, which were "rife . . . among Mexicans" at nearly 40 percent in the community, although these figures remained unverified. The report noted population size and demographics, calculating a total population of 90,000, of which nearly 60,000 were "Mexicans of the poorest class."[95] In the eyes of Sanger and Gamble, the reports underscored the need for family planning among Mexican-origin people, but they also revealed the intense antagonism of the Catholic Church toward the birth control movement, describing El Paso Catholic leaders as those of the "fanatical variety."[96] These observations helped create a clearer picture of the borderlands for Gamble and Sanger. Linking disease and poverty to "uncontrolled fertility" confirmed for birth control activists the need for population control measures among the great mass of Spanish-speaking people in the borderlands to protect a white American nation from decay. These reports affirmed the Catholic Church's oppositional intensity in the region and renewed birth control activists' spirit in contesting the Church's ire.

In later years, Gamble's interest in developing and promoting new population control technologies took him to other areas of the world, including Puerto Rico, yet he maintained a connection with the movement in Texas and the eugenic feminist advocates seeking to make birth control a part of public health across the state.

Birth Control, Infant Mortality, and Catholic Opposition

Birth control first entered public discourse in El Paso in 1933, as a public health response to high infant mortality rates. Dr. T. J. McCamant, El Paso's city-county health officer, led the charge that "some mothers had babies too often," endangering their lives and the lives of their newborns. There were El Paso mothers with "two babies, neither of which was one year old." And worse, Dr. McCamant knew of many thirty-year-old mothers with nine or ten children. "If we could raise the wage scale and regulate birth control, we would lower the infant mortality rate immediately," he declared.[97] The Mexican-origin community suffered the highest number of cases of infant mortality in the city.[98] Four years before Tracht asked the wage question to the members of the birth control committee, Dr. McCamant, one of El Paso's most trusted doctors, publicly acknowledged that raising salaries for the economically poor, mostly Mexican-origin women, undergoing disproportionate rates of infant loss would drive down these horrific figures. Correlations between family income, poverty, and infant mortality had been made nearly two decades before, as the Children's Bureau chief Julia Lathrop had published several studies on the topic in the *American Journal of Public Health*. Findings concluded that "a child whose father earned less than $550 per year was more than twice as likely to die as one whose father earned over $1,250" in 1919.[99] According to Melcher, other borderland states, such as Arizona, also suffering from high infant mortality rates among the Mexican-origin community were keen to these statistics.[100] And yet, in El Paso, the good doctor conceded that raising wages might be too difficult a task for residents of this borderland city to bear. As a public health measure, he believed birth control would be easier to employ despite federal laws prohibiting its dissemination. In addition to offering birth control, the city-county public health office had "plans to improve sanitary conditions in all parts of the city with special work in the Mexican section."[101]

Due in part to public outrage, predominantly from the Catholic community, city-county officials halted McCamant's campaign.[102] From the moment McCamant made the announcement, religious organizations were divided on the issue. The Catholic Church came out most forcefully in opposition. Rev. Fr. Joseph C. Garde from Immaculate Conception church stated unequivocally, "We are opposed to it on the grounds of morality. It is immoral to teach birth control."[103] After less than a month of backlash, McCamant concluded, "El Pasoans want babies. And the more the better with no newfangled teachings to interrupt their arrival."[104] Dr. J. A. Pickett, president of the El Paso County Medical Association, although a supporter of the birth control plan, added that while birth control was proper in some cases, in most others "it is a very dangerous thing for the public to know, it must be handled very carefully."[105]

Roman Catholics loudly opposed the city's attempts at providing birth control to poor residents. In 1934, lay Catholics, mostly Mexican American, staged protests outside drugstores accused of selling contraceptive devices and giving out birth control information. Part of a broader campaign against what the Jesuit priest Romualdo Benedet called "a nationwide drive against indecent moving pictures," Catholics picketed pharmacies distributing what they considered lewd information.[106] Cleofas Calleros, a well-respected Mexican American leader known for his work with the National Catholic Welfare Conference's Bureau of Immigration in El Paso, helped plan the boycott. Calleros was outraged that "in some drugstores when a customer buys something the clerk wraps up the article with a birth control leaflet inside."[107] He assured the press that women in the diocese were eager to lead the anti–birth control campaign. These public scuffles heightened tensions among local doctors who warned that birth control information, "if legalized, would fall into the hands of quacks and cause licentiousness among young people."[108] City fathers were torn on the significance of birth control in their city: some believed it held the power to diminish troubling infant mortality rates, while others thought it would promote promiscuity.

The year 1936 represented a major turning point in city- and county-wide discussions about infant mortality in the borderlands. Dr. McCamant's name appeared often in the newspapers that year as he touted a noticeable drop in infant mortality rates from years past—278 deaths in 1935 compared to 209 in 1936.[109] This was important since earlier that year the federal government had announced that Texas was the third-largest recipient of federal dollars apportioned under the Social Security Bill. In El Paso, the monies would head to McCamant's office.[110] Even as numbers began to show minor improvements, the pressure to continue presenting El Paso as a major Southwest health resort pushed McCamant and the city registrar, Alex Powell, to manipulate demographic figures to lower the infant mortality death rate among residents classified as "white."[111]

They justified the racial reclassification by noting that the high infant mortality rate among Mexican-origin families in the south side skewed the population data for "white infants" throughout the city.[112] Newspapers explained that "Four Texas cities, Dallas, Houston, San Antonio, and Forth Worth were following the new ruling" made by the US Census Bureau to classify "Spanish-speaking" people as "colored," which would have the effect of showing "a decrease in infant mortality rates among the 'white' race."[113] Because Mexican-origin babies accounted for most infant mortality cases in local data and because earlier calls for contraception had failed, city leaders believed changing the racial designation would allow them to mask the issue.[114]

Mexican Americans realized that in a city under Jim Crow, a nonwhite racial designation would mean further social and political marginalization. Spearheaded by Calleros, who two years earlier had led the fight against birth control, Mexican Americans pushed back against local politicians' efforts to simultaneously strip them of their political power and further racialize their community.[115] A group of twenty-five Mexican American plaintiffs placed an injunction against the city-county health unit's attempt to change the racial designation of people of Mexican descent and summoned McCamant and Powell to testify.[116] The protest garnered national attention as Senator Dennis Chavez of New Mexico derided the division of vital statistics for putting forth these changes on a federal level and denounced the Census Bureau for allowing such a change to be made with little discussion.[117] Two weeks later Chavez's local emissary traveled to El Paso to read a telegram "translated into Spanish," stating that vital statistics had acted in error in making the change. The telegram's signatory, Ernest Draper, representing the Secretary of Commerce, assured the senator and those protesting in El Paso that vital statistics would immediately make the correction.[118] Although Mexican American leaders were able to halt what could have been a devastating legal designation, the protest revealed the corrosive racial discord in the city, one that only heightened as the second push for birth control campaigns took shape.

Catholics Confront Sanger

Despite early opposition to birth control from Catholics in El Paso, Margaret Sanger toured the border city for the first-time in 1934 to lay the groundwork for a collaboration between public health officials and the birth control movement.[119] She met at the house of a local ally with forty El Paso doctors and their spouses in attendance, eager to discuss the importance of contraception in the borderlands. Sanger maintained that "no intelligence is being shown in the relief work, in work for charity when children of unfit parents, or poverty-stricken parents are brought into the world in an increasing number."[120] Sanger, already well versed in speaking publicly about the "need" for contraception among the poor, used words such as "charity" and "relief" as dog whistles for attacking the position of the Catholic Church and its charitable efforts among the poor. She also attacked the Comstock laws and the anti-pornography movement supported by Catholics when she stated that her birth control clinics were "taking the information out of the pornographic class and giving it out from the scientific centers, which take care of the individual needs of the women."[121]

Sanger's wrangling with the Catholic Church in El Paso mirrored the national dispute over birth control, one pitting Protestants and Jews against Catholics. In 1935, the *El Paso Times* emblazoned "Protestants and Jews Attack Catholic Birth Control Stand" on its front page. While the headline could have been taken directly from the squabbles in El Paso, this time the news came from New York. A contingent of Jewish and Protestant clergy had denounced Cardinal Patrick Hayes's condemnation of birth control during Sunday service the day before. The cardinal had suggested that rather than offer contraception to poor families, perhaps the "true lover[s] of the poor" and "true social scientist[s]" understood that society needed to "reorder our economic and social structure as to make it possible for people to have children and rear them in keeping with their needs." The Protestant and Jewish clergy countered that birth control was "necessary to prevent economic chaos."[122] These national arguments echoed and likely affirmed the sentiments of many local El Paso residents on both sides of the debate. Even as many Catholic El Pasoans pushed back against public campaigns for family planning, Sanger returned three years later with a serious bid to open a clinic.

Openly antagonizing the Catholic community who sought to silence her lecture the evening of February 24, 1937, Sanger welcomed the hullabaloo embroiling her second El Paso visit. Her lecture was originally slated for the Hilton Hotel, but Catholics organized by the Knights of Columbus called to say they would boycott the hotel if it allowed Sanger to speak. Fearing the wrath of the Hilton owners, who were themselves Catholic, and the angry parishioners tying up his phone lines and cluttering his desk with telegrams, the hotel manager canceled the event.[123] Goetting, with the help of Maud Phillips Harvey, wife of Charles Milton Harvey, president of El Paso National Bank, quickly moved the event to the Paso del Norte across the street. In a memoir dedicated to Sanger, Goetting later recalled that a "ludicrous" tone had shaped the fiasco as a "spokesman for the Roman Catholic Bishop said he would 'withdraw the blessing from God' if Mrs. Sanger spoke there [Hilton Hotel]!"[124] Sanger saw the attack as an opportunity to lambast the Church for opposing what she considered the perfect tool for ending poverty. "I cannot imagine any church that promotes the welfare of its people and its community and objects to birth control proposed in this program," Sanger declared. During her speech, she depicted the birth control movement as the foundation of a "great social principle," one that sought to end the misery suffered by the community's poor. A "conscious control of birth rate," Sanger argued, would end "wars, unemployment, relief burdens, child labor, disease and delinquency."[125]

Margaret Sanger melded together eugenic, neo-Malthusian, and ableist ideas against the welfare state to strengthen her pitch. She hoped to "see the day when parents will be made to *apply* [my emphasis] for a child or children," and when those parents "in ill health, and possessing sordid or moronic characteristics stood before the child, many a youngster would say, no thank you, I will wait for the next applicant."[126] At this point in her speech, she turned to the audience of more than 350 people and rebuked the "charitable" acts of keeping the so-called feebleminded alive. Sanger unleashed her ableist hostilities, stating: "You build palatial palaces to keep them [feebleminded] alive, while you are taxed to provide the means . . . each person is highly taxed for every inmate in the state's insane asylum. At various times these charges are allowed to go home on parole, to reproduce their kind, and I think that every official in every state and city heading an insane asylum bear the greater part of the responsibility of such an act."[127] As Lira observes, these "asylums" often operated as workhouses for those deemed eugenically unfit to reproduce and a continued danger to the public. These "inmates" worked during their involuntary internment offsetting the cost to taxpayers in states like California.[128] Nonetheless, connecting the so-called defective class to welfare abuse served Sanger's argument well, especially among El Paso's Anglo residents.

Sanger, who during her speeches in Tucson had prized compulsory sterilization campaigns in California, then promoted the use of sterilization in Texas. "Do not be afraid of the word sterilization," she declared, "It will figure largely in the future and is a thing needed for many types."[129] She was right to predict that sterilizations would become common across the country.[130] Dozens of states adopted sterilization laws to control the reproduction of women (and to a lesser degree men) who might pollute the national body politic.[131] Indeed, these laws were directed across the racial spectrum as poor white women, Black women, Mexican-origin women, and Native women were sterilized well into the 2000s.[132] White women's reproduction, in particular, came under scrutiny as eugenicists sought to rid the Anglo-Saxon race of feeblemindedness, simultaneously encouraging breeding by those with desired racial traits.[133] Texas, on the other hand, remained one of the few states that never passed compulsory sterilization policies. Although there was a nascent eugenic movement in Texas, libertarian convictions about consent laws and concerns over the disruption in the importation of cheap labor from Mexico prevented state-sponsored sterilization from gaining political traction.[134] Sanger was likely acquainted with the Lone Star State's reluctance to support sterilization. While touting the necessity of sterilization for the unfit, she proposed a more immediate remedy in El Paso: nonpermanent contraception.

After Sanger's fiery speech, Goetting recalled how audience members made the connection between poverty and the need for birth control "especially among the Mexican population" and how they believed it could help alleviate the "largest maternal and infant death rates" in the city. Proper education on the fundamentals of birth control, Goetting explained, would defeat the "ignorance and superstition among the poverty stricken."[135] Birth control was a benevolent intervention for eugenic feminists like Goetting and necessary to maintain control over a burgeoning pool of nonwhite workers whose existence raised racial anxieties in the borderlands.

Although there were many who agreed with Sanger's discourse, clergymen, lay Catholics, and community members expressed genuine concerns about the controversial topics Sanger addressed. Historian Harold L. Smith contends that, in cities like El Paso, the Church played an archaic and misogynistic role, oppressing women's voices.[136] El Paso's priests and lay Catholics certainly critiqued the establishment of a birth control clinic based on conservative beliefs about women, but they also advanced the idea that the so-called need for birth control was deeply tied to race and class. Some priests derided the birth controllers for suggesting that contraception could curb poverty and destitution on the city's south side. "To reach the perfect family," Rev. Daniel Quigley declared, Sanger would have the community "rejecting the teaching and example of the Perfect Family—Jesus, Mary, and Joseph. She would control poverty and pain by preventing life."[137] Ironically, the image of the "Perfect Family" was exactly what Sanger sought to exalt: a small, calculated, sacred household of three. Nonetheless, Rev. Quigley held to his belief that Sanger's ideas were cemented in perverse social engineering.

Another Catholic priest, H. D. Buchanan, proclaimed that birth controllers were ignoring the roots of poverty and labor issues in El Paso. Buchanan charged that wealthy El Pasoans did "not want to share any of our good things through reasonable taxation with those whose hard work was largely responsible for our prosperity, as we complain that women on relief continue to bear more children."[138] Deriding Malthus's treatise on overpopulation, its "dreary volumes" helping relieve "the painful strain on wealthy consciences," Buchanan slammed the birth control movement's obsession with contraception as the end-all solution to poverty. After "having attained a degree of luxury—from the hard labor of the less intelligent," Buchanan accused El Paso elites of abandoning the very people who had made them wealthy. Birth control activists and their moneyed financiers, he explained, claimed to care about eradicating poverty for working families, and yet they failed to directly support their domestic workers by paying decent wages.[139] Joining the clergy's backlash, white Catholic women such as Tracht also questioned economic inequality on the south side and the supposed links to overpopulation. She insisted that middle- and upper-class El Paso residents "examine" their consciences and ask whether they were paying their domestic workers a living wage.

We can recall the answer from Goetting, who agreed that some did "abuse the house servant wage." Still, Goetting believed that birth control would benefit those mothers by allowing them to have fewer children so they might better prepare themselves for higher-paying work. Goetting's comments, however, obscured the highly bankrupt education system afforded Mexican-origin people in the borderlands.[140] As a trained librarian, Goetting would have been keen to the racially stratified school districts serving Black, white, and Mexican children. While Black students were legally segregated into different schools throughout Texas, El Paso's de facto segregated school system focused primarily on preparing Mexican youths for vocational training.[141] City leaders sought to educate Mexicans in such a manner as to equip them for menial labor and service-oriented work to, in the words of historian Mario Garcia, "solve a major economic problem by adding to the productivity of its Mexican population." Organizations like the Women's Civic Improvement League suggested that young Mexican-origin women be instructed in proper housekeeping, cooking, and sewing so that "every American family would benefit."[142] Ultimately, antagonism from Catholic Church members did little to stop the birth control movement's forward march.

Sanger's sagacious use of Catholic hostilities and controversy to her advantage remained unparalleled. She advised Goetting and her followers to "fight Roman Catholic influence and power with influence and power. Get your most important citizens [in] back of you—doctors first, because birth control is medical; ministers to answer the Roman Catholic priests; as well as professional men and women—all groups of people."[143] Committee members put into practice Sanger's instructions, harnessing their political power to obtain money and positive press for the new clinic. El Paso's birth controllers became adept at influencing public perception of their campaign. Goetting explained: "To be sure of good publicity, we again followed Mrs. Sanger's advice in using power to attain what we were asking for." The birth control committee turned to one of its most prominent members, Hedwig Schwartz, the wife of the president of the Popular Dry Goods Company, the largest retail store in the city. Schwartz delivered a personal message to the editors of the *El Paso Herald Post* and the *El Paso Times*. She reminded the editors that the Popular Dry Goods Company was their best advertiser in both newspapers, and as Goetting recalled, "quietly, but most forcibly, [Schwartz] asked that the Mothers' Health Center (our official name) continue to be given good coverage and publicity . . . the editors were most agreeable."[144] What an inspired and manipulative move! To fight "Roman Catholic influence and power" with their own, the birth control advocates bribed news media outlets to write only positive stories about the birth control movement, which helped reframe public sympathies for the movement in El Paso. After this persuasive conversation, financial donations began to stream in, and the Mothers' Health Center committee gained ground in the fight for a clinic.

Nonetheless some residents continued to protest. Manuel Lopez, a Mexican-origin community member, understood his social and political marginalization and voiced his concerns with the birth control movement. In the local newspaper, he noted the racial undercurrents that saturated the demand for birth control in El Paso. Lopez critiqued Sanger's assumption that birth control would alleviate tax burdens on the rich so the wealthy could "assume their duty of establishing a virile race." Lopez accused the "Sangsters" of breeding those in South El Paso "like cattle in proportion to the demands of our menial labor." Like Tracht, Lopez also condemned the meager wages paid Mexican-origin people for their work as domestic servants, as farmworkers, and in the mining industries of the city, decrying the "$3 or $4 per week or whatever pittance the Sangsters will pay."[145] It seemed clear to Lopez that exploitative labor conditions and poverty wages produced the very conditions the "Sangsters" sought to curtail through the dissemination of contraception.

The very history that produced the US-Mexico border weighed heavy on Lopez as earlier attempts to control the Mexican-origin population—border quarantines, inspection stations, repatriation, and the latest campaign to change the racial designation of Mexicans on birth and death certificates from white to "colored"—predisposed some in his community against the possibilities of birth control. Lopez asked: "We are to be supervised in our most intimate relations . . . and beg for our God given rights?"[146] His statements recognized the nefarious thread imbedded in the campaign for birth control in the borderlands. White El Pasoans felt entitled to target Mexican-origin people as objects of surveillance and supervision in nearly every aspect of their lives, including their most intimate, sexual relationships. When they traveled across the border, when they became sick, when the economy was down, when labor was needed, when they were born, and when they died, white officials surveilled and recorded Mexicans' every move. As historian Alexandra Minna Stern states, "In the popular memory of El Paso residents, the construction of the border as a boundary that divided Mexico from the United States was connected most intimately to the implementation of the quarantine [1917] and the somatic invasion symbolized by disinfection and the medical exam."[147] Now, when Mexican-origin people decided to start a family, population control ideology constructed over time emboldened the "Sangsters'" supervision of Mexican-origin people's ability to do so.

Establishing the Mothers' Health Center

Some of the most civic-minded and progressive white women from El Paso sat on the board of directors for the Mothers' Health Center, the generic name given to the birth control clinic. Aside from a few Jewish women who were part of the early formation of the clinic, there were no other board members or clinic workers from any other ethnic or racialized group working at the clinic until the late 1940s. The lack of women from different social classes or racial and ethnic groups characterized the movement both locally and nationally.[148] Class affiliation produced strong allies among Protestant and Jewish women activists, forming the backbone of other important women-led organizations in the borderlands, such as the Young Women's Christian Association (YWCA).[149] The El Paso branch of the movement was no different—the organization's racial and class composition reinforced its eugenic feminist vision, one that sought to reproduce a sanctioned white middle-class vision of American citizenship by curtailing the reproduction of those they deemed unfit for it.

The list of those who sat on the board of the birth control clinic the year after it opened provides crucial evidence that the capitalist class in El Paso was thoroughly concerned with issues of uncontrolled fertility among the poor. The clinic's board of directors' roster reads like a who's who of the most politically and economically influential families in the community. Chief officers on the board included Goetting, wife of architect and general contractor Charles A. Goetting; Katherine McAlmon, wife of Mr. George G. McAlmon, owner of SW Surgical Supply Company; Beatrice P. Rathbun, wife of Mr. Donald Rathbun, owner and general manager of Rathbun Company, Inc. (a large chemical company); Jane Perrenot, wife of Mr. Preston Perrenot, partner in Perrenot and Broaddus (real estate company); Romain Howell, wife of Mr. Ben R. Howell, partner in Jones, Hardie, Grandbing, and Howell (law firm); and finally Mr. George Matkin, treasurer, the vice president of State National Bank.[150] Moreover, as instructed by Sanger, birth control activists sought advice from prominent medical professionals in El Paso, creating a medical advisory committee to bring legitimacy to their cause—Drs. Arthur P. Black, T. J. McCamant (the city-county public health physician who had tried to advocate for birth control just a few years before), Gerald Jordan, J. Leighton Green, and J. Mott Rawlings were the first to join. Rawlings's wife, Laura, was a founding member of the board of directors for the clinic.[151] These early advocates were critical to fundraising efforts in the months before the clinic opened. The well-connected board members wrote letters, made phone calls, and lectured on the benefits of birth control to organizations across the city. They contacted every women's organization and received replies from several, including the prominent YWCA leadership, which promised to "help in any way possible." Annual donations ranging from one dollar to twenty-five dollars offered various degrees of membership and access to the organization's voting apparatus and the annual luncheon gala at the end of each year.[152]

In April 1937, Goetting and fellow advocates opened the doors to the Mothers' Health Center. It was the 323rd such clinic opened since Sanger had started her work and the first opened on the US-Mexico border.[153] Goetting and the board of the Mothers' Health Center joined the Texas Birth Control League and aimed to make Texas an important state in the fight for birth control. Texas, like other states without specific legislation condemning the use of contraceptives, allowed birth control reformers to open clinics with relative ease. The committee used the "Mothers' Health Center," a name Sanger had used for clinics across the country, to tie El Paso's work to the broader birth control movement sweeping the country. They knew a euphemistic name—avoiding specific reference to birth control—would help patients feel comfortable visiting the clinic.[154] The vagueness of the name, however, caused problems for clinic staff as working-class El Paso mothers sought assistance for innumerable health issues afflicting their communities.[155] As one board member explained, "Many people thought we took care of mothers after their babies were born. Some thought we took care of babies."[156] The clinic's aim was to provide the means to control birth rates, nothing more. It was not interested in Mexican women's health concerns as mothers or anything else.

Despite their clear intention to lower the birth rates among Mexicans in the borderlands, the founders were unable to establish the Mothers' Health Center of El Paso in a Mexican neighborhood at first. Given continued apprehension toward their movement, activists had trouble securing a location on the south side. Some property owners remained squeamish about leasing their spaces to a birth control clinic. Instead, birth controllers opened their first clinic five blocks north of the train tracks that separated the south side from the rest of the city.[157]

Articles in the *El Continental*, a well-known Spanish-language newspaper, did their best to guide potential patients to this location. The newspaper was owned by a prominent Jewish publisher, Morris J. Boretz, and a Mexican attorney, Salvador Franco Urias, who represented clients on both sides of the border—although Urias did not last long as co-owner and editor.[158] Perhaps to align its interests with Anglo elites, *El Continental* ran small blurbs giving information to patients about the services of the clinic as well as background information about who would care for them: "Mrs. Emma Hensley is in charge of the clinic, having arrived from Mexico City where she took nursing courses and therefore speaks Spanish correctly."[159] Nurse Hensley was the only paid employee of the clinic. Doctors, receptionists, and all others were there on a volunteer basis. Even as the Catholic Church and others in the community opposed the clinic, it seems newspaper advertising, among other forms of communication, was successful, as women began to attend the clinic in large numbers. By July 1937 the Mothers' Health Center boasted 250 patients on its roster. Goetting was "jubilant over its financial stability and the response given to it[s] purpose and aim." Patients and donations were pouring into the clinic. Goetting told media outlets that "raising the money for the clinic has been the easiest part of its establishment."[160]

Birth control movement activists were determined to establish institutions that would successfully spread the gospel of family limitation across the city and promote what Betty Mary Goetting hailed as "intelligent family planning." Teaching reproductive discipline to the borderlands' community required an examination of "the consideration of the [family's] income, the mother's health, the right of the children to be wanted, well cared for, physically vigorous." Clinic staff also took into consideration the "child's possible heritage" and "the living standards to be maintained."[161] The Mothers' Health Center believed that the most obvious way to begin this work was by establishing strategic locations for its clinics. Although some city leaders were concerned that the clinic's first location north of the train tracks would attract all the wrong people—mostly young white women—birth control activists at the facility worked diligently for months and quickly opened two new branches on the "proper sides" of town—in the mostly Mexican-origin barrios south of the railroad tracks.

Goetting faced a major challenge securing space for birth control clinics in the city, as some continued to view the movement with disdain. Yet nearly three years after the first facility opened at 1820 East Rio Grande Avenue, in the residential neighborhood just north of the railroad tracks, the activists of the Mothers' Health Center celebrated the inauguration of its second clinic on 519 South Ochoa Street in Segundo Barrio. *El Continental* lauded the virtues and experience of its second nurse, Maude Gillespie, highlighting her residency at Hotel Dieu (the local Catholic-run hospital) and her work with the Red Cross in New Mexico.[162] The newspaper assured women that Gillespie spoke impeccable Spanish and that she would discuss birth control with curious mothers in their homes or at either treatment center location.[163] The clinic was nestled in the basement of the Iglesia "El Divino Salvador" established by the Presbyterian community in 1920. The church confirmed that it had no direct connection to the clinic but was merely renting the space to the organization.[164] Perhaps the good media coverage and the existence of patients heading to the north-side clinic provided the justification needed by some in El Paso's south side to open locations for the Mothers' Health Center to expand.

The birth control movement continued to grow as the years went on and always tried to maintain its clinics near or close to the south side. In 1942, it opened a third clinic, a tiny square building on a sliver of street between residential homes, on 3213 Rivera Street, in what was then considered east El Paso.[165] Two years later, the organization became an affiliate of Planned Parenthood Federation of America, continuing in its allegiance to Margaret Sanger, and changed its name to Planned Parenthood of El Paso (PPEP).[166] Energized by this newly made association and tired of renting, PPEP culled its resources to buy a lot at 1926 Arizona Avenue and built a clinic from the ground up in 1947.[167] Goetting's husband, Charles, an architect, provided the plans for the new building.[168] By 1950, the south-side clinic was moved out of its Presbyterian headquarters to 1009 East Second Avenue. The following decade Planned Parenthood had closed its smaller clinics to open a larger one in the heart of downtown. Across from today's El Paso Museum of History and diagonal to the monstrous Chihuahua baseball diamond, the robust, red-bricked building at 214 West Franklin Avenue still stands and was the main headquarters for PPEP in 1960.[169]

Religious Groups in Favor of Birth Control

Although the Catholic Church remained a thorn in the side of the birth control activists, other religious groups rushed to support them. Rev. Harold H. Wright, pastor at the Modern Liberal Church, chastised El Pasoans for their ill treatment of Margaret Sanger during her 1937 visit to the borderlands. "Such a massive act of inhospitality and intolerance demands a mass protest of all right thinking people here," he declared in the local newspaper. Rev. Wright continued, "Margaret Sanger's position in the world of social service demands courteous treatment and consideration. We of our group are committed to her program."[170]

As historians Tobin and Woodcock Tentler observe, the debate around birth control changed for many Protestant denominations and some Jewish groups after 1930. Sanger's *Birth Control Review*, no longer edited by Sanger at the time, engaged in vigorous debate in favor of contraception featuring some of the leading ecclesiastical voices of the period, including some fringe and ex-Catholics.[171] Protestant ministers from Pennsylvania, Maryland, Ohio, Indiana, Minnesota, and Texas exalted birth control in a special issue of the *Review* dedicated exclusively to the topic of religion and family planning. Rabbi Edward L. Israel, chairman of the Central Conference's Social Service Commission and longtime supporter of Sanger's activism, responded to continued antagonism by conservatives this way: "I for one do not condemn [Catholics and Orthodox Jews] for what they believe. My only condemnation is that they refuse to grant others that inalienable right of freedom of belief and conduct in personal life, which does not interfere with another's freedom."[172] While Rabbi Israel stressed the importance of the "freedom" to decide what might be best for each person and family, that language and spirit did not animate all corners of the birth control movement, especially as activists sought to curb racial degeneration amid massive economic devastation. The Great Depression and its aftermath proved incredibly valuable to birth control advocates with a clear example of how "intelligent family planning" could help mitigate poverty and what some religious leaders believed was an excessive reliance on welfare.

In El Paso, Sanger had expounded on the "dangers" of charity in her speeches as a dog-whistle attack against the Catholic Church and its parishioners, most of whom were of Mexican descent, for propping up the poor and genetically inferior. Some Protestant ministers reiterated her sentiments as the years wore on. During an interview with the local newspaper, Rev. W. H. Mansfield, pastor of Trinity Methodist Church, slammed El Paso's Sheriff Fox for not doing more to end the scourge of gambling among the city's poor. According to Rev. Mansfield, it was better for the sheriff to stay home since he had done nothing to solve the city's overwhelming "transient problem" and its use of "relief" funds. In contrast, Mansfield believed the Mothers' Health Center was doing the most to help this sector of society. After scolding the sheriff, the reverend replied to local Catholic leaders' contemptuous remarks of Mansfield's support of birth control clinics in El Paso: "I want to pay tribute to a group of women and doctors in this city who have provided a birth control clinic to which the poor can go . . . If you multiply a class of people that cannot afford to have children, you breed criminals. I refer to the great mass of people living in dire poverty and sickness. I know of one couple that got married and three generations of their families have been on relief."[173]

According to Mansfield, the birth control clinic was doing more to curb transient criminality than local law enforcement. Importantly, Mansfield thanked birth control activists for cutting the problem off at the root. Echoing Supreme Court Justice Oliver Wendell Holmes stating that "three generations of imbeciles were enough" in the infamous 1927 *Buck v. Bell* decision sanctioning compulsory sterilizations, Mansfield agreed that "three generations of families on relief" were also "enough." Since capitalists in Texas had decided that coercive sterilization might be viewed badly by Mexican-origin workers, the least they could do was support campaigns to discipline Mexican-origin people's reproduction to keep them and their children off the welfare line. Champions of birth control often conflated poverty and eugenic arguments about racial degeneration, as evidenced by Mansfield's final comments about the health among a certain sector of the community. "We have no right to bring a child into a home without being able to give that child the right kind of body to live in," he explained.[174] Given the high infant mortality rates and rampant tuberculosis—due largely to poverty and a near-complete disregard for proper social and economic infrastructure—affecting the majority Mexican-origin communities in El Paso, Mansfield's flippant condemnation of Mexican-origin people's reproductive health

MURDERS SHOW NECESSITY FOR BIRTH CONTROL

Chairman Says Crime Shows Need of Preventing Birth Of Criminal Types

FIGURE 2.4 Newspapers rallied around the eugenic need for birth control in the borderlands. "Murders Show Necessity for Birth Control," *El Paso Herald-Post*, April 7, 1938.

struck a painful chord. The next month the Mothers' Health Center board of directors agreed to send a letter thanking Mansfield for his unwavering support.[175]

While birth control activists did not often specifically invoke Mexican-origin community members as targets for their campaigns—especially given the initial pushback they received from the Catholic Church and some Mexican-origin men—they did invest great racist power in the euphemisms used to describe the clinic's patients. Birth control campaigns were directed at the poor, those suffering from ill health or disabilities, the less educated, and the so-called criminal class. To be clear, for many in the birth control movement, these characteristics were inextricable from each other. Goetting and the borderland birth control advocates hammered home the importance of incorporating eugenic and neo-Malthusian thought into their activism, focusing their efforts on disciplining the reproduction of these "types" (see fig. 2.4). One member of the birth control education committee expressed enthusiasm for their work because they shared birth control information with women considered "mentally unfit and undesirable[s]." In a 1938 newspaper article lamenting the recent murders of one family and another story of a mother who had killed her six children, the Mothers' Health Center board member proudly explained that they had taught the "birth control method to many mothers unfit for reproducing." She then observed that "one of the mothers who has been shown this method has the mind of a seven-year-old child." Finally, she reminded the journalist that their "syphilitic patients" were referred to El Paso's venereal clinic once they had left the Mothers' Health Center.[176]

With each reference to criminality, disease, poverty, and lack of education, birth control advocates built a borderlands lexicon that brought closer those individuals—most of whom were Mexican-origin people—suffering from these structurally produced deficits to the raison d'être for their activism. White women birth control advocates created knowledge through language along the US-Mexico border, especially as it related to Mexican-origin people's reproduction. Over time, these advocates racialized ideas about Mexican-origin people's reproduction by coding them in terms that were not explicitly racist but could be understood by those in the borderlands because of a shared historical and regional context. As we will come to see in the following chapters, there was no need for birth controllers to explicitly say that they were targeting Mexican-origin people, so when birth control activists said they were interested in curbing birth rates among the poor, the illiterate, the sick, or the "diseased from birth," most El Paso residents, including Mexican-origin people, knew who birth controllers were talking about. This linguistic sleight of hand is a hallmark of American racism, but in the borderlands it was specifically employed to protect white citizens from Mexican backlash—although it was never foolproof. Anglos in cities like El Paso often feigned ignorance when Mexicans confronted white residents' racist depictions and alterations to language to protect white supremacy. El Paso's attempt to change the racial designation of Mexicans from white to Black on birth and death certificates in 1936 is a perfect case in point.

White Women Soldier On

Debates between the Catholic Church, birth control advocates, and El Paso residents continued for decades—issues escalated once more in the 1960s when the birth control pill was introduced, making contraception easier to obtain. But as the years passed, memories lingered of earlier frustrations and confrontations as the white women on both sides of the debate carried the disputes forward. Nearly sixteen years after Tracht, Sanger, and Goetting came face-to-face in the Paso del Norte ballroom, attacking each other over the meaning of birth control in the borderlands, Tracht wrote to Sanger (see fig. 2.5). She had recently finished reading Sanger's autobiography and

FIGURE 2.5 Last Kodak of Margaret Sanger taken in El Paso, Texas, circa 1958. MS 316, folder 23, box 2, Betty Mary Smith Goetting Papers, 1910–1979, C. L. Sonnichsen Special Collections Department, University of Texas at El Paso Library.

was moved. She sent Sanger a note analyzing Sanger's troubled relationship with Catholicism—Sanger's mother had been a devoted Catholic, while her father scorned the family religion and lived his life as a "free thinker." Tracht wrote that this peculiar family dynamic had damaged Sanger. Despite Sanger being a "naturally gifted person," Tracht nonetheless concluded that Sanger could have "served God so well, had you been taught love."[177] Even if it was likely that the internationally renowned Sanger did not remember their first interaction in El Paso so many years before, Tracht stated that she had thought of Sanger many times over the years and hoped "you will realize my intentions toward you are kindly." Tracht believed that perhaps Sanger might welcome a devotional scapular with the Immaculate Heart of Mary, noting Sanger's interest in the Virgin Mary in her autobiography, and prayer book as a gift.[178]

Imagine Tracht's surprise when Sanger's reply arrived a week later with these words: "I remember you well . . . Many of us have never forgotten the outrageous arrogance of some members of your religion representing the Knights of Columbus, who, with dastardly affrontery, did everything possible to keep me from addressing a group of Americans . . . in the ballroom of one of the hotels." Sanger's characteristically strident prose cut deep as she informed Tracht that it was Sanger who knew more about the wretchedness of "Catholic hierarchy, celibates themselves" who had no business advising couples on matters of sex and family. At seventy-four,

Sanger's anger had only hardened around Catholic opposition to birth control, and she continued, even in the aftermath of Hitler's Germany, to expound on the eugenic necessity for contraception: "From their history, [Catholics] have only exerted the influence of ignorance and poverty and misery and illiteracy in all countries of the world. I have traveled; I have seen with my own eyes, the misery of human life, of family life, of sickly miserable children. I have covered the jails, where in most cases, eighty or eight-five percent of the inmates have been brought up and baptized in the Roman Catholic Church."[179]

Sanger, offended by Tracht's attempts at analyzing her family's religious position, declared that her childhood and life had provided endless examples for cementing the righteousness of her cause against the Catholic Church. "I had the constant examples in arrogance and abuse and lies in an un-American, un-civilized, un-Christian behavior, that any group could express toward another human being!"[180] Not accepting her own culpability in inciting Catholic ire toward her cause, Sanger's response to Tracht, and by extension to all El Paso Catholics, made clear that Catholicism kept them ignorant, poverty-stricken, infirmed, and filling up the jails. Sanger blamed Catholic obstinace, not capitalist exploitation emboldened by rampant racism, for depriving Mexican-origin people and all economically poor people from living full, complete lives.

Conclusion

Tracht and Sanger's final debate highlights the critical issues at the heart of the movement in the early years. First, it reveals the degree to which white women fought over the meaning of morality and activism within and at the margins of the birth control movement. Tracht and Sanger's quarrel suggests that not all Catholics agreed on the meaning and importance of birth control, but even as Protestant women gained ground in advancing their visions for social progress via the dissemination of birth control, alignments on the meanings of white middle-class womanhood were very much in flux. Second, unlike the assertions of other historians, the Catholic Church in El Paso did not always rely on orthodox teachings to preach against birth control. It critiqued the movement for its attack against the poor. Lastly, Sanger, Goetting, and the dozens of other white women in Texas and the greater Southwest mired in their own racial borderland hierarchies produced knowledge about the Mexican-origin community in the service of larger population control regimes. International population control zealots, such as Clarence Gamble, eagerly tapped into reports, files, and pamphlets often translated into Spanish, as these advocates' work spilled across national boundaries, especially among other Spanish-speaking populations in the Global South. This is the world white upper-middle-class women made to establish their roles as benevolent interventionists and eager eugenic feminists. Of course, their world did not exist in isolation from other worlds. Mexican-origin women in the borderlands had a different vision of reproductive care, one that centered their community and harnessed knowledge from the struggles of combating economic exploitation, social neglect, battling disease, and confronting infant loss. Their story is the heart of chapter 3.

In 1949, Bertha González married Alberto Chávez and, against her mother-in-law's wishes, continued to work (see fig. 3.1). They lived in Ciudad Juárez, first with his parents, but they soon found a place of their own. At the age of nineteen, she had had her first child, a boy. Soon after, González Chávez explained that her cousin "dragged me against my will to El Paso so I could get a diaphragm."[1] She could not remember the name of the clinic they attended, but they did spend some time in El Paso's downtown before heading to her appointment. Her use of contraception, she said, explained why there was a large gap between her first and second child—four years. Her second, third, and fourth children came in rapid succession: 1954, 1955, and 1956, respectively. Months after having her third child González Chávez and her husband migrated to Los Angeles. Money was tight. Baby number three was only five months old when they arrived in the City of Angels. With little economic support, she was unable to purchase spermicidal jelly needed for her diaphragm to function properly. Consequently, she became pregnant. Years later, González Chávez was still upset by that situation, as she recounted, "And like all men, they can't wait. Uh! They have their *needs*, so I couldn't use my—and then came my fourth son."[2] Although she had brought her first diaphragm with her to Los Angeles, as the years wore on and she was unable to use it properly, the diaphragm broke. After her fourth child, she acquired a new diaphragm and used it for nearly six years until her last child was born—the first one delivered in a hospital—in 1962.[3]

Despite being taken to obtain birth control "against her will," González Chávez knew a thing or two about reproductive control and reproductive health care because she had worked in the medical field starting at an early age. As she recalled, "I told a lie. I was 14 years old, but I said I was 16. And this is how I became a [nurse's] apprentice at the hospital."[4] Bertha González Chávez told this small fib to hospital management for her family's survival. Her father, Alfredo Benito González, had been a merchant in Ciudad Juárez, Chihuahua, when she was born in 1930. The family of five, three girls and two boys, along with her father and mother, Refugio López de González, had traveled throughout Mexico during the early years of González Chávez's

FIGURE 3.1 Bertha González Chávez, May 1949. Chávez Family Photo Collection, Los Angeles, California. Courtesy of Ernesto Chávez.

childhood to accommodate her father's work. Her father's business had provided for them. She recalled that "we were not rich, but we were also not poor."[5] She was twelve when her father became ill and could no longer continue to run his business. Within months, González Chávez and her eldest sister, Lupe, were forced to find work to help their mother and younger siblings survive. Before her apprenticeship at the hospital, González Chávez had worked for one of her cousins who had two babies very close in age and asked González Chávez to run errands to the market, cook, and change and wash diapers. While González Chávez did not mind this kind of work, she had hoped to do more. Her ambition might have stemmed from the fact that she had received a relatively good education. She attended a private Catholic school as well as public school; education had always been very important to her family, especially to her father. González Chávez finished her secondary education at night once she began training at the hospital. Her interest in medicine, however, stretched beyond nursing. She remembered that she had an aunt and cousin attending medical school and they had inspired her to have a "real profession" as a doctor, but at the time only nursing was accessible to her.[6]

When González Chávez and her sister began working in 1944, the hospital formalized their apprenticeship program through on-the-job training and night classes. González Chávez remembered how she had been trained by medical residents and other nurses at the hospital. She took exams, written and oral, to be certified. "Once you passed these exams," she explained, "then you received your certificate—the certificate was not much, but it was something. At the very least you could give patients injections, you could attend births, and all those other things."[7] In many ways, González Chávez was the beneficiary of one of the Mexican Revolution's greatest achievements which enshrined the right of every Mexican citizen to health care in its 1917 constitution—the first in the world to do so. While institutionalizing this right was not easy, especially given continued violence and warfare in the decades that followed, historians have shown that medical care became a critical nationalist endeavor in Mexico throughout the twentieth century.[8]

Through her training as a nurse, González Chávez learned much about reproductive health, contraception, and even abortion. By 1947, González Chávez's financial situation had changed, and at age seventeen, she went to work for Dr. Antonio Davalos, a well-respected abortion provider in Ciudad Juárez. She knew him from her time at the hospital, where he occasionally visited patients. Davalos had his own clinic and recruited González Chávez because he appreciated her skills as a nurse and believed her English proficiency, although limited, sufficient to help arrange visits between El Paso doctors who often crossed to perform surgeries in his Juárez clinic.[9] Despite attending Catholic primary school and catechism, González Chávez did not find working for Davalos repugnant nor did she judge the women who used his services. Instead, she found herself disparaging the men who, in her mind, had placed these women in such difficult circumstances.[10] For González Chávez, working with Davalos not only improved her economic situation, but she liked that he respected and appreciated her work.

In addition to working with Davalos, González Chávez made extra money to support her family by giving injections across several neighborhoods near her home. She remembered "so much sun exposure and walking and living on little sleep because in those days you had to give people their penicillin doses every three hours, day, and night, until the entire dosage was gone. So, it was day and night. Sometimes I would have to stay in people's homes, in their *ranchitos*, and they would give me a ride back in the morning."[11] Even though this endeavor was meant to increase her income, she sometimes worked without pay. According to González Chávez, "Many people could not pay; they had no money. Or they would pay toward the total over time, but it was something." Attending births, however, was better financially. "If we had a woman in labor, we could charge more, like 100 pesos, and later we charged up to 200 pesos. We knew that if we had a birth, that day we would buy more meat."[12] During these years, her sister Lupe had moved up the hospital ranks, becoming director of nurses. This meant that Lupe would need to live at the hospital, leaving her family behind. Chávez recalled that while her sister continued to help support her family financially, Chávez brought home the most money because of her neighborhood work.

In the years before and after González Chávez married, her life was bursting with intense reproductive care. During two long oral history interviews, with me in 2015 and her granddaughter, historian Marisela Chávez, in 1993, González Chávez recounted her adventures working to help her family survive after her father's illness. In laborious detail, González Chávez described her knowledge and understanding of and respect for reproductive health and care as she came of age in the post–Depression era borderlands. Although there was a nearly twenty-two-year gap between oral history interviews, her memory remained clear about how much she had enjoyed the work she had done and how it had shaped her life afterward. When asked why she worked so much aside from supporting her family, she said: "For me it was because I liked it, and it was better than staying home."[13]

While some may argue that Bertha González Chávez's life was unusual and incredible and likely not representative of the lives of most Mexican-origin women in the region at the time, I believe that her life was both *extraordinary* and *conventional* and that the lives of the people she worked with and for are critical to understanding what I call *reproductive care*. Following the path Chicana historians have made writing extensive histories about the lives of Mexican-origin women in the nineteenth- and twentieth-century borderlands, chapter 3 examines the lives of Mexican-origin women in the region from the vantage point of reproductive care.[14] This perspective expands our understanding of how—and perhaps why—Mexican-origin women, in the early parts of the twentieth century, participated in what today scholars and activists call reproductive justice.

Tracing the fluctuating social and cultural norms around sex, contraception, and abortion in both the United States and Mexico helps us see more clearly the turbulent society Mexican-origin women traversed in the years after the Mexican Revolution and Great Depression in the borderlands. Not only did they encounter white women birth control activists pushing for population control via contraception in El Paso, but they also confronted daily challenges to what reproductive justice scholars consider the third tenet of reproductive justice, the ability to raise children in safe and sustainable communities. As migrants, workers, mothers, wives, and community members, Mexican-origin women faced a barrage of obstacles simply to live out their lives while producing and providing opportunities for their children to thrive. Chapter 3 examines the circumstances that ground the reproductive care work of Mexican-origin women like Bertha González Chávez to reproductive justice. By examining the lives of women considered both extraordinary and conventional, I show how reproductive care tethered Mexican-origin women to historical forces that shaped their lives and how their engagement in reproductive care shaped their community's history and future.

Genealogy and Theorization of Reproductive Care

Reproductive care is critical to a broader theorization of histories of reproductive justice. While it is not the only way to understand and grapple with the labor of Mexican-origin women in the service of uplifting their own communities, it is an important framework for interpreting the dearth of sources that exist about their lives. Most of this chapter relies on the oral histories of several Mexican-origin women as well as historical data collected from the Planned Parenthood of El Paso archive, which help bring to life the complex and rich lives of Mexican-origin women living, working, caring, and struggling in the borderlands.

So what is *reproductive care*? It is the sometimes radical, sometimes conventional everyday actions of racialized, minoritized, and marginalized community members to comfort, support, and uplift each other amid the confines of state and nonstate suppression, surveillance, and capitalist exploitation. Reproductive care has often been used as shorthand for medical reproductive health services, such as access to contraception, abortion, Pap smears, pregnancy exams, perinatal care, cancer screenings, and more. These various forms of medical care can and should help Mexican-origin women abstain from having children if and when they want to or, conversely, support their ability to have healthy pregnancies and children as well.[15] Mexican-origin women demanding access to these critical reproductive health services are clear examples of reproductive care. In what follows, I extend reproductive care to account for how Mexican-origin women continued to care for—comfort, support, and uplift—members of their communities, (re)producing and maintaining safe and sustainable environments for their children, families, and future members, over decades while confronting state- and nonstate-sanctioned hostilities and violence, including denials of reproductive health care. This section offers a brief theoretical genealogy of reproductive care.

Reproductive care lives within a large overlapping and interlocking matrix of theories of social reproduction and reproductive racial capitalism, theories of care, Chicana feminist methodologies of resistance, and reproductive justice. An expansive constellation of feminist analytical tools produced and enhanced since the late 1970s, these theoretical frameworks have informed how I imagine reproductive care operating when examining and interpreting past *words* and *deeds* of historically marginalized and racialized people who labor in the service of their families and communities.

In reproductive care's universe, reproductive justice (RJ) is one of its primary stars. Revisiting the tenets of RJ to better express what relation it has to reproductive care, the pillars are (1) the right to have children, (2) the right not to have children, (3) the right to parent the children we have in safe and sustainable communities, and (4) the inalienable right to bodily autonomy. Reproductive care interprets *how* historically marginalized and racialized women have engaged these tenets and to what extent community concerns (nuclear family, extended kin circles, and broader involvement with friends and neighbors) informed their understanding of bodily autonomy, reproductive freedom, and self-determination. For instance, scholars documenting the forced sterilizations of Black, Indigenous, white, and Mexican-origin women throughout the twentieth century have shown how the state has engaged in denying racialized, poor women the right to have children. These examples underscore the injustices of important reproductive histories; however, reproductive care moves the analytical lens to an RJ analysis that is more than a denial of reproductive autonomy even when this is a central claim. Natalie Lira's recent scholarship at the intersections of reproductive and disability justice provides an excellent example. Not only did she push the field to examine the relationship between survivors of sterilization and the state, but more importantly, for enhancing reproductive care theory, Lira foregrounds survivors' relationships with each other.[16] Her research demonstrates that as sterilized individuals, institutionalized Mexican-origin women nonetheless continued supporting and uplifting those in their community (other institutionalized, racialized, and marginalized people), reproducing environs of care within hostile institutions, such as colonies for the so-called feebleminded. Those women confined in these institutions engaged in radical forms of community care–based *reproduction*. Despite the state stealing their fertility via coercive sterilization, institutionalized women produced spaces to engage with their own humanity reproducing love, understanding, tenderness, and support.

Reproductive care as a theory for historical analysis also makes heavy use of reproductive racial capitalism, social reproduction theory (SRT), and population control ideology. These theories make visible the mechanisms used to produce ideas about race, gender, and class over time and for what ends. They reveal how capitalism and white supremacy have accrued power and meaning through the continual exploitation and subjugation of land and labor since conquest. Studying white European settler's usurpation of land from Indigenous people and extraction of labor from the Black and Indigenous people they enslaved in the Americas at the end of the fifteenth century, shows how racial capitalism came to be. Reproductive care begins from the premise that this colonial history is necessary to understanding how racial formation co-constitutes gender and class formation throughout the nineteenth and twentieth centuries.[17] As Morgan and Weinbaum observe, the history of hereditary racial slavery, in particular after Britain (1807) and the United States (1808) formally ended the trade in human trafficking across the Atlantic, "places the battle over reproduction at the heart of modern racial capitalism."[18] The slaver's obsession with protecting its fetal chattel, making "children . . . the human biological commodities on which the entire system of hereditary slavery relies," and slavery's "commodification of reproduction and its living products" attempted to severe the kinship ties, familial bonds, and community concern critical for the enactment of reproductive care.[19]

While white Anglo-Saxons were themselves racialized, gendered, and classed in relation to other racialized groups during this time, reproductive care centers those at the very margins of the racial power structures these socially constructed hierarchies produced.[20] Reproductive care necessitates a rigorous understanding of the compounding historical effects extractivist regimes at the center of reproductive racial capitalism have had on the lives of Mexican-origin women, specifically; the generational accumulation of exploitation and loss; the consistent reinvigoration of subjugation under colonialism, capitalism, and neoliberalism; and how real people, enmeshed in these depraved histories, continuously reproduce cycles of concern, affirmation, and reciprocity for members of their communities.

Social reproduction theory helps bind reproductive care to reproductive racial capitalism by making visible the gendered aspects of reproductive care *labor*. Social reproduction theory (SRT) pinpoints the crevices in which reproductive care operates alongside and within extractive racialized and gendered capitalist labor regimes. Historian Tithi Bhattacharya explains how SRT's diagnostics work to make legible the lives of women laborers: "The fundamental insight of SRT is, simply put, that human labor is at the heart of creating or reproducing society as a whole." She clarifies this through a Marxist analysis of labor as the basis for capitalist exploitation, stating that "capitalism, however, acknowledges productive labor for the market as the sole form of legitimate 'work,' while the tremendous amount of familial as well as communitarian work that goes on to sustain and re-produce the worker, or more specifically her labor power, is naturalized into nonexistence."[21] Reading oral histories like the one provided by Bertha González Chávez sheds light on the process by which social reproduction is "naturalized into nonexistence." Work done to heal, such as giving injections or labor carried out to help birthing women, becomes naturalized as women's non-commodity-making work despite Chávez's wages. What reproductive care seeks to do is to view this potent social reproductive *power* as more than just an invisible support to the continued accumulation of capital. Reproductive care *is* labor power. Its significance, however, lies in an oppositional interpretation, one that views *labor power* as a form of care redistributed among marginalized communities for their human benefit and survival.

This oppositional interpretation is firmly rooted in Chicana feminist thought and theory. Reproductive care builds on Chicana and "US Third World" feminisms; concepts emerging from Chicana feminist such as Chela Sandoval's "methodologies of the oppressed," Emma Pérez's "decolonial imaginary," Gloria Anzaldúa's "La Nueva Mestiza," and Maria Lugones's "'world'-traveling" are critical to understanding how reproductive care illuminates the caring labor Mexican-origin women produced throughout the twentieth century. What these various lines of theoretical analysis maintain is the need for understanding the pluriverse—the multiple worlds racialized, working women must cross and navigate—and the possibility for *transformation* within these worlds.[22] These worlds exist simultaneously, forcing women of color into the practice of what Maria Lugones calls "'world'-traveling"—the necessary move between a "White/Anglo organization of life in the United States" and other, often intimate worlds of loving and care among women of color. "I affirm this practice as a skillful, creative, rich, enriching, and given certain circumstances, as a loving way of being and living," Lugones explains. She also concedes that often women of color engage in this "against our wills" to confront a "hostile" white supremacist patriarchal world.[23]

Reproductive care imagines the pluriverse of racialized and historically marginalized women in this spirit, as one that enforces coercive labor in support of capitalist extraction while this labor is simultaneously providing for their community in solidarity and love.[24] What remains critical in these assessments is what Chela Sandoval recognizes as a distinct interstitial space occupied exclusively by "US women of color" because they have long understood that race, "but also one's culture, sex, or class, can deny comfortable or easy access to any legitimized gender category, that the interactions between social classifications produce other, unnamed gender forms within the social hierarchy."[25] These experiences produce what Emma Pérez described as the "third space," the liminal zones between worlds, pushing back against narratives that seek to homogenize, invisibilize, or outright deny the existence of the experiences and lives of women of color.[26] Gloria Anzaldúa uses the Nahuatl term *nepantla* to mean the in-between "place/space where realities interact and imaginative shifts happen."[27] Reproductive care operates within these tensions and across multiple worlds. It is a term that makes visible the work of women who, despite the inhumanity they face as mothers, wives, workers, and migrants, will themselves to (re)produce kinship ties, familial bonds, and community concern that reproductive racial capitalism seeks to rupture.

Reproductive care, then, is a facet of labor power produced in a transformative third space. It is identified through actions and words in the service of communal intimacy and care—the often physical and always emotional work to make safe and sustainable communities for our children and future members of our communities. Miroslava Chávez García and Verónica Castillo-Muñoz have discussed this kind of community care using the term "intimacy" as it relates to the history of gendered affections in the US-Mexico borderlands. They suggest that intimacy is central to cultivating care among "parents, grandparents, children, siblings, and friends, who tell each other stories, listen, connect, and respond." Like reproductive care, they suggest that intimacy "is located within and across multiple spaces and frameworks," emerging in what Anzaldúa called the "third country."[28] It is through this third space, using Pérez's decolonial imaginary, that we begin to "see" and "hear" the power of reproductive care in the archive. As Peréz reminds us, the decolonial imaginary is how "the silent [re]gain their agency."[29] A decolonial imagination is necessary to read intimacy and care as labor power, further establishing a robust framing of reproductive care.

Through a reproductive care framework, Mexican-origin women's work matters along different community and self-realizing axes despite their labor's extractivist relationship to the accumulation of capital and, often, in support of the state. Bhattacharya, quoting excerpts from Marx's *Capital*, foregrounds important elements that animate critical aspects of reproductive care. "The materials necessary to produce the *worker* [my emphasis] in the image of her own needs and goals—be they food, housing, 'time for education, for intellectual development' or the 'free play of his [her] own physical and mental powers'—cannot be realized within the capitalist production process, for the process as a whole exists for the valorization of capital and not the social development of labor."[30] Racialized and marginalized women engaging in reproductive care are also necessarily part of the social reproductive process. Their labor, both in and out of the home, serves to enhance and subsidize capitalist accumulation for the bourgeois class. Reproductive care contemplates a world in which Bhattacharya's *worker*, in the first sentence, alternates in an ever-in-flux pluriverse with the identities of mother, migrant, sister, wife, cousin, daughter, and lover. Reproductive care is primarily concerned with the relationship of racialized and marginalized women to each other, their families, and their communities. It is not a relationship exclusively dictated by Eurocentric experiences of oppression and victimization, although it is certainly informed by them. It is a relationship of intentional actions, guided by care, love, and support in the face of repression, exploitation, and indignity.

Reproductive care is the active process of (re)establishing the binds of community care needed for existing in the pluriverse with the potential for imagining new futures. Reproductive care is one tactic within the broader spectrum of Chela Sandoval's "methodology of the oppressed," acting as a part of the "processes, procedures, and technologies" for "decolonizing the imagination."[31] The decolonial imagination is linked by its very utterance to newly emerging possible futures. There can be no greater example of decolonial imaginaries than working to produce hospitable environments for children and future members to live and survive. This is what brings reproductive care through reproductive justice to life: providing current and future members perennial environments from which to transform and be free.

Philosophers' definitions of care are helpful to understanding the underlying values needed for actions that constitute caring labor and reveal who has historically benefited from the values of care and its labor. For instance, political theorist Joan Tronto's assessment that certain values were used to define women's morality—especially in the late nineteenth- and early twentieth-century US context—gendered notions of "nurturance, attentiveness, compassion, and meeting others' needs." These values were "traditionally associated with women and traditionally excluded from public consideration" even as white women and men attempted to politicize them as moral justifications for white women's entrance into the political sphere.[32] While Tronto goes on to say that we must decouple the values that define care from gender, or from women's identities more specifically, the historical claim to a gendered analysis of care helps reinforce the importance reproductive care plays in understanding Mexican-origin women's lives in the past.

As white male capitalists and their female counterparts exploited Mexican-origin women's "natural tendencies" toward care—nurturing and raising white children, cooking and cleaning in the homes of their white employers, and toiling in their fields and factories—Mexican-origin women were nonetheless denied the social and cultural capital that came with the maintenance and preservation of white domesticity and white productivity.[33] This denial of not only social and cultural capital but also material capital—low wages—produced what Marxists refer to as alienation from care labor. As a corrective to the disassociation caused by capitalist exploitation, I argue that Mexican-origin women engaged in nurturing, with compassion and dignity, the lives of the members of their communities. Mexican-origin women engaging in reproductive care labor helped minimize the painful effects of capitalist exploitation, racialization, and everyday oppressions. Their work was more than simple harm reduction. Mexican-origin women engaged in reproductive care to anchor their humanity and dignity to their families, children, communities, and possible futures.

The preceding theories infuse reproductive care with meaning not only to further theorize reproductive justice in history but also to make visible the care labor needed to make reproductive *justice* possible. Racialized, minoritized, and marginalized community members provide reproductive care as reproductive labor, defined as radical or quotidian actions used to comfort, support, and uplift each other amid the confines of state and nonstate suppression, surveillance, and capitalist exploitation. Because reproductive justice maintains that people can have the children they want to have or they can have no children at all and they deserve to raise their children in safe and sustainable communities, then it requires a theory of labor that decenters capitalism and the state as the only sources wielding the power to produce and consume. Reproductive care accounts for the loving labor produced by Mexican-origin women grounded in their own humanity.[34]

Therefore, reproductive care is attentive to philosophers of care and their insistence that care is fundamentally political. Tronto, for instance, shows how caring values and care itself have been both gendered and racialized as to be made invisible. Rather than deconstruct these assertions, I use them as diagnostic tools, examining historical relations of care that occlude a fuller understanding of the complex and nuanced lives of economically poor, Mexican-origin women in the borderlands. Even as caregiving and nurturing have been viewed by dominant theorists as gendered *burdens*, feminist care theorist Asha Bhandary aptly notes that "identifying the domain of caregiving as a domain for human genius" yields a place from which to recuperate one's dignity and a sense of mutual/communal responsibility.[35] In the history that follows, I weave together these various theoretical strands to bring reproductive care to the fore of Mexican-origin women's lives. Reproductive care makes visible what was rendered invisible (and even perhaps unthinkable) by reproductive racial capitalism, patriarchy, and the arrogance of white settler history.

Sexuality, Care, and Control in the Late Nineteenth- and Early Twentieth-Century Borderlands

Reproductive care brings greater significance to the historical context surrounding the lives of women like Bertha González Chávez. Different from the world upper-middle-class women lived in in the United States and Mexico, working-class *fronterizas* contended with changing definitions of sexual morality that over time came to set the foundation for undue surveillance and critique of their families, their sexuality, and their supposed inability to control their reproduction. Ungirding this borderlands history is the degree to which changing definitions of sexuality became linchpins in processes of racial and gender formation of working-class Mexican-origin people in the region. More important for reproductive care and a deeper understanding of Mexican-origin women's lives and labor are the demystification of their use of contraception, their knowledge of reproductive health, and sexuality. Let us momentarily return to González Chávez's cousin's referral to a birth control clinic in 1950. Passing such information to her cousin was certainly an act of reproductive care in the moment but also indicative of longer histories of reproductive knowledge that remained private or obscured. To better contextualize the lives of Mexican-origin women in the borderlands requires a comparative transnational analysis of the years before and after the Mexican Revolution in both the United States and Mexico with a focus on changing sexual mores, new legal structures, and gender and racial formation.

People have always found ways to control their reproduction.[36] Historian Nora Jaffary observes that Indigenous people in Mexico used various kinds of contraceptive and abortifacient herbs before the Spanish conquest. With the arrival of Spanish colonizers and the ebbs and flows of the colonial period and the period of Mexico's independence, the significance of and interest in controlling access to contraceptives and abortion knowledge changed. Even as the Catholic Church weighed in during and after the colonial period and medical professionals took charge in earnest at the end of the eighteenth century, midwives, *boticarios*, and laywomen knew how to help bring about a return of the menses or help induce an abortion throughout these periods.[37] Jaffary and others note that "contrary to the misconception of the timelessly enormous size of Latin American families," studying Mexico City reveals that nearly half of the married women in the city had either no children, only one child, or two children in the early nineteenth century. "It seems unlikely," Jaffray concludes, "that nearly half of the female population of urban Mexico had managed to limit family size so drastically without recourse to either contraception or abortion."[38]

By the mid-nineteenth century, moral panics struck the United States, a leader in the industrial world, and Mexico, a nation on the precipice of industrialization, and both nations adopted strict laws against the proliferation of information related to sex.[39] In the United States, men like Anthony Comstock and Horatio Storer determined that easy access to information about sex, sexuality, contraception, and abortion bred licentiousness and should be criminalized when found in the hands of nonspecialists.[40] In 1865, Storer, a former professor of obstetrics and gynecology at Harvard, led the charge against abortion, writing an "entire volume of anti-abortion propaganda" directed at the main culprits of its use: married women.[41] Eight years after the end of the Civil War, Comstock, the leader of an anti-obscenity crusade, helped establish the Comstock laws regulating the exchange of so-called pornographic material and information related to reproductive control via the US Postal Service.[42] Although Storer's campaign sought to elevate the medical profession, the moral panic against access to abortion and contraception had more to do with changing demographics and falling birth rates among white Anglo-Saxon Protestants.[43] As immigrants from Eastern Europe, China, and Mexico arrived en masse and as formerly enslaved Black people reclaimed their freedom, Storer asked if the westernmost regions of the United States "shall be filled by our children or by those aliens? This is the question our women must answer; upon their loins depends the future destiny of the nation."[44] By the end of the nineteenth century, nearly every state in the United States barred abortion except when physicians, and physicians alone, deemed it necessary.[45] It bears mentioning that Mexico experienced a similar crisis in morality, bringing forth several criminal statutes governing various forms of reproductive control.

While in the United States physicians and moralists led the charge, producing a barrage of state and federal regulations against abortion and contraception, in Mexico legal theorists provided the grounding for such changes. Outlined by liberal Mexican jurists in the shadow of the 1857 War of Reform and the short-lived attempts at imperial domination by Maximilian Habsburg in 1863, Mexico's 1871 Código Penal sought to streamline and reform colonial law and the penal system altogether.[46] One of the central concerns of the 1871 code was "its heightened articulation of the importance of public honor in Mexican society."[47] The penal code gave detailed expression to how Mexico's judicial system would regulate and control abortion and infanticide. As historian Elizabeth O'Brien maintains, "a tacit acceptance of, and participation in, fertility control . . . was couched in a social-salvation rhetoric that alternately heeded, reformed, or rejected Catholic reproductive doctrines."[48] Elite women in Mexico could avail themselves of medicalized abortion as a means for "salvation" if the pregnancy was unwanted.[49] Much of it was linked to notions of public morality and protecting the honor of families whose "private legal matters" could not be "contained within the sphere of domestic regulation."[50] Punishments differed, for instance, in cases where people sought to abort offspring conceived in legitimate unions from cases of those who sought to end pregnancies from illegitimate ones. The former would be more severely punished than the latter, presumably because the latter would protect or even restore a family's honor.[51]

The political nature of these moral panics tells us much about whom these laws were for, who was initially meant to be controlled and surveilled. As Foucault reminds us, these laws were first intended to control the emerging bourgeoisie. The "new distribution of pleasures, discourses, truths, and powers," Foucault contends, was for "the self-affirmation of one class rather than the enslavement of another."[52] In Storer's anti-abortion crusade, these laws were meant to protect white Anglo-Saxon Protestant birth rates by denying white middle-class married women easy access to their own reproductive control. While these laws intended to regulate more than demographic loss, they also produced a matrix from which other hierarchies around sexuality and control would emerge. Foucault suggests that with "this investment of its own sex by technology of power and knowledge which it had invented," the upper class "underscored the high political price of its body, sensations, and pleasures, its well-being and survival."[53] By the end of the nineteenth century, the Comstock laws in the United States and the Código Penal in Mexico set the stage for the cultural self-affirmation of the upper classes in each country. In the ensuing decades, these policies were infused with eugenic purpose to maintain order among the working class and to define an emerging nationalism.

The cult of domesticity that governed women of both the American and Mexican bourgeoisie during this time is one critical site for understanding the intersections of a growing nationalism and concern for and reproductive control over a rapidly expanding and racially nonwhite proletariat. In the United States, the cult of "true womanhood" reified piety, purity, submissiveness, and domesticity among middle- and upper-middle-class white women, reestablishing the special need for separate spheres between men and women during a cultural moment in flux. During a time of rapid demographic change, when the working class was no longer exclusively white, gender and class alliances reformed to protect white supremacy. As Amy Kaplan suggests, the cult of domesticity united bourgeois American men and women under the guise of "manifest domesticity," wherein the nation becomes an extension of the home and, "men and women become national allies against the alien, and the determining division is not gender but racial demarcations of otherness."[54]

In Mexico, the cult of domesticity had a more blurred connection between the bourgeoisie and the nascent working class. Historian William French observes that during Porfirio Diaz's dictatorship, an "increased emphasis on domesticity and the exaltation of motherhood" led various kinds of education for women, including industrial schools (escuelas industriales para señoritas) in border states like Chihuahua.[55] Unlike any other issue, women's education "linked moral reform, gender, and class."[56] As conceptions of sexual purity and public honor came to govern the social thinking of the emerging American and Mexican bourgeoisie, these notions became tied to middle-class standing but also informed working-class people's own ideas about sexuality and reproductive control.

As both countries experienced extreme authoritarianism in the late nineteenth and early twentieth centuries—in Mexico, the so-called peasant class, including mestizos and Indigenous people, faced the wrath of the dictator Porfirio Diaz, while in the United States, Jim and Juan Crow policies further segregated and subjugated working poor people of color—ideas about how the working class should comport itself in the realm of sexuality, family, and reproduction took on greater political salience.[57] Thus, in the US-Mexico borderlands, these sometimes competing and at times complimentary visions of sexual morality and reproductive control intertwined as Mexican-origin women traveled back and forth across the border to care for others and care for themselves.

Contraception and Reproductive Care in the Early Twentieth-Century Borderlands

Historians of Mexican American history suggest that the use of contraception in the early twentieth century may not have been "widespread" among the Mexican immigrant community in the United States. This was not only due to "strict cultural sanctions . . . emanating from the Catholic Church" and moralistic codes lingering from the cult of domesticity that gripped the middle class in the United States and Mexico toward the end of the nineteenth century but also because the Comstock laws made this information unlawful to disseminate and thus difficult to obtain. George J. Sánchez observes that "Mexican women were unlikely to have access to the occasional private physician who might be willing to give such advice."[58]

For some people in the United States and Mexico, the use of contraception indicated lackadaisical attitudes toward sex and disinterest in the preservation of virginity before marriage.[59] More directly, contraceptive use was associated with vice and sex work.[60] One example historians use to affirm these attitudes is a set of encounters documented by a male interviewer who worked on behalf of Mexican anthropologist Manuel Gamio, who produced a watershed study of Mexican migration in the 1920s. While helping Gamio collect the experiences of Mexican farmworkers, Luis Felipe Recinos engaged in what Recinos described as consensual sex with Mexican-origin women interviewees he met in Los Angeles dance halls in 1927.[61] These young women frequently worked as "taxi dancers" in dance halls, offering male patrons a dance for a price.[62] Recinos frequented these establishments for his "research" and recounted in detail his sexual encounters with the women he met as well as recording their conversations and what he considered interesting aspects of their lives. Recinos labeled these documents "Life of Elisa Morales and other data about prostitution, etc." and

"Life of Gloria Navas and data about prostitution."[63] Yet none of what Recinos described could be considered sex work. Rather, through his insistence and pestering of Elisa Morales over several days and through sheer desire and eagerness of Gloria Navas, Morales and Navas engaged in what appears to have been consensual, unpaid sex with Recinos. As Vicki Ruiz explains, for many in the Mexican-origin community, Morales and Navas may have been examples of American's "corrupting influence" on Mexican-origin women.[64]

Upon further analysis, however, these encounters provide us with a rich understanding of reproductive control and reproductive care in the decade after the Mexican Revolution and before the Great Depression. Fleeing the turmoil of extreme poverty, violence, and social upheaval in the years after 1910, Elisa Morales and Gloria Navas came to the United States as child refugees of war as the revolution took hold in Mexico. Although their parents became the generation of "PEASANTS WITHOUT LAND AND PROLETARIANS WITHOUT JOBS [emphasis in original]," as one Chicana historian has put it, Morales and Navas experienced the liminal space of "neither from here nor from there" that is characteristic of first-generation migrant children.[65] Morales's and Navas's experiences were captured as part of Gamio's research studying the lives of Mexican male laborers in the US Southwest, and despite Recinos's unethical ethnographic process, he managed to obtain vivid portraits of working-class women living complicated lives.

Elisa Morales was born in Hermosillo, Sonora, Mexico, around 1906. She migrated with her parents to the United States as a child—first to Tucson, Arizona, where she was raised, and then to Los Angeles. She considered herself "Spanish" and not "Mexican." Her father hailed from Spain, but her mother and siblings were Mexican born. When Recinos first met Morales at the "Latino" dance hall, he had insinuated they have sexual interactions from the beginning, but Morales had slowed him down, exerting control over her sexual urges and his. Over the course of several days, she bided her time, dancing with Recinos and allowing him to take her, her best friend Anita, and Morales's sister out to dinner after the dance. Morales made sure her inner circle of family and friends were fed and that Recinos paid every time. She also told Recinos that she lived with one brother, her mother, and Anita to share the burden of paying rent. Morales accompanied her mother every Thursday and Sunday to the hospital, where her other brother received treatment for tuberculosis. Morales talked about her sister who worked with her as a taxi dancer. Her sister's husband was a tailor whose salary was not enough to keep her and her children afloat. Her sister "did not like American customs" and hoped to return to Mexico someday, but for now she danced to make ends meet.[66] Morales told Recinos that her sister and her mother were "different" from her and that she was free-spirited.[67] She understood that to a man like Recinos, her life seemed to embrace libertine attitudes at odds with "traditional" early twentieth-century Mexican and US sexual mores.

At the dance hall, Recinos also met Gloria Navas, a twenty-five-year-old taxi dancer, whom he interviewed for his research. After a long night of dancing, "riding" around in her friend's car in Los Angeles, and spending Recinos's money at a second nightclub, Navas returned with him to the apartment she shared with two friends, Ponchito and Gustavito, and asked Recinos to stay. While Morales had pushed off his advances for a several days, Navas became indignant when Recinos insinuated an "exchange" should be made for what might come next. Navas told Recinos that she "paid her own rent" and was unequivocally "free." She liked him and wanted to have sex with him. So she did.[68] Afterward, as the sunrise peeked over the hills and Recinos began dozing off, Navas reminded him that he was there to interview her about her life. He dutifully obliged. As it turned out, she too was born in Hermosillo, Sonora, in 1902. As a young child, Navas had emigrated from Mexico with her parents and siblings to Tucson, Arizona, and then to San Francisco, California. At eighteen years old, she married, moved to Pasadena with her husband, a carpenter, and had two children.[69]

Navas spent much of her interview describing her reproductive life as a mother and worker. She spoke extensively about her pregnancies, having experienced life-threatening labor with her first child. A physician, who later became her good friend, said she should not have any more children. She became pregnant once more before she divorced. This time, her doctor cautioned, would be the last time she had children. Navas had not been pregnant since. This doctor, Navas told Recinos, had helped her take care of her reproductive needs and assisted her friends in acquiring birth control when they needed it.[70] Her two children were living with a "very Catholic" elder Irish women in San Francisco, and as soon as she was ready, Navas would bring them to Los Angeles permanently. Navas sent her children money every week. She made good money as a taxi dancer, she said, between $25 and $30 a week—sometimes more.[71] She told him that she had had many jobs, including as a singer and dancer. She performed Spanish dances, including the "Jarabe Tapatío," for audiences across the state of California. Navas had also worked as a waitress, laboring more than twelve hours a day, receiving little pay, and hating it.[72] She much preferred her job as taxi dancer, making better money and working the hours she wanted. In fact, her pay exceeded the amount most Mexican-origin laborers made a day. Her wages were at least double what agricultural workers made and were likely on par with what laborers in mining, factories, and railways were paid in the 1920s borderlands.[73]

At various intervals during the interview, Navas exclaimed that she "was absolutely free" to dance for a living, enjoy life with her friends, and care for those in her extended kinship circle.[74] She related the following: "Many think that Gustavito is my sweetheart because we live together in the same home and because we love each other very much and when I've brought my children to Los Angeles, he takes them on trips, and although that could mean nothing in particular, it is not true, Gustavito loves me very much because I've taken *care* [my emphasis] of him when he didn't have friends or money, so I have been to him more than a sister, and he has done the same for me. We don't care what they say about us."[75] After her proclamation of care for Gustavito, Navas also described her connection to the Catholic Church and religion. Although she did not attend church every Sunday, when she did go, she took communion and confessed her sins to the priest. She insisted that she harmed no one, she never stole, and she "lived from my own work." And "when I go with a young man it is not out of interest or money, but because I want to and I don't hide from anyone because I have no one who tells me what to do, nor do I want that." She reiterated that it was "best to be free and do what one likes."[76] She threaded the needle between morality and reproductive care in a way that was counter to a patriarchal, heteronormative, nuclear traditional family. For Navas, being a "good person" meant that she took care of herself and the people she loved by the sweat of her own brow while simultaneously finding pleasure in her life.

Although the lives of Morales and Navas may seem extraordinary, their stories give us a powerful window into the pluriversal worlds of Mexican-origin working-class women in the post–Depression era United States and their deep knowledge of and consideration for reproductive control and reproductive care. Morales and Navas both understood the utility and importance of contraception and reproductive health care as they found physicians, or people who claimed to be doctors, to give them access to regular checkups and contraceptives. After one sexual encounter with Morales, Recinos noted that the young woman "washed with powders given to her by an American doctor" to prevent pregnancy.[77] According to Navas, her physician willingly supplied her friends with pessaries, while Morales used douches to avoid pregnancy.[78] This is not far off from the experiences of other Catholic working-class women in cities, such as Chicago, in the 1920s. As Angela Fritz observes, "Although many Polish Catholic immigrants may have fulfilled their public religious obligations by sending their children to parochial schools and generously giving to the collection plate every Sunday, in private many working-class women maintained that birth control was less a moral issue than a personal choice influenced by both economic and medical necessity."[79]

In addition, Navas and Morales provided reproductive care not only in their sharing of information and knowledge about reproductive health but also as friends, lovers, mothers, sisters, daughters, and workers. Both women supported their families financially. As Navas noted, a large portion of her pay went to provide for her children; Morales mentioned that she gave much of her earnings to her mother.[80] These two women were critical reproductive caregivers within their kinship circles, offering their broader community consideration, joy, love, and economic support outside the nuclear heteronormative patriarchal family ideal. Note how Morales made sure that everyone in her friend group ate well while in Recinos's company and on his dime. Navas recounted the different jobs she had tried before landing on taxi dancer—one that seemed to pay the best and offered her the most "freedom" to care for those around her in her own way. Critical to their reproductive care labor is the transformative aspect imbedded in it—both women understood that they were different from the generation before them. They were part of an emerging generation of women who would leave behind traditional expectations of respectability and chart their own path.

Morales's and Navas's stories have remained unexamined, as Mexican-origin women's sexuality and use of contraception in this period largely show up as part of state campaigns criminalizing and racializing sex deemed deviant and in need of state control. Most of the literature concerning Mexican-origin people's sexuality rests on archival materials from the early twentieth century. These documents highlight the state's tracking of so-called dysgenic traits and its attempts to control deviant sexual behaviors, notably homosexual ones, especially among racialized communities.[81] Coercive sterilization mandates and forced detention were state correctives to control sexual deviancy and supposed human defectiveness and used to "justify the policing of entire working-class families and intervene in the lives of Mexican-origin women, denying them freedom, privacy, and reproductive autonomy."[82] With this backdrop, especially the heightened surveillance in California during this period, Morales's and Navas's stories take on greater valiance. Sexual pleasure in or outside marriage and the use of technologies to prevent conception would surely have been markers of deviancy. Viewed from this angle, their words and deeds and their desire to have their sexual lives documented for posterity—recall Navas reminded Recinos that he was there to interview her—become themselves radical acts of reproductive care. These narratives push against homogenizing stereotypes of Mexican-origin women as only always poor working mothers.[83] Finally, Navas and Morales did not exist in this pluriverse alone. Navas's and Morales's friends and acquaintances likely believed they too should have control over their bodies and their lives to uplift themselves and loved ones around them.

Birth Control and Reproductive Care in the Post–Depression Era Borderlands

Although the impetus for the birth control movement's activism is covered in chapter 2, it bears recognizing that a possible antidote to birth controllers' eugenic feminism is reproductive care. Despite their public altruism, birth controllers masked their coercion with the language of care.

For instance, among birth control leaders there was little focus on Mexican-origin mothers' confrontations with infant mortality. While public concerns for infant mortality first brought the issue of birth control to the fore in cities like El Paso, most of what has been written about the topic centers the lives and work of white leaders and reformers' attempts at curbing the astronomical rates of infant death they believed was caused by overpopulation. As birth control activists peddled contraception as a cure-all for population control, it is possible to imagine that Mexican-origin women believed contraception could be one tool for protecting their children from ill health and infant death while also producing the conditions for raising the children they had in safe environments. After all, birth control and raising wages had been Dr. T. J. McCamant's, the city-county public health officer, solution to the infant mortality crisis in 1933. Viewing Mexican-origin women's use of birth control through the frameworks of reproductive care requires an honest assessment of the compounding markers of trauma and pain caused by poverty, marginalization, exploitation, and infant death. As Anglo borderland activists leaned into the idea that their domestic workers knew nothing of birth control and would need lots of coaxing to enter the clinic, a look at the actions of Mexican-origin women and their relationship to Texas birth control clinics in this period suggests otherwise.

Finding testimonies of Mexican-origin women who were interested in or had already visited the clinics in the borderlands was no easy feat. Their words were often filtered through other mediums and people. In the wake of the El Paso Mothers' Health Center inauguration, birth control activists fielded questions from members of the community about the clinic's services. One query arrived from a boy who stated, "'My mother is anxious to learn how to keep from having a baby every year . . . and I do hope she can get this information so that my brother next to me can finish his schooling in the High School and won't have to stop and work for the little children in the family as I have to do.'" Mrs. L. O. Dutton, member of the Mothers' Health Center of El Paso board of directors, reported that she had spoken with a "young Mexican boy" who called the clinic asking for birth control information for his mother and her three friends. None of the women spoke English, but all "four women wanted to come to the Health Center as soon as it was open," she assured.[84]

In one way, Dutton's anecdote about the young boy's mother and her friends represented a kind of advertising for the clinic. For birth controllers, Dutton's story suggested that their rhetoric of social uplift was working among the Mexican-origin community and animating Mexican-origin women's desires for birth control. Viewed another way, this instance can also represent a radical act of reproductive care of the boy on behalf of his family. Perhaps Dutton revealed the content of this call to the newspaper without the consent of the boy and his family. It is likely he believed, along with his mother and her friends, that advocates at the clinic would respect his inquiry and act with discretion, so he spoke openly. He described how his mother was "anxious to learn how to keep from having a child nearly every year." [85] Interacting with the clinic on his mother and her friends' behalf, perhaps at her behest because of the language barrier, provides a window into a moment of familial openness about family planning seen by some as an aberration despite the need of many American-born Mexican children to act as cultural brokers for their parents and relatives. However, given the profound impact the Depression had on Mexican-origin people in the Southwest, especially the issue of deportation via repatriation, frank discussions of child-spacing and family limitation in that context may not have been so rare. The boy's generous act of translation reveals that notions of shame surrounding issues related to sex, reproduction, and birth control were not necessarily shared among all members of the Mexican-origin community. For many white birth control activists, contraception was framed as an individual act of control and protection against overpopulation, but for Mexican-origin women, especially those at the margins of such thinking, contraception offered possibilities and opportunities for families and their broader community to survive and possibly thrive during a moment of economic deprivation and government hostility.

Much like Recinos's interviews, white women birth control activists served as intermediaries between Mexican-origin women's words and the world. Newspapers captured some of what they would say, but generally these exchanges were funneled through interviews with board members or nurses at the clinic and meant to make the birth control movement and its advocates in the borderlands look good. Patient interviews in local newspapers provided free advertising for the clinic and were rarely done outside the watchful eye of clinic staff or board members. These kinds of interviews were meant to comfort donors as well. Firsthand accounts of the power of birth control affirmed that their money was being used to keep birth rates low among potential welfare recipients. One newspaper account reassured donors, and the public at large, that well over 500 mothers, wives of American Works Progress Administration (WPA) workers, had been cared for at the clinic. An interview with a clinic patient who first stated that her husband was a WPA worker was meant to highlight that data point. She also made sure to thank the "mothers of El Paso who started the clinic."[86] For birth control advocates, these interviews and press engagements provided moments of great spectacle, lauding their arduous but necessary labor among the mostly Mexican-origin women clientele in the community. As mentioned in chapter 2, Goetting took Sanger's advice to heart and made sure newspapers offered the clinic the best publicity.

Sometimes the clinic and press conspired to demonstrate a deep lack of empathy and care for clinic patients, even as patients attempted to tell their stories, especially in the shadow of devastating infant loss. As the birth control clinic celebrated its one-year anniversary in February 1938, The El Paso Herald-Post described how the birth control clinic's nurse, Emma Hensley, "presented" a twenty-eight-year-old mother, whose name remained unknown in the article, to a crowd of thirty birth control advocates and donors as a prime example of the women the clinic sought to assist. Depicted in the newspaper as a woman with limited English skills, she was asked by clinic board members to explain her rationales for attending the clinic. Holding her "round-faced, black-eyed infant," she said: "I am married eight years. I have seven babies. My husband is in WPA. I am 28. I came to the

Health Center. I was thin and I worry very much. The nurse and the doctor helped me. Now it has been 11 months since I have a baby. This baby is the first baby I have nursed. I am so happy. I have new suit. Baby has new shoes. My husband love me more because I am pretty."[87] The voice of this young Mexican-origin mother was eclipsed by the white women in attendance congratulating themselves on their magnanimity toward her specific demographic. Goetting later quipped, "We are getting results."[88] Yet this mother's story tells us that she believed the use of contraception after her seventh child had contributed to better physical and mental health and the well-being of her family. For eleven months she had not been pregnant, helping her regain her strength and perhaps even rekindle affections toward her husband. She also felt more beautiful. The newspaper noted that she "beamed" as the young mother "point[ed] to her waved her."[89] Her small baby had new shoes, and she expressed happiness as she stated that this baby was the first of her children she was able to nurse. Birth control advocates certainly manipulated her pride in acquiring a modicum of control over her health and life as they sensationalized her words to elevate their mission in the borderlands. Still, her story reveals multiple worlds at play. It is possible that she considered access to birth control part of giving greater care to her family, lifting her spirits and mind, and perhaps providing an example to other women in her community.

Although Mexican-origin women's unvarnished thoughts about reproductive control are scarce in the historical record, their actions are not. Three months after the inauguration of the clinic in 1937, the El Paso Mothers' Health Center boasted 250 patients on its roster.[90] Patients and donations were pouring into the clinic. By its six-month anniversary, the clinic had served 407 women. Early clinic records were sparse and not always accurate; quarterly reports were often used to publicize the clinic's success and not necessarily to keep strict medical records about patients. A quarterly report from 1937 showed that out of 190 patients, 127 were considered new patients, 121 were advised on the use of birth control, and six were not advised due to sickness or pregnancy. Describing these new patients, the clinic reported seventy-eight patients as Catholic, forty-three as Protestant, one as Mormon, one as Jewish, and four as non-professing. Under "nationality"—a category that evidently described both race and ethnicity—they listed eighty as Mexican, forty-one as American, three as "colored," and one each as Italian, French-Canadian, and French. From these scant figures, it appears many of the clinic's patients were Mexican and Catholic.[91]

Despite the paltry records documenting women's reproductive experiences in their own words, clinic data allows some inferences to be made about the reproductive lives of the women who sought care at the El Paso Mothers' Health Center. The quarterly assessment registered six case histories describing the socioeconomic backgrounds of the patients, four of whom were Mexican-origin women. One entry read: "Patient age 28, married 13 years, 6 living children, 4 spontaneous abortions, 12 pregnancies. Husband laborer, works part time. Referred by City-County clinic." While the city-county health clinic could not officially sponsor the birth control clinic, it nonetheless sent patients whom were believed to need contraceptive information. In another case, the report described a patient's difficult circumstances and home life: "Patient Mexican, 29 years, blind, married 14 years, 4 living children; several abortions. Husband 60 years, drinks and does not care to work. Was also taken to office of one of our clinic doctors, as she could not follow instructions, and he took care of her." The use of "abortion" as a reproductive category in this case study could indicate either miscarriage or the intentional termination of pregnancy.[92]

The July 1937 quarterly report revealed further information about the reproductive lives of working-class women in the city. Another case on the list stated: "Patient Mexican, 34 years, married 10 years, 4 living children, 9 pregnancies, 1 still-born child, 3 children died before reaching 3 months of age, 1 spontaneous miscarriage. Husband laborer earns $7.00 weekly. Woman walked part way from Smelter to the Center. Case referred to the Center by physician."[93] The smelter in question was the American Smelting and Refining Company (ASARCO), whose workers and their families lived in "Smeltertown," located nearly five miles away from the clinic.[94] That a patient walked this distance in the desert's summer heat for information about birth control or basic access to reproductive health services underscores the need working-class people had for health care. The number of living children compared to pregnancies recorded in these documents emphasizes the real problem of infant mortality and lack of prenatal care for working-class women in El Paso. Although Dr. Arthur P. Black, the chairman of the clinic's Medical Advisory Board and the preparer of the clinic report, brusquely laid out the reproductive tragedies of each patient, their miscarriages, infant deaths, still-born babies, and abortions, the report did reveal the intent of working-class Mexican-origin women to access reproductive health services.

Clinical services at the Mothers' Health Center expanded over the years as advancements in technology and demand brought a greater variety of contraceptives to clinics across the country. In 1937 there were few options available to women. Informational pamphlets, available in English and Spanish from the El Paso clinic, instructed patients to wash, douche, and use spermicidal jelly with a cervical cap. Pamphlets describing the "rhythm method" show that physicians also prescribed periodic abstinence.[95]

As the Mothers' Health Center expanded its reach, more dramatic stories of appreciative women were reported in the local press. The description of a "poorly-clad illiterate Mexican woman [who] suddenly kissed the hand of a doctor at the El Paso Mothers' Health Center" underscored the ideas constructed about Mexican-origin women and their supposed gratitude for being taught the power of reproductive control. The article described the Mexican-origin woman as "just 33 years old, the mother of eight children, two of them dead," as she expressed gratefulness for the reproductive health care she had received. The news article maintained that "there will be no more babies for the ailing mother to bear or care for. The clinic has shown her a way to a little future happiness and a less burdened life. She has been taught birth control."[96] Her case had been explored in greater detail in the clinic quarterly report and contradicted the newspaper's accounts. Dr. Black reported that she likely had epilepsy and that two of her children had died before turning six months old. He remarked that she had killed one of the infants "while having a spasm." A third child around twelve years old had recently died "after complaining of a headache." The physician noted that "because of her inability to follow instructions, was taken to office of our clinic doctors who used his own supplies." She had most likely been fitted for a diaphragm and then sent for a follow-up with Dr. Black. Her reaction to his care had surprised the veteran doctor as she had shown her "appreciation [in an] unusual manner—wanted to kiss doctor's hand."[97] While the newspaper's depiction of her as poor, infirmed, and illiterate—but now free from the burdens of procreation—was meant to exalt the work of birth control activists among wealthy community members, we can and should reimagine her enthusiasm for birth control in relation to her difficult reproductive life. According to Dr. Black's report, she had lost three children in the span of her thirteen years of marriage, and one of the children may have accidently died by her hand. Her husband, who was a tailor, likely did not make enough money for her to seek proper medical services for her epilepsy, and so she had confronted these tragedies with her family and community as support. To the Anglo doctor and the local press, her act of tenderness and gratitude may have seemed overblown and reinforced their condescending position toward her. But perhaps her excitement over the possibility of future health and more control over her reproductive life, the ability to parent the children she had in a safer environment, moved her to show reverence for the doctor's support offering him a peck on his hand.

The media and activists celebrated the dissemination of birth control among working-class Mexican-origin women, but the actual arrival of hundreds of patients reveals these women's intention to take control of their bodies and lives, highlighting what one scholar calls the precarious connection between choice and coercion.[98] Clinic reports from 1937 to 1938 document the large groups of women who attended the clinic during the nine months after it opened. With a total number of 604 patients, over 265 were considered revisits (women who had attended the clinic more than once), signifying their concern not only with birth control but perhaps their reproductive health overall. Of those considered new patients, nearly 339 women, clinic records listed 205 as Mexican and 211 as Catholic.[99] Amid the campaigns for and against birth control and despite harassment, women attending the clinic were steadfast in acquiring basic reproductive health services.

Staggering numbers emerged in the annual report for 1938–1939, published by the Mothers' Health Center in conjunction with the Birth Control Clinical Research Bureau in New York City. By this time clinic staff had better classification data and reported that nearly 1,170 patients had attended the clinic. The report showed that they had served 556 new patients, but, perhaps more importantly, they had 614 revisits. High numbers of women were returning to the clinic. The document categorized the new patients by religion, nationality, and race: Mexican 378, American 150, Negro 5, Syrian 4, Chinese 2, and other 17. Religions included Catholic 364, Protestant 131, Jewish 2, and other 59. Mexican women again dominated the representational case studies presented in the report. The Mexican-origin women represented in the case studies report disclosed at least one abortion or miscarriage, and all had lost at least one of their children. Of the 556 new patients, 514 were advised on the use of birth control, while 42 were turned away "on account of pregnancy or illness."[100] Even as some women were turned away, others continued to stream in. Their determination to use clinic services complicated Goetting and Sanger's racially motivated birth control crusade.[101] While activists lauded their own efforts to bring "superstitious," ignorant women into the light of reproductive regulation, patients themselves calculated their needs by either returning for more assistance or simply using what they needed without going back.

Mexican-origin women navigated rhetorical and material minefields, maneuvering through a pluriverse of hurdles, as they sought access to reproductive health services during the late 1930s and early 1940s. As eugenic and overpopulation discourse increased in fervor and as Catholic harassment intensified, they nonetheless continued to seek out care. They did so precisely because their economic and social marginalization produced structural barriers to proper health in El Paso. The Mexican-origin patients at the clinic experienced infant and child loss, miscarriages, and other debilitating health effects working as domestics in private homes, as laundresses, or as factory workers for the very people who sought to control their reproduction for eugenic aims.

Despite the racial and class hierarchies that dominated the birth control movement and clinic in the borderlands, Mexican-origin women still managed to assert their concerns. Faint echoes can be heard through Planned Parenthood of El Paso archival materials. In 1941, board members agreed to provide more information about the clinic in Spanish, no doubt a recommendation made by the patients themselves, who may have sought greater clarity about the services provided at the clinic. And, although none of these women were hired, the board of the birth control clinic submitted the names of "Mrs. Garzapania (Social Worker), Mrs. Vidal (Mexican nurse), and Mrs. Carrasco (Social Worker)" for full-time positions at the clinic.[102] While the three Spanish-surnamed women workers, including one who was identified as a "Mexican nurse," might be beneficial to the birth control movement's mission, it also indicated the possibility that patients asked for more Spanish-speaking health care providers. This also shows that Mexican-origin women actively sought to work at the clinic, not only to support the dissemination of contraceptive information but also to serve their community. Perhaps many Mexican-origin women openly sought employment at the clinic to bring their voices to the movement and influence its aims and mission, but these kinds of interactions were not recorded by PPEP board members. Even as the press and clinic reports documented their reproductive tragedies to bolster fundraising schemes, Mexican-origin women took advantage of the medical care offered to them at the birth control clinic to empower themselves and their families. Despite their words and deeds being filtered through the work of Anglo birth control advocates and an Anglo press, Mexican-origin women nonetheless braided together concerns for reproductive control and health care with the need to protect, uplift, and support their communities.

Reproductive Care in the Borderlands

Some historians have interpreted the noncoercive use of contraception as an individual act of bodily autonomy. Reproductive care opens the aperture for understanding the significance of contraceptive use as something that is both an individual and community act of care. For instance, when Bertha González Chávez discussed her use of contraception in the years after she married, she provided a forthright yet critical description of the power and impact wielding reproductive control had on her life and the life of her family.

Like González Chávez, hundreds of Mexican-origin women visited birth control clinics in El Paso in the 1940s and 1950s. Planned Parenthood of El Paso records shows that an average of seventeen *new* patients a month attended the clinics from 1945 to 1954 for contraception.[103] During those same years, an average of fifty-two women a month were considered *old* patients, meaning they had attended the clinic once before and were returning to the clinic for services. For the months with available data, approximately 5,586 women were considered returning patients in that nine-year period.[104] While these may not seem like astronomical figures given the population size of the El Paso–Ciudad Juárez region—roughly 253,051 residents in 1950—these were substantial figures for the time. It is critical to note these were the days before the introduction of the contraceptive pill.[105] After 1960, PPEP began to offer various forms of the Pill, and numbers of people seeking birth control increased precipitously, not unlike in other regions of the United States.

Mexican's generational understandings of sexuality and its connection to contraceptive use were commonly associated with lax American morals and their undue influence on young Mexican Americans. For instance, historian Elizabeth Escobedo describes the shock of Aurora Preciado, a native of Mexico, when she realized her pompadour-wearing daughter was hiding birth control in her dresser drawer in 1945 Los Angeles.[106] What this chapter has shown, however, is the degree to which Mexican-origin women in the United States and Mexico had complex understandings of their bodies and reproduction. Their relationship to sex was not necessarily a traditionalist one, and knowledge of contraception was not exclusively a trapping of American culture.

Some women acquired knowledge from each other; from physicians at PPEP who instructed patients in the use of diaphragms, the rhythm method, and abstinence; and from other health professionals. Diaphragms, as González Chávez herself recalled, were fitted to each individual person and necessitated an intrusive vaginal exam that not all women were willing to have—what one historian referred to as "an exercise in embarrassment."[107] González Chávez explained that her cousin took her "encontra mi voluntad," or against her will. Given her background as a nurse and midwife, she likely knew to expect an intrusive examination and was hesitant about it. Or maybe she wondered if she might be seen by someone in her community who disapproved. There could have been numerous reasons for her caution in acquiring birth control, and yet she nonetheless used contraception successfully on and off for twelve years. She even went so far as to acquire a new diaphragm after her first one broke. Like the hundreds of women who attended the birth control clinic in El Paso, González Chávez returned to the clinic for care during her reproductive years not only to obtain reproductive services but also to engage in reproductive care for herself and her family. When she could, González Chávez used birth control to help space her children so that she could work and continue to provide for them at times of economic strain, first as a recently married woman in Juárez in 1950 and again as a recent arrival in Los Angeles in 1955.

Further still, this was not González Chavez's first encounter with different forms of birth control. During her time working at the General Hospital in Juárez, she recalled women who received tubal ligations. She explained that these were done with the consent of the patient. González Chávez recounted how women would enter the hospital to have ovarian cysts removed and doctors would ask patients if they wanted the sterilization procedure. Similarly to what anthropologist Iris López has documented about Puerto Rican women, for some Mexican-origin women, having "la operación" ended the difficulties of dealing with contraceptive devices that could fail or caused side effects and could be viewed as a "pragmatic stance . . . [toward] the church telling them what to do with respect to birth control . . ."[108] Although González Chávez's time as a nurse in Mexico must be understood through the history of Mexican medical practice at the time. In the 1920s and 1930s, Mexico had begun a practice of eugenic sterilization. As O'Brien observes, "Obstetrics after the Revolution showed strong clinical continuity from the late nineteenth century, in which doctors pursued interventionist surgeries on racially marginalized women as part of a larger national project that pathologized Mexican women and disparaged their biological capacities."[109] Mexico's racial landscape was influx during these years, as important national thinkers such as Manuel Gamio and José Vasconcelos (discussed further in chapter 6) articulated anxieties about the so-called "Indian problem" and argued for various kinds of social-engineering projects to incorporate Native peoples into the Mexican nation. O'Brien contends that while there was a robust eugenic movement in Latin America, "Latin eugenics was not some foregone, culturally rooted phenomenon. . . ."[110] Rather, physicians, medical professionals, and the state paid close attention to the German experiment and rejected its extremist genocidal positions.[111]

Therefore, when González Chávez first entered Ciudad Juárez's hospital in 1944, eugenic concerns regarding reproduction were certainly part of the clinical context. Yet, her recollections of her experiences with doctors there did not connote these ideas outright. She recalled that sometimes the doctors would not ask the husband for consent as was the custom. "No," the doctors would not ask, she said, "because you know some of these husbands wanted to have all the children that God could give them!" González Chávez continued, "As I used to tell my friend, 'What idiots!'"[112] She interpreted these interventions as moments of reproductive control and dignity for the female patients she encountered. For González Chávez these were moments to fight patriarchal and heteronormative ideas about reproduction and bodily autonomy. Her admonishment of men who "wanted to have all the children that God could give them," calling them "idiots" and her discussion of this critique with her friend reveal the degree to which women discussed these hypocrisies with women friends and family, providing a kind of discursive reproductive care amid the spread of eugenic ideology in Mexico.

The experiences of González Chávez and her cousin and of Elisa Morales and Gloria Navas, as well as of the hundreds of women who attended El Paso's birth control clinics, widen the possibilities for understanding the full lives of Mexican-origin women as they traversed the twentieth-century pluriverse. Despite the many histories of state-mandated reproductive coercion that dominate the literature of Mexican-origin women's reproduction, there are nonetheless glimmers of reproductive autonomy centering the reproductive health decisions Mexican-origin women made for themselves and their communities. Many women of González Chávez's generation and before faced a panoply of reproductive injustices in their day-to-day lives, mainly due to what Chávez called *la pobreza* (poverty). Poverty played a starring role in the everyday lives of Mexican-origin people in the decades before and after the Mexican Revolution, the Great Depression, and the Second World War. Despite the violence of poverty, Chávez's story and the stories of the other women presented in this chapter bring to life nuanced histories of Mexican-origin women's relationship to sexuality and reproductive control. These narratives shine a light on specific markers of material deprivation, social marginalization, and economic exploitation that characterized their ability to fight for different ways to provide care within their communities. Their lives and experiences show that reproductive control, care, and justice are not so easily disentangled, nor should they be.

A transnational approach to understanding how the lives of these women unfolded on both sides of the border in conversation with the political changes occurring in Mexico and the United States disrupts facile interpretations of Mexican-origin women's supposed prudishness or religious conservatism toward sexuality and contraception. True, not all women wanted access to birth control, nor did they seek information for reproductive health services. Equally true, working-class Mexican-origin women are not a monolith. Poverty and lack of access to resources for reproductive health care and the time needed to acquire available resources dominated the everyday lives of Mexican-origin women. Finding time to care for one's own health, especially given the myriad responsibilities of work, home, and family, may have precluded many a working woman from inquiring about birth control and other health services. Generalizations about Mexican-origin women's inherent sexual timidity also denies the influence of moral panics in both the United States and Mexico that were deeply tied to reestablishing gender, race, and class roles in the aftermath of industrialization.

In the post–Depression era United States, birth control campaigns entered a protracted struggle, grappling with the roots of eugenic racial degeneration and white population decline as well as managing a much-desired, easily exploitable, nonwhite labor class. From forced deportations to calls to end dependence on welfare and the push for Mexican-origin women to use birth control, Mexican-origin people's supposed predisposition toward poverty placed them in the crosshairs of excessive government- and nongovernment-sponsored surveillance. If only this attention had changed the structural and systemic obstacles that created poverty. It did not. On both sides of the border, exploitative labor conditions and extractive policies forced many Mexican-origin people to the live in abject or near-abject poverty for generations—these cycles continue today. And still, as Anzaldúa posits, Mexican-origin women engaged their "pluralistic mode—nothing is thrust out, the good, the bad and the ugly, nothing rejected, nothing abandoned."[113] As they face structural and systemic oppression, Mexican-origin women provided reproductive care for themselves, amid the good, bad, and ugly, and sought to uplift their communities with dignity, genius, and an eye toward the future.

4 *Se Aguanta*

Borderland Internationalism, Overpopulation, and Reproductive Control

In the 1950s and 1960s, Mexican-origin women in El Paso experienced a marked increase in aggressive birth control campaigns. These were explosive decades for contraception; an array of new technologies including the Pill, spermicidal foams, and intrauterine devices (IUDs) emerged, augmenting older tools like the diaphragm. Women had never seen such diverse birth control technologies in their lifetimes.[1] PPEP continued directing its advertising at women in the most economically depressed areas of El Paso, specifically the Mexican-origin, mostly working-class wards south of the train tracks. As years passed, PPEP expanded its reach to women across El Paso County. The organization launched educational campaigns sharing new birth control equipment with women in door-to-door campaigns that advertised new pharmaceuticals—it explicitly called one major campaign "Knock on Every Door." While PPEP promoted the utility of birth control for greater reproductive autonomy, it also continued to distribute materials dramatizing what it perceived to be the perils of overpopulation from the perspective of Anglo upper-middle-class El Pasoans. Working-class women received an onslaught of birth control information and contraceptive devices in their homes and places of work in the decades after World War II as PPEP expanded its concerns for population control to an international arena. At the same time, Planned Parenthood Federation of America attempted to distance itself from openly supporting eugenic ideology due in part to the horrors of the Holocaust.

Cold War obsessions with population increases, especially within communist countries, inflected mid-century anxieties about overpopulation and helped reshape old rationales for birth control into new technological advancements in contraception. Bombarded by news articles proclaiming that the United States' food reserves were "sav[ing] vast areas of world from disastrous famines" and that Russians rejected the "reduction of population or birth control" cemented for many El Pasoans that, while eugenic justifications for engineering better races was now out of vogue, a concentrated effort to curb population growth was not.[2] Internationally, population control advocates proclaimed that Malthus, not Galton, reigned supreme.

This was merely a magician's sleight of hand, however, as concerns for population size and fitness for reproduction had shifted to highlight specific regions of the world—namely in the Global South—as the culprits for resource depletion through out-of-control fertility. Organizations such as Planned Parenthood Federation of America pivoted toward a less overt call for social engineering via negative eugenics and more toward solving the problem of so-called overpopulation among the poorest communities on the planet.[3] Population control ideology merely became a global movement, becoming naturalized and imbricated through discourses on foreign aid as a "tax burden" for Americans after World War II. For instance, PPEP had a special fixation with family planning in Japan, proclaiming that in the years since V-J Day, Japan's population had seen a marked increase representing an "untold increase in the tax burden of America, which has pledged itself to support its former defeated enemy."[4] PPFA auxiliaries, such as Planned Parenthood of El Paso, began ginning up support for constraining the reproduction among the global poor, notably in Latin America, Africa, China, Japan, and India.[5]

Planned Parenthood of El Paso became a model of the internationalist work others might do.[6] It had always claimed that both quantity and quality of people were at issue in the borderlands. As such, it had never deviated from its intended audience. PPEP merely intensified its campaigns, and Mexican-origin women were mercilessly targeted for reproductive control. The organization did soften its message, removing direct references to a woman's lack of "eugenic fitness" from its advertising. In this way, El Paso is a prime site to examine how eugenic thinking was naturalized in the movement and how birth control advocates continued developing a borderlands lexicon that allowed them to speak about population bombs without directly naming the Black and brown people they accused of orchestrating the explosion. It was understood by many donors, though, that the continued rationalization for offering free contraception to the poor was to curb the fertility of those considered "unfit" for reproduction.

Chapter 4 examines how PPEP's birth control campaigns became more forceful due in part to a confluence of forces that connected borderland efforts for population control to international aims addressing overpopulation at its reproductive roots. Bolstering PPEP's long-established fears about overpopulation among Mexicans in the region, international population control advocates made the borderlands central to experimentation, testing, and research of new contraceptive campaigns and devices. Various players on the international scene, including Clarence Gamble and Margaret Sanger, produced a perfect circle of co-constitutive anxieties they had exalted since the 1930s, homing in, once again, on Mexican-origin women's reproduction in the borderlands in the 1950s and 1960s. This chapter connects the international efforts of population control advocates in the US-Mexico borderlands to older testing sites, such as Puerto Rico, as Spanish-speaking people from Spain's former colonies became the main test subjects for new birth control technologies. Furthermore, this chapter explores how even as Mexican-origin women attempted to use new contraceptive devices and pharmaceuticals and showed enthusiasm for joining PPEP's efforts in providing critical reproductive health information to their own community members, the PPEP board of directors remained indifferent to and often skeptical of Mexicanas taking care of their own reproductive health needs.

William Vogt's Maria in the Borderlands

One clear iteration of an aggressive reproductive control project was the campaign to offer contraceptive devices door-to-door. This mode of dissemination saw its origins in Planned Parenthood Federation of America's neo-Malthusian obsession with averting a "population explosion" and expanding its international arm with Planned Parenthood World Population.[7] Although Sanger had invested money in producing simpler—"dummy-proof"—contraceptives, it was not until major philanthropists, entrepreneurs, and pharmaceutical companies jumped in that new contraceptive technologies emerged en masse. This postwar population control movement included wealthy financiers, such as John D. Rockefeller III, Levis Strauss, Clarence Gamble, and others. William Vogt, the director of Planned Parenthood Federation of America, joined their contingent as one seeking to heighten concerns for overpopulation's deleterious impacts on the environment.[8] Elite El Pasoans had conflated overpopulation with poverty, destitution, and racial degeneration in south-side barrios and were alarmed by an impending population bomb since at least the late 1920s.[9] Sanger, along with Goetting, peddled support for clinics in the borderlands, marrying eugenics with demographic doom. William Vogt's PPFA directorship in the 1950s reinvigorated an urgency for population control and found fertile ground in the borderlands.

Known as the father of the modern environmentalist movement, Vogt penned *Road to Survival* (1948), which enumerated countless environmental catastrophes that could befall a population left to its own devices. His best-selling book opens with a series of fictional vignettes, portraying people in various parts of the world confronting what we today call "climate change." Vogt's *only* female character is "Maria," an indigenous woman from Michoacán, Mexico. She, like her more than "twenty-three million [Mexican] compatriots," is indifferent to the impacts of how Mexico's poverty—lack of access to water, food, and clothing—will influence the foreign policy of the United States, Vogt writes. Maria only sighs and mutters, "*Se aguanta*—one must bear it." This phrase, Vogt suggests, is the most "common on the lips of the women of her people."[10] Vogt constructed his fictional Maria by embellishing tropes about Mexican-origin women, likening her to poor women in developing nations around the world. Her indigeneity harkens back to those who modernity has left behind. In his story, Maria is also illiterate and has recently lost her baby due in part to a lack of water in her region—this last revelation he delivers by describing how her now-empty rebozo once held her infant on her back.[11] Her meager existence, Vogt explains, is inextricably tied to the fate of millions of others around the globe due in part to overpopulation.

Vogt provides a simple mathematical formula for addressing the indiscriminate rise of populations. The letter "C" in his equation stands for what Vogt termed "carrying capacity," or the ability of an area of land to provide for the population on it. Without a clear understanding of this critical equation, by men of science and politics, he contends that "at least three-quarters of the human race will be wiped out."[12] Vogt's *Road to Survival* was in line with early twentieth-century demostopic literatures, such as David Starr Jordan's *The Blood of the Nation* and Madison Grant's *Passing of the Great Race* and *The Conquest of a Continent*, discussed in chapter 1, although they explicitly decried the decline of the white race and white civilization. Vogt couched his demographobia in clear Malthusian terms.[13] Vogt believed he could foretell the "'history of the future'" by providing a graph of population increases over time and the depletion of natural resources on another, the lines had overlapped and were increasingly growing apart.[14] Vogt's ideas were vital in shaping the international family planning movement in the years after World War II.[15] His participation in this postwar population control iteration of the birth control movement preceded his time as director of Planned Parenthood Federation of America. During his directorship, Vogt helped reorient PPFA's mission to provide "cheaper contraceptives, education and incentives to increase demand, and linking food aid to population control."[16]

In 1953, Vogt brought his message to the US-Mexico borderlands after he attended a global population control conference spearheaded by Sanger and her new International Planned Parenthood Federation (IPPF) in Bombay, India, the year before.[17] Lady Dhanvanthi Rama Rau of India, a powerful champion for contraception in one of the world's most populous countries, was critical in bringing Sanger; Vogt; Elise Ottesen-Jensen, a Norwegian-Swedish sex educator activist; and C. P. Blacker, the secretary of the Eugenics Society, together to hash out specifics about IPPF.[18] They wanted to make birth control a "cornerstone of the welfare state" and fundamental to the struggle for women's rights in India and around the world. Sanger also secured Blacker, who, according to Ottesen-Jensen, was potentially a racist, to be IPPF's new director.[19]

Months after the success of the Bombay conference and the establishment of the IPPF, Vogt arrived in El Paso praising the gains made in India and its effects on the rest of the world. He spoke at various meetings and luncheons around the city, declaring that "the meeting in Bombay clearly established India's leadership in that field [family planning]."[20] For Vogt, the conference was a call to arms for all those interested in arresting war and famine. Addressing members of the Kiwanis Club and at a public meeting at the Southern Union Gas Company, Vogt stated that "it is when we come to the larger problem of how to provide food and the other necessities of life for a hundred million people in the next 15 or 20 years that we see the momentous importance of Planned Parenthood."[21] His celebration of the Bombay conference in El Paso set the groundwork for Rama Rau's visit to the borderlands later that year. Sanger sent Goetting word that Rama Rau's lecture "will be a wonderful boost to our cause" in El Paso.[22]

Vogt's best-selling book and his work with the international movement for Planned Parenthood made him a huge draw. As he lectured on scarcity, poverty, and war, many middle- and upper-middle-class El Pasoans who attended his talks could easily resurrect Vogt's fictional Maria. While she was meant to be a stand-in for all economically poor, third-world women, in the US-Mexico borderlands, Vogt's Maria was exactly who El Paso elites and ascending middle-class Anglos pictured when they linked overpopulation to their southern neighbors in Mexico. She was not a fictional character but a real, flesh-and-bone person they all knew too well. Now, with Vogt's help, white borderlanders were affirmed in making Maria the nexus to overtaxed land, never-ending war, famine, and environmental devastation.

Considering these challenges, Mexican-origin women like Bertha González Chávez and the hundreds of women attending clinics in the 1930s and 1940s were the mirror opposite of Vogt's Maria. They defied racialist expectations, using what services and supplies they needed from the birth control clinic and leaving aside what they did not. As Vicki Ruiz has stated of the settlement movement in the El Paso, "Mexican clients, not missionaries, set the boundaries for interaction."[23] The same rings true for PPEP clinics, even though doctors, clinic staff, and board of directors convinced themselves that Mexican-origin women's enthusiasm for contraceptive information was due to their educational campaigns alone. PPEP advocates could not *imagine* that Mexican-origin women understood for themselves the benefits of these contraceptive tools.

Thousands of Mexican-origin women from Mexico and the United States attended PPEP clinics as women took advantage of the various technologies that came and went like the tide. Pharmaceutical companies regularly offered substantial financial support to clinics willing to use their clientele as human guinea pigs. Planned Parenthood of El Paso exploited these conditions. This bounty of human need and excitement provided doctors, Planned Parenthood advocates, and pharmaceutical companies with ready test subjects in the borderlands as new and sometimes untested technologies made their way to local communities.

Mining the Archives for Moments of Reproductive Liberation and Care

Although women from both sides of the border attended the Planned Parenthood clinic since its opening in 1937, scant information exists about their lives, desires, and concerns as they entered the clinic in search of reproductive health services. While myriad documents exist tracing the history of the white women who founded Planned Parenthood of El Paso, the doctors and advocates who worked toward its mission, and other organizations who supported its efforts, few sources exist in PPEP archives that vividly describe the patients themselves.

What we do know about the thousands of women who risked social and cultural stigmas to visit PPEP's birth control clinics is gleaned from clinic data, forcing us to rely on patients' actions rather than words—as clinic figures often omitted personal testimony—to attempt to understand their motivations and experiences.[24] Chicana feminist Chela Sandoval's "differential mode of oppositional consciousness" and its connections to reproductive care help further underscore the significance of grappling with clinic data sets, number of returning patients, number of patients changing from one contraceptive to another, and number not returning to the clinic at all. When reviewed critically, data can attest to the heterogeneity of a group that often is lumped onto a generic axis of race, gender, sexuality, and class. As Ruiz reminds us, "There is no single hermetic Mexican or Mexican-American culture," nor is there a singular, victimized, or heroic Mexican-origin women.[25] Information collected from PPEP materials reveals that not all Mexican-origin women's reactions to changing mores and access to different reproductive or contraceptive resources neatly lined up together. In other words, working-class, Mexican-origin women accepting contraceptive materials and reproductive health care services defies simple categorization; they were complicated women leading pluriversal lives.

Thus, examining *how* we know about Mexican-origin women's participation and activism will be as critical as *why* Mexican-origin women were key to the movement for reproductive care and liberation as they faced an international conglomerate of the richest people on the planet hell-bent on controlling their fertility—and as you continue reading, you will see that this is not hyperbole! While it is important to "excavate new histories" of reproductive autonomy, I also heed Blackwell's advice that we remain "attentive to how that knowledge is produced . . . question[ing] the politics surrounding existing modes of knowing and systems (archives) of knowledge."[26]

Asking questions about privacy and agency, for instance, helps complicate birth control clinic sources and the production of knowledge around Mexican-origin women's engagement with contraception. It is possible that some Mexican-origin women did not feel comfortable championing their use of contraceptives because birth control was still very much stigmatized. For Mexican-origin Catholic women, who represented the vast majority of those using clinic services, a need for discretion would have been paramount as artificial birth prevention was considered a major offense against God and Church.[27] But, as I concluded in the preceding chapter, concerns about infant loss and commitment to reproductive and community care could have assuaged their fears about contraceptive use.

We might view the lack of women's voices in the archives not simply as an act of erasure or a lack of women's agency (although there are clear moments of erasure and denial of agency interlaced throughout PPEP sources) but also as a call for privacy, to keep to themselves their intimate reproductive choices. The politics of privacy complicate the role Planned Parenthood of El Paso's programs played in reaching women in the barrio. As anthropologist and legal scholar Khiara Bridges maintains: "To be poor is to be subject to invasions of privacy that we might understand as demonstrations of the danger of government power without limits." The case of PPEP, a nongovernment actor taking on the role of the state, raises deeper concerns about private, nonprofit organizations acting in place of state agencies especially as they tried producing social programs for the poor. There are often few avenues for communities or individuals to hold private agencies accountable—at least the state offers some, albeit minimal, recourses for holding itself accountable to its people. Bridges argues that so-called privacy rights often do not extend to the poor in general and to poor women and mothers of color in particular, emphasizing how "one would expect that if the Constitution contains individual rights and liberties that restrict state power, it would prevent precisely what poor women endure with respect to state intrusions into their private lives."[28]

PPEP's family planning programs were an intrusion into Mexican-origin family's private lives. Although PPEP received no government funding at the time, the organization nonetheless sought to fill what it believed was a state vacuum in disciplining the private reproductive decisions of El Paso's laboring class. PPEP's apprehensions about privacy regarding its mostly Mexican-origin women patient base was virtually nonexistent. In 1959, PPEP's lone social worker, Elizabeth Patterson, retired from work with PPEP because she was "unwilling to go into the homes of strangers, unsolicited, and initiate a discussion of such a personal matter as contraceptives." While she disagreed with the position of the Roman Catholic Church on the subject, she admonished PPEP's methods, recognizing that "I can see no value and perhaps some harm from canvassing a Roman Catholic neighborhood with the purpose of inducing persons of this faith to go counter to their religious training and to what they themselves may believe to be wrong."[29] PPEP paid Patterson no mind. It eagerly established the "Knock on Every Door" campaign and hired field-workers to comb neighborhoods south of the train tracks, engage potential patients, and leave pertinent information, regardless of people's interest in the clinic, at their front door. This program did little to protect the privacy of potential clinic patients as neighbors and others in the community could easily bear witness to those women who allowed Planned Parenthood social workers into their homes.

In addition to its door-to-door efforts, PPEP also sent out field-workers to visit women entering pre-and postnatal care and often planted field-workers at local maternity hospitals and clinics or entrusting local physicians with special clinic hours offering information about contraception. As early as 1939, PPEP board members secured office space with Dr. Malloy in Ysleta.[30] It took several decades of pushing the idea, but finally in 1958, PPEP secured cooperation from Newark Maternity Hospital, the large Methodist hospital located in Segundo Barrio, to assist in the dissemination of birth control literature.[31] El Paso's General Hospital offered similar support the following year.[32] Even before the "Knock on Every Door" program was instated, PPEP social workers often made uninvited house calls. They were tasked with visiting the "new mothers" noted in the Daily Court Recorder, suggesting that a personal visit might do more to convince women to use birth control than their normal "baby letters" sent to new parents.[33] PPEP sought to build a vast dragnet among local government agencies, such as El Paso General Hospital, County Health Unit, City-County Health Unit, Child Welfare, and Family Welfare agencies, that would allow it unfettered access to "needy" and vulnerable populations via a steady stream of referrals.[34] Although some Mexican-origin women had been recruited early on to help in some clinic work, it was not until 1959 that PPEP allowed one of the first Mexican-origin clinic staff members, Cristina Nevarez, to interview patients in Spanish and engage in fieldwork.[35] In the years that followed, Nevarez paved the way for several Mexican-origin women field-workers at PPEP who served their communities in Spanish—offering countless Mexican-origin women vital reproductive health care.

Even though some social workers like Elizabeth Patterson were ushered out of homes in South El Paso, allowing Planned Parenthood volunteers into their homes could also connote a subversive act in favor of Mexican-origin women's own autonomy, contradicting social norms that stigmatized the use of birth control. As one woman whom I interviewed explained, "*Nosotras nomas calladitas*; we used birth control, but quietly."[36] While the "silence" of Mexican-origin women in the history of the birth control movement has long been understood as a cultural admonition for contraception, Mexican-origin women participated in the movement as active seekers of reproductive autonomy and later as volunteers and clinic staff educating their own communities.[37] Moreover, women's abilities to make choices about their bodies outside the dominion of the Catholic Church, their husbands, and others in their community, who did not agree with their use of contraception, would be worth protecting by keeping their connections to the clinic and birth control to themselves. As Ruiz reminds us, women of color "have not had unlimited choice. Race and gender [and class] prejudice and discrimination with their accompanying social, political, and economic segmentation have constrained aspirations, expectations, and decision-making."[38] Therefore, as white women *publicly* championed the use of birth control, including abortion, as a "right to privacy," Mexicanas and Chicanas in the borderlands championed privacy through silence as they protected themselves from the prying eyes of nonstate and state actors.

To get a clearer picture of their involvement in the movement for reproductive freedom necessitates a more nuanced framing of how people become active participants given their location to power and oppression. Blackwell contends that we need to "complicate our notions of social movements and political subjectivities in order to see the multiple sites of contestation, production, of political knowledge, and registers of meaning that women of color navigate [to] formulate new theories and politicized identities to constitute themselves as political subjects."[39] In this case, Mexican-origin women's resistance to, ambivalence of, and compliance with various contraceptive methods can only be known through the murmurs they left in clinic documents. These data points tell a story if we listen.

For instance, from 1945 through 1950, the average number of new patients receiving clinic services annually neared 1,100, and the average number of returning patients was approximately 1,600.[40] In the "new patient" category, the clinic saw a marked change since its establishment in 1937 when it saw an average of sixty-seven new patients per month. By 1945, PPEP saw an average of ninety new patients per month.[41] Although these numbers may seem relatively small, Catholic Church officials and community members exerted enormous pressure on women to avoid PPEP clinics. Moreover, the sexual undertones of birth control—that it would cause promiscuity among its users and general immorality—kept many away. After the invention of the Pill and the emergence of other new contraceptive technologies, as well as a Catholic generation more likely to defy Church doctrine, clinic records boasted that in the twenty-seven years since it opened, PPEP's clinics had served a total of 14,440 patients. The largest proportion of these patients attending in the years after 1960.[42]

On Gynecological and Reproductive Violence

As PPEP amassed patients eager to avail themselves of its services, it confronted resistance from patients complaining about improper care. Patients disclosed complicated and at times inappropriate interactions with doctors, leaving some women without appropriate care. One year, the PPEP medical committee lambasted a doctor who did not give women pelvic exams, "nor [was] he using a fitter for deciding the size of diaphragm to prescribe." Women in his care would endure "rush[ed] . . . examination[s] so that he is very rough—at one clinic [session] he saw 15 patients and was through and ready to leave in 15 minutes!"[43] Additionally, he would "not examine old patients who have missed one or [more] periods."[44] For decades, doctors worked on a volunteer basis in the clinic. Later, residents from local hospitals also became part of the PPEP medical staff. It is unclear if the physician mentioned in the PPEP medical committee's notes was an established doctor or a student, but his demeanor with the mostly Mexican-origin, working-class patients is telling of his inability to see his PPEP patients as sentient, flesh-and-blood humans.

Reminiscent of historian Deirdre Copper Owens's examination of gynecological procedures invented through the experimentation on enslaved Black women in the antebellum South, Mexican-origin women in this scenario were denied the most basic human emotion—feeling pain. As Copper Owens contends, "black women remained flesh-and-blood contradictions, vital to [physicians] research yet dispensable once their bodies and labor were no longer required."[45] Racialized notions of Black and Mexican-origin women's capacity to endure extreme discomfort or their "natural abilities" for childbirth, often used as counterpoints to wealthy white women's reproductive fragility, anchored the medicalization of women's reproductive health at the intersections of race, gender, and class during the nineteenth and twentieth centuries.[46] Women's proximity to poverty—using public clinics or hospitals—put them in grave danger of being employed as guinea pigs—often against their will—for all manner of educational purposes, especially pelvic exams, well into the latter part of the twentieth century.[47] Whether the previously mentioned doctor was a student or a veteran physician and whether he actually examined fifteen women's vulvas and vaginas (standard practice for a gynecological exam) in fifteen minutes, his brutality with patients was noted by clinic staff and the medical committee. His brusque care exemplifies obstetrical violence via obstetrical racism, specifically related to gynecological examinations.[48]

From the PPEP medical committee's notes on the matter, it is clear that patients were critical in bringing the doctor's terse bedside manner to the attention of his superiors at the clinic. Patient complaints forced the PPEP's medical committee to issue a memorandum addressing proper care in its clinics. Committee members feared that this doctor's actions were causing other patients to reject gynecological exams. Nurses noted that women arrived at the clinic refusing to have pelvic exams but still requested birth control, prompting the committee to address the situation.[49] In the end, the committee decided that doctors at PPEP must comply with national and local regulations that made a proper pelvic examination part of the basic care offered to patients and a prerequisite for receiving birth control. Although patients were not directly quoted in the organization's missives, their objections to painful, rushed, careless procedures and inappropriate care emerge as faint whispers expressing their wish to protect themselves and each other.

While PPEP publicly celebrated its intensive educational birth control campaigns, it knew its mission would be dead in the water if patients did not positively review clinic services by word of mouth. Patients forced PPEP to streamline its services, including the creation of standard procedures after the incident with the doctor discussed previously. Not only could a patient anticipate standard conduct during appointments, but she could also explain the process to friends and family interested in birth control as someone who came from similar families and community. As one board member noted in 1961, "word of mouth [is] still our best source of patients."[50]

Emerging Technologies and Demographic Shifts

By the 1960s, during an initial visit, women could expect a thorough explanation of contraceptives available and a thirty- to forty-minute lecture on the purposes of the clinic—PPEP board members tried to maintain bilingual (English and Spanish) access to all clinic information. Three clinic sessions were offered every week, with a different attending clinician at each session, and volunteers from the PPEP board or from other women's organizations in the city administered duties at the front desk. The clinic also offered marriage counseling and managed infertility cases on a referral basis only. Although the national policy was to offer birth control to married women exclusively, Planned Parenthood of El Paso made contraception and reproductive care available to anyone referred to by a doctor, clergy, or agency "no questions asked."[51]

During this same decade, low-income patients now had more contraceptive choices, some opting not to use the diaphragm and instead choosing birth control they could administer themselves without an invasive fitting from an unknown doctor. Thousands of women from across the county rushed PPEP clinics after less physically intrusive contraceptives arrived: the miracle pill, among others. PPEP clinics began dispensing Enovid—the first birth control pill—in 1960. The organization described the arrival of "new and simpler methods of contraception" among them Emko a spermicidal foam; Enovid; and Koromex A, a contraceptive jelly.[52] What had been a consistent flow of women accessing the clinic soon turned into a flood as these easier and less intrusive contraceptives became available. By the end of 1960, over 836 new patients had registered for some form of birth control and 757 women were returning patients. The clinic prescribed a total of 2,363 contraceptive aids, including diaphragms, pills, jellies, and foams.[53] The following year, the number of new patients in the PPEP records jumped to approximately 1,335 with about 943 returning patients. Clinic records registered a 115 percent uptick in supplies with approximately 5,082 apportioned in 1961.[54]

A new demographic had become increasingly interested in the clinic's distribution of contraceptives. A 1961 clinic dispatch noted that "ethnic data shows a remarkable change . . . for the year [up] to July 1960 the center had 18 Anglo patients," and by the following year up to the same month, there was an increase of "194 Anglo patients."[55] As mentioned in previous chapters, PPEP's exclusive mission was to bring poor, Mexican-origin women—Black and Native women to a lesser degree—into the bright light of natal control. Supporting the birth control needs of Anglo women was certainly not on its agenda. Internal memos show the increase of Anglo patients left clinic staff and PPEP board members flummoxed. By 1962, after an article reviewing the history of the Pill appeared in the *Saturday Evening Post*, special mention was made of the ten new Anglo patients accepted to PPEP clinics.[56] A month after these women became clinic patients, the board of directors discussed whether dispensing Enovid to so-called financially stable women—a euphemism for Anglo—conflicted with the clinic's mission to serve the poor. Among the solutions proposed was instituting a sliding scale whereby women would pay "Ten percent of the 'take home pay,' minus 50 cents for each child."[57] By summer 1962, however, board members stated that "if a patient desires Enovid, regardless of income, she must be permitted to have it."[58] The contraceptive revolution quickly became a challenge to the borderlands movement's principal intentions. Records do not expressly mention the ethnicity of all the facility's patients during these years, but the specific reference to Anglos receiving birth control suggests PPEP's concern, or at least its surprise, in this demographic shift. Even as more affluent, white women sought PPEP for their birth control needs, likely because they could circumvent discussions with their family doctor and could easily pay, El Paso clinics remained largely focused on poor Mexican-origin women.

Experimentation in the Borderlands

The confluence of emerging technologies and eagerness among many PPEP patients for access to these new contraceptives provided Planned Parenthood with a ready patient base for experimentation and clinical trials of cutting-edge contraceptive technologies. In these years, PPEP became a critical site for research and testing. Although greater contraceptive "choices" emerged at the time, those options did not always translate into safer alternatives for women—what contemporary scholars of long-acting reversible contraceptives (LARC) have termed "agency-without-choice."[59] Women in El Paso visiting PPEP clinics made birth control decisions filtered through the national and local organization's necessity to control the type of contraception offered due in part to clinical testing needed to get new contraceptives on the market.

One transnational aspect of the experimental history of the contraceptive pill in the borderlands is that, as historian Gabriela Soto Laveaga contends, a Mexican chemist named Luis Ernesto Miramontes was "the co-discoverer of the chemical compound that led to the global production of oral contraceptives."[60] Once the wild yam barbasco—only found in Mexican jungles—was singled out as producing synthetic progesterone, the main chemical necessary for the Pill, Miramontes's laboratory developed it in 1951.[61] In the United States, the Pill's history centers Dr. Gregory Pincus as the discoverer of the Pill and his work with Planned Parenthood Federation of America (PPFA), through the auspices of Margaret Sanger. By 1955, pharmaceutical companies in the United States had claimed the discovery for themselves, with Dr. John Rock, a well-respected fertility specialist, selecting Searle Pharmaceutical's contraceptive formula over the one patented first by Miramontes.[62]

While Enovid emerged as the first birth control pill on the market, side effects and other health concerns pressured scientists to continue their research for a better option.[63] PPFA and the Margaret Sanger Research Bureau funded and supported the study of contraceptive devices and pharmaceuticals in their clinics.[64] PPFA national medical director Mary Calderone wrote to a potential drug company explaining that the clinics nationally "'have a total of 10,000 new patients yearly,'" which would undoubtedly excite executives yearning to produce more clinical research needed for FDA approval of these new contraceptives.[65]

According to PPEP documents, hundreds of women attending its clinics in the early 1960s served as case studies for Enovid—once the drug had already been brought to market. Calderone made several trips to El Paso to ensure that proper records were maintained to support the clinical data for these new contraceptives. Calderone first visited in November 1961, nearly a year after the Pill was introduced in the borderlands. She explained to clinic staff and board members the singular importance of keeping proper documents related to Enovid's distribution. "Numbers will become important" as a "surge" of patients would begin to clamor for oral contraceptives. Calderone also called for properly trained staff at the clinics in preparation for the swell of new patients.[66] The following year Calderone sent a letter to the PPEP board recommending it employ a pharmacist to accurately dispense the medication, guaranteeing that women could only receive the Pill with a prescription. Board members and doctors suggested that perhaps their clinic would be free from inspection since they sought to make no profit on the drugs.[67] The matter was postponed, and PPEP continued to provide Enovid to all those who desired it. Later that year, the Pharmaceutical Association reassured PPEP that it could continue dispensing Enovid without professional pharmacists, expressing that it "could no longer open the vials, and dispense single pills, and the patient's name, case number, etc. will now have to be noted on the vial." Although no pharmacist was needed, some restrictions were placed on the distribution of the Pill.[68]

Calderone was right; PPEP saw the number of patients skyrocket in the following years. From January to July 1962, nearly 7,000 women visited PPEP's clinic, far exceeding the total numbers for 1960 and 1961 combined; this increase is perhaps due to the popularity of and diversity in birth control technologies that had emerged. In a period of six months, there was an increase of more than 52 percent as women inundated the clinic.[69] By January 1962, PPEP board members boasted that Planned Parenthood of El Paso had more women using Enovid than any other such facility in Texas—it is unclear how it verified this, although its close relationship with Dr. Calderone could have facilitated such information from the national organization.[70] End-of-the-year numbers disclosed a total of 12,841 clinic visits to PPEP in 1962.[71]

Despite enthusiasm for the Pill, issues with the oral contraceptive began to surface. In June 1961, a small, nondescript blurb appeared in the *El Paso Herald-Post* describing the Food and Drug Administration's (FDA) ambiguity toward Enovid. The FDA was not "worried about undesirable effects; [it] just says it doesn't have sufficient evidence to be sure."[72] Although the FDA made it clear that women were to use Enovid for no more than two consecutive years, PPEP was slow to follow orders. Not until February 1963 did clinics in El Paso begin to comply with FDA guidelines, restricting the use of Enovid.[73] At this point they had a "52% delinquency rate of Enovid patients," or patients who had failed to return to fill their prescriptions, but they had nearly 309 patients "waiting to go on the [new] study."[74] Furthermore, the Searle Corporation, the pharmaceutical company that developed Enovid, offered to help pay for the new study in El Paso.[75] As board members meandered through research guidelines, checked patient files, and considered side effects, nearly half of the recorded Enovid patients had, seemingly of their own accord, stopped taking the Pill.

That over 50 percent of Enovid patients, most of whom were Mexican-origin women, stopped taking the Pill highlights potential moments of *autonomy* as well as *agency-without-choice*. Many of these women made reproductive health decisions regardless of instruction from clinic doctors, nurses, or PPEP staff. There are dozens of reasons why a person might decide to stop using birth control; harsh side effects are certainly one of them, and planning a pregnancy is another.[76] It is also true that they made decisions about their reproductive health without adequate information as to the possible side effects or other long-term effects of certain drugs, suggesting agency without a choice to explore the full spectrum of consequences to their health.

While some historians have remarked on the ethical commitments of the originators of the Pill, namely Dr. John Rock's concerns for side effects, the same cannot be said for other physicians and trials that took place in the 1960s.[77] Planned Parenthood of El Paso's medical committee glossed over Enovid's potential side effects until May 1963. Committee doctors discussed the 1961 deaths from thromboembolisms of two women who had been taking Enovid and explained that "if after a patient uses the drug Enovid for a full two years and reports ill health, she *may* [their emphasis] have a case against the drug. Therefore, the patient has a choice when she *begins* [their emphasis] taking Enovid, as she is aware of the two-year limit."[78] Although patients may have had a choice when to start the medication, little is known about what patients were told concerning complications with the Pill prior to this date and afterward. The drop-off in Enovid use may point to complications that some PPEP patients encountered. As the number of women willing to use Enovid began to wane, board members suggested that "a more intensive program of education for patients regarding the Enovid pills" was needed.[79] Doctors on the committee acknowledged the need for a diversity of pills and introduced Ortho Novum, a new oral contraceptive pill, which became available to the clinic in November 1963.[80]

Not until April 1964 did clinic records describe women complaining of side effects from Enovid. Despite the FDA suggesting time limits for the use of Enovid, doctors on PPEP's medical committee urged a "long term study of enovid [sic]" be completed in late 1963.[81] Clare Nowers, the clinic nurse, reported that the study was well underway in 1964. She noted that there were 137 women on a two-year trial, 30 women on a two-and-a-half-year stretch, and 25 women on a three-year timetable being monitored in the study. Women left the research study, Nowers cited, due to side effects, some of which caused pigmentation on the face. She added that nearly 117 patients were now using Ortho Novum "with a low percentage of side effects."[82] Although clinic records do not specifically discuss the concerns of individual patients, many did suffer side effects, and perhaps clinic staff—doctors and nurses—attempted to minimize their concerns to continue providing clinical studies to pharmaceutical companies. As Nowers acknowledged, "a certain number of case studies were promised this year" to the Searle Company as PPEP continued receiving program funding for its clinical data.[83] It is also possible that the mostly Mexican-origin patients minimized concerns to keep receiving birth control. Perhaps those patients who stopped taking Enovid feared that they too might suffer side effects such as facial hyperpigmentation that could draw undue attention from family and community if discoloration in the face had become a sign of birth control use.

As mentioned previously, many Mexican-origin women sought to keep their contraceptive use private. Despite the proliferation of contraceptives technologies in the 1960s, birth control remained taboo for many people. Not until 1965, when President Lyndon B. Johnson heeded population control advocates cries over the impending population bomb, did birth control become part of public policy and discourse in the mainland United States.[84] This was the same year the US Supreme Court case *Griswold v. Connecticut* annulled the last remaining state law against contraception for married couples.[85]

Although patients raised red flags about side effects and the safety of medication like Enovid, Planned Parenthood of El Paso continued to add new and seemingly untested pharmaceuticals to its swelling inventory. In the spring of 1964, the medical committee suggested that "the center must stock all kinds of pills." Parke-Davis, a pharmaceutical company located in

Detroit, Michigan, was "anxious" to bring a new Pill to the market. The head of the PPEP medical committee, Dr. Avner, arranged for Parke-Davis to deliver 10,000 to 20,000 pills to its El Paso clinics.[86] Women in El Paso experienced an increase in advertising campaigns for clinic services as studies into oral contraceptives intensified. To draw more patients, board members devised different programs using traditional forms of promotion and new outreach projects that would "educate" the community about the importance of birth control. Members from PPEP's public relations committee suggested placing clip-out forms in local papers like the *El Paso Herald-Post* and *El Paso Times* as well as the Spanish language newspapers *El Fronterizo* and *El Continental*.[87] By July 1964, PPEP received a total of 104 replies. The Spanish-language newspapers' advertisements netted thirty-four requests from community members exclusively interested in birth control. The English-language papers promoted more than contraception; they also offered marriage and infertility counseling.[88] One PPEP committee member suggested that perhaps sending letters to "mothers of girls about to be married, the names of the girls to be gotten from the society pages," would translate into more patients for the clinic. Women received coupons for fifty cents off tubes of spermicidal cream and jelly, as well as a reduced price for contraceptive pills. These money-saving strategies resulted in 105 new patients by the end of the year.[89] As clinical studies became increasingly important for the creation and supposed improvement of contraceptives, more bodies were needed to fill clinic space, providing a relatively inexpensive model for producing clinical and reproductive control knowledge in the borderlands.

Many working-class, Mexican-origin women in El Paso were on the receiving end of Planned Parenthood's intensive educational campaign, reaching them through newspapers as well as their places of employment. PPEP's public relations committee conferred with private businesses to distribute information about birth control to women at their place of work. In 1960, it sent birth control literature to the women garment workers at the Farah Manufacturing Company and those laboring at the Golden Motors plant.[90] Several years later, PPEP inaugurated the "Industrial Campaign," sending letters to executives of local industries and factories, "especially those employing large numbers of women." The missive suggested "that a way of reducing employee turn-over is to lower the number of unwanted pregnancies among employees through a program of education."[91] Committee members began working with Safeway grocery management and other supermarkets to place birth control pamphlets in women-employee bathrooms.[92] The same year the United States ended the Bracero Program (1942–64), intended to bring only male contract labor from Mexico to the United States precisely because the government hoped Mexican men would not establish families on US soil. PPEP recommended employers around the city place birth control and clinic information in women's paychecks.[93] The 1960s became a pivotal moment for labor organizing among Mexican-origin people, as they demanded greater rights not only as farmworkers, denied them under the Hartley Labor-Management Relations Act of 1947, but also as factory workers.[94] Mexican workers, including women, had shifted from mostly agricultural work to industry-based labor as early as the 1930s in Texas.[95] Although Mexican-origin women were involved in labor organizing at least since the early twentieth century, the 1960s and 1970s brought the birth control movement, an emerging Chicano/a movement, and labor movement, both in factories and in the fields, together in the borderlands for the first time.[96] Mexican-origin women in cities like El Paso remained deeply imbedded as domestic workers far into the late twentieth century.[97]

Even as PPEP staff worked with farmworkers in El Paso's Lower Valley distributing birth control information and the spermicidal foam Emko, they also sought to market its services to reproductive-age women in the city. Mexican-origin women workers found themselves bombarded by requests to control their reproduction. Women were needed not only to secure further studies on reproductive technologies but, in this case, also to preserve a blue-collar workforce.

The "Knock on Every Door" Campaign's Colonial Roots

Despite its enthusiasm, Planned Parenthood of El Paso did not innovate the door-to-door contraceptive campaigns; it emerged instead in the colonial periphery of Puerto Rico. The border city and the small Caribbean island were part of a much larger conversation on the significance of population control and colonial rule during the 1950s and 1960s. As borderlands historian Pablo Mitchell notes, the "lingering colonial presence in the [borderlands] region in the twentieth century" drives the relationship between Mexican-origin people and Anglos—one that predates the Treaty of Guadalupe Hidalgo and carries on to the present.[98] The "Knock on Every Door" program was a perfect example of how ideas and strategies about overpopulation, population control ideology, and reproduction were transported from one colonial place to another and back again. Recall that Clarence Gamble had asked birth control advocates in El Paso for their Spanish-language pamphlets before his first trip to Puerto Rico in 1938 (chapter 2). By 1964, PPEP board members, as part of their "reports committee," were reading accounts of the "birth control movement in Puerto Rico" into their organization's meeting minutes.[99]

By the summer of 1965, Planned Parenthood of El Paso had contacted the Sunnen Foundation, a nonprofit organization whose founder had connections to Puerto Rico's birth control movement, to secure a large supply of Emko spermicidal foam for its project over the next two years.[100] Only six months into the pilot program, board members had already hoped to secure funding and products to extend "Knock on Every Door" for the next two years. When Joyce Compton, the head of the pilot program in El Paso, contacted the Sunnen Foundation for material support for its contraceptive distribution program, she was tapping into the vestiges of an eight-year project sponsored by Joseph Sunnen and Clarence Gamble.

Sunnen, an industrialist and self-made millionaire from St. Louis, Missouri, after traveling the world and visiting some of the globe's poorest regions, decided to make it his life's work to reduce the planet's population. During a vacation in Puerto Rico, Sunnen encountered like-minded population control promoters, most notably Gamble (see chapter 2 for more on Clarence Gamble in Texas), and in 1956 set forth the "Sunnen Project."[101] Among the project's main objectives were advancing Puerto Rico's welfare by reducing its birth rate and, most importantly for El Paso, "furthering planned parenthood [sic] objectives elsewhere by demonstrating effective action in Puerto Rico."[102] After donating large sums of money to various family planning organizations in Puerto Rico, Sunnen returned home to create the ultimate contraceptive for those "lower-income persons not familiar with the idea of birth control."[103] First labeling it "Sanafoam," Sunnen enlisted the help of the Margaret Sanger Research Bureau for quick clinical tests. By the end of 1958, Sunnen was manufacturing and shipping the newly named "Emko" foam to the Family Planning Association in Puerto Rico.[104]

To fully exploit this new contraceptive technology, the Sunnen team created a special door-to-door program, distributing information and spermicidal foam free of charge to people across the island, the same population control crusade that later found its way to El Paso. Area supervisors were hired to enlist hundreds of volunteers interested in promoting birth control. Well-known and respected neighborhood community leaders, after a brief training session, were entrusted to dispense the product and explain its purpose and use. As historians Annette Ramírez de Arellano and Conrad

Seipp explain, "volunteers were free to choose their own ways of getting people to use Emko; these included making house calls, holding group meetings, showing films, setting up storefront clinics. . . ."[105] Although the Sunnen Foundation began to reduce its efforts in Puerto Rico by 1963, other areas of the continental United States sought out the easily dispensed spermicidal foam for use in areas deemed overpopulated by local residents. Thus, these strategies and new technologies were imported from the US colony of Puerto Rico to a lesser-acknowledged colonial site: the US-Mexico border.

Emko in the Borderlands

In neighborhoods across south El Paso, Mexican-origin women, like their Puerto Rican counterparts, could expect field-workers knocking on their doors offering up pamphlets and other informational literature about PPEP and distributing Emko spermicidal foam. PPEP initially hired Alice Aguilar, a Spanish-surnamed staffer, to spearhead the new program. She was tasked with preparing "leaders in neighborhoods not easily accessible and set up meetings in homes to dispense Emko foam and show our slides." Aguilar was soon unable to perform her duties.[106] According to PPEP staff, this was due to "prejudice of neighbors, husbands, and priests," although PPEP was only temporarily deterred by the community's supposed "prejudice" toward its contraceptive campaign.[107] Records show that a woman as far away as San Elizario, a small town on the outskirts of El Paso composed of Mexican-origin residents, contacted the clinic offering to "distribute samples in the [public health] clinic" and in her home; she already had six people visiting her home for information.[108] Despite the ire of neighbors, spouses, and the Church, some Mexican-origin women sought to participate as PPEP volunteers, informing their communities of clinic services and birth control.

Notwithstanding initial setbacks, the project committee began to outline the purpose of the "Knock on Every Door" campaign by the end of 1964. The program's aim was to:

> Go to women of the lowest income groups and give them our literature and a reply card on the first call; on the second call the reply card will be picked up and free Emko Vaginal Foam will be given to those desiring it. The field worker can also make an appointment at the Center if the client is interested in another method of birth control.

At the end of the month each housewife who accepted the Emko will be contacted again with an offer of additional free supplies. All this will be done by home visiting, block by block, by part-time field workers hired and trained for this project. A large map of the city will be used to chart the field workers' progress.[109]

In the final month of 1964, the "Knock on Every Door" pilot program reached a total of 609 women, 366 women registered interest in birth control, and 25 made the trip to the clinic.[110] Women received over 168 bottles of Emko, and 154 household members came home to find birth control notices on their doors.[111] Given the success of the first month, board members decided to expand and submit the program to the city's local War on Poverty Program, started nationally by Lyndon B. Johnson earlier that year, to access federal funds for their cause.[112]

"Knock on Every Door" became a central campaign for Planned Parenthood and engendered a contraceptive revolution for women in the barrio. With spermicidal foam brought directly to their doorstep, Mexican-origin women found it difficult to escape PPEP's family planning crusade. In March 1965 alone, Planned Parenthood delivered 650 letters to women who consented to a visit, while 457 found the organization's mailing attached to their front door, and over 192 potential patients were given Emko bottles. Five part-time field-workers interviewed 552 women, 19 of whom immediately became patients. However, another 260 decided they were not interested in the services of the clinic. This massive project resulted in a paltry 3 percent of those contacted using the clinic's facilities, while more than 44 percent of women who were visited turned Planned Parenthood field-workers away.[113] Sources say little about why field-workers were turned away—one might imagine that receiving in-person calls from the local birth control clinic may have been jarring to some residents, or perhaps unsuspecting husbands, grandparents, or children opened the door or women simply made the decision to refuse field-workers entry. Perhaps Elizabeth Patterson's 1959 assessment was partially true, that "inducing" persons of the Catholic faith to birth control might be counterproductive to PPEP's mission.

While PPEP grappled with dismal clinic enrollment through its new program, it did accomplish another major goal: educating the public about birth control. In its first major six-month report to the PPEP board of directors, "Knock on Every door" field-workers detailed new changes that would better integrate the program in low-income neighborhoods. Newly hired field-workers would have to be bilingual and between the ages of thirty and forty-five years old, and they would need to "have a suitable personality" enabling "them to go from door to door offering Birth Control information; the services of the Planned Parenthood Clinic; and mainly to offer and demonstrate the use of the contraceptive foam EMKO."[114]

It is unclear what happened to Alice Aguilar, the Spanish-surnamed woman initially hired to direct the "Knock on Every Door" program whom we might assume spoke Spanish. From the report's own conclusions, we might infer that the new director hired mostly English-speaking field-workers not of reproductive age. Field-workers' recommendations that PPEP would need to hire reproductive-age, Spanish-speaking women as field-workers—if the organization were to make any headway with residents in the mostly Mexican-origin neighborhoods of the city—seem absurdly obvious, especially since PPEP had a history with its first Spanish-surnamed field-worker in the months after Elizabeth Patterson retired. Hired in 1958, Cristina Nevarez, the first Spanish-surnamed worker to transition from front desk clerk to PPEP field-worker, began interviewing potential PPEP patients in the summer of 1961 and had gained a substantial rapport with women in Segundo Barrio and Chihuahuita.[115]

Additionally, the report suggested that PPEP recruit community volunteers who would inspire confidence in the message and product.[116] From this first accounting of the program's progress, it is clear that directors took little consideration of Puerto Rico's nearly decade-long experiment. And yet the Sunnen Foundation sent PPEP hundreds of free Emko bottles for continuation of the program. Along with those, it shipped pamphlets (in English) titled *Population Dilemma, Too Many Americans,* and *Planning Your Family,* designed to educate and proliferate the gospel of population control.[117]

By the end of the year, after "trials and errors, consultations, changes almost weekly, financial snags, frustrations trying to hire the right Field Workers, endless hours of work given by the Committee . . . rejection of the Project by some individuals" the "Knock on Every Door" team was happy to announce their program was a huge success.[118] They had interviewed approximately 6,548 "housewives," distributed 3,288 bottles of Emko, and delivered over 16,484 pieces of literature discussing the importance of birth control. Of the total interviewed, 539 women had decided against birth control. The report preparer observed that their lack of interest was "partly due to their age, religious beliefs, or just plain negativism."[119] Rita Taylor, chair of the pilot program committee and report preparer, did not cite tactical strategies on the part of field-workers as a possible reason for women's rejection of birth control.

Field-workers covered a vast terrain as they traveled into areas beyond Segundo Barrio and Chihuahuita in South El Paso. They visited women as far southeast as Ysleta and Socorro—a fifteen-mile drive from the city center—and El Paso's western edge in Smeltertown near the border with New Mexico. Poor women in the areas around Ft. Bliss and Concordia Cemetery along with those living in what was then considered "East El Paso" received Emko foam and information.[120] Field-workers added ten "neighborhood stations" across El Paso and one in Ciudad Juárez where volunteers could distribute Emko to interested women.[121] While field-workers did spend time in Ciudad Juárez, El Paso's sister city in Mexico, little was recorded about their advancements in the city that many PPEP board members perceived to be ground zero for overpopulation.

According to Taylor's final report, field-workers contended with what she considered unexpected and at times harrowing experiences as they walked paved and unpaved streets to encourage the use of birth control in El Paso. One field-worker "had to help a midwife deliver a baby in a home," while another had her path "sprinkled with Holy water" for it was believed that "the devil had been to her home and tried to sell his works." During these visits, "angered husbands" shouted: "None of your business, señorita, I run this household" when their wives were queried about birth control.[122] This smattering of vignettes confirmed for PPEP board members, who, in the 1960s, continued to be overwhelmingly white and upper-middle-class El Pasoans, that they were working to upend great ignorance and "machismo" in communities south of the train tracks.

Field-worker encounters provide insights into the various ways community members opposed the intensity of population control campaigns in their homes, even as their resistance sometimes reinforced heteropatriarchal norms via angry husbands or an omnipresent Church.[123] It might be that women who turned away strange, English-speaking field-workers were protecting themselves and their homes from charlatans peddling unknown pharmaceuticals.[124] These encounters also reveal how, like in the case of the midwife, community members utilized the benevolent spirit of field-workers to their advantage. In her report's final words, Taylor still emphasized that "there is also the grateful volunteer and the patient that assures the Field Worker that this [birth control] is the answer to her prayers."[125] Even as some women in the community may have shunned the door-to-door program, final patient numbers for 1965 were nonetheless impressive as El

Paso clinics registered 24,069 visitors, almost 4,000 more than in the previous year.[126]

The Power of Long-Lasting Contraception

The "Knock on Every Door" program ran concomitantly with PPEP's internationalist efforts promoting intrauterine devices (IUDs) for patients in their clinics. A "cheap, convenient and safe" technology requiring "a minimum of both personal and professional attention," IUDs became part of population control advocates' arsenal to promote contraception on an international scale. Leading organizations like the Population Council, established in 1952 in Williamsburg, Virginia, enthusiastically provided multimillion-dollar grants to support "institutions in twenty-five countries" testing the effectiveness of IUDs.[127] While the Emko spermicidal foams could be delivered to women in their homes with little medical intervention, other more permanent technologies were presented as a better prophylaxis for the poorest members of El Paso's community.

Early in 1965, doctors on PPEP's Medical Advisory Committee discussed the use of intrauterine devices. Dr. S. L. Avner, who eagerly solicited various contraceptive pills for use in the clinic in years prior, suggested that IUDs be used only for the "indigent patient." Many doctors and clinic staff believed that even when contraceptive information was clearly explained to patients, many could still not use materials properly. Furthermore, the insertion of an IUD was touted as needing a medical practitioner for its removal and thus was viewed as a more permanent form of contraception—one step removed from tubal ligation. For these reasons, Avner stipulated that "both husband and wife should sign the papers, and that caution should be exercised." According to the other doctors on the committee, there existed numerous causes for restraint. Some feared the possibility of infection, and others noted the importance that "no device be inserted without the consent of the husband." Dr. Paul Huchton formed the consensus among the all-male medical committee to favor the use of IUDs. Huchton backed this new technology for "the poverty group," which would be "properly controlled" by his medical staff.[128]

Huchton's position was in line with that of Planned Parenthood Federation of America's President Alan Guttmacher—a beloved physician and champion of contraception. Historian Rickie Solinger points to Guttmacher's "unselfconscious" assessment of the ways in which "race and class affected a woman's ability to be a successful chooser and user of the birth control pill." For many population control advocates, including Guttmacher, "Private (white, middle-class) patients were good users," while those patients relegated to clinics, often poor women of color, were not.[129] Like his colleagues in the borderlands, Guttmacher believed in the security of IUDs because "once the damn thing is in, the patient cannot change her mind."[130]

While consent forms were recommended for the procedure, giving women the opportunity to agree to the insertion of a tiny contraceptive device in the uterus, the husband's permission was needed to complete the procedure. Greater attention was placed on obtaining the husband's permission to insert an IUD in his wife rather than attaining her consent or addressing concerns over the risk of infection.[131] In fact, this is one of the few times husbands and consent forms are discussed in the vast PPEP archive. PPEP rarely considered husbands as active agents in their own reproduction even as concern for their consent seemed paramount in this instance. IUD use caught on slowly in the clinic; in September 1965, only about six women had used the new contraceptive as compared to over ninety patients taking the Pill.[132] Physicians from Chihuahua, Chihuahua, on the other hand, grew interested in the technology and visited Planned Parenthood the following month in order to gain greater insight for some of their military hospitals across the line.[133] In this way, El Paso became a literal gateway, a new frontier in transmitting population control strategies and technology to developing nations such as Mexico with little need for incentives.[134]

Elites Remain in Control

Rather than engage with patients' desires or interests in birth control needs, services, and the availability of contraceptives, these assessments were mostly subject to pharmaceutical companies' impulses and demands from PPFA, the PPEP medical committee, and board members. For instance, the PPFA and the Searle Company, Enovid's distributors, decided to drop what they called the "Twenty-Five Month Club Enovid program." Clinic staff was given less than four months to complete the final examinations and reports of patients in the program.[135] It is unclear how women in the program may have interpreted this rushed move. Complications with or worsening side effects of the Pill likely factored into the determination to terminate the Enovid program. Once the clinical trial ended in El Paso, no mention was made regarding patient perceptions of the Pill. That same month, the medical committee advised the clinic to suspend Pap smears for women from Ciudad Juárez because of "financial hardship to the center" since they generally provided this service for free and asserted that "medical treatment for the indigent Cd. Juarez [resident] is very difficult."[136] The doctors elected to serve on the medical committee recommended that Juárez women coming to the clinic for reproductive care be left without recourse. Fortunately, clinic board members felt it was a "moral obligation to inform any patient about a positive Pap Smear" even if the "medical follow-up and treatment was not necessarily our problem."[137] Making their decision in opposition to the medical committee, the board decided that Pap smears would be given to all patients, regardless of their ability to pay. While in the latter case board members sought to protect vital patient services from "money-saving" strategies by the medical committee, the abrupt end to the Searle trial likely left an unknown number of women without their contraceptive of choice.

The best example of the top-down approach PPEP took to provide reproductive health and direct attempts at population control was its "Knock on Every Door" campaign that closed out the technologically turbulent 1960s.[138] The campaign continued well into the next decade and became a huge clinical achievement for the Sunnen Foundation and a landmark program for PPEP. In 1966, almost 1,050 bottles of Emko foam were given to women across El Paso. PPEP conducted a small survey of 100 women. All the women were of Mexican origin from South El Paso, averaging about five or more children and taking part in the "Knock on Every Door" project (see fig. 4.1). Of this small sample, twelve continued to use Emko and twenty-two became clients of the clinic. With nearly a quarter success rate among those becoming new patients, Planned Parenthood of El Paso recommended that "home visiting should continue to be stressed as an effective method, both for education and service to the women in the low income areas."[139]

In 1967, a financially strapped PPEP sought the Sunnen Foundation's help to continue its work.[140] Sunnen funded a special "Emko survey" in order to support the "Knock on Every Door" campaign, paying Planned Parenthood of El Paso $15 for each patient it retained as a user of its product.[141] Committee members announced that by the end of that same year, 1,816 women were registered Emko consumers, meaning nearly $27,240 for the clinic through this project.[142] After a year, the Emko survey raised the amount per patient to $25, as field-workers continued to canvas low-income neighborhoods for women willing to join the study.[143] Hundreds of women were recruited for the special Emko survey, while doctors and the Emko Company set to work learning from this borderland population.

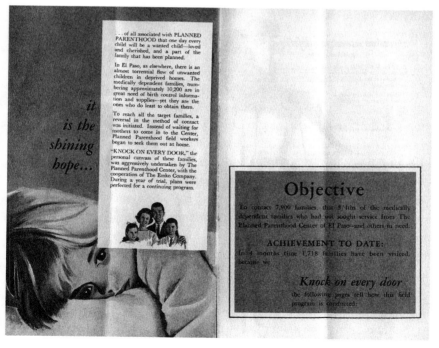

FIGURE 4.1 "Knock on Every Door" pamphlet, cover, middle panel, and back panel. The cover of the pamphlet places El Paso symbolically at the center of the American nation with a disconnected hand gently wrapping on the doors of countless women needing birth control. The first page of the pamphlet shows a sad, listless, blonde-haired child juxtaposed behind a panel describing the "torrential flow of unwanted children in deprived" El Paso and in the world. The perfect nuclear family, two children, one to replace each parent, is pictured over the languid child, reinforcing mid-century overpopulation concerns. The last page of the pamphlet explains that this door-to-door campaign confronts those women who have avoided the clinic because of "plain procrastination, as well as timidity." MS 316, folder 41, box 1, Betty Mary Smith Goetting Papers, C. L. Sonnichsen Special Collections Department, University of Texas at El Paso Library.

Dr. Gray Carpenter, chairman of the Planned Parenthood of El Paso medical committee, and Dr. John Barlow Martin, assistant professor of OB/GYN, Washington University School of Medicine, St. Louis, Missouri, wrote a short but enlightening summary of the El Paso Emko campaign and survey published by the American Association of Planned Parenthood Physicians in April 1969. Carpenter and Martin explained that the "noteworthiness of this program lies in its unique approach in recognizing the characteristics of the population, i.e., an unusually low motivated and disadvantaged group."[144] Mexican-origin women from the poorest areas in El Paso were overwhelmingly represented in the study, as they continued to represent the largest racial demographic at the clinic.

Carpenter and Martin surmised that five major factors—including that the field-worker was of the same ethnic background as those surveyed and that a non-prescription contraceptive [Emko] was left with the patient—"played a vital role in motivating the El Paso subjects to an unusually high degree for such an ethnic population and cannot be overemphasized."[145] By the second year of the program, PPEP had learned a valuable lesson. It needed Mexican-origin field-workers to create the cultural networks of reproductive care necessary for establishing trust among the Mexican-origin community across the city and beyond. Mexican-origin field-workers knew the community they served, and it was through their hard work, pounding the pavement across El Paso's desert streets, that made the greatest impact on the program's success.

The report's data supported PPEP's notion that Mexican-origin women, as an "ethnic group," lacked motivation—reinforcing stereotypes of Mexicans as lazy and passive. Without the driving force of field-workers, who established "personal relationships" with Mexican-origin women, their use of Emko would have been doubtful, the doctors surmised. Carpenter and Martin first compared the "previous pregnancies" of those surveyed to those they identified as a "normal population," using 1960 US Census data. The doctors concluded that "the child bearing incidence of the subject population is greater than that of the general population."[146] Women in the study with over five previous pregnancies represented about 11.2 percent in the study, while among the so-called normal population, women pregnant over five times only represented 4.8 percent.[147] Their data did not account for stillbirths and miscarriages. Nor did they consider the high infant mortality rates that had been a long-standing issue in South El Paso for decades. Carpenter and Martin used their figures to establish the supposed hyperfertility of Mexican-origin women while not accounting for the lack of access to health care of the impoverished study group. The doctors concluded that forty-five out of the 1,778 women in the study discontinued the use of Emko "because of [an] undesired pregnancy." To calculate the effectiveness of a given birth control method, Carpenter and Martin employed the Pearl Formula (Index), used in these kind of clinical trials. They tabulated that roughly 3.14 per 100 women who were part of the study for a year became unintentionally pregnant. This low number showed, at least superficially, that Emko foam performed better than creams and jellies, which had a success rate of 6.33 per 100 births per women versus the least effective rhythm method, which they figured at a rate of undesired pregnancies of 16.13 per 100 women over a year.[148] Contemporary discussions by doctors and scientists, however, have described problems with the use of the Pearl Index, as "contraceptive failure rates decline with duration of use . . . women most prone to fail become pregnant early after starting use, so over time the group of continuing users becomes increasingly composed of those least likely to fail."[149] Over time women became better at using the contraceptive foam, and Martin and Carpenter's study did not account for proper or improper use, merely the supposed effectiveness of the chemical product.

Carpenter and Martin marveled at the success rate of the borderland study. The physicians underscored the importance of PPEP's "Knock on Every Door" program, in particular "its ability to elevate the desire of a poorly motivated group of women to accept a birth control concept." Their study revealed that "there was a significant reduction of approximately 1,000 to 1,600 births among the 1,778 women during the period of time while they were enrolled on the study."[150] The doctors insisted that a better Pearl Formula Index would emerge among a group of women "more highly motivated to use a method."[151] They also suggested that while not "statistically significant," the data showed that among the sixty women with more than twelve years' education, none became pregnant.[152]

Like others in the birth control movement, Martin and Carpenter presumed a "lack of motivation" toward contraception as an inherent characteristic of undereducated, impoverished women in developing nations.[153] Their fixation on Mexican-origin women's supposed apathy toward birth control, something they considered an immutable denominator for this population, colored all aspects of their study. Yet the doctors never defined what they meant by "low motivation" or assessed what they considered to be "low motivation" among the women they studied. Similar to Puerto Rico's brush with Emko, this term often meant the inability of one contraceptive to dramatically affect population growth.[154] Even as women continued requesting Emko, PPEP decided to suspend "seeking new patients" because field-workers did not have the resources to revisit such a tremendously high number of patients in the summer of 1968.[155] While doctors suggested that field-workers' strategies seemed to engender a higher rate of positive outcomes with the use of Emko, they simultaneously denied the eagerness of women in the barrio who sought out reproductive information and technologies.

As 1968 came to a close, board members decided the Emko project would end in January and reinvest all the monies collected in a similar program.[156] Just as Planned Parenthood of El Paso wrapped up the year, the Emko Company came to the border city in order to film and document the progress of its impressive project.[157] After a triumphant study, Emko debuted the documentary film *Knock on Every Door* during the annual Planned Parenthood board meeting in 1970, showcasing the person-to-person program's success. The *El Paso Times* discussed the film and program at length, explaining that the "target of the project were [sic] the 10,200 medically dependent families in El Paso." Indeed, the film would put El Paso on the map for clinical studies in reproductive technologies as the Emko Company sought to show the film around the country.[158] And while Sunnen's invention failed at its intended purpose, to dramatically curb the population of Puerto Rico and El Paso's poor, it did become a financial success. Sunnen established the Emko Company and began turning a profit just a few years later. Historians Ramírez de Arellano and Seipp contend that the company was grossing roughly $4.5 million in sales worldwide by 1968.[159] Historian Laura Briggs suggests that in Puerto Rico, "neither [Clarence] Gamble nor Sunnen was the benefactor of birth control on the island; that role was taken up by the pharmaceutical companies."[160]

Although the door-to-door program was not as successful in Puerto Rico, the film's El Paso focus made clear that PPEP's field-worker campaign promoted "enthusiasm" for contraception, shaping Emko's victory in the borderlands. Local newspapers reinforced Carpenter and Martin's assessment that the program's triumph relied on the "personal canvass [that] was aggressively undertaken, with volunteer workers doing the footwork."[161] The *El Paso Times* maintained that "the film stresses the effectiveness of the program and its ability to motivate a heretofore unmotivated group of women."[162] None of these stakeholders made mention that this supposedly "unmotivated group" of Mexican-origin women had been using birth control through PPEP clinics since 1937. The newspaper's posturing was meant to affirm PPEP's missionary work in El Paso's barrios, drawing on racialist tropes about Mexican-origin people. As Loretta Ross observed within the African American community, "If a decline in African-American birth rates occurs, the population experts usually ascribe it to poverty, coercive family planning, or other external factors, ignoring the possibility that we Black women were in any way responsible for the change."[163] Similarly, PPEP advocates' incredulity at Mexican-origin women's sincere interest in birth control stunted the El Paso movement. Many in the borderlands saw PPEP as a top-down organization, a neocolonial structure that sought to benevolently intervene in Mexican-origin women's reproduction without recognizing their humanity or will.

One aspect of the study that critically contested the perception of Mexican-origin women as apathetic toward birth control were the dozens of Mexican-origin women, who, over the course of six years, helped survey some of the most economically depressed neighborhoods in El Paso. As the El Paso Times underscored "the field workers were highly dedicated and motivated and had the same ethnic background as those they were serving."[164] While doctors and Planned Parenthood board members decried the lack of interest in birth control from the Mexican community they sought to serve, they simultaneously elided the enthusiasm, "dedication and motivation" from the Mexican-origin women directly engaged in the program as volunteers and patients. Because this aspect of the study did not fit PPEP's narrative of the "indifferent Mexican woman patient," it remained unexamined by doctors and clinic staff.

Mexican-origin women in El Paso were caught between the desire to control their own reproduction and the outside forces that sought to stigmatize and dominate the process. Given the numerical data available and the lack of testimonials, it is difficult to ascertain exactly why some women continued to attend PPEP, why others never returned, and why many never stepped inside. Perhaps some women were concerned with their ability to determine the growth of their families and desired greater autonomy over their reproduction. Those who chose not to return were perhaps disenchanted with the level of care at the clinic, while growing concerns over long-lasting side effects of the Pill may have frightened others away.[165] Women who attended the clinics but then failed to continue with the program may have felt caught between wanting to limit their fertility and PPEP's focus on population control. Or perhaps there were simpler reasons, such as moving away or wanting to become pregnant. Although doctors touted the success of the "Knock on Every Door" campaign and hundreds of women joined the project both as clinical subjects and field-workers, it is still unclear to what degree this invasive project was welcomed into the community. Aggressively canvassing poor areas in El Paso likely gave the program a distasteful tinge of coercion that kept some women away, while others may have felt compelled to comply. Lack of personal testimonies in clinic files could indicate a striking disregard on the part of Planned Parenthood staff and board members to archive the desires, cares, and concerns of women receiving birth control in El Paso or an attempt at protecting patients' privacy. However, given PPEP's general indifference toward its patients as active agents of their own reproductive health care, the former in the preceding scenario is probably true.

Furthermore, the dearth of information concerning Mexican-origin women field-workers and other clinic staff and their interest in educating community members about the significance of birth control reveals the prejudice that continued to plague PPEP as it dismissed Mexican-origin women's interest in joining the family-planning movement as advocates. Always battling the curse of what historian Peggy Pascoe and Vicki Ruiz call the "native helper," Mexican-origin women were only ever seen as "subordinates," never as potential leaders or organizers in PPEP's hierarchy.[166]

Women like Irene Robledo, who was hired as a clinic assistant in the 1960s, are a prime example of PPEP's incredulous stance toward Mexican-origin women birth control advocates. Robledo was asked by the then PPEP nurse—Francis Porth—to conduct "re-check examinations" on patients coming in to renew their birth control prescriptions. Board members reported that when the clinic director attempted to discuss this highly unorthodox method with Porth, she had responded "in a flippant and even obstreperous manner."[167] It was clear, however, that Robledo had been trained to do clinical work. Porth clearly had faith in her skills. During that same meeting, board members also noted that Robledo had tendered her resignation because she was offered a $40-a-week job at an insurance company. Board members suggested they raise Robledo's salary to try to keep her since "she gives the lectures in Spanish, does most of the clerical work, helps with the luncheons, maintains the reception desk, assists all the clinicians, and does the domestic work."[168] Despite being a one-woman family-planning machine, Robledo did not receive a second thought from board members. During the meeting, they tabled the matter because they were unsure about giving her a raise. Meanwhile, Cristina Nevarez continued to work as a field-worker for many years until the "Knock on Every Door" program began. Later, Maria Elena Hernandez was hired as a clinic assistant in 1964 and

FIGURE 4.2 Maria Elena Hernandez (Gutierrez), clinic assistant (right), with Bernadine Thomas, executive director of PPEP (left), August 7, 1967. Both women are standing in front of a 1966 Chevrolet Sport Van originally meant as a gift from a Washington, DC, organization to the Mexico City birth control clinic. Unable to clear customs, the automobile was gifted to PPEP to help with its dissemination efforts in the borderlands. "Meeting Minutes April 1967," PPEP records, box 2. Photograph, MS 348, Folder 3, Box 150, El Paso Herald Post Collection, C. L. Sonnichsen Special Collections Department, University of Texas at El Paso Library.

worked well into the late 1960s, often supporting the clinic when it had no registered nurse on duty (see fig. 4.2).[169] It is unclear to what degree women like Robledo, Nevarez, or Hernandez internalized the population control rhetoric of the organization, but perhaps the board's lack of enthusiasm for their work tells us that these women likely sought to join the clinic to help women in their communities on their own terms.

Although Mexican-origin women's reproductive autonomy is addressed through the filter of PPEP's institutional documents, this chapter provides an initial baseline for rethinking how Mexican-origin women engaged with reproductive health services and contraception during a moment of intensifying population control hysteria. By the early 1970s, as Elena Gutiérrez points out, private citizen groups and organizations were working alongside national governments to bring greater financial and political security to the population control movement. As the William Vogts of the world died, the Paul Ehrlich's arrived. Ehrlich's 1968 best-selling *The Population Bomb* introduced a new generation to the "perils of overpopulation."[170] At the same time, Mexican-origin women in El Paso had been maneuvering through white people's overpopulation anxieties and population control ideologies since the 1930s.

Clinic data tells part of their story. In 1970, PPEP admitted approximately 1,308 new patients, clinic doctors performed nearly 3,936 medical exams (including 3,312 Pap smears), and over 696 vials of various forms of the Pill were apportioned. Almost 300 women received IUDs, and roughly 300 other forms of birth control (like Emko, the diaphragm, and other creams and jellies) were dispensed to the hundreds of new and returning patients.[171] These astounding figures reveal that in the face of population control hostilities, Mexican-origin women still managed to carve out small spaces for autonomy in their reproductive health care.[172]

Although PPEP formulated innovative ways to bring women to the clinic to address concerns about overpopulation, Mexican-origin women used PPEP clinics for their own reproductive health needs, regardless of the broader socioeconomic implications associated with reproductive services. Despite social pressures, changes in contraceptive technologies and health concerns, and international movements focusing on overpopulation, statistical analysis shows that thousands of Mexican-origin women from some of the most marginalized barrios in El Paso and Mexico made decisions about birth control, were active clinic participants as patients and advocates, and sought to attain self-determination through reproductive care. From this vantage point, Vogt's fictional Maria spoke of "*se aguanta*" not as bearing the suffering of a precarious life but as enduring, surviving, and (possibly) thriving under the weight of racist international population control campaigns.

5 Chicanas' Holistic Vision for Reproductive Care

· ·

Wherefore the health needs of the Chicano community have been grossly ignored in the past.

Wherefore the health services available to la raza [sic] are shockingly inadequate.

Wherefore La mujer Chicana has carried the greatest burden of deprivation in the area of mental and physical health within the community.

Therefore, be it resolved that the IWY [International Women's Year] conference endorse more quality health, ambulatory, and comprehensive health care programs for the Chicano community which emphasize the total needs of la Raza, not emphasize only family planning but allow Chicanas the right to choose in all areas of health services.

—Luz Gutierrez, 1977

While the 1960s had introduced new contraceptive technologies to millions of women across the country and the population control movement gained momentum at home and abroad, the civil rights movements of the 1950s and early 1960s had transformed the legal and social landscape, opening new pathways for the generation that followed. Radical young people—mostly women and people of color—impatient with what they viewed as slow, incremental change demanded nothing short of revolution in the face of increasing racist, sexist, and economic tensions. Hastened by the previous generation's focus on challenging the legal strictures that controlled access to the ballot box, segregated education, and denied equal job opportunities, so-called militant Brown and Black youths rose up to "fight the power!"[1]

Health care became a critical site for demanding revolutionary change. Along with organized groups such as the Black Panthers and the Young Lords, Chicana/o activists also demanded equity and equality in their ability to access good-quality health care. For the International Women's Year Conference of 1977, Chicanas across the state of Texas were asked to write resolutions to present to a broad international audience about the plight of the Chicana in the United States. Chicana activist Luz Gutierrez from Crystal City, Texas, succinctly captured her frustrations in a handwritten resolution transcribed in the epigraph. [2] As a Chicana, a woman of Mexican descent, Gutierrez believed the Chicano community received "shockingly inadequate" health care. Chicanas carried the heaviest burden of "deprivation" of mental and physical health. Further still, Gutierrez emphasized that health care should include more than just family planning and that it was critical that Chicanas have a choice in what health care they received. Gutierrez outlined a holistic vision for health care, one concerned with what she called the "total needs" of the community. For Gutierrez, family planning was not enough. Given the political context of the time, her statement was a nod in recognition of the rise of coercive sterilization campaigns in Los Angeles, California, as well as the nearly fifty-year history of organizations like Planned Parenthood Federation of America that continued to shore up harmful overpopulation discourse.[3] By the time Gutierrez wrote her resolution, however, there were already several Chicana/o community clinics attempting to make her demands a reality.

The history of one such clinic established by Chicana activists in South El Paso embraced Gutierrez's holistic vision of health as early as 1968.[4] The clinic focused on expanding health care through reproductive care in the barrio. The women and men who founded the first Chicana/o-run health clinic, initially named the Father Rahm Clinic, in South El Paso were part of a larger *movimiento* of Chicana and Chicano activists fighting for self-determination and a radical upending of the status quo in the late 1960s and early 1970s.

Chapter 5 tells their story, alongside PPEP's continued push for population control measures in the borderlands. Instead of supporting Chicana/o activists fighting for self-determination and greater access to health care, PPEP worried that it was not rightfully benefiting from federal dollars apportioned for family planning during the same years Chicano movement organizations received funds from the state. While El Paso is not normally discussed as the epicenter of Chicano movement mobilizations, the city nonetheless played an important role in linking organizers and leaders from across the Southwest—including from California, Colorado, Arizona, New Mexico, and greater Texas—to address a host of injustices in their respective communities. An important aspect of collaboration between organizations and leaders across the different states was their attention to health and quality of life for Mexican-origin people. El Paso was also not known for women's liberation organizing that described much of the women's movement in this period. However, the work of Chicana activists as they sought to provide health care to their community brought together the aims of these distinctive movements for social justice in the borderlands. This chapter puts Chicana/o activism in conversation with organizations such as Planned Parenthood and the Catholic Church and shows how these groups shaped the politics of health care and reproductive care along the US-Mexico border.

Health Care and Chicana's Visions for Self-Determination

By the 1970s, the Mexican-origin community in the borderlands had been the central locus of public health campaigns that sought to surveil and control the transmission of diseases, such as tuberculosis and typhus, across and along the US-Mexico border for nearly a century. Historians have paid close attention to how disease and its containment became a specific project, a product of settler colonial and imperial systems, for the racialization of Mexican-origin people. Over time, "diseased Mexicans" became one avenue from which doctors, public health officials, and the state gained knowledge about and power over a racialized community susceptible to ill health because of lack of resources and extreme poverty.[5] Rather than act as a medium for actual health care for impoverished communities in the Southwest, public health departments were weaponized as an extension of state surveillance against these communities. Thus, in the late 1960s and early 1970s, Chicanas and Chicanos, as an organized contingent, fought back. They clamored for greater access to health care, including physical and mental health services. As Gutierrez mentioned previously, Chicanos and Chicanas wanted to choose for themselves the kind of health care they needed and deserved.

In El Paso, various Chicano- and Chicana-run organizations, supported by the US Office of Economic Opportunity (OEO), dotted the landscape of South El Paso and helped bring the plight of Mexican-origin people into the light. Project Bravo, Volunteers in Service to America (VISTA), Project MACHO (Mexican Americans for Culture, Honor and Organization), and the Juvenile Delinquency project (charged with addressing issues of increased gang activity in the area) organized residents of Segundo Barrio. Pete Duarte, who was a founding member of the Father Rahm Clinic and later became the executive director of Thomason General Hospital, explained: "The concerns articulated by the people of the Southside were similar to those voiced by the poor throughout the country: the unavailability of services, the insensitivity of providers, the high cost of services, transportation problems, the long waiting periods at public health facilities, language barriers, and the institutionalized racism inherent in the delivery of health services to this segment of society."[6]

As Duarte tells it, several Chicana mothers came together in *Los Seis Infiernos* (Six Hells) tenement buildings, known as some of the worst and most neglected housing in El Paso's south side, to discuss the dearth of health care services. The buildings were owned by the director of the city-county health department, Dr. M. D. Hornedo, and another slumlord named Esteban Alba. According to Duarte, the women chose this location in part to embarrass Hornedo and the city writ large for allowing such neglect and poverty to persist in the Mexican-origin community. Fighting for "greater self-determination in all aspects of life," Chicana/o activists and residents of El Paso's south side came together to set the foundations for a community-focused clinic.[7]

The call for self-determination among Chicanos and Chicanas in the movement was one premised on a host of cultural, social, intellectual, political, and spiritual ideas that sought to exalt the needs of the community and instill ethnic pride. As activists were quick to remind people, however, the Chicana/o *movement* was not a homogenous one. Chicanas had specific notions of what self-determination meant to them, based on the intersections of race, class, sexuality, and political affiliations. What can be gleaned from movement literature of the time is clear: Chicanas rallied to support greater access to education, employment opportunities, labor protections, political representation, and health, including unfettered access to abortion and birth control on their terms.[8] At the Mexican American National Issues Conference of 1970, Chicanas advocated for what activists today call "reproductive justice" issues. As historian Marisela Chávez explains, the women articulated a slew of demands, but their specific concerns for abortion rights and access to childcare were "referred to as women's issues by Chicano advocates and society at large." Chávez observes that "the women at the workshop couched their demands for choice and childcare in rhetoric familiar to the Chicano movement, equating the right to abortion with 'self-determination' and demanding childcare centers that would instill ethnic pride."[9] In 1971, during the first national Chicana conference held in Houston, over 600 Chicana activists from all over the country came to engage in workshops, panels, and conversations about "Sex and the Chicana" and "Marriage—Chicana Style." Socialist Latina activist for Chicana liberation Mirta Vidal wrote that "Raza women" were calling for "free, legal abortions and birth control for the Chicano community, controlled by Chicanas," as well as demanding equal pay for equal work.[10] Chicanas were not alone in articulating a reproductive justice vision in their calls for self-determination that went beyond racist population control campaigns. Women of color activists in diverse movements pushed for more dynamic reproductive health care visions that decentered racialist family planning projects. For instance, historian Brianna Theobald observes that Native women activist gathered to discuss the meaning of sovereignty in the late 1970s. Katsi Cook, a Mohawk activist and mother, helped establish the Women of All Red Nations (WARN) in 1978 and called on Native women to "expand[ed] conceptions of sovereignty" to include land and "'sovereignty over our own bodies.'"[11]

Despite Chicanas' unabashed defense of reproductive liberation, Chicanas' articulation of self-determination was often cited in relation to a holistic vision of community care, one that sought to provide justice and equality for all members of their community, including children and elders. Tejana Chicana activist Martha Cotera explained self-determination this way: "We have lent our professional skills, and ourselves to the arduous task of making local institutions responsive to the majority population's needs, in this case, Chicano."[12] The "arduous" labor of making and remaking local institutions and systems responsive to the Chicana and Chicano community was reproductive care in action. Cotera continued, "We have assisted in a very dynamic effort for self-determination of a total Chicano community."[13] In places like South El Paso, Chicana and Chicano leaders—many of whom were professionals working in the fields of social work, medicine, and education—came together with Mexican-origin members of the community to insist on greater accountability and justice from city leaders; local, state, and national institutions; and the federal government. A major aspect of the self-determination ethos sought to build solidarity through Chicana/o-run institutions and organizations accountable to the community. Chicana activism in this regard becomes a central pillar of reproductive care, premised on a transformative vision for human dignity, mutual responsibility, and strengthening community networks of justice and care.

Mexican-origin women had worked to support and used the services of organizations, such as Planned Parenthood of El Paso, and other clinics offering birth control information including Newark Maternity Hospital and El Paso General Hospital, as acts of self-determination and reproductive care in the years before the Chicana/o movement. As the Chicano/a movement grew in strength and fervor, Mexican-origin people sought a kind of health care that centered their lives and was attentive to their experiences. Even as activists like Gutierrez were critical of family planning campaigns and demanded comprehensive community-centered health care, calls for self-determination by Chicanas necessarily included access to reproductive health care and childcare—issues fundamental for advancing reproductive justice. Incorporating these community visions for care became paramount as Chicana and Chicano organizers gathered to establish a clinic in El Paso's Segundo Barrio.

"The Mexican American: Quest for Equality"

Nearly a decade before Gutierrez's remarks to the IWY, a report by the National Advisory Committee on Mexican American Education titled "The Mexican American: Quest for Equality" asked the question "The Mexican American: How Have We Failed Him?"[14] Chicanas and Chicanos replied: let us count the ways. Dozens of US government reports confirmed frustrations among Mexican-origin people. The governments had done little to mitigate political marginalization, as well as ease social and economic neglect in their communities. The American G.I. forum and Viva Kennedy generation, those who had rallied for greater access to opportunities in education and labor and in the late 1950s energized their community to elect the first Roman Catholic president, felt betrayed; they continued to be part of a forgotten constituency in the Southwest.[15] After John F. Kennedy's assassination, the new Texan president, Lyndon Baines Johnson, promised to transform America into a "great society" by waging war against poverty and inequality to produce better living conditions for the most marginal in the country.

Mexican American activists in Texas and across the Southwest pressed Johnson and his administration for support, especially as they sought funding for local efforts to combat poverty and the violence it wrought in their communities. One journalist admonished Johnson for not having done enough for the "Mexican-Americans in the President's own backyard of South Texas."[16] El Paso's Chicana/o movement made this clear when Johnson arrived in the borderland city to sign the Chamizal Treaty with Mexican President Gustavo Díaz Ordaz, formally ending the dispute over territory between the United States and Mexico in October 1967. Simultaneously, as part of his War on Poverty program, Johnson's administration scheduled meetings in El Paso with Mexican American leaders from across the country.[17] It named the compilation of testimonies delivered during the event "Mexican American: A New Focus on Opportunity." Johnson administration officials gathered for two days of hearings of the Inter-Agency Committee on Mexican American Affairs.[18] This was an important opportunity for leaders of Johnson's administration, including the secretaries of Agriculture, Labor, Health, Education, and Welfare (HEW), and Housing and Urban Development, to hear about the barriers Mexican-origin people faced in the United States.[19] As one El Paso newspaper put it, the idea of a conference on Mexican affairs was "a sound one" because Mexican Americans represented the "second largest minority group in our country. Those people have problems and those problems should be aired."[20] Prominent Mexican American leaders and scholars, such as Ernesto Galarza, Gilberto Esquivel, and Patricia Jaquez, presented extensive studies detailing the state of the Mexican American community in the United States as it related to education, labor, and housing, among other critical issues.[21] Even with so much attention on these issues, Chicano activists threatened to boycott and protest the talks, creating a schism within the national Mexican American leadership and more radical activists in the Southwest.[22]

When Johnson declared that the second day of hearings would be canceled so that participants could be shuttled to the Chamizal ceremony, those disenchanted with the sessions "spilled out of the hotel and joined José Angel Gutiérrez, Corky Gonzales, and Reies López Tijerina, who were picketing in front."[23] Giving rise to what would later become "La Raza Unida," local and state organizations, including Mexican American Youth Association (MAYA) of South El Paso and Mexican-American Political Association (MAPA) of California, demanded less talk and more action toward justice in housing, education, political representation, and greater access to employment.[24] Attendees of the conference also joined the protest, and an alternate conference was held at the Sacred Heart Catholic School gymnasium. Dr. Ernesto Galarza, who was named chairman of the new La Raza Unida "solidarity movement," emphasized that this adjacent conference was in no way a repudiation of the Johnson administration's attempts to bring Mexican American concerns to light.[25] Rather, it was a chance for the community to speak. In the spirit of calls for self-determination, activists declared that "the time of subjugation, exploitation, and abuse of human rights of La Raza in the United States is hereby ended forever."[26] In addition, they offered an eight-point declaration of rights that included "the right to organize community and labor groups in our own style."[27] As one activist, Frank Moreno Martínez, later wrote, "It was in El Paso where La Raza Nueva was given form."[28] Although Los Angeles emerged as a hub of the Chicano movement, this event left a lasting impression on young Chicanas and Chicanos, particularly those living in South El Paso, as well as city leaders and Anglo residents.

La Raza Nueva's vision came on the heels of Mexican-origin youth-led protests months before Johnson's visit to the borderlands. Young Chicana and Chicano activists had taken to the streets demanding action from the city about the conditions of their barrio. In the shadow of the 1965 Watts Rebellion in Los Angeles, which came to symbolize the anger of African Americans pushed to the edge by state-sponsored neglect and violence, one El Paso journalist surmised that "the idea of a Watts-like outbreak [in El Paso] suddenly did not seem at all far-fetched."[29] South El Paso residents protested squalid living conditions, economic exploitation, lack of access to education, police brutality, and the denial of health care. As Chicano scholar Benjamin Marquez argues in his landmark study of Chicanos in South El Paso, the sustained obstinance of Anglo leadership to avoid complying with federal housing regulations produced catastrophic consequences.[30] On January 4, 1967, Ismael Rosales, eight, his brother Orlando, seven, and their little sister, Leticia, four, were pronounced dead after their tenement building caught fire due to an unventilated gas heater. The *El Paso Times* captured images of the gruesome scene as firefighters worked to revive the three children while their parents and two older siblings were taken to Thomason General Hospital to receive treatment—all four survived.[31] Chicana/o activists took their deaths as a call to arms and hundreds took to the streets in protest.[32]

City officials could not deny the squalor Mexican-origin people were subjected to in South El Paso. As early as 1960, Federal Judge R. E. Thomason and then Mayor Raymond Telles (the first Chicano-elected to a leadership position in El Paso's history) remarked that "living conditions [in South El Paso] are a disgrace to civilized society."[33] The City of El Paso's Department of Planning conceded in July 1967 that "the story of South El Paso has been the same since the beginning." Quoting the *Herald-Post* newspaper in 1922, the report cited that "there is no toilets [sic], there is garbage on the vacant lots . . . The City should solve the problems of Chihuahuita [neighborhood in South El Paso], it's a shame." Over forty years later, the Planning Department concluded that "today, the same problems exist."[34]

In the 1960s, South El Paso neighborhoods, including Chihuahuita and Segundo Barrio, like other disenfranchised communities across the country, were the subject of numerous academic studies.[35] As one journalist noted, "Anthropologists, sociologists, youth and social workers have long studied the Second Ward [Segundo Barrio]." However, "if someone wanted to make a study of the nearly total impotence of this approach, South El Paso would be a good place to go."[36] Although the Johnson administration had declared a war on poverty in 1964 and some cash had started reaching borderlands communities, poverty and appalling conditions still characterized El Paso's south side by the end of the decade. The 1967 city planning analysis summarized its findings of buildings like Los Seis Infiernos this way:

> [They] are in fact the worse housing condition that exists in the City today. The typical tenement is deplorable for the simple fact that individual units are denied the basic needs of a family shelter. Housing amenities such as water, open space, pride of ownership, area for child play, toilets, and bathing facilities are for common use. These facilities in the common use area (courtyard), so typical of tenement housing in South El Paso are the true root of the slum condition. Accepted conditions of South El Paso such as high density and aging structures are diseased by the total failure of common use space. Almost all tenements in South El Paso deprive thousands of El Paso citizens from the basic needs of our society.[37]

El Paso city planners unequivocally stated that these living conditions robbed thousands of Mexican-origin people in South El Paso from the "basic needs of our society." What they did not acknowledge, however, was this level of poverty was created by design. Wealthy Anglo residents and Anglo politicians had consistently disinvested in South El Paso for decades, opting instead to champion the discourse of organizations such as Planned Parenthood of El Paso, which insisted that Mexican-origin people were poor because there were too many of them. PPEP's nearly thirty-five-year refrain exalted high, uncontrolled fertility, not intentional social neglect and exploitative labor conditions, as the culprit for producing poverty in the Mexican-origin communities of El Paso. Even as Mexican American advocates and Chicana and Chicano activists tried to pull back what one Texas government worker called the "cactus curtain" to reveal the squalor and deprivation their communities were subjected to, organizations such as PPEP refused to accept their complicity in enabling a narrative that blamed Mexican-origin people for these injustices.[38]

Reproductive Care and Justice versus Population Control

As the Johnson administration sought to address social unrest and poverty nationally, borderland organizations, like Planned Parenthood of El Paso and the Father Rahm Clinic, attempted to confront these issues from different cultural and community vantage points due, in large part, to those seeding these diverse movements. The Anglo women of PPEP stayed the course. Since establishing the clinic in 1937, PPEP maintained that disciplining the uncontrolled fertility of women in South El Paso and other poverty-stricken areas of the city would, over time, reduce poverty and crime and help quell social unrest. PPEP's prescription was wholesale use of contraceptives by all women in the barrio. In contrast, Chicana and Chicano activists in South El Paso believed a more holistic approach was needed to tackle poverty in their community. This schism, especially among Chicana and white women activists, was indicative of larger quarrels within the women's movement at the time.[39]

The women's liberation movement helped shine a light anew on issues related to contraception and abortion just as major legal cases such as *Griswold v. Connecticut* (1965), allowing married couples to use contraception without state criminalization, produced massive shifts in accessibility to birth control. The PPEP board of directors, however, was not of this generation. Throughout the late 1960s and early 1970s, in meeting minutes and other communication, PPEP leaders said little about the growing visibility and agitation of now-famous "women's libbers" such as Betty Friedan, Gloria Steinem, and Shirley Chisholm. Logics of population control overshadowed other political struggles that might have made PPEP a more feminist organization.

Chicanas working for the Father Rahm Clinic were likewise not inspired by women's liberation movements per se despite overlap with goals for women's reproductive freedom and power to care for their families. For Chicana activists establishing the foundations of the clinic, reproductive freedom was part of larger concerns for liberation and community transformation that were deeply tied to fighting structural and historical racism in El Paso. Amelia Castillo, the first executive director of the Father Rahm Clinic, explained her desires through the language of self-determination for Chicanas and Chicanos. She emphasized that a major emphasis of the Father Rahm Clinic was to "increase Chicano awareness and expertise in as many fields as possible for the purposes of furthering our ability to bring to our respective communities more than mere bandaide [sic] assistance in the face of severely limited irrelevant and inadequate service delivery."[40] Therefore, the Father Rahm Clinic was meant to provide not only community health care, a transformational act given the lack of health care access in South El Paso, but also a space for new epistemologies of care, one premised on the production of knowledge by, for, and about the community.

Chicana and Chicano activists made real part of their eight-point declaration of rights when they began to organize institutions in their communities "in our own style." Part of what they termed self-determination was the ability to pursue new models of community care that situated Chicanas and Chicanos as both mediators and recipients of care. They brought reproductive justice to life, paying special attention to the third prong of this framework, to make and sustain suitable environments to raise and nurture the next generation of children. From that angle, Chicanas and Chicanos contested the top-down, population control rhetoric of white, upper-middle-class organizations, such as Planned Parenthood of El Paso, as they established a holistic mode of community health care.

Very little has been written about the history of Chicanas and Chicanos and health during the Chicano movement, in particular the creation of community clinics in the late 1960s and 1970s.[41] While the abortion rights movement came about because of the second-wave women movement's call for greater "reproductive rights," as articulated by mostly white feminists, Chicanas engaged in legal battles against forced sterilizations in Los Angeles and elsewhere. The Mexican American Legal Defense and Educational Fund (MALDEF) created a small organization called the Chicana Rights Project in the early 1970s to document cases of forced sterilizations of Chicanas in California and Texas. Although the Chicana Rights Project focused on reproductive rights, it was most concerned with sterilization abuse and was not necessarily interested in aggressively advocating for legal access to abortion.[42]

In other words, Chicanas' concerns about reproductive health and rights manifested themselves differently than those of their white counterparts. As white women sought sterilization on demand as a voluntary decision, Chicanas insisted on a waiting period for fear of sterilizations performed under duress and without their consent.[43] The differences in each group's concerns stem from the birth control movement's early days when eugenic reasoning was used to problematize the fertility of poor women of color on the one hand while exalting the fecundity of white, mainly upper-middle-class women on the other. By the 1970s, the question of reproductive "rights" did not materialize evenly across different racial groups of women because not all women experienced access to reproductive health care equally or equitably. Therefore, when Chicanas in El Paso's Segundo Barrio established a clinic in 1968, which sought to provide comprehensive health care, including reproductive health services, in their community, they fought against a population control ideology that for decades had stigmatized their reproduction as excessive and their leadership as ineffectual or nonexistent.

Chicanas were not necessarily fighting for reproductive rights explicitly, but they were, as reproductive justice activist Loretta Ross contends, "fight[ing] for the necessary enabling conditions to realize these rights."[44] This is not to say that Chicanas in El Paso were disinterested in the legal strictures that denied them access to reproductive freedom—their demands for proper access to health care were not directed exclusively at the state. Rather, they oriented their reproductive care labor toward collecting resources and shoring up community-based institutions. For instance, Kathy Flores's often cited article "Chicano Attitudes toward Birth Control" recommended that Chicanas should oversee their own sexual health education as counselors and instructors. To combat "machismo" and dispel myths about birth control among community members, Flores suggested that a "sex education course could be taught with Raza doing the teaching."[45] Flores, like other Chicanas, believed in addressing both the material and epistemological deficits caused by decades of segregation, exploitation, and exclusion. Chicanas could and should provide each other with the knowledge to care for their own bodies on their own terms.

Chicana and Chicano efforts to expand access to health care can be understood as a critical example of reproductive justice through reproductive care. Chicana and Chicano activists understood too well that poor living conditions, the spread of treatable diseases, the lack of education, police brutality, and exploitative work impinged on women's abilities to experience good reproductive health outcomes for themselves and their families. Furthermore, South El Paso activists were not alone in reasoning that good health care was critical to community flourishing. As historian Johanna Fernández maintains, many young revolutionaries were "following the example of the Cuban experiment, which made dignified healthcare for all a signature of revolutionaries around the world."[46] The Cuban health care experiment could connect its lineage to the Mexican Revolution, which pushed Mexico to enshrine the right to health care for all its citizens in its 1917 Constitution. Even though health care provision itself remained precarious and mired in eugenic ideologies in Mexico, the ideal that it should be a civil right traveled across the US-Mexico border and likely influenced Chicana and Chicano activists in the borderlands. While the founders of the Father Rahm Clinic were in line with other politically situated groups at the time, such as the Black Panthers, the Young Lords, and the Brown Berets, who also created neighborhood health care clinics in their communities, they also made health care as a basic right a transnational vision for liberation.[47]

The significance of Chicanas' reproductive health activism is made more striking as it crossed paths with population control advocates, such as Planned Parenthood Federation of America, the most well-known and respected reproductive health organization in the world at the time. The movement for access to birth control in the United States began in the early twentieth century, and as leaders of the movement, particularly Margaret Sanger, sought to broaden its aim, connections between population control, eugenics, and contraception began to form. As we saw in the preceding chapters, Sanger, Goetting, and their ilk sought "the incorporation of reproduction control into state programs as a form of social planning."[48] Planning and control were different sides of the same coin. Historian Linda Gordon suggests that for many in Sanger's organization, birth control was first and foremost a tool to "achieve a goal greater than individual freedom."[49] After World War II, scholars argued that the extreme tactics implemented by the Nazi regime left the eugenics movement—including many who advocated for birth control—scrambling to rebrand itself. Some began to focus on the issue of overpopulation.

By the 1960s Planned Parenthood Federation of America was fully ensconced in the global battle to stem overpopulation, and in 1961 it joined forces with the World Population Emergency Campaign (WPEC) to become Planned Parenthood Federation of America-World Population Campaign.[50] Planned Parenthood of El Paso's "Knock on Every Door" project was the local example of global attempts to curtail populations in the "poorer regions" of the world. Coupled with population increases in places like India, China, and Mexico, population control activists found new resolve in their convictions about birth control. By the 1970s Planned Parenthood was the vanguard of the overpopulation crusade.[51]

As the focus on overpopulation became part of public discourse, civil rights movements became more militant. Considering Vietnam War activism and earlier civil rights struggles, Chicana and Chicano, Black, and Puerto Rican youths organized to bring greater access to food, housing, and health care to their neighborhoods. Thus, concerns about population were complicated by demands for economic equity and racial justice. In El Paso, the proximity to the border, a seemingly expanding Mexican-origin community, and the growing social unrest of Chicana/os served to foreground local anxieties over and mirrored national preoccupation with overpopulation and quality of population—not necessarily quality of life—in the region.

Amelia "Amy" Castillo and Social Work as Reproductive Care

Rather than focus on racialized ideas of hyper-fertility and its dubious connections to poverty, Chicana and Chicano activists viewed their economic marginalization as part of a larger struggle for social justice. The Father Rahm Clinic became one of the most important examples of the Chicano community organizing around issues of health and family planning. Founded by Chicana activists on the south side, "The Father Rahm Clinic was conceived by the dreams of the people in the Mexican American barrio called Second Ward in El Paso, Texas."[52] The first paid members of the staff were all Chicanas: Amelia Castillo, a social worker; Mary Márquez, a registered nurse; Lupe T. De Anda, community aide; Gloria Amador, as secretary; and Maria-Elena Martínez, as a part-time clinic coordinator.[53] Although formally established in 1968, the Father Rahm Clinic did not receive US Public Health Service federal funding for its work until June 1970; in the early days small grants and community support kept it going. The founders and initial members of the clinic staff were community organizers, professionals, and residents; many had long ties to activism and social reform efforts in El Paso. Amelia "Amy" Castillo, as she was known to friends and colleagues, the first executive director of the Father Rahm Clinic, was an outspoken social worker who had cut her teeth in the early 1960s working with Family Services of America—a program funded by the United Way—in Segundo Barrio.

Castillo was born on a peninsula along the Rio Grande just a few miles from Fabens, Texas, in a covered wagon on October 6, 1934—the same year Margaret Sanger first visited El Paso.[54] She was the youngest of six children, two died before she was born, and her mother was the lone breadwinner in the family. Although Castillo never knew her father, her devoted *abuelita* supported Castillo throughout her childhood in Carlsbad, New Mexico, while Castillo's mother worked as an "indentured servant" for a chicken farmer in West Texas. During her oral history interviews with me, Castillo recalled that her mother never went to school but taught herself how to read and write. Bearing witness to her mother's determination, Castillo knew she wanted to go to college and return to serve her community. In 1954 she registered at El Paso's Texas Western College and majored in business administration. Unable to find work after graduation in 1958, she decided to heed the advice of a friend and take the Texas social welfare worker exam. After a year of working for the state, Castillo enrolled at Our Lady of the Lake University Worden College in San Antonio to complete a master's degree in social work. She received a full scholarship and interned as a medical social worker at M.D. Anderson Cancer Center in Houston during her time in school. "I was able to help individuals facing cancer and they were Hispanic, and I was able to use my *español mocho, de manita, de Nuevo Mexico* to assist in reducing their stress, their fear, their loss of hope," Castillo remembered during our 2016 interview.[55] With a master's degree in social work, Castillo returned to El Paso to marry her sweetheart, Fernando Castillo, and begin a career as a social worker in South El Paso in 1962. Later she would become an expert in grant writing, assisting many in the community, including Project Bravo, in accessing funds from the Johnson administration's War on Poverty programs.[56]

After her Family Health Services of America supervisor changed jobs and was replaced with a "racist skinhead, named Waggoner," who only wanted therapy and marriage counseling for the wealthy, white residents of El Paso, Castillo decided it was time for a change.[57] She became the first Chicana social worker at William Beaumont Army Medical Center at Fort Bliss in El Paso and gave consultation to command regarding what she called "mental hygiene" and "mental health" for soldiers on and off the field. Even as she broke barriers at the military hospital, Castillo said she longed to return to her work in Segundo Barrio.[58]

During these same years, the State of Texas, via the National Institute of Mental Health (NIHM) and the Social and Rehabilitation Services (SRS), began offering grants to further train social workers. In 1966, the Department of Social Work at her alma mater, Texas Western College, known later as the University of Texas at El Paso (UTEP), recruited Castillo to help rewrite a grant application to receive monies from those funds. It was missing what she called the "cultural component," a viewpoint and understanding of the Mexican-origin community in El Paso. Colleagues in the department concluded that Castillo could write a firsthand account of what was needed in South El Paso and help them win the grant. With Castillo's help they did, and they received economic support, including a grant from HEW for $26,060. This HEW grant would finance "U.T. El Paso Undergraduate Social Work Faculty and Curriculum Development Project," meant to place "emphasis on the recruitment and education of bilingual Mexican-American students, particularly those who are economically and educationally disadvantaged."[59] Castillo was named "Field Experience Instructor" for the grant. Once her colleagues saw that Castillo could win important grants, some in the department began to feel threatened, she recalled. After establishing curriculum and securing grants to produce more social workers from the Mexican-origin community, the mainly white, all-male faculty in the department began to push Castillo out. After two difficult years at UTEP, Castillo was recruited by Chicana activists to help establish the Father Rahm Clinic in South El Paso, and she left to support her community.

A Clinic at the Intersections of Reproductive Justice and Care

At this point, Castillo had been a social worker for nearly a decade, and she had extensive knowledge of how to write award-winning grants and had attempted to recruit more Chicana and Chicano students to become social workers at UTEP. Joining the group of activists who started the Father Rahm Clinic in Segundo Barrio as the first executive director of the facility seemed the next logical step in her desire to support her community. She took on an advocate role in the clinic and sought out "*promotoras,*" or field-workers, from South El Paso to canvas the neighborhood and document "the lack of healthcare with R.E. Thomason [El Paso's General Hospital], the inaccessibility, unavailability, racism, distance, policies, everything that would interfere with our population getting health care."[60] For Castillo, health care was "todo, todo, todo," including reproductive health services and battling police brutality. "The community called for a program that would help them; it was the community that drew me back, and now that I know more about grant writing . . . we survived and we survived beautifully, and we addressed police brutality, the first thing!"[61] Young Chicano men, brutalized by police, she recalled, were the first patients at the Father Rahm Clinic on the corner of Virginia and Third Avenue in Segundo Barrio.

Concern for police brutality, the police's harassment of and violence toward Chicano youth, had deep roots with the clinic's history and identity. In the early 1950s, a Jesuit priest named Harold Rahm had come to live and work in South El Paso, where he dedicated his efforts as a conscious Catholic minister toward the Mexican-origin youth of the area. First, he created a youth theater group, and then he pushed for economic and social investment to ease the effects of violent, degrading poverty in Segundo Barrio.[62] By 1954, Father Rahm, who "style[d] himself a 'natural beggar,'" had "finagled, hustled and wheedled" equipment and support to turn the basement of the Our Lady's Knights of Columbus (KC) into a youth center at 515 South Kansas Street.[63] Led by Mexican American members of the Knights of Columbus, Father Rahm, and community youth, the project to transform the KC's basement into a place where young people could gather, learn crafts, play, and ultimately "battle against juvenile delinquency" left an indelible mark on the community of South El Paso for several reasons.[64] First, it showed others outside the barrio that Mexican-origin people could organize all sorts of people, including union members, painters, and builders, to support a cause for their children. Second, it demonstrated that community leaders could influence members of the Catholic Church to support meaningful community projects. And lastly, it signified to Segundo Barrio's youth that they were worth fighting for and that they had every right to join and shape that fight.

Father Rahm understood the need for young people in South El Paso to see their worth in the present but also to work toward the future. "We must look ahead, though," he said to journalists in 1954. "In a year or so we are going to have to build another building, bigger than this, if we are to keep up this work."[65] After ten years of laboring in Segundo Barrio, the Reverend Father Rahm left for Brazil to continue his ministry of young people in that country's poorest neighborhoods. Although the youth center did not end police brutality, the center and the work of Father Rahm produced the foundations for community-led organizations and activists to carry on this labor in the decades that followed.

When community members came together to build a new center for community care, one that would confront the violence of police brutality and provide proper health care, they named it after the man who had championed them less than a decade before.[66] With its inspirational name in tow, the Father Rahm Clinic not only sought to address the dearth of health services in the community but also began to investigate why there was such little accountability to the community in the realm of health, medical services, and social services (see fig. 5.1).

One of the first things clinic organizers did was assess the current availability of health care for the Mexican-origin community in the area. At the time, health services remained geographically distant, housed within El Paso's general hospital and therefore inaccessible to many without transportation. Father Rahm Clinic field-workers, called *promotoras*, ran experiments, taking their young children to R.E. Thomason, registering them, and then documenting how long it took for them to receive treatment. According to the promotoras' findings, children waited a minimum of five hours to be seen regardless of their issue.[67] Amy Castillo used promotoras' informal studies as evidence for grants that supported the work of the Father Rahm Clinic. After several attempts, she obtained small grants from the National Urban Coalition and the Zales Foundation in 1970 and then finally received a large enough grant to train community staff members

FIGURE 5.1 "Interview #5 in apartment door with promotora (field workers)." MS 637, Box 2, Amelia Mendez Castillo Papers, C. L. Sonnichsen Special Collections Department, University of Texas at El Paso Library.

as health professionals.[68] With the help of Republican Senator John Tower of Texas, the Department of Health, Education and Welfare (HEW) awarded the Father Rahm Clinic over $300,000 (which was about $2,442,769 in 2023) to start a family health center.[69]

Castillo developed a "self-concept" grant, focused on youth mental health, including discussions about self-esteem and dignity, that was approved for the children of Segundo Barrio.[70] She recounted, "how the children didn't have toys, they'd never seen themselves in an upright mirror, you know, to develop their own self-concept . . . everything was broken around them."[71] She explained, "How can they go out and fight the system? When they have no food, no clothing, lack of sleep, cause they're all piled up—*todos juntos*—they don't have a place to rest. They have no wellness. So how can we expect them to grab the concepts of our system?"[72]

For Castillo and the other activists who worked alongside her, including Pete Duarte, Mary Márquez, and Lupe T. De Anda, justice for their community—fighting against police brutality, poverty, lack of access to education—was premised on bringing health and wellness to the barrio.[73]

The Father Rahm Clinic also received funds for women's health as it expanded its networks, collaborating with other South El Paso community groups such as Project Bravo. The clinic sponsored programs around the community that provided women with complete medical examinations. Castillo noted that many times women bore babies but never had follow-up medical visits after delivery. Countless cases of cervical and uterine cancer were detected after the Father Rahm Clinic implemented its new reproductive health program.[74] Domestic violence issues were also addressed during physical exams as well as women's desires to obtain birth control. Castillo called on José Cázares-Zavala, a student resident working at R.E. Thomason, El Paso's General Hospital, to help expand this aspect of the clinic. At the time, the clinic lacked money to buy contraception or to purchase the instruments to conduct full physical exams, but R.E. Thomason, recalled Castillo, received "lots of money for family planning."[75] According to Robert Taboada, the Program Administrator for R.E. Thomason's Family Planning Services, the general hospital had received large sums of money used for family planning since 1971. It allowed their family planning program to exist not only at the general hospital located at 111 Fullan Street, over an hour walk from Segundo Barrio, but also at several satellite locations, including the nearby townships of Canutillo, Alamito Complex, Clint, Moon City, Henderson, Ysleta, and El Paso's Northeast. R.E. Thomason's family planning program incorporated services that "helped individuals freely determine the number and spacing of their children in as healthy a manner as is possible."[76] After decades of birth control and population control advocates fighting for acceptance, the words "family planning" had taken on a new significance during the Vietnam War era. As Elena Gutiérrez explains, by 1970 the Nixon administration folded in national concerns about the "population explosion" into their platform, adopting the Family Planning and Research Act. They funneled plenty of federal dollars into family planning programs across the nation. Simultaneously, Nixon's administration created the Office of Population Affairs headed by the Department of HEW that awarded the Father Rahm Clinic with its largest grant.[77]

Although family planning was connected nationally and locally to population control campaigns vis-à-vis the Office of Population Affairs and Planned Parenthood of El Paso, Chicanas and Chicanos like Castillo and

Dr. Cázares-Zavala focused on the immediate needs of Mexican-origin women by directly funneling those population control funds toward community care programs.[78] After some discussion, Dr. Cázares-Zavala agreed he could hold a women's clinic twice a week, first at the Father Rahm Clinic location, and then at the Houchen Settlement House to guarantee greater privacy for patients. He also agreed to prescribe contraception to the women who wanted it, because as Castillo explained, "they will ask you about it!" According to Castillo, Dr. Cázares-Zavala sent women to obtain their birth control from R.E. Thomason: "Let them [the hospital] feel it,' he said."[79] He wrote patients prescriptions for contraceptives that they received free of charge through the hospital's family planning program. Dr. Cázares-Zavala also provided women from Segundo Barrio with complete physicals, including blood work, Pap smears, pelvic exams, and all other manner of health tests. Castillo and Dr. Cázares-Zavala called it the Women's Care Clinic, facilitated by Castillo through the auspices of the Father Rahm Clinic. Later, Dr. José Cázares-Zavala became a member of the Medical Advisory Committee of Planned Parenthood of El Paso in 1973 and worked at its clinics.[80]

The work of Castillo and Cázares-Zavala was in line with the thinking of Chicanas in the movement who believed that reproductive liberation lay in greater access to birth control and abortion on their own terms. During the 1971 Raza women's conference in Houston, Chicana activists wrote a seven-point plan addressing "Sex and the Chicana." In it they made clear that birth control and abortion were critical to their liberation because "as Chicanas we have the right to control our own bodies."[81] To do so they believed that they should "destroy the myth that religion and culture control our sexual lives" and that those who believed in religion should "interpret the Bible, or Catholic rulings according to their own feelings, what they think is right, without any guilt complexes."[82] Castillo was similarly inclined to this religious interpretation as she faced the Catholic Church in El Paso.

As the Father Rahm Clinic's reproductive health programs expanded, Castillo recalled that a rumor began to circulate insinuating that abortions were being performed on-site. Castillo, a self-described devout Catholic, explained the issues that surrounded the lack of information about reproductive health in the barrio: "The [Catholic] Church would not provide the 'education' . . . because it was taboo, you don't talk about sex, you don't talk about prevention, there was no education, and no clinics."[83] El Paso's Catholic Bishop, Sydney M. Metzger, "was receiving information from his 'santuchos' [male parishioners] that we were having abortions and dispensing medication—like the Pill."[84] Castillo went to see Metzger and unabashedly explained to him, "I am the mother of six [children] and not once has the Church given me money for a medical exam or for medication. There has been nothing developed by this diocese, not one thing about the human body . . . now if you provide it [proof of abortions at the clinic], we'll stop whatever we're doing at Father Rahm."[85] Bishop Metzger nonetheless suggested the name of the clinic could cause confusion among parishioners. He worried that community members might believe the Father Rahm Clinic was sanctioned by or working under the auspices of the Catholic Church. Castillo retorted, "Well, you just have to take my word for it. There has never been an abortion, no miscarriages, not one single crisis. But if there has, I want proof." She remembered that the bishop fell silent. Because of the clinic's reproductive health component, the Church and other community residents demanded that the Father Rahm Clinic change its name. By 1973 it was known as Centro de Salud Familiar La Fe (see fig. 5.2).[86]

El Paso, an All-America City

Just as the Father Rahm Clinic began to take shape and gain momentum, the city of El Paso was thrust into the national spotlight. The March 1970 issue of *Look* magazine, a competitor to *Life* magazine and dedicated to photojournalism, along with the National Municipal League, released the names of the winners of the coveted "All America Cities" contest. Given to cities and townships that exalted democratic values, the award symbolized civic participation in local politics. El Paso, Texas, was the largest city on the "All America Cities" list. The Sun City rushed to capitalize on the distinguished honor and local news showcased headlines like "El Paso Named All-America City" splashed across the front page of the *El Paso Herald-Post*. Attached to this headline was a photograph of Mayor Pete De Wetter with other members of the Chamber of Commerce celebrating the triumph. They held a congratulatory telegram from President Nixon, and all eagerly wore the All-America Cities symbol—a red, white, and blue shield—as a patch on their coat jackets.[87] As one article explained, "The Chamber of Commerce, the City, and various business firms are making plans to incorporate the All America City shield design into their letterheads." And if this were not enough to bolster the importance of the award, "bumper stickers with the symbol will soon break out all over the city as the full import of the honor attributed to El Paso is understood."[88] Indeed, as the weeks passed, businesses on both sides of the border sought to link themselves to the award.

"Centro de Salud Familiar"

November 3, 1973

Mrs. Amy Castillo, MSW, ACSW
El Paso, Texas

Dear Amy:

On behalf of the Board of Directors and the Staff of
the Father Rahm Family Health Center, it is with a deep sense
of appreciation and sincere gratitude that we extend our heart
felt thanks for taking time off of your busy schedule in order
to help us become more educated in the broad implementations
of health services for the benefit of the poor and needy in our
community.

We have labored long and hard, and now it seems like
all our efforts to establish one of the first Family Health
Centers in Texas is about to bear fruition.

If other Chicanos, regardless of their profession or
stature in life, will join their brothers in other needed
endeavors, such as you have done here, there is no reason why
we should not triumph in the end.

From the bottom of our hearts, thank you.

Sincerely,

Manuel de la Rosa
Chairman, Board of Directors
Father Rahm Family Health Center

715 East Fourth Street   •   El Paso, Texas 79901   •   915/532-5940 - 532-5949

FIGURE 5.2 Letter from Manuel de La Rosa to Amy Castillo. MS 637, box 7, Amelia
Mendez Castillo Papers, C. L. Sonnichsen Special Collections Department,
University of Texas at El Paso Library.

The same month the *Look* article appeared, disputes erupted over Planned Parenthood of El Paso's desire to join city-county health clinics. Some county officials determined the new relationship between private and public entities as a necessary step and a means to address a public health concern: overpopulation. Others, specifically the Catholic Church, felt this nexus would disproportionately target poor, mostly Mexican-origin families, whose poverty city officials and Planned Parenthood leaders viewed as self-inflicted and caused by too many babies. As Chicanas and Chicanos sought community self-determination through the creation of localized infrastructure programs, specifically the Father Rahm Clinic, Planned Parenthood continued to support contraception as a means of quelling social unrest among what it viewed as rowdy, ballooning populations. The tensions caused by the desire to expand birth control access in city-county clinics mirrored national and local concerns about overpopulation and the supposed menace of young Black and Brown so-called radicals.

The initial response to the *Look* magazine award seemed to affirm what many elites in the city long hoped to celebrate: civic and democratic progress on the border. City managers were thrilled, and many turned to congratulate the group that first applied for the prize. The League of Women Voters, composed of wealthy, steadfast white club women, sought to highlight El Paso as a socially progressive place. Mrs. J. Max Quenon, president of the El Paso League of Women Voters, and its vice president, Mrs. John Tullis, had the idea to apply for the coveted award and pushed to include some of the city's most impressive projects. The jury composed of *Look* magazine executives and members of the National Municipal League wanted to highlight towns, suburbs, and cities that were front runners in community participation, specifically in the fields of "mental health, job training, and birth control."[89] The League of Women Voters outlined the Mayor's Youth Opportunity Program, which provided young people in the community the chance to become involved in civic affairs. Quenon and Tullis included St. Joseph Hospital's plans to aid an estimated 15,000 alcoholics as well as "care for the narcotic sick, the mentally retarded and 80- and 90-year-old geriatric population."[90] While El Paso was recognized for its efforts to address alcoholism and palliative care for those with mental health issues and the elderly, birth control was noticeably omitted from the award application. Planned Parenthood of El Paso was a strong force in the community, making the absence that much more striking.

The *Look* article did highlight some of El Paso's "social problems," namely its disgruntled "Mexican-American" population. "The largest 1969 winner (pop. 350,000) has so far accomplished least in brick-and-mortar terms," the piece chimed. Projecting into the future, *Look* responded to its own critiques by suggesting that El Paso was having a "spiritual awakening," led by Mayor De Wetter. The mayor was forcing El Pasoans to confront a "half-century of indifference toward its Mexican American poor." His youth program was an attempt to quash what the magazine termed "Brown Power militancy among angry chicano [*sic*] youths" by including young "Mexican-Americans" into the city's urban renewal plans. According to the article, the mayor's efforts, not Chicana or Chicano activism in South El Paso, deserved recognition for bolstering the requirements for the prestigious All-America City honor.

Look celebrated the twentieth anniversary of the All-America award by "remind[ing] the reader—especially the young reader—that an All-America City award recognizes citizen participation in democracy."[91] The citizenry of El Paso was, according to historian Oscar Martínez, 57.3 percent Mexican-origin by 1970.[92] A truly democratic space would require their full participation, yet as the city worked to address health issues, it struggled to include the Mexican-origin community in civic and political life. The article examined the condition of many Mexicans in South El Paso and concluded that they were "locked in feudal poverty on the city's south side, [and] *they* [my emphasis] provide[d] de Wetter with enough negative housing, health and employment statistics to fill a target-area textbook." Even as *Look* magazine sought to draw attention to the inequality in South El Paso, it still could only blame the survivors of racist marginalization and not the systems and Anglo leadership that produced their deprivation.

The All-America award bestowed by a Midwest magazine (*Look*'s headquarters were in Des Moines, Iowa) called forth a national and historical dialogue about poverty and democracy in the United States. This national conversation drew a direct link between Franklin Roosevelt's New Deal policies in the 1930s to Johnson's War on Poverty in the 1960s. One critical rhetorical construction used to highlight the plight of the poor began with one of FDR's fireside chats in 1932 foregrounding the economic pains of America's "forgotten man."[93] Farmers, factory workers, and miners emerged as FDR's forgotten Americans. Despite their hard work and sacrifice, these white men were in danger of losing their homes and farms during the Great Depression, and FDR sought to provide a plan to protect these men from losing a pivotal centerpiece of American democracy: property. Thirty-six years later, Johnson dusted off the rhetoric of the "forgotten man" to describe the poverty and political marginalization of Native peoples in the

United States. While the "American Indian" served as a critical figure in the mythmaking of the United States as a "symbol of drama and excitement" of the colonies and early republic, Johnson conceded that "for two centuries, he [Native American man] has been an alien in his own land."[94] For Johnson, investing in roads and water management on or near reservations, education, housing, and health was central to incorporating Native peoples into the broader democratic project.

Tying these rhetorical threads together, the *Look* article sought to highlight Mexican-origin people as part of this "forgotten man" narrative. In a caption under the photograph of two presumably Mexican-origin children from South El Paso, *Look* proclaimed that "El Paso's unfinished business is to fulfill promises of a better deal for its forgotten Mexican-Americans."[95] Yet *Look*'s award seemed to prize the charity of white El Pasoans for attempting to address the rampant poverty and political marginalization of the city's Mexican-origin workers who remained the backbone of the borderland economy. The All-America award sought to highlight white El Pasoans' supposed altruism despite its lack of material results for the majority Mexican-descent community.

Even as the Johnson administration and popular magazines like *Look* acknowledged the state's neglect of historically marginalized and racialized communities using the "forgotten American" narrative, by the end of the 1960s this vein of thinking had been eclipsed by a growing white backlash. Peter Schrag's 1969 "The Forgotten American" essay in *Harper's* magazine articulated growing white working-class resentment and has been used to signify the public pronouncement of a new neo-conservative movement in the United States. As Schrag wrote, "While he [white working-class man] is making more than he ever made—he's still struggling while a lot of others—'them' (on welfare, in demonstrations, in the ghettos) are getting most of the attention."[96] FDR's 1930s fledgling white working class was now Schrag's disgruntled and ignored white American. These national racial tensions filtered through cities like El Paso, as Chicanas and Chicanos continued to fight to make their plight not only known but accepted by Anglo leaders.

PPEP, Birth Control, and Public Health

While the city celebrated the not-so-well-deserved All-America City award, Planned Parenthood of El Paso was a few months into organizing new programs for 1970 shaped by local and national fears of a population explosion. For many in PPEP, the Malthusian prediction El Paso birth control activist had long feared was finally coming to pass.[97] PPEP's educational efforts to combat the fertility bomb included showing films at schools, churches, hospitals, and other welfare organizations in the city that dealt with reproductive issues. Films with titles like "The People Problem," "Population Ecology," and "Children by Choice" were scattered throughout the meeting notes.[98] In addition, PPEP's Education Committee leadership asked board members to think about new ways to increase the patient load, since it had begun to dwindle in recent months.[99]

During the early months of 1970, Planned Parenthood of El Paso reached dozens of organizations, groups, and individuals with a message that connected birth control to population control. This may be one reason why some in the city, particularly from the Mexican-origin community, reacted negatively to Planned Parenthood requests to make birth control information available through county health clinics.[100] Speaking visits from population control supporters were not necessarily helpful to Planned Parenthood's cause. Lee Loevinger, one such speaker, a well-respected jurist in the Kennedy administration who had spearheaded anti-trust legislation, suggested "compulsory birth control" was on the horizon.[101] Speaking at the Texas Daily Newspaper Association conference in El Paso, Loevinger "attributed the rise of such protest groups as blacks, students and anti-this or pro-that, as being formed simply because individuals want recognition as individuals not because of the cause."[102] Rather than view the work of Chicanas and Chicanos in Segundo Barrio as a process of self-determination through community engagement and reproductive care, Loevinger viewed demands for social justice as mere self-aggrandizement and symptoms of a population out of control. He leaned into Schrag's hypothesis that a white backlash against social justice organizing was on the horizon. Like Sanger's push for compulsory birth control before a similar audience in El Paso in 1937, Loevinger declared: "You may not agree, but our children are going to live to see compulsory birth control . . . Only when we control the population will society be back in control of itself. The family of two children must become the average and the norm. If we make this much of an adjustment in our attitudes, we may preserve our basic values and ethics; otherwise, we surely will not."[103] So moved was Betty Mary Goetting, the honorary president of Planned Parenthood of El Paso, that she clipped and neatly pasted the article in her scrapbook, alongside the countless articles that emerged as Planned Parenthood fought to make birth control part of the city's public health regime.

Later that year, PPEP board meeting minutes revealed substantial political obstacles that could prevent PPEP plans from moving forward with its public health campaign for contraception. PPEP records described the entanglement as "Planned Parenthood vs. City, County Health Board, County Commissioners and the City Council."[104] Enmeshed in this public debacle were not only city and county social services but also the United Fund, a large financial supporter of Planned Parenthood. The relationship between the United Fund and PPEP had been complicated from the onset with many Catholic organizations openly boycotting its affiliation. Planned Parenthood was no stranger to hostilities from the Catholic Church and many in the Mexican community whom the Church purported to represent. As the drama unfolded, PPEP board members sought to "request statements from the City, County, Health Board, and United Fund saying whether they have been unduly influenced by strong Catholic elements."[105]

The United Fund became one of the main financial contributors to PPEP in the early years, and any financial changes from the United Fund to the clinics could radically alter services. The United Fund consistently felt pressure from the Catholic Church and affiliated groups since the early twentieth century to remove Planned Parenthood from its roster of supported organizations. Faced with economic uncertainty, PPEP turned to the state for assistance. Rather than compromise its overpopulation projects, PPEP strove to "obtain federal funds from the Health, Education, and Welfare department for their program, and that such funds would be much more easily available if the Planned Parenthood applicants could work in conjunction with El Paso City-County Health Unit."[106] As it began to see other organizations receive monies from the War on Poverty war chest, the board decided to obtain "government money" in 1969. As discussed in PPEP documents, "previous attempts have been unsuccessful," but "since the Public Health Board and Project Bravo are also eligible for funds for family planning we need to move quickly in order not to be excluded."[107]

Project Bravo worked hand in hand with the Father Rahm Clinic to assist in the formation of family planning projects, but according to Amelia Castillo, Planned Parenthood of El Paso never made an attempt to join forces with groups led by Mexican-origin activists in South El Paso.[108] If the goal was to end poverty in Segundo Barrio and assist the community, surely Planned Parenthood should have been enthusiastic in its support of the Father Rahm Clinic. Instead, PPEP ignored Chicana and Chicano attempts to address social marginalization and increased its overpopulation rhetoric. The same month that *Look* magazine exalted El Paso's civic engagement,

PPEP unveiled plans to chase public funds and join with the city-county health department in order to make overpopulation a public health cause.

The Catholic Church and Mexican Politicians Counter PPEP's Plans

In March 1970 during a County Commissioners Court hearing, commissioners voted to OK the use of city-county health clinics for the distribution of contraceptive information and devices. Newspapers noted that despite objections from Bishop Sidney M. Metzger of the El Paso Catholic Diocese and some Mexican American commissioners, the court voted to approve Planned Parenthood's request.[109] Although powerful Mexican American commissioners Richard Telles and Rogelio Sanchez voted no, the project moved forward ready for a vote from the city council, which shared the budget for the clinics with the county.[110]

As the program received a green light from county commissioners, voices of dissent grew loud. Al Velarde, president of the Catholic Church's Social Action Committee, presented a lengthy letter from Bishop Metzger at the commissioners' meeting. The communiqué outlined three main reasons for Metzger's objection to the proposed plan:

> (1) The physical dangers arising from the use of the pill have prompted the recent requirement that warnings about the harmful effects of the use of the pill must be issued whenever it is dispensed; (2) Family limitation is not the proper solution for serious social problems causing poverty, such as low wages, lack of adequate educational opportunities, sub-standard and-or over-priced housing etc.;
> (3) The determination of family size is essentially the obligation of the parents themselves, while inclusion of a birth control pill project in a public health program implies governmental coercion and an invasion of family privacy.[111]

Though the bishop's main message sought to condemn the relationship between the city-county health department and Planned Parenthood, he also played on the underlying racial and class concerns from the mostly Catholic and Mexican community in the city.

Metzger's first critique concerned the Pill itself and perceived side effects. The Pill was introduced in 1960 as the ultimate advancement in contraceptive technologies, and Metzger brought up congressional hearings about its dangers and risks to patients that had hit the limelight by the 1970s. Metzger contended that this contraceptive method should not be given to the greater public. Excerpts from the congressional hearings published in the *El Paso Herald-Post* a month before PPEP moved to publicize its intent to join city-county clinics were telling. Congress solicited the testimony from Planned Parenthood Federation President Dr. Allan F. Guttmacher, who believed the Pill was a profoundly important tool in the war against overpopulation. Guttmacher had cautioned the committee: "With world population soaring and bringing in its wake malnutrition and starvation, overcrowding and increasing illiteracy . . . it would be foolish to abandon use of this particular contraceptive."[112] Guttmacher accused Senator Gaylord Nelson (D-Wis.) and the hearings on the "pill" of "being highly inflammatory and hav[ing] panicked the public." In fact, one of the headlines in the *El Paso Herald Post* read: "Pregnancy More Dangerous Than the Pill! Says Dr. Guttmacher." It was clear that Guttmacher believed the Pill was an important tool in the war against overpopulation. Guttmacher had long insisted on family planning as the ultimate remedy for overpopulation. When Planned Parenthood Federation of America added the "World Population Emergency" suffix to its name, it hired Guttmacher as the president.[113] Guttmacher had been a welcomed visitor to Planned Parenthood of El Paso luncheons and fund drives since 1956 and had extolled the virtues of population control at every speech.[114] During his first talk in the borderlands, Guttmacher was sure to justify fear of overpopulation declaring that it would "aggravate the food problems and affect living standards."[115] His remedy for overpopulation, entangled in eugenic arguments, brought into question the intentions of PPEP and helped underscore Bishop Metzger's second argument.

Metzger's next point served as a rebuttal to Guttmacher's warnings about overpopulation, but his concerns also traced a longer history of the birth control movement in El Paso. Since Margaret Sanger's visit to El Paso in 1937, birth control was lauded by many wealthy, white women city leaders as the singular solution to the city's social problems. Residents of Segundo Barrio were the main targets of campaigns against social degeneration in the city, and birth control movement activists encouraged this connection. Metzger derided eugenic arguments made by some in the birth control movement insisting that "prescription of anti-ovulant pills to treat individual pathological conditions is a matter to be determined between physician and patient and is not properly the concern of public health programs."[116] His contention referenced discussions riddled with eugenic ideas and ideologies that dominated the birth control movement in the 1920s and 1930s. Moreover, Metzger declared that "children are not the cause of poverty which has indeed many causes, gravely low wages, lack of adequate educational opportunities, substandard and or overpriced housing, to name a few."[117] His statement was a direct indictment of the social and economic neglect of south-side barrios. He scoffed at Planned Parenthood's motto—"every child, a wanted child"—stating, "It is far too simplistic to assume or to assert the children of the poor are unwanted or unloved."[118] While Chicana and Chicano activists sought to address the lack of social services and funding for social welfare programs in places like Segundo Barrio, Metzger delineated the hypocrisy with which Planned Parenthood attempted to confront similar issues. Yet, even as Bishop Metzger criticized the societal neglect of families in South El Paso, Amelia Castillo maintained that the Catholic Church under Metzger's leadership had done very little in terms of addressing the poverty the bishop decried.

Metzger's third objection focused on the state's interest in advocating for birth control using public health clinics. According to Metzger, "It is claimed that such a program never contemplates ever a hint of coercion on the individual recipients of any welfare program, but this is not always the case."[119] Highlighting the public push of family planning programs, Metzger observed: "The determination of the size of one's family is essentially the obligation of the parents themselves and this natural right is theirs whether they be rich or poor."[120] For the bishop, decisions about reproductive health should not be made at the mercy of state entities, given the interest the state had in controlling welfare programs.

Metzger's final remarks to the commissioners emphasized the pressure some in the community might feel when confronted with contraceptives at local public health clinics, explaining how "it may be stated policy that participation in a welfare program imposes no obligation, the recipients of welfare have protested against the intrusions on their privacy."[121] As Khiara Bridges observes, poverty-stricken people are rarely afforded considerations for privacy.[122] Although PPEP had a controversial history with the Catholic Church in El Paso, PPEP had involved private companies, such as Emko, in its distribution efforts. According to the Church, state clinics promoting Planned Parenthood's mission would allow government and corporate interference in private matters.

Missing from Bishop Metzger's stern opposition to the plan, however, were overtly religious claims that birth control collided with Catholic dogma. The clergyman made almost no reference to religion as a major motive for refusal of the project. Perhaps doctrinal visions of the Catholic Church had affected earlier moves to thwart Planned Parenthood.[123] Again, historical memory would remind many in the community that fervent religious arguments only helped divide the city as it had in the late 1930s and 1940s when the contraceptive movement first began. Misogynistic arguments about a woman's proper place in the family and her subservience to her husband did not hold the same sway in the 1970s, particularly considering changing social and cultural ideas about gender and race and especially given recent changes within the Roman Catholic Church itself. Although Pope Paul VI had signed *Humanae Vitae*, the encyclical condemning the use of contraceptive technologies in 1968, the cat had been unceremoniously released from the bag. As journalist Robert Blair Kaiser explains, "Priests were starting to accent the positive" use of contraception— not directly, of course, but by counseling married couples that the sexual act was a "unique mystery of total self giving" and that couples should decide how many children they had based on "their own circumstance."[124] Surveys in Europe, the United States, and Canada confirmed what ecclesiastical fathers knew would not change despite the encyclical, Catholic couples were using birth control without fear of committing mortal sin.[125] Thus, Metzger, likely well aware of the recent tensions among Church leaders and local priests and their tepid support of contraception, steered clear of religious overtones but helped draw attention to economic and social concerns.

El Paso's bishop was not the only person to oppose the nexus between the city-county health clinics and Planned Parenthood of El Paso. Richard Telles, one of the county commissioners who voted against the plan, spoke out during the proceedings. Telles questioned the legality of the use of public clinics to advocate for a private cause. He also pleaded with the court on behalf of the poor. The *El Paso Times* published his declaration: "How long would the rich last if we eliminated the garbage collectors and ditch diggers who are the poor? . . . We have failed the poor. There are those who say we are giving them too much and it turns my stomach every time I hear that. We are not giving them enough care. It is the Mexican-Americans doing all the dirty work and we should do more for them."[126] Telles, a longtime political figure in El Paso whose older brother Raymond Telles was the United States' first Mexican American mayor upon his election in El Paso in 1957, defined the debate in terms of upper- and middle-class residents shirking their civic responsibility to *care* for the poor, most of whom were of Mexican origin.[127] While Metzger did not directly mention the Mexican-origin community in his dissention of the birth control project, Telles insisted they would be the main targets for reproductive control. The *Look* article highlighted stark economic and racial disparities in El Paso, which confirmed for Chicanas and Chicanos what they had long hoped to address: the marginalization of the Mexican-origin community in El Paso. For more than eighty years, Anglo residents attempted to drive a wedge between questions of economic exploitation by city elites on the one hand and the financial degradation of the Mexican-origin community on the other. Political figures like Telles, as well as Chicana and Chicano activists, sought to shimmy out the block that prevented residents from seeing the direct connections between low wages, deadly living conditions, lack of access to education and job opportunities for Mexican-origin people, and the oppressive labor conditions of this same community in El Paso.

For decades, Anglo residents indulged in xenophobic renderings to produce and maintain fears about overpopulation as the singular culprit for poverty in El Paso's Mexican community. Anglo leaders believed a combination of high immigration and uncontrolled fertility were to blame for an "explosive" population that consequently caused the economic devastation of Mexican-origin people in El Paso. On the day the "All-America City" article was published, the *El Paso Times* highlighted the immigration status of some residents of the south side and their connection to social problems there. Discussing Mayor De Wetter's trip to Washington, DC, to secure funding to build affordable housing in El Paso's south side, the press acknowledged the lack of infrastructure many "resident aliens" faced as they sought refuge in the barrio. The mayor "made it clear [to DC politicians] that if the US government is going to allow thousands of poor Mexicans into El Paso to live and work, then the United States is going to have to foot some of the bill to alleviate the social problems caused and encountered by these aliens."[128] The mayor's comments conflated Mexican American residents with newly arrived immigrants as a means to divorce the city of its civic and social responsibilities toward its residents who had populated the city since its inception. Oscar Martinez confirms that in 1970, 80.3 percent of Mexican-origin people in the city had been born on US soil. Less than a quarter were immigrants to the city.[129] Wealthy El Pasoans benefited greatly from the migration of "thousands of poor Mexicans" at the turn of the twentieth century, which helped spur El Paso's industrial, agricultural, and service sector economies.[130] Many, including 1930s' birth control movement activists, sought to address poverty in the barrio by imposing ideas about family limitation while refusing to address economic exploitation and deplorable living conditions. The racist discourse that bound uncontrolled immigration, overpopulation, poverty, and the Mexican-origin community in El Paso remained strong since the 1930s.

Many El Pasoans took to the newspapers to proclaim their support for the fight against overpopulation and the need for birth control in the city. In the *El Paso Times'* section "Speaking the Public Mind," resident Roy H. Huntley proclaimed, "I believe it is worthy to note that thinking people, be they socialist, capitalist, or any other ideology are in agreement on this issue. In order to keep the earth inhabitable we must limit population."[131] Huntley, like others in the city, underscored the fact that "thinking people" would easily discern the importance of controlling populations. He implied that those who were against population control were likely inconsiderate at best or idiots at worst about family limitation and poverty-induced social ills.

In the *Herald-Post*, another concerned resident expressing support for PPEP sought to involve the national so-called radical militant youth movement in the population control controversy. Belittling Telles's remarks by likening them to those of Stokely Carmichael, the Trinidadian-born Black political activist, Mrs. C. M. Boone declared: "If Stokely Carmichael's charge is true, that drugs are a tool of whites to dull the minds and ambitions of blacks in the ghetto, then it is also true that the Planned Parenthood's Association's aim is to limit the number of births of Mexican-Americans, as Richard Telles seems to believe. One assumption is as realistic as the other."[132] Associating Telles, a middle-of-the-road public servant, to Stokely Carmichael, who coined the term "Black Power," was a discursive tactic aimed at radicalizing middle-of-the-road politics.[133] Although Telles was a longtime Mexican American civic leader, he was no Brown Power radical. For Boone, Telles's conflation of birth control with controlling Mexican American birth rates was as ludicrous as Carmichael's assessment that whites invented drugs to keep Black people subservient and numb to their social realities.

Boone's alignment of Telles and Carmichael is telling, given that the Black Power leader was seen as a radical on the national stage. Telles's views were more conservative, and he did not espouse the same antiestablishment, anti-colonial rhetoric as Carmichael. Boone sought to link them in the minds of white El Pasoans, who feared not only the uprisings of militant Brown and Black youth around the country and in El Paso proper but also the supposed population explosion within those very same groups. Population control advocates were making similar connections nationally, as they homed in on overpopulation in so-called urban areas and connected these "out-of-control" populations to social unrest across major cities in America.[134]

During the weeks that the birth control fiasco droned on, Chicana and Chicano youths continued organizing in El Paso. As Mayor De Wetter attempted to soothe concerns of marginalized groups in Segundo Barrio through the development of outreach programs, many young people took to the streets to expose the rampant discrimination in the border city. Focusing mainly on deplorable living conditions, on March 22, 1970, members of the Mexican American Youth Association (MAYA) marched to "protest housing, education, and job conditions." Others from Union de Inquilinos, MACHOS, and MECHA also sought to join the protest. Tony Marín, a MAYA leader, responded that they could no longer simply "wait for better housing" and jobs. Furthermore, when asked about education Marin proclaimed: "We cry for justice because too many students are pushed out by a system that does not understand the culture of the Mexican-American. Racist teachers and racist books should not block the way for a better education."[135] Up to this point, newspapers and city officials alike refused to explicitly call the degradation in South El Paso racist. Although Metzger accused city and county officials of attacking the fertility of poor families in Segundo Barrio and Telles underscored the disproportionate targeting of Mexican-origin residents for reproductive control, neither directly called it racist. Chicana and Chicano activists, however, directed their ire at policies they deemed racist, bringing to light decades of the city of El Paso's structural marginalization and institutional racism against the Mexican-origin community.

Population Control versus Reproductive Justice

The fight to have PPEP join city-county clinics failed. Weeks after the county commissioners decided to approve the measure, city-county health board members recommended that the city council nix the plan.[136] Since county and city monies funded the health agency, a no vote from the city would inevitably kill the nexus. The recommendation, however, was made during an executive meeting—a session closed to the public—and County Judge Colbert Coldwell, a staunch supporter of PPEP and city-county birth control union, jumped to reprimand Dr. Laurence Nickey, the head of the health board, for discussing the matter in private. Furthermore, the judge declared the voice of the health agency would have no standing with the commissioners' court since it had already voted and hoped that the city council would stand steadfast in favor of the clinics.[137] Coldwell angrily demanded the resignation of all members of the city-county health board. He remarked that the "Health Board was 'presumptuous' in making the recommendation [to City Council] to reject the request, particularly after the County Court had officially voted to approve it."[138] As the drama wore on, Mayor De Wetter received letters from clergymen in favor of and against the measure to marry Planned Parenthood services with city-county health clinics. Several ministers from Protestant churches in El Paso urged the mayor to strongly consider the idea, while representatives from the Catholic Church stood in opposition.

Nonetheless, the health board was resolute in opposing the board with two Spanish-surnamed physicians, Dr. Joe Román and Dr. Raúl Rivera, as the most vociferous opponents of the agreement. The health board blocked the plan, citing: "Legality of permitting private organizations to use health clinics built with . . . federal funds; whether or not the Board was setting a precedent in designating family planning as a health service; what legal liability might exist on the part of the city and county if any birth control device recipient filed suit, claiming injury . . . whether approval would open a 'Pandora's box' of applications from various other health-connected organizations; and information from a survey to be conducted as to whether the people want or need such a program."[139] Rivera concluded that "the Board should not get involved in something that is not a public health issue, but a moral and religious issue."[140] Coldwell, who attended the meeting, remained silent on the matter. Perhaps the impending city and county elections that followed in May kept him quiet.

Most telling about the fight over birth control in publicly funded clinics was the city-county health board members' final concerns. Did "the people want or need such a program?"[141] Clearly, poor residents needed health care since the Father Rahm Clinic had garnered so much support from local activists and leaders in the barrio. While Planned Parenthood continued to frame the use of birth control as a tool to combat overpopulation, residents of south-side communities created comprehensive health programs that included family planning as a matter of self-determination and justice. Political and civic leaders determined that neither city nor county funds should be used to bring greater access to family planning, I believe, because they could not completely guarantee that these clinics would not launder PPEP's message about overpopulation to a greater swath of the Mexican-origin community. The religious intolerance and moral objection of some of the Spanish-surnamed physicians on the health board likely saved the city and county from further marginalizing a community in desperate need of health care access, but we will never know for sure.

Community Clinics and Reproductive Care

Despite the contentious debates between politicians and activists about birth control, economically marginalized Mexican-origin women continued to use PPEP clinics and the Father Rahm Clinic to address their reproductive health needs. During the two months of the controversy, PPEP had 247 new patients and conducted over 699 medical exams.[142] The Father Rahm Clinic program, assisted by Amelia Castillo and Dr. José Cázares-Zavala, took a more holistic approach to reproductive health. According to media accounts, the Father Rahm Clinic fielded 171 requests for assistance the first month after it opened. By December 1970, Amelia Castillo confirmed that it had aided over 91 families, providing 250 dependents with "evaluative and personal assistance services by the staff and over 560 telephone and office inquiries for information and referrals a month were processed by the staff."[143] As community members spread word of how others might receive care at the Father Rahm Clinic, services for more community care expanded.

The late 1960s and 1970s ushered in a movement to train more people of color as medical professionals and to create additional clinics centered on the desires of those in the community.[144] The Department of Health, Education, and Welfare (DHEW) newsletter, "For Your Health: A Su Salud," published an article dedicated to the Father Rahm Clinic. It stated that "the Father Rahm Clinic, a community based organization, has made tremendous strides in a two-year pilot demonstration to improve and develop adequate, accessible, and available health care services in South El Paso."[145] By 1972, the Father Rahm Clinic identified four major gaps in health care for its community: (1) availability of medical care, (2) family planning services, (3) the creation of health and health-related information and referral services, and (4) greater community involvement in the decisions regarding healthcare in the barrio.[146] The recent acquisition of buildings from the Newark-Houchen Board of Directors helped expand the Father Rahm Clinic programs for El Segundo, the article reported.[147] As historian Sandra Enríquez explains, expansion was necessary for many reasons, including that the clinic "became a vehicle for training the next generation of health professionals."[148] Receiving these major grants forced the clinic to focus on professionalization of its staff, causing it to lose the "informality" that made it easier for patients to "approach medical personnel with their medical health problems." As Pete Duarte surmised, this made some of the militant Chicanas and Chicanos involved in the "ethnic empowerment" of communities of South El Paso view the clinic's professionalization and bureaucratization as a "co-optation—an ethnic betrayal in return for fiscal support from external sources."[149] Still, the initial purpose of community-created institutions representing the interests and addressing the concerns of Segundo Barrio residents remained at the core of Chicana and Chicano activist and leaders' agitations in the years that followed.

The Father Rahm Clinic was part of a larger movement across the Southwest that believed health and community care were intrinsic aspects of self-determination, social justice, and ethnic pride. David Hayes-Bautista, professor of medicine and director of the Center for the Study of Latino Health and Culture at the School of Medicine at the University of California, Los Angeles, described his initiation into the field of community-run health care beginning with a phone call from parent organizers in Oakland, California's Fruitvale community in 1970. They had three complaints they hoped he, a young medical student at University of California, San Francisco, could help them correct. Their demands were simple: "The first was the scarcity of physicians practicing in the area. The second was the near total lack of Spanish-speaking physicians. The third was the high cost of medical care for those without medical insurance. And the parents wanted to do something about all three."[150]

Like the south-side residents of El Paso, the Oakland parents sought out community members who were obtaining graduate degrees or had some professionalization for guidance. As Hayes-Bautista recalled, after cobbling together $240 and "a lot of dreams," they opened Clinica de la Raza a few months later.[151] Meanwhile in Crystal City, Texas, a crew of Chicana and Chicano activists came together to form a Health Action Committee in 1970 as an investigatory arm for city residents of the rural Zavala County—fewer than 11,000 residents. By 1974, they had opened a small clinic offering medical services for the mostly Mexican-origin members of their community.[152] Energized by community activism during these years, medical graduate students from Texas, California, Arizona, New Mexico, and Colorado established the National Chicano Health Organization.[153] During these same years, Chicanos in San Antonio, Texas, began the "Chicano Health Career Institute," a program established by the Chicano Health Policy Development, Inc., an organization meant to reach across the state of Texas to help young Mexican-origin people address their communities' health care concerns.[154] Young activists viewed health, including reproductive health and family planning, as part and parcel of the larger struggle for social justice in the barrio. They established new institutions offering services that centered community needs in the present with an eye toward securing greater health futures. Their models were successful. Many, including the Father Rahm Clinic (Centro de Salud Familiar La Fe), continue their work today, over fifty years later.

Conclusion

When *Look* magazine declared El Paso an All-America City in 1970, city officials did little to acknowledge the work of Chicanas and Chicanos in South El Paso. Although racial and class tensions through calls for population control dominated discussions about access to contraception, local leaders ignored the voices of those who tried to address the social ills caused by so-called overpopulation. Like many white dominated cities attempting to confront political and social upheaval, city leaders took matters into their own hands without engaging the specific concerns from those most affected. It seems likely that a citywide discussion of reproductive health, stripped of its inflammatory population explosion rhetoric, might have neutralized the backlash from the Catholic Church and would have been welcomed within the Mexican-origin community given the use of family planning programs promoted by the Father Rahm Clinic. That Planned Parenthood's purpose in expanding birth control throughout city-county clinics aimed to address what it considered a "major public health issue," namely overpopulation, then surely Chicana and Chicano attempts to establish a clinic addressing general health and well-being of the Mexican-origin people of Segundo Barrio would be praised. It was not.

As city representatives scrambled to confront *Look* magazine's critiques, the health needs and major strides of the Mexican-origin community continued to be, in the words of Luz Gutierrez, "grossly ignored." The All-America City award not only outlined the city's marginalization of Mexicans in the community, but it also foregrounded the paternalistic vision of city leaders as they sought to tackle decades-old structural neglect through programs that discounted the work and needs of Chicanas and Chicanos in their community. For instance, at the end of 1970, under the auspices of the mayor's $21.9 million urban renewal project, the city acquired the infamous Seis Infiernos tenement, where the Father Rahm Clinic activists got their start. Residents protested because while the city planned to turn the 120-unit building on the 600 block of Ochoa Street in South El Paso into sixty-two-bedroom apartments, it had yet to find adequate living arrangements for the hundreds of residents currently living there.[155] Planned Parenthood of El Paso board members often echoed the city's thoughtless engagement with the Mexican-origin community. Its focus on population control coupled with a disregard for an organized Mexican-origin community revealed the tangled and undemocratic history of El Paso, one premised on the economic exploitation of those it presumed expendable and outside the reach of proper citizenship but in desperate need of reproductive control.

6 Battling Mexico's Growth

Population Control, Neoliberalism, and Reproductive Autonomy

· ·

The paradox of Mexico is that it tries so hard to make so much progress but always seems stuck on the treadmill of debt, unemployment and overpopulation.

—*New York Times*, February 13, 1988

One cool Los Angeles evening in May 1987, Guadalupe Arizpe de la Vega held an event in Beverly Hills, California, to discuss the work of her organization in Ciudad Juárez, Mexico. De la Vega held captive the audience of three dozen attendees as she spoke about her organization's family planning mission in Mexico. De la Vega, the founder of Federación Mexicana de Asociaciónes y Empresas Privadas (FEMAP), represented a "light in the darkness" for the members of the Southern California Population Crisis Committee.[1] They responded positively to her groundbreaking work, battling Mexico's growth by providing contraception to economically poor women across the country.[2] In her talk, De La Vega noted how "demographic and environmental tensions increase each day and have a strong impact on natural resources. Increasingly, they determine the quality of life on our planet."[3]

The Southern California Population Crisis Committee, an offshoot of the Washington DC-based Population Crisis Committee founded in 1965 by William Draper, a wealthy financier consumed with fears of overpopulation, was primed for de la Vega's neo-Malthusian talking points. Echoing rhetoric that connected environmental devastation to overpopulation, De La Vega enthusiastically placed Mexico at the forefront of major global family planning efforts. Many international organizations recognized her efforts via "Mexico's national population program" even garnering a United Nations population control award as well as the Margaret Sanger Award from Planned Parenthood in 1985 (see fig. 6.1).[4]

De la Vega plied the audience with sobering statics describing how Mexico's population had grown from 20 million in 1940 to 80 million inhabitants by 1986. Demographic projections foresaw an increase of over

FIGURE 6.1 Guadalupe Arizpe de la Vega (center) accepting the Margaret Sanger Award from Planned Parenthood Federation of America alongside fellow winner, Mechai Vivavaidya of Thailand, and Dr. Allan Rosenfield, national chairman of Planned Parenthood Federation of America. (*Planned Parenthood Review* [Winter 1986]: 43). Box 7, Planned Parenthood Federation of America Records Group II (PPFA II), Sophia Smith Collection of Women's History, Smith College, Northampton, Massachusetts.

23 million people by the year 2000.[5] Mexico's supposed rapid expansion kept many of Southern California Population Crisis Committee members, such as director-at-large Ben Lohrie, up at night. Lohrie, who expressed some doubt that de la Vega's contraceptive campaigns would alter these numbers, was nevertheless supportive, as he believed that overpopulation would be a disaster for those living on both sides of the US-Mexico border. "Up until now, they [undocumented Mexicans] have had the safety of El Norte. That's closed down now. You can't hire illegal aliens anymore," he lamented.[6] Lohrie's mournful tone likely came as a response to US President Ronald Reagan signing the Immigration Control and Reform Act (IRCA) in 1986, which penalized employers for knowingly hiring "illegal aliens."[7]

Others in the audience openly wondered how de la Vega, a practicing Catholic, confronted the Catholic Church in Mexico. Her clinics, she explained, were less like Planned Parenthood in the United States because they offered pre- and postnatal care. She reasoned that otherwise "no one in [Mexico] would go." In addition to assisting Mexican women with access to better health care, helping them have healthier pregnancies and babies, FEMAP offered women information about birth control. These charitable efforts and de la Vega's high social standing ingratiated her with the Catholic Church. "I don't have any problem with the bishop. He's a very good friend of mine. Our bishop has never opposed our (family planning) cause," de la Vega responded. She lauded the local Church, stating that "even priests send people to the clinic to have tubal ligations," and she remarked how nuns as volunteers for FEMAP performed charitable acts delivering babies.[8] "Bishops and priests understand the tremendous need for family planning," de la Vega declared to the crowd. Operating in a Catholic country where abortion was illegal, de la Vega expressed the Church's support for her family planning agenda as a critical way to "prevent abortions."[9] Guadalupe de la Vega's very persona assuaged the crowd's skepticism. She was often likened to Grace Kelly in the media, dressing stylishly and wearing her platinum-blonde tresses gently framing her face. Her affluence certainly strengthened her public appeal. De la Vega's charm and movie star air, along with her family's reputation in the borderlands, influenced important community leaders and donors to support her cause.

De la Vega had unequivocally committed her life to the family planning movement in Mexico. In the 1970s, this meant a profound fixation with overpopulation as the family planning movement's global mission was indistinguishable from population control advocacy in the latter part of the twentieth century. As the opening epigraph contends, overpopulation became a major economic and social concern for Mexican officials and global policymakers in the 1980s. The year before de la Vega's visit to Beverly Hills, Mexico's incoming and outgoing presidents both agreed that "Mexico's overpopulation was a backdrop to all of Mexico's problems."[10] The focus on overpopulation was a relatively recent concern since the government—although never coming to an overwhelming consensus—had maintained a mostly pro-natalist stance for much of the twentieth century. Historian Ana Raquel Minian explains that from 1821 to the early 1970s, "the country's policy makers tended to cast population growth as essential for economic growth and nation building."[11] These issues not only included questions of reproduction but also overlapped with concerns for immigration to and emigration from Mexico and its connection to labor.

While some Mexican officials had cast emigration as a potential danger to Mexico's national goals of modernity, order, and progress after the 1910 revolution, other Mexican policymakers and social scientists promoted circular migration, whereby Mexican workers would go to the United States to learn new techniques and technologies, bringing back their newly acquired knowledge to support the modernization of their home country.[12] This latter group supported the institutionalization of circular migration through the Bracero Program (1942–64), the binational US-Mexico guest worker system that led to the emigration of over four million Mexican men during and after World War II. Over a decade after the Bracero program ended, Mexican and US officials met privately to discuss ways Mexico might offset its now "chronic" overpopulation problem. The Mexican government suggested that the US government turn a blind eye to undocumented migration as it was vital to mitigating Mexico's unemployment issues.[13] Yet other stakeholders in Mexico and abroad believed a robust birth control campaign could do the work undocumented immigration to the United States could not: stem the birth rate among poor Mexican women.

Guadalupe de la Vega took up the population control mantle in the early 1970s with support across the US-Mexico border from Planned Parenthood of El Paso. De la Vega's spirited concern for Mexico's population issues resembled the activism of Betty Mary Goetting in the 1930s. There were deep connections between the two activists and their organizations. FEMAP represented the culmination of activism and advocacy on the part of the international family planning movement with ties to Planned Parenthood Federation of America (PPFA), the International Planned Parenthood Federation (IPPF), and Planned Parenthood of El Paso (PPEP). A deeper exploration of these connections provides a broader history of one of the borderlands' most powerful family planning institutions, showing how, over time, FEMAP became central to health and reproductive control in Mexico and a critical space for health care for El Paso residents as well. Along with Clinica Familiar La Fe (formerly the Father Rahm Clinic), FEMAP offered health care for residents in the Ciudad Juárez-El Paso metropolitan area. Yet, unlike Clinica Familiar La Fe, a pluralistic organization focused on community leadership and care, de la Vega, with support from very wealthy financiers, directed FEMAP's mission alone.

FEMAP and de la Vega's story is a critical turning point in the transnational movement of ideas about family planning and population control ideology in the US-Mexico borderlands—a region that for decades had experienced a ramping up of immigration controls. Despite the end of the formalized binational Bracero program at the end of 1964, the need for Mexican labor did not recede, and migration continued. Border Patrol and immigration controls became more coercive and brutal, particularly as multinational corporations, known as maquiladoras, began to appear in border communities along Mexico's north, attracting potential laborers to the region.

The proliferation of maquiladoras in Ciudad Juárez and other border cities is critical to the story of population control and the dissemination of contraceptives in Mexico's northern borderlands. As Guadalupe Arizpe de la Vega worked to bring greater awareness of contraception to Mexico, her husband, Federico de la Vega Mathews, became a central figure in establishing the exploitative maquiladora system in Juárez that was originally meant to "replace" the Bracero program by employing male workers. Over time, however, maquiladoras came to rely almost exclusively on the labor of impoverished Mexican women.[14] US manufacturers were "invited to move their factories south" to Mexico's northern border, and with Mexican federal subsidies, they built massive industrial parks in cities like Ciudad Juárez.[15]

After de la Vega Mathews's death in 2015, the *El Paso Times* editorial board declared that his name is a synonym for "development in Juárez (in) its support of education, the maquiladora industry, health and sports, which now transcend generations."[16] The newspaper noted that the family's most "important legacy" was the establishment of FEMAP "to address health and human development concerns in Juárez," a model "widely duplicated across Mexico and in US border areas."[17]

Chapter 6 maps out the history of FEMAP by tracing its connections to population control as labor control in conjunction with expanding family planning campaigns during the 1970s and 1980s. Guadalupe de la Vega's establishment of FEMAP in the borderlands is intimately tied to the lineage of neo-Malthusian activists and eugenic feminists, such as Betty Mary Goetting and Margaret Sanger. In earlier chapters, we followed the activism of Goetting and Sanger as they sought to oppose overpopulation by addressing Mexican-origin women's supposed hyperfertility. De la Vega's work is an extension of their movement. Not only did de la Vega receive support from Planned Parenthood of El Paso in her early quest to open a birth control clinic in Juárez, but she framed her crusade as one that would impact industrialization and modernization along Mexico's border by clamping down on Mexico's excessive population growth. Furthermore, her family's links to industrialization in northern Mexico, specifically the maquiladora industry, made de la Vega a complicated figure in the fight for greater access to family planning. Her public altruism and feminist leanings obscured other intentions deeply tied to what became a central motor for the Mexican economy in the 1980s and 1990s: cheap, exploitable, accessible feminized labor in factories a stone's throw from the US-Mexico border. This chapter charts the work of de la Vega and FEMAP, in line with the activism started by Goetting and Sanger before her, and how population control ideology crossed the border and laid the critical groundwork for labor control through the discipline of Mexican-origin women's reproduction.

Eugenic Feminism and Demographic Disasters in Mexico

Guadalupe Arizpe de La Vega's work and FEMAP's existence emerged from a longer history of eugenicists, demographers, scientists, doctors, philanthropists, political scientists, eugenic feminists, and other activists who sought to revive Thomas Malthus's eighteenth-century theory of population growth and resource depletion. Though many lauded Malthus's ideas in his day, Malthus's true legacy resides in the twentieth century's population control movement.[18] His treatise on population growth and the subsequent resource collapse that was sure to follow became a canonical idea for those interested in controlling and disciplining populations for different ends. Since the turn of the twentieth century, scientists, wealthy financiers, and activists in the United States and Europe had been consumed by what they believed to be rampant population growth among the "unfit" mostly marginalized, poor communities the world over; it was not until the 1950s and 1960s, however, that nation-states endorsed these endeavors explicitly to stem overpopulation and began to enact their own programs.

Historians have shown how Mexican scientists' and politicians' interest in population *quality* and *quantity* stretched back to before the revolutionary period and strengthened as concerns grew for the nation's ability to modernize properly and quickly after 1910.[19] Historian Alexandra Minna Stern explains that eugenics became the "handmaiden" that bound ideologies of heredity, such as mestizophilia and biotypology, together as science and policy changed and adapted over time.[20] After the 1910 revolution, policymakers and politicians attempted to socially engineer a population based on *mestizaje* ("the Black, the Indian, the Mongol, and the White"), or what Mexican philosopher José Vasconselos called *La Raza Cósmica*.[21] As Stern maintains, "The cult of the mestizo was a critical component of nationalism . . . [and] the 'mestizophilia' that characterized the postrevolutionary years was intimately linked to the emergence of a eugenics movement . . ." in Mexico.[22] In this way eugenics in Mexico developed differently from a US context. One key deviation concerned US eugenicists' obsession with an imagined white Anglo-Saxon racial purity as a critical component for human superiority. The "demodystopias" that shaped eugenic thinking in the United States—namely David Starr Jordan's, Lothrop Stoddard's, and Madison Grant's fears that white demographic decline would hasten the end of white civilization in the United States—did not exist within a Mexican context in the early parts of the twentieth century.[23]

Mexican eugenicists sought ways to address Mexico's "social problems" through a mishmash of sources, including "from the French medical art of puericulture, from Italian demography and criminology, from British biometrics and anthropometries, from US psychometrics, physiology, and endocrinology, and from other Latin American reconstructions."[24] The very existence of eugenic analysis signaled Mexico's emerging position in the international scientific vanguard.[25] Biologist Laura Suárez y López-Guazo contends that, as early as 1910, pamphlets concerned with the "hygiene of the species" were published in Mexico. The following year, *El Diario* published American Cuban writer Blanche Z. de Baralt's summary of British physician and eugenicist Caleb Saleeby's *Eugenic Feminism*, making a more gendered assertion.[26] Tucked among "beauty secret" articles and wrinkle cream advertisements, Baralt's summation of Saleeby's ideas promoted the notion that women could and should be at the forefront of proper breeding through marriage. While Baralt acknowledged that Saleeby's ideas were not novel in and of themselves, it was Saleeby's commitment to a "militant feminism" and his "declaration in favor of women's right to vote" that made his call for women's promotion of eugenics so important.[27]

Historian Emma Pérez reminds us that feminist demands for greater autonomy were part of Mexico's revolutionary nationalist milieu in the 1910s and 1920s. Toppling Mexico's thirty-five-year dictator, Porfirio Diaz, Pérez maintains, was an act by women and men protesting Diaz's neocolonial relationship with the United States, in effect demanding "Mexico for Mexicans." Mexican women, then, created their own feminist spaces within this nationalist moment in Mexico.[28] Ideas about reproductive control—later seen as part of US foreign intervention into Latin American politics—were not part of this neocolonial relationship at the time. By 1916, the first Feminist Congress was called to order in Yucatán, helping establish the Feminist Council calling for "women's emancipation" in Mexico.[29] The following year, a Regional Workers Convention was held in Tampico, where women workers demanded the right to "prevent unlimited procreation" as it might interfere with a worker's livelihood or when it might imply the degeneration of the species.[30] This culminated in a massive scandal after a pamphlet published by Margaret Sanger titled "La Brújula del Hogar" made the rounds in feminist circles around Mexico in 1922.[31] As one Mexican scholar put it, "the Mexican state's contraposition [to birth control] was establishing Mother's Day" the next year.[32] Still the "militant feminism" exalted by Saleeby via Baralt's promotion of his work in 1911 was not outside Mexican women's consideration at the time. Many Mexican women across the country were committed to a revolutionary nationalism that included discussions of family planning because of rampant maternal and infant mortality rates. As historian Nancy Stepan Leys observed, by 1929, "a new Mexican Society of Puericulture (Sociedad de Puericultura) . . . had created a eugenics section, where issues of heredity, disease, infantile sexuality, sex education, and birth control—radical ideas for their time and place—were discussed in relation to the care of the child."[33]

Mexican feminists' sustained interest in reproductive control, however, was not responsible for major shifts or changes in family planning and fertility. While feminists were interested in *planificación natal* during and after the Mexican revolution, some scholars have wrongly attributed falling fertility rates to a concerted effort by feminists to promote birth control around the country.[34] As demographer Gustavo Cabrera explains, the interruption of demographic expansion during the Porfirian era was linked to deaths and social changes caused by "armed struggle, the 'Spanish influenza' epidemic, Mexican emigration to the United States, and the decline in the birth rate resulting from the temporary separation of married couples and the postponement of new unions."[35] Of course, it is difficult to determine an exact cause for demographic decline since census results for those decades remain in question.[36]

Others have gone further to argue for a deeper analysis of the "demographic disaster" Mexicans experienced during the revolution. In his article "Missing Millions: The Costs of the Mexican Revolution," demographic historian Robert McCaa asks if the Mexican Revolution was the worst demographic disaster since the conquest.[37] Stern and others suggest that between 1910 and 1917, Mexico lost nearly 5 percent of its population and infant mortality soared due in part to the lack of food and potable water, which produced the proliferation of gastrointestinal diseases.[38] As discussions of overpopulation centered on Mexican-origin people's supposed hyperfertility in the decades after the revolution in US cities such as El Paso, it is important to note the demographic catastrophe that preceded a demographic upswing in the years after 1930 in Mexico.

While there were attempts to revive interest in family planning throughout the early parts of the century, Cabrera maintains that in the aftermath of the various periods of national violence and war, the Mexican state's focus was in increasing its population. The Mexican state, led for decades by the Partido Revolucionario Institucional (PRI), viewed the expansion of its population as inextricably linked to economic development and a strengthening of its nationalist aims. The government's pronatalist stance based on spurious connections of unending modernization and development via population growth established ideas that led to Mexico's high fertility rates as compared to other Latin American countries and the United States. As demographer Amado de Miguel contends, this belief supported the political aims of the PRI, religious conservatives, and demographers in the country for nearly sixty years.[39] Another Mexican scholar stated more succinctly that the Mexican state's philosophy during this period boiled down to "gobernar es poblar," or to govern is to populate.[40] The Mexican state concentrated its efforts in improving health programs, access to medical care, and reducing high mortality rates among its citizens. From 1940 to 1970, Mexico's population expanded exponentially and by 1970 boasted 50 million inhabitants.[41] As late as 1971, after international efforts had begun providing Mexico with family planning infrastructure and population control advocates marked Mexico as too densely populated to progress in a modernizing world, President Luis Echeverría continued to exalt Mexico's rising fertility and its connections to unending economic development.[42] By 1975, as Mexico City hosted the first United Nation's conference on women's issues, concerns about reproductive rights and population policy had been a critical element to the conference along with greater access to education, health care, and employment opportunities for women.[43]

Therefore, contrary to popular beliefs, high fertility rates were not a timeless or inherent aspect of Mexican-origin people's culture or biology. Rather, extensive family sizes were in many cases produced via state forces seeking economic and social development in twentieth-century Mexico. Scientific studies and theories about Mexican-origin women's innate hyper-fertility were, in fact, racist constructions.[44] US birth control activists, anti-immigrant eugenicists, and later population control advocates and demographers had charged Mexican-origin women with unhinged procreation since the days of C. S. Babbitt. This racist logic based on cultural stereotypes of blind Catholic devotion, superstition, lasciviousness, ignorance, and a deep love of family constructed Mexican-origin women as naturally profusive procreators. These bigoted conclusions manifested themselves throughout the twentieth century in US population control schemes, immigration and welfare debates, and racializing projects that from their inception determined Mexican-origin women (and later all Latinas) as suffering from excessive fertility. Some demographers and historians of Mexico suggest that the dramatic rise in fertility rates among Mexican-origin women was manufactured by the Mexican state in the twentieth century—partially in response to a "disappointing" nineteenth century and the "demographic disaster" during the revolutionary period.[45]

What Mexico saw as a model of third-world development driven by state-led capitalist efforts, others saw as a population out of control.[46] As economist Zadia Feliciano states, "Mexico had one of the fastest-growing populations in the world during the 1960s, almost three times the annual growth rate (1.2%) of the United States and almost two times the annual rate of Canada (1.8%)."[47] By this point, most demographers of the period had already adopted the "demographic transition theory," making reductions in fertility rates critical to the "modernization process."[48] Mexico's population growth occurred just as developed nations openly supported population control advocates in their aims to curb populations they deemed "explosive." India and China had already begun their own efforts at population control a decade before, and by the 1970s, as historian Mathew Connelly maintains, international organizations such as the UN Fund for Population Activities, the World Bank, and USAID were harnessing the power of population control policies beyond family planning.[49]

El Paso: On the Doorstop of a Population Explosion

Movements for international population control placed Mexico's burgeoning populace at the center of Planned Parenthood of El Paso's mission. PPEP felt compelled to prevent Mexico's population from spilling over the border. In 1963, regional director and former president of PPEP Cornelia Love Owen faced a crowded El Paso Kiwanis Club meeting to engage in what newspapers called a "frank and open discussion of a controversial subject." She declared a population emergency in Ciudad Juárez—El Paso's sister city—stating that its birth rates were the highest in the world, placing "a problem of international scope at El Paso's doorstep."[50] Since the turn of the twentieth century, white Texans had warned of a human deluge washing across the national border from Mexico. Even as Texas agriculture, cattle ranching, manufacturing, and domestic service greatly benefited from the constant flow of human labor crossing the border, the specter of being overrun by Mexicans had been a consistent narrative in the state.

While immigration controls were strengthened at various points throughout the century, soothing some racial anxieties, many in the birth control movement continued to put forth the idea that strict fertility control was needed, consistently attacking the twin problems of immigration and overpopulation.[51] Owen compared Juárez's numbers, 63 per 1,000 births, to those in all communist China—45 per 1,000, nearly a decade prior to China's draconian one-child policy. These comparisons were common in the borderlands as PPEP often gestured to Juárez and, by extension, South El Paso as places in danger of becoming *India* or *China*, two internationally recognized countries whose populations were deemed out of control. That same year, in a letter to PPEP's president, one PPEP member and well-respected public relations guru in El Paso, Bill Lynde, suggested similarly when he wrote, "I don't think you can spend much time walking the streets of Hong Kong or Singapore or Calcutta or Cairo or Caracas (or South El Paso) and still labor under the impression the more babies the merrier."[52]

Owen went on to remind her audience that higher fertility rates raised the "cost of welfare, the Aid to Dependent Children program and operation of health and hospital services" and, potentially, cost the city thousands of dollars, as women sought underground abortions in Juárez and then crossed back to El Paso hospitals for extended care.[53] She stated unequivocally that PPEP was "concerned with quality rather than quantity of children."[54] Her statement is telling in that, by the 1960s, eugenics and its focus on "better breeding" had been subsumed due in part to revelations of Nazi atrocities during World War II and supplanted by neo-Malthusian concerns for population quantity in relation to natural resources. Yet championing child-spacing for the "protection" of mother and child was intimately tied to notions of eugenically fit families.[55] Her statement was also a direct attack against the Mexican state's pronatalist ideology. Owen suggested Mexico cared more about quantity than quality of its citizens.

What Owen and Lynde posited as a major concern for El Paso—an out-of-control Mexican population that threatened the United States from inside and outside the national border—quickly became part of the borderlands' media landscape. The 1960s saw dozens of newspaper articles denouncing falling birth rates among whites in Texas and the United States writ large while simultaneously sowing the seeds of fear as journalists declared that not only was Mexico's population growing exponentially, but lands for agriculture and industry in Mexico were "becoming scarce."[56] One 1967 headline announced, "Birth Rate in Texas Has Dropped to 30-Year Low," with Texas's health department statistician, John Pokorny, suggesting that it was "the birth control pill" fulfilling its promise. State birth rates were as low as they had been in 1950, Pokorny stated, and, importantly, the rate of population per 1,000 fell to a low not seen since 1930.[57] Pokorny could not prove conclusively that contraception was to blame for this precipitous drop in birth rates since "scientifically you can't point to anything definite because the studies that might prove it just haven't been done." Yet Pokorny concluded that the Pill, having been released in the US mainland in 1960, "must be one of the reasons."[58]

It was clear Pokorny was not the only person who thought so, and correlations between falling birth rates among whites and contraception were made succinctly by *El Paso Times* editor and the newspaper's vice president, W. J. Hooten, in 1967. In his well-established "Everyday Events by W. J. Hooten," he surmised that falling birth rates among the white population would soon prove disastrous. "The non-white population is increasing much more rapidly that the white population," he stated. And while birth control was "operating efficiently among the white race," contraception was not working well among nonwhites. Therefore, he cautioned that "the white race all over the world had better be taking a look at its hole card" or it was going to be in "real trouble before too long."[59] This shows how the specter of a disappearing white race—what white supremacists at the turn of the twentieth century called *race suicide* and white nationalists today call *race genocide*—was being recalibrated by mid-century.[60] As in the past, El Paso's press largely centered white El Pasoans' concerns in most city matters; Hooten had certainly done so for decades. As scholar of English Jonna Perrillo explains, through his column, Hooten had delineated public discussion in favor of bilingualism—the teaching of Spanish in El Paso public schools in the 1940s—to help protect the social status of Anglo children and their "ability to compete in a growing border city where more citizens spoke Spanish than English."[61] Hooten's 1967 concerns for a vanishing white race were in line with his past support for protecting Anglo supremacy in El Paso.

Although historians are charged with tracing change over time, we must watch for repetition in ideology and rhetoric. As Emma Pérez reminds us, there are critical moments when tracing repetition, "the manner in which rhetoric is repeated to serve similar kinds of purposes," enlightens seemingly new interests in old subjects.[62] In this case, concerns for overpopulation in the borderlands had been part of public discourse since the Mexican Revolution drove men and *women* across the US-Mexico border into El Paso. By the 1930s, when Betty Mary Goetting and Margaret Sanger marketed the necessity for birth control because of supposed overpopulation in El Paso's south-side barrios, neo-Malthusian ideas, demanding smaller families, had blended with eugenic philosophies touting an end to high fertility among the poor and hereditarily "unfit." In the borderlands, technologies employed to control Mexican-origin women's reproduction changed, while the desire of white residents to do so never swayed. The steady drumbeat of "birth control, birth control, birth control" as the miracle that would save a historically white city from the perils of the reproductive aftermath of Mexican immigration only became louder as the century wore on.

Overpopulation, Maquiladoras, and the de la Vega Dynasty

During these same years, Guadalupe Arizpe de la Vega became an active member of the population control movement in Mexico. Her entrance into the birth and population control universe was akin to Margaret Sanger's story. In 1912, Sanger, a nurse working in the immigrant enclaves of Brooklyn, New York, witnessed the death of Sadie Sachs, a young mother of three children, from a botched, self-induced abortion after she had begged Sanger for birth control information weeks before. De la Vega, like Sanger, also claimed a woman's traumatic abortion story as the impetus for her activism. In the late 1960s, de la Vega read a newspaper account about a young mother of nine children who had attempted to stab herself in the abdomen to abort her tenth pregnancy. De la Vega later visited the mother in jail and inquired as to why the mother did not practice family planning. To de la Vega's surprise, the woman "lacked the most basic knowledge about preventing pregnancy." She was inspired to help the mother obtain legal counsel, beginning her life's work educating poor women about the importance of family planning.[63] This powerful narrative became part of de la Vega's persona later in her life—for instance, when CNN's Anderson Cooper honored de la Vega as a 2010 recipient of the network's CNN Heroes award for her dedication to FEMAP, de la Vega repeated the narrative.

In the early days of her career as an advocate for contraception, however, de la Vega combined a charitable spirit with a deep desire for economic development and population control in Ciudad Juárez and greater Mexico. Her philosophy was in line with the work of her husband, Federico de la Vega Mathews, an important financier in the US-Mexico borderlands and one of the founders of the maquiladora industry in Juárez. The de la Vegas were *fronterizos* by birth.[64] Guadalupe de la Vega was born Maria Guadalupe Arizpe de la Masa to her parents Emilio Arizpe and Elena de la Masa in Monterrey, Nuevo León, on March 10, 1936. She was born the same year

El Paso attempted to change the racial designation of Mexicans in the county from white to "colored" to numerically correct the horrendous infant mortality data showing high death rates among Mexican-origin infants. Though the attempt by public health officials failed—due, in part, to major backlash from the Mexican American community—this event served as a critical turning point in bringing the birth control movement to the borderlands. In some ways, this chronology brings de la Vega's life into the borderlands constellation of reproductive health activism joining women like Betty Mary Goetting on the population control side of the spectrum and Amelia Castillo fighting for reproductive freedom on the other. Although de la Vega sought to align herself with relief and welfare efforts, specifically lifting poor Mexican women out of poverty, her concerns for overpopulation and her husband's businesses severely complicate her altruistic mission in the borderlands.

While Guadalupe de la Vega's family connected their lineage directly to Mexico's northern border, Federico de la Vega Mathews was born in El Paso, Texas, on September 1, 1931, to Artemio de la Vega and Kathryn Mathews. His mother was born at the turn of the century in Midland, Texas, and his father hailed from Asturias, Spain.[65] De la Vega Senior immigrated to Mexico at the age of fourteen, arriving in Ciudad Juárez in 1928. The Asturian rose to prominence over the years, becoming a central figure in industry and commercial enterprises as well as land development.[66] Federico continued his father's businesses. In collaboration with various other Mexican industrialists of the region, including Antonio J. Bermudez, Fernando Borreguero, and Alfonso Murguia, de la Vega Mathews expanded his family's reign in the region in education and development and as one of the masterminds behind the maquiladora system across Mexico's northern border.[67] Later, de la Vega Mathews established Grupo De La Vega, a consortium of companies including Almacenes Distribuidores de la Frontera, operating Del Río and Superette y Oasis convenience stores as well as Inmobiliaria De la Vega y Altec Purificación (Agua Alaska), Operadora Alpic (Domino's Pizza), Petrol gas stations, and distribution of Carta Blanca beer. For decades, he held the monopoly of beer contracts in Ciudad Juárez, amassing a fortune.[68]

As Mexican historian Luis Aboites Aguilar surmises, it was high unemployment and massive tax shortages that paved the way for the birth of the maquila system in Mexico's northern borderlands.[69] The maquiladora system—foreign-owned assembly and manufacturing factories, mostly in the garment and electronics industry—was part of Mexico's Border

Industrialization Program (BIP) initiated in 1965 as Mexico saw the detrimental effects of ending its Bracero program with the United States. Thousands of people returning from the United States and others newly arrived from Mexico's interior found themselves in Mexico's northern borderlands. With this new program, borderland magnates, like de la Vega Mathews, in conjunction with the Mexican state, sought to "provide employment and to foster economic development" using foreign industry to create and manage these assembly plants.[70] As US public health scholars noted in the 1980s, the rapid growth of the maquiladora system, expanding from approximately fifty-seven plants in 1967 to nearly one thousand in the late 1980s, caused massive strains on access to housing and health care in the region. While the Mexican state had guaranteed health and wellness as a right under the 1917 constitution—establishing the Instituto Mexicano de Seguro Social (IMSS) through legislation in 1943—the maquiladora system had placed great strain on the few recourses that existed in Ciudad Juárez.[71] FEMAP became part of the public–private health care ecosystem that had developed in the decades since. Guadalupe de la Vega's inauguration of a family planning center, just as maquiladoras expanded their reach across the nearly two-thousand-mile stretch of the Mexico-US border, could not have come at a more opportune time.

Linkages between Guadalupe Arizpe de la Vega's population control advocacy and her husband's business deserve further scrutiny as scholars have rightly argued how maquiladora work became women's work in the latter half of twentieth century.[72] Historian Vicki Ruiz observed that "maquiladoras prefer[red] young women on the assembly line."[73] Industrialists' predilection for a young, single, female workforce was evident early on. One *El Paso-Herald Post* journalist confirmed, "A Juarez labor force comprised of some 70 percent women workers account for 4,000 jobs created by twin plants in Juarez since 1966."[74] Accompanying his news story in the paper were various pictures including one of hundreds of women waiting in a long line outside the Antonio J. Bermudez Industrial Park and RCA plant in 1972. Bermudez, along with Federico de la Vega Mathews, were godfathers to the maquiladora system in Juárez.

By the 1980s, several important data points were established for women working at various hierarchies of the maquiladora system. For instance, electronic industries preferred younger women than those in garment shops, an average age of twenty-one to twenty-seven respectively. Those assembling electronics were also better educated, averaging a total of eight years of schooling, than women working as seamstresses with only six years. Most importantly, electronic assembly plants preferred unmarried women, often requiring them to show medical examinations that were "nothing more than a 'simple' pregnancy test," likely confirming a negative result.[75] Policies that prevented women from starting their jobs until maquiladora administrators could verify workers' menstrual cycles became part and parcel of companies' labor management strategies.[76] This kind of reproductive control—one that was integral to Mexico's rising maquiladora system—needed guidance from someone who understood what was at stake if women workers did not get adequate access to family planning. Ciudad Juárez would become a perfect case for testing the limits and borders of population control via reproductive labor and biological reproductive control championed by Guadalupe de la Vega.

The birth control movement in cities like El Paso had made working women's family planning decisions at top priority for decades. In 1964, PPEP board of directors launched the "Industrial Campaign." Sending letters to executives of local industry and factories, especially those employing "large numbers of women," PPEP suggested that a pivotal way to "reduce employee turn-over" was to lower the number of unwanted pregnancies among their women workers.[77] Although women workers had historically been on the frontlines of demanding access to contraception in the early twentieth century, from feminist workers in Mexico to activists like Emma Goldman in the United States, by mid-century it was industrialists who sought to harness birth control's potential for a well-managed and maintained workforce. Contraception was not simply about reducing population size, but its greatest possibilities lay in disciplining and controlling women workers during their reproductive years.

In her 1983 groundbreaking study *For We Are Sold, I and My People: Women and Industry in Mexico's Frontier*, anthropologist María Patricia Fernández-Kelly describes in elucidating detail the trajectory of the "border industrialization program" and its overreliance on young women workers as a central tenet of its business model in Ciudad Juárez. She concedes that, unlike other areas in Mexico, the country's border areas, in particular Ciudad Juárez, saw rapid demographic changes and increases in population.[78] Border cities like Tijuana, Mexicali, and Ciudad Juárez also represented the most densely populated cities in the Mexico-US borderlands. As other scholars have noted, these cities represented major migration hubs, making them gathering places for Mexicans seeking to cross the border to the United States.[79] Migrants coupled with high birth rates "exerted much pressure upon the border communities' capacity to provide for their citizens' welfare."[80]

While Fernández-Kelly's use of "citizens' welfare" refers to the city's inability to provide employment and basic housing to its rapidly expanding population, I extend this to mean what we now call the "social safety net"—programs offering low-income and working poor communities access to housing, health care, education, and food. Extending the meaning of "citizen's welfare" helps contextualize the history of FEMAP and Guadalupe de la Vega's rise as Ciudad Juárez's philanthropic Polaris. According to FEMAP's own narrative, de la Vega established the first birth control clinic in 1973 as a "civil, private, non-profit association, when the first [Mexican] population policy was approved and when the maquiladora industry began in our region, making it [FEMAP] a pioneering institution in the field of family planning and community work with volunteer fieldworkers, focusing its work especially on maternal and child health."[81] FEMAP, like PPEP and Clinica La Fe, filled in a health care gap the state could not or had refused to occupy on either side of the borderline.

Unlike Clinica La Fe, however, PPEP and FEMAP were not community-organized clinics. They were top-down institutions built by affluent crusaders, shaping social norms they believed they had the moral obligation to influence. Over time, these clinics became fundamental to the very infrastructure of the city. De la Vega's birth control clinic preceded the formation of Consejo Nacional de Población (CONAPO) in Mexico. CONAPO, installed by presidential decree, provided a nexus to the Mexican state between organizations, scholars, financial institutions, and other sectors of the government dedicated to reshaping and recalibrating the "reproductive patterns in Mexican society," likely to benefit Mexico's economy and the management of the state.[82] The state had no interest in questioning FEMAP or surveilling its work since de la Vega supported—with her own money—the state's population control dictum. Her family, insulated from state oversight and spearheading Mexico's new nationalist demographic mission, earned cultural capital, allowing the de la Vegas' smooth trajectory as the people's oligarchs.[83] FEMAP's significance—its far-reaching tentacles encircling nearly every social service needed in Ciudad Juárez—outlasted Planned Parenthood of El Paso. But in the early days, when De la Vega was seeking support for FEMAP, she reached across the border to her counterparts in El Paso and found a receptive audience. PPEP had been monitoring Mexico's rise in the movement since it noted the establishment of Mexico's first birth control clinic in Mexico City in 1959.[84] As historian Martha Liliana Espinos Tavares maintains, even before the Mexican state had formally accepted birth control as a tool for combating overpopulation, private organizations and representatives from the Population Council and the Ford Foundation had expended resources to help private Mexican citizens start their own clinics.[85] De la Vega later tapped into those resources as well. Meanwhile, 1973, the year Guadalupe de la Vega opened the first birth control clinic in Ciudad Juárez, became an auspicious year for reproductive freedom and population control in the Texas-Mexico borderlands. Indeed, it would be a year that would shape local, national, and international plans for access to reproductive health care and bolster claims that overpopulation was one of the greatest threats facing humanity.

1973: An Auspicious Year for Reproductive Control

The year 1973 represents a pivotal moment in women's history as the United States Supreme Court decided that under the Fourteenth Amendment women were guaranteed a constitutional right to abortion as a matter of privacy. The fight for abortion rights had been a signature demand of the women's liberation movement of the late 1960s and 1970s. The liberalization of abortion restrictions had also been a centerpiece of some in the population control movement as well, including prominent leaders such as Richard Bowers of Zero Population Growth (ZPG) and the National Association to Repeal Abortion Laws (NARAL).[86] The mutual support between some second-wave feminists and population control advocates caused many within the Black, Chicano/a, and Puerto Rican youth movements to equate abortion with genocide.[87] Although many women celebrated the decision of *Roe v. Wade* in January 1973 as a major victory for reproductive freedom, other women, namely poor women and women of color, continued to point to the growing numbers of coercive sterilizations in the South and Southwest as a sign that the fight was merely just beginning.[88]

In the borderlands, Planned Parenthood of El Paso had been slow in its public response to the issue of abortion. Only three days before the high court's decision in *Roe V. Wade* sparked a firestorm across the nation, PPEP publicly addressed abortion. As it celebrated its Thirty-Sixth Annual Planned Parenthood of El Paso meeting, Sarah Ragle Weddington—the Texas attorney who argued the landmark abortion decision before the Supreme Court—gave the event's keynote lecture, titled "The Law and Planned Parenthood."[89] She urged the El Paso audience and PPEP leadership to join her and others to help pass more laws in Texas protecting and supporting women's access to reproductive health care. The following year, Dr. W. Taft Moore, the first man to preside over PPEP, expressed the organization's unease with the high court's decision on abortion, stating, "At this time we as a board seem uncertain as to the qualitative extent of our obligation concerning the question of abortion."[90] In Ciudad Juárez, the abortion issue remained on high alert as clandestine abortion clinics and providers proliferated there in the years before *Roe*. Juárez residents—politicians and the Catholic Church in particular—were sensitive to references made in United States and Mexican newspapers calling their city "the largest abortion mill" in the Western hemisphere.[91]

Overpopulation fears, however, rarely failed to draw concern. In his 1974 address, Dr. Moore insisted that while abortion remained a touchy subject for their local organization, PPEP's interest in population control endured. "You would think we could relax—but no!" he wrote in the meeting's program. He continued: "The birth rate in the United States is approximately 15 per 1,000 population. Ours in El Paso is 30 per 1,000, and that of Juarez is one of the highest in the world at 49 per 1,000. Our goals in Planned Parenthood aim at the very core of many, if not most, of the world's problems. Without overpopulation, there would be no energy crisis. Pollution is a function of overpopulation. Welfare and excessive taxation are results of pool [*sic*] family planning. We must work harder to reach more people, especially in this area with its exaggerated need."[92] Local PPEP leadership's enthusiasm for combating high fertility rates matched national and international concerns for global overpopulation. All human crisis led back to one critical issue: too many people on the planet, most of them lying in wait across the border in Ciudad Juárez, Mexico.

Texas politicians voiced similar fears. George H. W. Bush, then ambassador to the United Nations and an already well-known name in Texas after his brief stint in the US House of Representatives representing Texas's Seventh District, put forth his vision for population control, writing the foreword to Phyllis Tilson Piotrow's often-cited *World Population Crisis: The United States Response* (1973). Despite his conservative leanings, George Sr., like his father Prescott, was a proponent of family planning—both men were supporters of Planned Parenthood Federation of America.[93] As a US representative, he recalled how "perplexed" he and his male colleagues were to confront "famine in India, unwanted babies in the United States, poverty that seemed to form an unbreakable chain for millions of people—." Even with his disdain for "big government," Bush heeded the words of then Planned Parenthood of America President Alan Guttmacher, supporting a robust investment in family planning services. "So we took the lead in Congress in providing money and urging—in fact, even requiring—that in the

United States family planning services be available for every woman, not just the private patient with her own gynecologist," Bush wrote.[94]

On the international front, Bush was "impressed" by the lobbying of William Draper, the founder of Population Crisis Committee, and his stance that "economic development overseas would be a miserable failure unless the developing countries had the knowledge and supplies families needed to control fertility."[95] According to Connelly, Draper had been the most interested in focusing on Mexico as the center of population explosion woes. Draper seemed to be the "catalyst" for opening Mexico up to the population control movement brokering a "$1.2 million" funding deal between Mexico's minister of finance and the UN Fund for Population Activities to be executed by Mexico's secretary of the interior rather than the Mexico's minister of health.[96]

Bridging national and international concerns for economic development and political stability, Bush synthesized the US government's position toward family planning at home and abroad. The late 1960s and early 1970s saw a demonstrable turn from private foundations' and organizations' financial support of overpopulation studies to governments' financial investments in research on the subject.[97] Bush, and other Texas politicians, such as President Lyndon B. Johnson (as discussed in chapter 5), led government efforts in support of family planning as central to curbing poverty, eliminating out-of-wedlock births, and most importantly curtailing a population explosion from below.[98] De la Vega's work coincided nicely with the efforts of PPEP and Texas politicians—Republican and Democrat—to put population control at the center of transnational border policies and action.

In 1973, Guadalupe de la Vega opened her first clinic in the same location where FEMAP's Hospital de La Familia sits today. Nestled between the two major international bridges connecting Ciudad Juárez to El Paso, the clinic faced Calle Malecón connecting foot traffic from the Santa Fe Bridge to the clinic's left with Stanton Street bridge on its right. Easily accessible to residents in both Ciudad Juárez and El Paso's south-side barrios, de la Vega's clinic offered at first only family planning—various forms of birth control and educational materials. Over time and due to the great need in the community, the clinic began offering various forms of reproductive health services, including maternal and infant care. According to de la Vega, the clinic "was just a few rooms and was not equipped for delivering babies." But as the story goes, "De La Vega opened the doors to a desperate woman in labor"—starting a decades-long expansion process.[99] Only three years later, de la Vega had been welcomed to sit on PPEP's board of directors. PPEP's 1976 president's report devoted one line to de la Vega's major accomplishment: "Board member Lupe de La Vega succeeded in opening a birth control clinic in Cd. Juarez, a city with one of the highest birth rates in the world."[100] This was the same year Patrick O'Rourke presided over PPEP's leadership after spearheading the hunt for an activist to open birth control clinics in Juárez just a few years before. After de la Vega joined its board, the hunt was over.

FEMAP: Borderlands Health Care Enigma

FEMAP's internal workings remain, for the most part, unknown. Unlike PPEP's large cache of internal documents, there has been no formal avenue for accessing FEMAP's archives. Newspaper reports and scholarly investigations into the organization's programs offer opportunities for understanding FEMAP's programs and services. One major continuity among the various reproductive health clinics in the borderlands was the use of the "promotora" or "field-worker" model. In 1984, a US newspaper described FEMAP's field-worker efforts:

> The Mexican Army, hotel operators, cigarette vendors, tavern owners all are part of Evangelina Martinez Salmon's clientele. She's not selling a product. She's selling an idea: family planning. In her spare time and that can mean up to 15 hours a day the Juarez elementary school teacher commands a team of 500 volunteers who distribute free contraceptives and health information to the people of this border city. With the trunk and back seat of her battered 1970 Mercury Cougar jammed with birth-control [sic] pills and condoms, the chain-smoking Mrs. Martinez races down rutted streets, stopping to talk with almost every woman of child-bearing age she can find . . . Mrs. Martinez's green Cougar, nicknamed the "Parrot," is regarded as a symbol of the de la Vega program. She drives the car at high speeds from more settled areas of the city into shantytowns flung up by thousands of migrants from Mexico's rural areas. She negotiates dry riverbeds and mud—clogged ditches or speeds through a hairpin turn without missing a puff on her Benson and Hedges. "I never go in reverse," she says. "Every step forward there are new people." In 2½ hours one recent day, she distributed 400 pills and 500 condoms. She lets almost no one capable of having children get past her. "How many children do you have?" she asked

one woman on a wind-swept street. "Nine," was the answer. "Why didn't you have an operation (sterilization)?" "My husband didn't want me to." "OK, we'll operate on him." She passes out free passes to a clinic that is part of the program. Women receive tubal ligations, Pap smears, intrauterine device insertions, venereal disease screening and other health services. Babies also are delivered.[101]

Evangelina Martinez Salmon's enthusiasm and wares did not appear as if by magic. De la Vega, interviewed later in the article, recruited Martinez to the cause—selling the "idea" of family planning to the poor and working-class women of Juárez. At first, Martinez described her incredulity at de la Vega's concern for these women. She did not "trust" de la Vega. She even threw a rock through the windshield of de la Vega's car. But in the end, "Mrs. de la Vega persisted, and Mrs. Martinez relented."[102]

Martinez said she began to see dramatic results as she brought others into the fold. When she first began soliciting reproductive-age women with de la Vega (see fig. 6.2), they reached women with large families, as most had six or seven children. As Martinez recruited more promotoras and they managed to branch out farther into the city's colonias,[103] family sizes dropped to an average of three children per woman, Martinez stated.[104] Dr. Enrique Suarez Toriello, a physician associated with FEMAP, argued that there was still much to be done. Although FEMAP "reaches 39 percent of married women of child-bearing age in Juarez, the program covers only 7 percent of unmarried, fertile women," Dr. Suarez observed. Many in the latter group were teenagers.[105] FEMAP's insistence on reaching the younger demographic aligns with maquiladoras' desire for younger women and girls—unmarried and without children—for factory work.[106]

According to Fernández-Kelly, between 1978 and 1979, "fully 21% of the female workers in Ciudad Juárez's maquiladoras are between the ages of 16 and 18." Of the workers in her study, over 57 percent were single women, and the majority in this group, over 69 percent, "were daughters living with their parents."[107] Nearly 64 percent were born outside Ciudad Juárez; most were from Chihuahua, Durango, and Coahuila, although most had lived in Ciudad Juárez for more than a decade.[108] A majority of young women workers had little to no previous work experience. Of those who did have earlier work experience, many had labored as maids in El Paso at very young ages, between thirteen and fifteen.[109] Maquiladora managers prized young, unmarried, and childless workers for their potential productivity and to pay them low wages. Fernández-Kelly's ethnographic work reveals that

FIGURE 6.2 Guadalupe Arizpe de la Vega, 1986 Planned Parenthood International Advocate Workshop El Paso. MS 286, folder 10, box 13, Planned Parenthood Records, C. L. Sonnichsen Special Collections Department, University of Texas at El Paso Library.

maquiladora managers and promoters hired women over men because "of their putative higher levels of skill and performance, because of their quality of their hand work, because of their willingness to comply to monotonous, repetitive and highly exhausting assignments and because of their docility," discouraging unionization efforts.[110]

And still, there were thousands of working mothers among the maquila proletariat. Some married, others widowed, separated, or divorced, overseeing the "proliferation of female-headed households'" in the expansion of the maquiladora system.[111] Over time, their wages became critical to the sustainability of their families—children, parents, and siblings. As Fernández-Kelly concludes, "most maquiladora workers can hardly be considered as supplementary wage earners."[112] Given these figures and insights, it is critical to view FEMAP's distribution of birth control among working-class girls and women of Ciudad Juárez as having multiple goals and objectives.

First, the organization's adherence to Mexico's family planning mandate imposed by international and domestic concerns for overpopulation put FEMAP in the good graces of these various actors. Lifelong members of the Partido Revolucionario Institucional (PRI), the de la Vegas did well to oblige the government's mission.[113] Additionally, most of FEMAP's budget relied exclusively on private fundraising. International efforts were already underway, supplying de la Vega with private financing and various kinds of contraceptives. In the decades that followed, local industry began to "invest" in her version of community health care, outside her own family's financing of FEMAP's endeavors. Second, interest in disciplining women's reproduction went beyond population control directives from the state or international agencies. FEMAP's contraceptive campaigns supported reproductive domestication of the local workforce, educating women to be both better workers and world citizens. The maquiladora management's decision to employ women with "acute economic needs" represented, as Fernández-Kelly maintains, "the use of the most vulnerable sector of the population" to achieve "greater productivity and larger profits."[114]

Lastly, the *need* for population control stretched past the anxiety-riddled discourse and rationale that too many people on the planet was bad. Rather, in the case of the Ciudad Juárez-El Paso region, the model served the "demographic transition theory" enhancing a modernization process informed by a fledgling neoliberalism, one brought into full bloom during the 1980s by the fall of the Soviet Union, the rise of Ronald Reagan in the United States, and Margaret Thatcher in the United Kingdom. As eugenics was the handmaiden to a spectrum of ideologies bringing science and policy to bear on reproduction in the early twentieth century, so too was overpopulation discourse a handmaiden to neoliberal policies and structures meant to discipline a demographically massive group of women workers. FEMAP provided an essential nexus point for addressing economic and immigration woes, health care gaps, and continued empowerment of borderland oligarchs.

Population control advocates in the United States took notice. By the 1980s, the next generation of population control advocates began to take the reins of the movement. Like their intellectual elders, these men were also concerned with overpopulation, immigration, and reproduction. Garrett James Hardin, an ecologist and professor at the University of California Santa Barbara who dedicated his early career to curbing overpopulation via the promotion of contraceptives and abortion, began to inquire about the de la Vegas' organization in the borderlands. Hardin associated with countless population control advocates and xenophobes, often with too much time and money on their hands. One such associate, William Thaddeus Rowland Jr, was a businessman, and had spent much of his life serving as a board member of prominent organizations, including Planned Parenthood of Essex County, Council of World Affairs, and the American Foreign Policy Association.[115] In 1985, Rowland, along with Hardin, founded the Action Committee of Americans for Population Issues (ACAPI), a "binational organization" created between Mexican and US citizens (see fig. 6.3).[116] Hardin and Rowland believed organizations, such as IPPF, were not strident enough and more concrete connections between Mexico must be made to turn the tide on immigration and overpopulation. The de la Vegas initially agreed to join them.[117]

The members, seven Americans and seven Mexicans, first met at the de la Vega home in May 1986 to discuss the direction of the organization. According to notes from the meeting, Guadalupe de la Vega sought to convince Hardin and Rowland that it was possible to offer reproductive services focused on population control while also paying close attention to women's needs. "Women must have control over their own fertility—often, this is the first decision they have made," she said. She also made sure to point to differences in attitudes between the United States and Mexico, stating, "Family planning in Mexico is a human right. In the US family planning is related to abortion. Not so in Mexico."[118] Hardin, however, later pushed two critical issues to de la Vega, "immigration and abortion," explaining that these would "have to be faced sooner or later." Those comments seemed to dash hopes for the meeting. While Rowland seemed to believe things had gone well, the air cooled between the de la Vegas, Hardin, and Rowland. In the months that passed, Guadalupe de la Vega expressed concern over the ACAPI's mission, suggesting that perhaps this could disrupt FEMAP's money streams. Hardin, in a letter to Rowland, responded brusquely to de la Vega's fears. "Of course she is wrong, but it is just another proof that those who have a project in the area we are addressing, are worthless to us," he said.[119]

It took nearly a year to convince her, but eventually de la Vega came around to the idea that the connections Rowland and Hardin offered them went beyond access to birth control. Rowland reported in a missive to Hardin that "Lupe finally understands that ACAPI is not just more family planning. She is now enthusiastic about getting the businessmen of Mexico and the United States involved."[120] According to records (see fig. 6.4), they met again in 1987, but this time without Guadalupe, to discuss how population

MEETING FOR THE CONSTITUTION OF THE ACTION COMMITTEE
OF THE AMERICAS FOR POPULATION ISSUES

FEMAP

PARTICIPANTS

1. Mr. Thad Rowland, businessman, co-founder of Bertholon-Rowland Agencies.

2. Mr. Luis Acle, White House Associate Director for Public Liaison.

3. Mr. William Chip, lawyer in Washington, member of the National Advisory Board of the Federation for American Immigration Reform.

4. Mr. Garrett Hardin, a well-known writer on demography and ecology.

5. Mr. Mark d'Arcangelo, Vice-President of the General Electric Company.

6. Mr. Sam Taylor, representant in Mexico of the Agency for International - Development.

7. Mr. Robert Fox, formerly Senior Analyst at Inter-American Development - Bank on social and demographic issues.

8. Mr. José Luis Palma, from the General Division of Family Planning, - - Ministry of Health.

9. Mr. Eduardo Cantú, businessman from Ciudad Juarez.

10. Mr. Leopoldo Peralta, businessman and member of the Board of Directors - of the Family Orientation Center of Queretaro, Mexico.

11. Mr. Federico De La Vega, businessman and member of the Board of Directors of the Centros Materno-Infantil y de Planeación Familiar of Ciudad Juarez.

12. Mrs. Guadalupe A. de De La Vega, President of the Mexican Federation of - Private Family Planning Associations and Director of the Centros Materno-Infantil y de Planeación Familiar of Ciudad Juarez.

13. Mr. Ernesto Barraza, Executive Director of the Mexican Federation of Private Family Planning Associations (FEMAP).

14. Mr. Enrique Suarez, Director of Education and Training of FEMAP.

15. Ms. Gabriela Durazo, Director of Socio - Demographic Studies of FEMAP.

FIGURE 6.3 List of initial participants in ACAPI on FEMAP letterhead. Hardin and Rowland were grateful that the de la Vegas had introduced them to important government and business leaders in Mexico interested in supporting their cause. Uarch FacPap 14, folder 1986a, box 23, Garrett Hardin Papers, Department of Special Collections, University Libraries, University of California, Santa Barbara.

To: Board Members of ACAPI and others who may be interested

From: **THAD ROWLAND**

April 8, 1987

Freddie De la Vega, Mark D'Arcangelo and I (Lupe De la Vega was prevented from coming because of a prior engagement.) met with Joe Hood in Dallas on Sunday, April the 5th. Joe was hired to direct the activities of the committee headed by Freddie and Mark.

Joe points out, and Freddie confirms, that the forthcoming election of a new president in Mexico gives us a window of opportunity. They, and Time magazine, agree that the next president will be one of three persons. Two of these are known personally to either Mark or Joe, and they are sure they will have no difficulty getting an audience with the third. In order to fine tune the procedures outlined below, the two of them plan to meet, during the week following Easter, with the potential next-presidents best known to them.

While our conference was devoted mostly to economics, we took time out every half an hour and spent a minute advising ourselves that the survival of our patient depended on the curing of a long term ailment: Excess population growth. It is necessary to keep the patient alive at the present time, which is dependent greatly on improving the economic condition.

Freddie seems to think that the Maquiladora program is something that should rate in history along with the discovery of the internal combustion engine. He certainly did a good job of selling me, and I believe the other two, (1) that the maquiladora plants in Mexico should be operated only by U.S. companies and not companies of any other country, and (2) the U.S. companies should have their maquiladora operations done only in Mexico and no other country. He wants to see the maquiladora plan greatly increased. He had his answers all ready for my questioning the opposition of U.S. labor to this expansion.

In keeping with my theory that the 35-40% of the rural population of Mexico must be stopped from feeding its surplus population to the cities of the country and to the U.S., I suggested that the Mexican government build and equip plants in or near population centers of 5, 10, 20 or 25,000 and give these plants to the U.S. banks in settlement of indebtedness due them. The banks in turn, would sell these plants for dollars to U.S. companies who would use them in processing some portion of their work on some of their products. The whole deal would be pre-arranged, with the plants being built to the specification of the eventual purchaser. Of course, the purpose of these plants providing employment in these less intensive populated areas would not only be to stop the out migration, but to reduce the birth rate.

☐ 804 FLEETWOOD PLAZA
HENDERSONVILLE, N.C. 28739
704-693-5893

☐ ACAPI
1615 17TH ST. N.W.
WASHINGTON, DC
202-387-1378

☐ 1977/GULF SHORE BLVD., N.
APT. 701
NAPLES, FL 33940
813-263-3819

Please reply to address checked.

FIGURE 6.4 Notes about April 1987 meeting in Dallas with Mark D'Arcangelo, Thad Rowland, Federico de la Vega Mathews, and Joe Hood. Uarch FacPap 14, Folder Rowland 1986–1987, box 23, Garrett Hardin Papers, Department of Special Collections, University Libraries, University of California, Santa Barbara.

control and the maquiladora business could help each other. "Freddie," as Rowland wrote in notes of Federico de la Vega Mathews, seemed only concerned with discussing the maquiladora business.

For de la Vega Mathews, the issue was clear. He wanted to bring important US investors to Ciudad Juárez to exploit the existing population for their labor. De la Vega had "sold" Rowland on the idea that maquiladoras could help reduce birth rates among Mexican women if they stuck to Rowland's theory that rural populations must be "stopped from feeding its surplus populations to the cities" of Mexico and the United States. Maquiladoras had the power to not only keep women from reproducing but keep Mexicans from migrating; maquiladoras were the ultimate form of population control. As Rowland tabulated the numbers, he concluded that "this mountain seems so high. It seems unscaleable [sic]." And yet they would soldier on.[121] It is unclear how much more assistance ACAPI provided the de la Vegas and vice versa; little is known after these interactions. In the ensuing years, Hardin became increasingly obsessed with the "Benjamin Wattenberg thesis" that posited two major emergencies would collide, ending Western civilization.[122] Unceasing population growth from the Global South coupled with the so-called "birth dearth" among whites would collapse the white societies Europe and the United States had created. Perhaps this preoccupation caused him to end his relationship with ACAPI in November 1986.[123]

Expanding Transnational Population Control Networks

Rowland, however, did leave FEMAP and the de la Vegas with an important idea to maintain financial support for their work. As one critical way to expand FEMAP—he hoped they would be able to control fertility and immigration throughout Mexico and Central America—Rowland recommended they create a nonprofit arm in the United States as an easier way to "channel $ to Mexico."[124] FEMAP did just that in 1992, establishing the FEMAP Foundation in El Paso, Texas. This new branch of the organization sought to reframe the infrastructure of citizens' welfare and the expansion of private philanthropy in the borderlands. This relationship helped occlude the exploitation and harm done by global industrial capitalism as experienced through the maquiladora system, one justified via neoliberal philosophies quickly spreading around the globe. Like Gilded Age philanthropic projects, FEMAP, a nonprofit, private organization, allowed for millionaire corporations and wealthy industrialists, on both sides of the line, to white-wash profits in the name of community care.

While never addressing better working conditions, better pay, access to education, or solid infrastructure—the root causes of poverty in the borderlands—philanthropists whose wealth was intimately tied to exploit-ative maquiladora businesses, like the de la Vegas, accumulated incredible cultural capital and power by controlling most major community projects. For instance, news media reported FEMAP had received $45,000 from Coo-per Industries, Inc.—a publicly traded electronic parts company—to be ad-ministered by the FEMAP Foundation on the US side of the border in 2000. This followed a similarly large award given by Cooper Industries, Inc. the year before. H. John Riley, the president and chairman of the company, stated the purpose of these grants was to "strengthen partnerships between community service organizations and local Cooper Industries facilities." Cooper's management "desires to enhance the quality of life and improve the resources available in these communities."[125] By 2000 the FEMAP Foun-dation, founded by Adair Margo, friend and supporter of prominent Texas Republicans such as George W. Bush, had received over $1.5 million in fi-nancing for FEMAP in Ciudad Juárez.[126] Recent scholarship critiquing the "nonprofit industrial complex" has rightly pointed out the hypocrisy of cor-porate sponsorship of such institutions and how these organizations oper-ate much like "'shadow governments' doing the work that the government has essentially outsourced to the private sector."[127] FEMAP's charitable works bolstered the image of extraordinarily rich and well-connected fam-ilies in the borderlands who also had economic interests in a well-managed and controlled workforce.

De la Vega proved to be what population control advocate Jean Van Der Tak called a "transducer"—a "new type of professional who [can] bridge the 'communication gap' between the academic demographer and the pop-ulation program practitioner or policymaker."[128] De la Vega quickly filled the gap between Mexico-US borderland multinational corporations and lo-cal charitable projects. She advanced Mexico's population policy, providing family planning education and contraceptives via door-to-door promotoras, extending population control campaigns started earlier in the century.

As de la Vega's FEMAP kicked off, many of the movement's giants had al-ready died. Towering figures, such as Clarence Gamble (1966), Margaret Sanger (1966), William Vogt (1968), Alan Guttmacher (1974), William Draper (1974), John D. Rockefeller (1978), and Lady Rama Rau (1987) had passed. De la Vega could be counted among the new generation of population control advocates, such as Garrett Hardin, Thad Rowland, philanthropist Cordelia S. May, and "mastermind" of the anti-immigration movement John Tanton.[129] While Hardin, Rowland, May, and Tanton were ardent xenophobes, zero-population crusaders, and white supremacists, de la Vega exhibited a softer, gentler vision centering family planning for the good of neoliberalism.

Following the meetings with the Americans, she moved quickly, joining organizations and institutions started and funded by the elder generation of population control visionaries who had since died off. She became a board member of PPEP in 1976 and in 1979 was on the board of directors' roster for the International Fertility Research Program (IFRP).[130] De la Vega appears to have been the only representative from the Global South—other members included Sharon Lee Camp, chairperson of the Population Crisis Committee, and Dr. Torrey Carl Brown, director of Health Care Programs at the John Hopkins Hospital. Dr. Elton Kessel, a medical doctor focused on public health and family planning, established the IFRP in North Carolina with support from the University of North Carolina at Chapel Hill in 1971.[131] In the foreword to Kessel's book about his work in the family planning and population control movement, Reimer Ravenholt, head of the Agency for International Development's population division, described Kessel as being "cut of the same cloth as Dr. Gamble and knew well how to get the best results from limited funds."[132] Kessel came under Gamble's tutelage when Kessel became executive director of Gamble's Pathfinder Fund, another international organization focused on family planning and curbing overpopulation, in the 1960s.[133]

With support from Kessel and organizations like the IFRP—its connections to USAID and Pathfinder Fund—de la Vega became part of the expanding lineage of population control movement activists, inheriting vast resources and government collaborators older generations had only dreamed of. Elder movement champions, such as Rockefeller, Gamble, and Sanger, had laid the groundwork for the innovations and transformations that occurred by the end of the century; de la Vega continued their efforts. She carried their fears and anxieties, as well as the financial and cultural resources they created, to expand her family's empire into the twenty-first century.

Mexico: A Population Control Miracle

In a few short years, to the astonishment of demographers, politicians, and population control activists the world over, Mexico became a population control role model. One *New York Times* headline exclaimed: "Mexico's Birth

Rate Seems Sharply Off." The article went on to explain how census experts and demographers in the United States noticed a "stunning" change in Mexico's fertility rates. US Census Bureau statistics revealed fertility figures going down from forty-two births per one thousand in 1975 to thirty-three to thirty-five births in 1979. Data showed population growth in Mexico in a clear decline, from an average of 3.2 percent in the early 1970s to between 2.4 to 2.6 percent at the end of the decade.[134] President Echeveria's successor, Jose Lopez Portillo, had promised this level of decline by 1982—the good news had arrived early. Although demographers and other population control leaders cautioned the public over the early figures, many at the time agreed that Mexico's intense birth control campaigns, improvements in the lives of women, and mass emigration of young men had created this new Mexican miracle.[135]

By 1984, demographers and population control experts were calling Mexico a "success" on population—Ciudad Juárez's FEMAP its guiding star. According to media accounts: "In Ciudad Juárez, one of Mexico's fastest-growing cities (population 900,000), the local family planning group has arranged for 6,000 women to be sterilized and has brought 40,000 families into its program."[136] Population control advocates responded enthusiastically to the news. "If you compare where Mexico was in the early 1970s . . . with where it is now, you can count on the fingers of one hand the number of countries that have been able to match its success," explained William McGreevy, an economist at the World Bank. Family planning advocate and director of the Washington, DC-based Population Crisis Committee Dr. Joseph Speidel called Mexico "one of the great success stories in family planning."[137]

In conjunction with Mexico's national birth control campaigns instituted by CONAFO, using massive publicity campaigns, including the production of a telenovela that inculcated rural and urban Mexican families on the benefits of family planning, FEMAP played a critical role in Mexico's borderland success.[138] In 1987, when de la Vega joined the Population Crisis Committee (PCC) event in Beverly Hills, she presented members with tangible accomplishments. She explained that in 1982 FEMAP had reached nearly 50,000 Mexican women in and around Ciudad Juárez; by 1987, de la Vega touted a 620 percent increase in the number of women linked to FEMAP's clinic network—over 360,000 women were receiving some form of birth control via FEMAP. Demographic figures continued showing a steady decline, down to 2.4 percent in 1986.[139]

Immigration and labor concerns nevertheless tempered enthusiasm for this massive demographic "accomplishment." Between 1960 and 1980 the Mexican labor force had added nearly nine million people, and projections described a labor force increase of nearly 20 million by 2000. The *Los Angeles Times* asked, "How can the Mexican economy accommodate such a large increase in workers? Where will they go?" State department officials had some ideas. One such agent, newly returned from UN Conference of Population, replied, "That is why some people in the United States want to enact stiffer immigration laws."[140] As historians of US immigration note, calls for stricter immigration laws generally follow a period of economic distress in the United States—the Great Depression ushered in mass deportations of Mexican-origin people in the late 1920s and throughout the 1930s. In the late 1970s, as Jimmy Carter took office during a recession, some politicians once again called for tightening up immigration controls to prevent further economic troubles. As one *New York Times* reporter declared, "We are now witnessing yet another 'rediscovery' of the illegal alien." Various "special interest groups," he stated, "rush to blame him [the immigrant] for every imaginable problem afflicting American society, from high unemployment to rising crime rates, escalating social service costs, overpopulation, and balance-of-payment deficits."[141]

One of the vilest examples of overpopulation rhetoric and xenophobia colliding were the documented forced sterilizations of hundreds of Mexican-origin women at the Los Angeles County Medical Center (LACMC) in the late 1960s and early 1970s.[142] Doctors and residents at LACMC felt justified in administering permanent birth control as the discourse of overpopulation, fear of an ever-browning America, untethered immigration, and the supposed hyper-fertility of Mexican-origin women rose to a fever pitch. Forced sterilizations—consent given under duress or not given at all as laboring women were already under the effects of pain medications—would solve what hospital physicians believed were the roots of many social problems: the uncontrolled fertility of women of color. Elena Gutiérrez observes, of research done at the time, that studies found that of the many "cases of coercive sterilization reported, none documented abuses against white women."[143] US physicians perpetrated these human rights violations just as the global movement for population control supported similar coercive measures abroad.[144] For decades population control advocates trotted out the same winning ponies—the specter of overpopulation, labor troubles, and immigration—to redirect the public's gaze from extractive capitalist policies producing rampant inequality and destitution. What's new in this equation is the degree to which Mexican population control activists, such as de la Vega, shored up these ideas in the latter part of the twentieth century.

Population Control and Labor Control in a Borderland Context

Taking a borderland framework, de la Vega made these connections clear during her Beverly Hills event in 1987: "Many issues of great significance such a migration, population growth, pollution, trade, tourism, education, poverty, and political changes challenge the well-being of our countries as never before. Social disorders in Mexico brought about by a socioeconomic crisis would trigger distress in the United States."[145] The "social disorders" affecting Mexico, in this case high unemployment and poverty, had the frightening potential of traveling north across the border, she cautioned. This transnational position had been part of PPEP's vision since the 1930s. Local borderland population control advocates had long used the US-Mexico's porous border as justification for sustained birth control campaigns in both countries. Finally, after decades of work, Mexican activists were taking the reins of population control efforts.

By the late 1980s, however, the sustained positions and policies of borderland population control advocates flew in the face of established scholarship by Mexican and Chicana academics, such as María Patricia Fernández-Kelly and Vicki Ruiz, both writing and publishing throughout the 1980s. Fernández-Kelly's and Ruiz's research refuted the charge that Mexican-origin women's supposed "hyper-fertility" caused poverty and moral and social decay and was to blame for an impending population crisis. Rather, their studies reveal how neoliberal thinking, one that sought to monetize and therefore devalue every aspect of human existence, had been central to the expansion of the Border Industrialization Program, making central to its mission the exploitation of Mexican women workers in the borderlands. Following the work of sociologists such as Devon Gerard Peña, Ellwyn Stoddard, Marta C. Lopez-Garza, Susan Tiano, James Russell, and Fernández-Kelly studying the maquiladora system at the time, borderlands and Chicana labor historian Vicki Ruiz synthesized the historical present of the maquiladora system in a 1988 paper titled "Mexican Women and Multinationals: The Packaging of the Border Industrialization Program." Weaving together their analysis, Ruiz reminds us that despite the difficult experiences maquiladora workers faced, "labor militancy [was] not unknown in the maquiladoras as women attempt to exercise some control over their work lives."[146] Strikes and union organization, critical forms of reproductive care, were not uncommon among women workers on the factory floor, but most often they employed what one sociologist called *tortugismo*, "operatives deliberately slow[ing] their routines to that of 'a turtle's pace.'"[147] These coordinated but often "subtle acts of subterfuge" represented "a cathartic release helping women cope with a less than ideal work environment."[148] Women in the maquiladora system found moments of maintaining autonomy and control over their social reproduction and labor, and they also found similar solace in access to birth control.

Even as population control rhetoric dominated FEMAP's contraceptive campaigns in Ciudad Juárez, women such as Evangelina Martinez Salmon and Maria de los Angeles Rodriguez were enthusiastic about the possibilities available to them if they were able to plan their families. In the days before FEMAP's public family planning programming, Maria de los Angeles Rodriguez queried her sisters for information about contraception. She would ask them: "'How do you keep from getting pregnant?' and they would reply 'Oh, I guess I'm just lucky.' Imagine that!" Marrying at seventeen and having her first two children one after the other, Rodriguez was "convinced" she needed to do something. She received information about birth control through FEMAP's field-workers and began taking contraceptive pills after her second baby was born. Through FEMAP's program, Rodriguez became "such a believer in family planning" that she, like Evangelina Martinez, joined FEMAP as a promotora in her neighborhood. "I have given out information about it in my Catholic Bible School," Rodriguez declared.[149] She likely worked with Evangelina Martinez, who oversaw nearly 500 of FEMAP's volunteer field-workers in Juárez.[150] The interactions women workers had with FEMAP's promotoras foreground the reproductive care labor Mexican-origin women had engaged in for decades. They did not necessarily internalize the overpopulation rhetoric but did promote contraception and access to reproductive services to each other as a tool that could provide them some control over their lives.

The Catholic Church's position in Mexico remained silent toward contraception, granting a space of cultural indifference readily exploited by population control advocates, promotoras, and women seeking birth control. In Maria de los Angeles Rodriguez's case, the priest knew she was distributing information about family planning to her church group. His "tolerance" of this practice reflected the Roman Catholic Church's position toward birth control campaigns in Mexico at the time.[151] Ciudad Juárez's immediate history, as a place where underground illegal abortions thrived, may have softened the Catholic Church's position toward de la Vega's enterprise. If abortions were kept under control, as de la Vega assured them her work would do, the Church would not interfere with FEMAP. De la Vega stated clearly that FEMAP did not condone or offer abortion access in its clinics. "We tell them [women seeking family planning] the only thing you can do to prevent abortions is family planning."[152] The Mexican state compensated the Catholic Church's ambivalence toward its national population control program by "refusing to abolish criminal penalties for abortion." Mexican officials touted a decrease in "abortion-related health complaints" because of its widespread family planning campaign.[153] As demonstrated by historian Elizabeth O'Brien's research on the history of abortion in Mexico, the Catholic Church's ambiguity was not a new phenomenon but part of negotiations between the government and the Church since the colonial period. Expanding anthropologist Lynn Morgan and Elizabeth Robert's theorization of "reproductive governance" in Latin America, O'Brien posits that history provides a clear vantage point from which to understand how ideas about abortion and contraception were "refracted" through a "Catholic lens."[154] This reproductive health merger between Church and state suited the political, social, and cultural needs of a tumultuous Mexican nation. Thus, contrary to the Catholic Church's official position in the United States, the Church in Mexico did not take a hardline stance against the Mexican government's population control policies, nor did it stand in the way of wealthy philanthropists peddling contraception or working women using it.[155]

Conclusion

As the maquiladora system proliferated in the Mexico borderlands, the United States sought to capitalize on the booming transnational model embracing neoliberal capitalist policies through the 1994 North American Free Trade Agreement (NAFTA). Canada, the United States, and Mexico were to "open their borders" to free trade of goods and capital; in return, the United States closed its borders to immigration. The Clinton administration oversaw the proliferation of massive immigration changes nationally and locally. Along with launching federally funded programs such as Operation Gatekeeper in 1994 and the Illegal Immigration Reform and Immigrant Responsibility Act of 1996—part of Clinton's "tough on crime" program—states passed their own immigration laws, such as California's Proposition 187, also known as the "Save Our State (SOS)" initiative.[156] Ramping up militarization of the border, criminalizing immigration, and denying migrants basic access to health care, housing, and education in the United States represented the culmination of the fundamental cruelty and extractive nature of neoliberal policies in the borderlands. At the same time, Northern Mexico in general, but Ciudad Juárez in particular, saw an exponential rise in what feminists in the region began to call *feminicidio*—the murder of women and "the state-sponsored impunity for the murderers"—as thousands of women and girls of all ages went missing and then their bodies were found defiled and mutilated in the Chihuahua desert. As geographer Melissa Wright contends, these murders became a turning point in extreme borderland policies that devalued human life in favor of neoliberalism. Wright observes how feminists, "activists and families protested a governing discourse that blamed women for the violence, and in so doing disrupted a capitalist logic that reaped value from the devaluation of women as a social group."[157]

While nation-states provided capital and goods free passage across borders, human labor remained confined to the zones where it could be easily exploited, controlled, and discarded. In the case of Mexico's maquiladora system, this meant restricting the movement of women workers and curbing their reproduction. Because this was a binational ordeal, NAFTA's brutal policies crippled women garment workers, most of whom were Mexicanas and Chicanas, in El Paso.[158] Renewed xenophobic fears of "hordes" of fertile Mexican women crossing the border into the United States revived calls for population controls across the United States, breeding new insidious terms like "anchor babies" to refer to the children of undocumented parents, supposedly stealing welfare and health care resources through the US Fourteenth Amendment and birthright citizenship.[159] As philosopher Natalie Cisneros explains, these fears reinvigorated century-long anxieties about the "problematic of alien sexuality" and specter of nonwhite mothers producing US citizens.[160]

Immigration anxieties, fear of overpopulation, and a demand for cheap labor went hand in hand in the borderlands. Panic over excess populations spilling north of the border consumed Planned Parenthood of El Paso from its inception, but by the 2000s, these concerns had become national policies in both the United States and Mexico. Guadalupe de la Vega became a critical transducer of information between local and international governments, wealthy financiers, the Catholic Church, and women workers all with opposing and nonetheless synchronous reasons for supporting family planning. FEMAP's programming became a model instituted across Mexico's northern border and continues advancing access to vital health care today. Yet de la Vega and FEMAP's role in institutionalizing population control policies cannot go unexamined as the twenty-first century brings concerns for reproductive health care access and justice to the fore of borderland politics once more.

Epilogue

Our Reproductive Futures Past

. . . .

I'm Roman Catholic, I have six children, and I had my six children in nine years. I adhere to my own faith; so that's my faith, *my* faith. But I am adamantly pro-choice because I feel that that decision needs to be made by each woman and her own health care provider, her own faith, or whatever decision-making matrix she uses. It's not [a decision] that I feel I can make for each woman.

—Leticia Van de Putte, interview with author, 2021

In 2013, State Senator Wendy Davis made headlines attempting to filibuster anti-abortion legislation in Texas. As the end of the session drew near, Davis's seldom-mentioned Democratic colleague Leticia Van de Putte, a Mexican American lawmaker representing San Antonio, declared, "At what point must a female senator raise her hand or her voice to be recognized over the male colleagues in the room?"[1] Hundreds of activists watching the tense debate in the Senate gallery erupted in cheers and applause lasting so long the session expired before the bill passed. In subsequent interviews, Senator Van de Putte doubled down on her statement, saying she protested for the women of Texas, fighting for their rights to reproductive control and bodily autonomy. Media accounts of that day have often erased her statement, attributing the hoopla and all that came afterward to Davis's filibuster alone.

This erasure is not accidental. It is part of a longer history of denying reproductive autonomy and reproductive agency to Mexicanas, Chicanas, and Latinas throughout the twentieth century. The history of the movements for reproductive rights and the legalization of abortion are often viewed as "white women movements," presumed devoid of critical interventions by Latina, Black, Native, and Asian women. The history of coercive sterilization, however, is replete with oppressive narratives about poor women and women of color. One of the main things I set out to do in this book is to bridge this historical gap. How do we make sense of Chicana politicians like Leticia Van de Putte and her unequivocal defense of reproductive autonomy? What role did Mexican-origin women play in advancing ideas for reproductive liberation and care in the twentieth century? And how does the history of the US-Mexico borderlands shape their protracted struggle for reproductive freedom?

One way to answer these questions is to place women like Senator Van de Putte and their explicit support for reproductive rights in historical context. Van de Putte's "pro-choice" position has a historical lineage that is worth investigating. When she was sixteen years old, Senator Van de Putte's mother, Isabelle "Belle" Ortiz, sat her down to give her "the talk." It was 1970, and the women's liberation movement gained greater attention with each passing day. Women across the nation demanded access to childcare and equal wages for equal work as well as access to reproductive health care, including the right to have an abortion and access to contraception. Isabelle Ortiz told her daughter that this new generation of women had it harder than her own. Society in the 1950s had given Ortiz limited opportunities. Middle-class women, like Isabelle, were trained to be housewives, or if they received schooling beyond a secondary education, they could become teachers or nurses or secretaries. Van de Putte's generation had it worse, her mother insisted. They were to be *pathbreakers* and, by extension, *pathmakers*. If Leticia made a mistake, her mother explained, Leticia could not fault her husband; she had only herself to blame. To keep a steady course, to get a good education, and to move onward on her own, Ortiz told her daughter that she would need to know about birth control. Senator Van de Putte's mother was clear, controlling her reproduction—when to have children and how many—would be the key to the future senator's success.[2]

Through college, Van de Putte faithfully used the services at the local Planned Parenthood to stay on track and finish her studies. The birth control pill became her main source of contraception. Despite her Catholic faith and the Church's strict policies against contraception, she made a choice to use birth control like thousands of other Catholics during this period. She completed her degree in pharmacology from the University of Texas at Austin in spring of 1979. One year prior, she married Pete Van de Putte at St. Paul's Catholic Church in San Antonio.[3]

As stated in the epigraph, Van de Putte went on to have six children in the first nine years of her marriage. Her first daughter, Nicole, was born May 1980, one year after she graduated from college, and her last child, Paul, arrived in 1989, one year before she became a state representative for San Antonio's District 115.[4] During these early years mothering her young children and working as a professional pharmacist, Van de Putte joined several civic organizations that shaped her political outlook and provided the grounding for her career in the Texas state legislature. As her biographer, Sharron Navarro, contends, Van de Putte "was like many Chicanas at the time, intimately involved in the organizing and mobilizing that formed the backbone" of political activism in their communities.[5]

Leticia Van de Putte went on to have a well-respected career in Texas politics. She was the leading Chicana politician in the Texas House of Representatives until 1999 when she decided to run for Twenty-Sixth District in the Texas state senate representing San Antonio. Van de Putte was a Texas state senator for nearly sixteen years when she retired in 2015. During her tenure as state senator, Van de Putte was an ardent supporter of women's reproductive rights, often campaigning for education and access to health: two critical topics ungirding Mexican-origin women's autonomy.[6]

Van de Putte's story is all the more compelling because of the combination of her identities, a Catholic, middle-class, Mexican-descent Texas politician. The involvement of Chicanas and Mexican-origin women, regardless of where they fell on the social-economic spectrum, in the reproductive rights movement remained unthinkable. For too long, scholars and the public have nurtured stereotypes wrapping the reproduction of Chicanas, Mexican-origin women, and by extension all Latinas and its supposed excesses in a blinding Catholic faith. Catholicism has been inscribed as antithetical to a more progressive and modern Protestantism.[7] In the borderlands, Mexican-origin people's culture and community became inextricably linked to the Catholic Church—in both the United States and Mexico. Yet, as Chicana religious scholar Susana Gallardo has stated of Chicana Catholics, they "practice a diversity of beliefs and behaviors that range within and beyond the institutional framework of the Church."[8] This was also true of Catholic, Mexican-origin women in the decades before the Chicana/o movement, who, despite the Church's doctrine against the use of contraceptives, sought birth control from established organizations as early as the 1930s. We have been told that Mexican-descent women and other Latinas never cared about the fight for reproductive freedom because the Catholic Church forbade it.[9] Van de Putte's life and the history and lives of Mexican-origin women in this book tell us a different story. So much can be gleaned from the lives of Mexican-origin women, such as Bertha Chávez, Amelia Castillo, Leticia Van de Putte, and even Guadalupe de la Vega. These women and so many more in the borderlands represent the diversity of thinking and attitudes toward reproductive control and freedom that strike at the heart of homogenizing discourses about Mexican-descent people and their families.

As I have disentangled the history of Mexican-descent women's reproduction, reproductive care, and control, I center questions of religion, gender, race, and class to understand how this history has remained invisible
for so long. Rhetorics of racial inferiority, interwoven with discourses of superstitious Catholicism, plagued Mexican-origin people since before the
US war with Mexico in the nineteenth century. Anglo settlers' racialist
machinations justified the founding of the Texas Republic in 1836 and the
expansion of the United States' empire in the decades that followed.
Chicana/o scholars have spent decades documenting the history of Mexican-
origin people's racial formation in the Southwest, sometimes extending
this process of racialization over the border into Mexico, and its connections
to the usurpation of land, forced assimilation, and exclusion from citizenship culminating in oppressive working and living conditions throughout
the twentieth century. This combination of anti-Mexican views and religious
bigotry produced a damaging environment for Mexican-origin people in the
borderlands.

I traced the history of Mexican-origin women who sought and claimed
access to reproductive health services in the twentieth-century borderlands,
later becoming activists in the movement for reproductive health care in
their communities and beyond. Advancing projects for basic access to health
care, especially reproductive services, was not easy for Mexican-origin
women as they confronted numerous obstacles. Beginning in the 1930s, the
Mothers' Health Center of El Paso, founded by Anglo Texan Betty Mary
Goetting, with help from birth control pioneer Margaret Sanger, offered
contraceptive advice and materials to the Mexican-origin community.
Wealthy, progressive Anglos touted birth control as a critical tool for demographic management in one of the largest border crossings of the Southwest: El Paso. Population control ideology premised on the notion that
birth control was necessary to help curb the birth rate of Mexican-origin
people became a hallmark of the organization's vision as it affiliated with
Planned Parenthood Federation of America in 1945. Desires for stringent
forms of population control informed Planned Parenthood of El Paso's
(PPEP) policies well into the 1980s and spilled over the border into Ciudad
Juárez as women like Guadalupe Arizpe de la Vega took on the cause along
Mexico's northern frontier. Although PPEP became a critical site for wealthy
white women's activism in the borderlands, it also became an important
space for Mexican-origin women to access contraceptives and other forms
of reproductive health care in the decades that followed. Even as PPEP leaders' rhetoric racialized Mexican-origin women's reproduction as "exces-

sive" and in need of control, poor women, most of whom were Catholic and Mexican, used its services year after year.

In documenting the long and nuanced history of Mexican-origin women's tenuous connections with Planned Parenthood, one of the largest and, at one point, most powerful family planning organizations in the world, a multiplicity of reproductive health histories emerge. While historians have long focused on the legacy of Margaret Sanger, her advocacy for contraception, establishing Planned Parenthood, and making "birth control" an international phenomenon, few have taken a critical look at how this history was complicated along the US-Mexico border, especially its links to the logic of border enforcement and immigration controls.

Reproductive Justice in the Borderlands: Articulating a Theory of Care over Rights

In this book, I stress the idea of *care* rather than *rights* when discussing the history of Mexican-origin women and reproduction. While white women feminists have claimed legal rights over access to abortion, contraception, and other reproductive health services under the guise of the "right to privacy," Mexican-origin women and Chicanas demanded a totality of health care, foregrounding the ideals of what scholars call *reproductive justice* (RJ). Given their second-class status as citizens not only in the United States but also in Mexico—a gendered racism that permeates both sides of the border— Mexican-origin women put forward an articulation of justice informed by theories of care. Feminist philosopher Virginia Held contends that the "central focus [of care] is on the compelling moral salience of attending to and meeting the needs of the particular others for whom we take responsibility."[10] Beginning in the 1920s, Mexican-origin women began to take over the "care economy" as laundry workers, nannies, and domestic workers across the Southwest. Middle-class and upper-class white women paid their Mexican-origin counterparts to raise their children, clean their homes, and feed their families. Mexican-origin women were charged with "taking responsibility" for their white dependents as well as their own children. Simultaneously, Anglo elites denied Mexican-origin communities' access to resources such that derelict housing, lack of sewage and plumbing, bad roads, and nonexistent health care came to characterize the "Mexican" areas of cities like El Paso. To survive this institutionalized neglect, Mexican-origin women built their own communities of care within these neighborhoods, adapting charitable resources, such as Planned Parenthood clinics, to their own needs. As Chicana sociologist and reproductive justice scholar Elena Gutiérrez observes, Latinas have played significant roles "in the development of both mainstream reproductive rights efforts and community-based reproductive health and sexuality agendas" in ways that remain illegible to the larger public.[11]

RJ is a theoretical tool that helps reframe, analyze, and reassess reproductive injustices of the past, illuminating the complex gendered racism along both sides of the border. Four major pillars encompass the RJ philosophy: the human right to have children, the right to not have children, the right to parent the children we have in safe and sustainable environments, and the right to possess full bodily autonomy. Feminist activists of color came to this definition in 1997 when they launched a national movement consisting of several women of color organizations.[12] Spearheaded by activist-scholar Loretta Ross, the movement for reproductive justice is fast becoming an important theoretical praxis across academic disciplines. As a historian, reproductive justice has opened new ways for me to convey the lived experiences and activism of Chicanas and Mexican-descent women and their connections to the fight for reproductive liberation in the twentieth-century borderlands. RJ helps us better interpret the actions of Mexican-origin women and Chicana activists as they fought for reproductive services and health care for their communities based on mutual respect, dignity, and self-determination. As workers in the care economy, laboring in homes of Anglo families, Mexican-origin women demanded access to the same care they provided their white dependents.

An RJ framework also brings together decades' worth of Chicana feminist scholarship that has remained on the margins of discussions about reproductive autonomy and freedom. In tracking this nearly one-hundred-year reproductive health and control history, I highlight what Chicana anthropologist Patricia Zavella calls the "analytic of *poder* (power)" that "signals the ability of structurally vulnerable people to develop skills or capabilities and aspire to better conditions or even wellness."[13] I tried not to overstate nor deny Mexican-origin women's *poder* as they confronted their husbands and families, eugenic feminists, the Catholic Church, doctors and nurses, and various forms of state structural oppression to eke out small and large doses of bodily autonomy.

This is a difficult task given that the records and sources used to write this book were mostly written from the perspective of what Emma Pérez calls the "colonialist" vantage point. Historians writing about the lives of historically marginalized and colonized people must often engage the archive in an oppositional fashion, reading against the grain to hear the voices of those who were not meant to be heard, those who were meant only to exist as a backdrop to more important historical forces—think nineteenth- and early twentieth-century concerns for progress and modernity. Pérez critiques those who mimic this colonialist subordination by suppressing the historical lives and experiences of Chicanas and Mexican-origin women in Chicano historiography. She insists that "Chicana, Mexicana, India, mestiza actions, words spoken and unspoken, survive and persist whether acknowledged or not."[14]

Building on Pérez's insight, I sought to locate the words and actions of Mexican-origin women through a vast reproductive control ecosystem built largely by white women-led organizations. White women collected and archived material highlighting their achievements, lauding their activism in the public and private sphere. This cache of information became a central component of this history. No such archive exists exclusively dedicated to the work of Mexican-origin women and Chicanas in the movement for reproductive freedom. White women birth control advocates, and later historians, erected and reinforced a tough veneer that encapsulated, intentionally or not, the singular significance of white women's activism in the movement. This has allowed the idea that Chicana and Mexican-origin women played little to no role in the battle for reproductive freedom to persist.

While many of the sources used in the book come from the usual centers of archival power, library collections, government records, newspaper accounts, and private collectors, I employed oral histories and Chicana feminist thought and experience to flesh out the narratives presented. Chicana and Latina scholars have written extensively about their mothers and grandmothers, theorizing notions of "motherwork" as "subtle strategies" for resistance.[15] Memories of their mothers and grandmothers, women living and working in the United States, Mexico, and other Latin American countries stretching back to the earliest days of the twentieth century, serve as vital counternarratives to the thousands of documents collected by Planned Parenthood Federation of American and Planned Parenthood of El Paso that rarely documented their patients' thoughts or concerns. Weaving together historical evidence with feminists of color's articulations of resistance and resilience provides a more nuanced understanding of the lived experiences of Chicanas and Mexican-origin women and their connections to reproductive care and control.

This book is more than a historical accounting of past reproductive violence, although I certainly write about this too; examining how Chicanas and Mexican-origin women survived what seemed like insurmountable obstacles to provide care for themselves, their families, and their communities. Chicana theorist Chela Sandoval describes this position as a "differential mode of oppositional consciousness," a consciousness that entails "grace, flexibility, and strength" and like "the clutch of a car provides the driver the ability to shift gears . . . permit[ing] the practitioner to choose tactical positions, that is, to self-consciously break and reform ties to ideology, activities which are imperative for the psychological and political practices that permit the achievement of coalition across differences."[16] Though Sandoval was naming the moves made by Chicana feminist activists, similar conclusions can be drawn about the Mexican-origin women and Chicanas who maneuvered around, between, and among white women birth control activists, the Catholic Church, politicians, and their families to access resources for themselves and their communities. The editors of a recent groundbreaking anthology about Chicana activism have used the phrase "Chicana *movidas*" as a shorthand for the kind of "flexible consciousness" Sandoval articulated.[17] Therefore lives and issues of Mexican-origin women cannot be, as Vicki Ruiz argues, "boiled down into a dialectic of accommodation and resistance but must be placed within the centrifuge of negotiation, subversion, and consciousness."[18] Mexican-origin women and Chicanas made tactical shifts, reducing speed or accelerating when necessary, to survive an environment that often sought to violently suppress their existence or outright kill them. Even when white progressives in the borderlands attempted to bring forth some magnanimous or seemingly altruistic measure, like birth control, to "uplift" the Mexican and Mexican American community, it was presented as a tool that would surely benefit the white population as well. As it turns out, even when white people are well meaning, they are still self-serving.

In this way, this book bridges traditional historical methodologies with a wide range of disciplines to, as Chicana historian Deena González quipped, reassess the old order of things.[19] This *old order* includes birth control histories that focus on the lives and work of white women and their cursory interactions with communities of color, historians of the borderlands who continually ignore the lives of women and women-led social justice movements, and Chicana/o histories that have yet to fully grapple with histories of reproduction. Locating the lives of those lingering in historical obscurity necessitates a braiding together of various fields and disciplinary methods to show how Mexican-origin women participated and shaped one of the most important women's social justice movements of the twentieth and twenty-first centuries: the movement for reproductive liberation.

By following the lead of reproductive justice scholars who see border-lands thinking and theorizing by Chicana scholars as critical for an expansion of RJ as an analytical framework, we begin to see new avenues of analysis, including a deeper theorization of reproductive care. Exalting the significance of Gloria Anzaldúa's mestiza consciousness, reproductive justice scholars write, "We need a *new* language that would provide an analytical anchor to engage issues both within and beyond US borders to build strong connections between political organizing and theorizing by women of color [emphasis in the original]." For me, this new language is not so much creating new words or ideas to understand the role of Mexican-origin women in this movement, but rather to reframe older histories about *rights* to focus on *care*. This subtle shift brings forth what reproductive justice scholars assign to Anzaldúa's analysis of "living in the borderlands, or interstices of rigid boundaries."[20] Chicana historian Marisela Chávez has taken this a step farther, coining the term "bridging activism" to show how Chicanas "built densifying webs of interconnection between organizations, with some women serving as bridges that brought others onto new activist paths."[21] Chávez revives Anzaldúa and Moraga's bridge metaphor from their revolutionary 1981 anthology *This Bridge Called My Back* to bring forth new ways of making visible generational reproductive care among Chicana activists. For decades Chicana feminists have insisted that to appreciate the lives of Mexican-origin women living in the borderlands, working-class women existing in various economic and social states of *in-betweenness*, it is necessary to view their lives from different positions relative to geography, access to citizenship and civil rights, as well as their concerns for and work in their own communities.

Centering *reproductive care* provides a new location from which to examine mutualist and communitarian networks that defy categorization under (neo)liberal concerns for *civil rights*.[22] Care also allows us to view informal practices of reciprocity and support as activism by those in liminal relationships with the state—migrants, immigrants, undocumented people, and those perceived as such despite their legitimate claims to citizenship. What is the meaning of care in this context? I follow the work of feminist philosophers concerned with theories of care who have articulated care as principle and practice (both affective and material) that "are the central values in human life."[23] Care is an affective feeling, one that conveys compassion, trust, and understanding and is the foundation for love. Feminist ethicist Asha Bhandary also pushes us to think about caregiving and labor as critical to human existence. Uniting this assessment with Chicana feminists' analysis of differential consciousness rooted in acts of resistance to white supremacy, a theory of reproductive care emerges. In other words, we've got to care to survive; we've got to care for each other to break free.

The Mexican-origin women in this book were workers, mothering their children and the children of their employers; they cleaned and kept order in the homes of their *patrones* and laundered the clothing of hundreds of people in their communities. Many of them simultaneously worked in oil refineries, in factories sewing clothes for major American manufacturers, in fields picking cotton and other agricultural goods, and in electronic facilities preparing new technologies on assembly-line floors on both sides of the US-Mexico border. While many Mexican-origin women organized throughout the twentieth century, fighting for higher pay and greater protections, they often relied on each other and their families, neighbors, and coworkers when the government and their workplaces neglected their civil and human rights. This labor history becomes critical to connecting reproductive labor and reproductive care to the broader history of Mexican-origin people in the borderlands. This book unites the long history of exploitative reproductive labor with Mexican-origin women's ability to control and care for their reproductive health.

While securing reproductive *rights* continues to be a critical aspect of reproductive justice, its significance has not always been central to *all* women or reproducing people. As we have seen in other aspects of our society, the gains made by activists of color demanding civil rights in the 1950s and 1960s—access to suffrage, education, and the end to segregation—are currently hanging by a thread. As I pen these words, *Roe v. Wade* is gone, and more extreme legislation to end all manner of human rights continues to find its way to the desks of right-wing governors across the country. What happens when the law is not there to protect our dignity or our humanity?

I believe we can learn from the spirit in which our mothers and grandmothers organized and cared for each other decades before. Mexican-origin women and Chicanas attempted to create networks that spread beyond a reliance on "civil rights" to access reproductive health care, especially when their claim to citizenship and legal status as Americans was so precarious. In El Paso, Mexican-origin women accepted the charitable offerings from organizations like Planned Parenthood on their own terms, using what they needed when they needed it. As white birth control advocates applauded their gains—defeating "superstitious Catholic ideology" by teaching Mexican women about contraception—birth control leaders rarely acknowledged the humanity and consciousness of their patients, who were making decisions about their bodies and families every time they stepped into the clinic.

As years passed, many patients attempted to join PPEP, to take on volunteer roles to help inform their community about the power of reproductive autonomy, but PPEP hardly allowed Mexican-origin women to take on leadership roles. Not until the 1950s did Spanish-surnamed women appear as volunteers or workers in the clinic, and certainly their names did not appear on the coveted board of directors list. Many of the Mexican descent women hoping to join PPEP in its early days sought to expand the services of PPEP into some of the poorest sectors of the city, not necessarily to join the crusade for population control via contraception. These divergent goals reveal how historically marginalized people use politically and economically powerful institutions for their own interests.[24] From Bertha Chávez to Amelia Castillo, Leticia Van de Putte, and Guadalupe Arizpe de La Vega, there existed millions of Mexican-origin women who resisted facile categorization. These women were not an anomaly, but given this rich history, it seems for too long historians of reproduction have denied their complex humanity.

I had several goals in mind when I wrote this book. First, I hope the words and *actions* of Mexican-origin women and Chicanas examined here help us reimagine current and future movements for reproductive liberation. Today's Latina-led efforts are rooted in longer legacies of negotiation and resistance, giving those in the past their due and those in the present a stronger foundation from which to fight. Texas has become ground zero for anti-reproductive justice political efforts as well as scalar reproductive justice movements. Those in the latter group need history to ground their struggle.

Second, this book was conceptualized and written over a ten-year period of white feminists reckoning with demands made by feminists of color around issues of reproduction. As white women scholars sought to defend the legacies of activists such as Margaret Sanger, organizations like Planned Parenthood nearly buckled under the weight of denying her involvement in the eugenics movement. In 2021, Alexis McGill Johnson, a Black activist and the newly elected president of Planned Parenthood Federation of America, wrote a searing op-ed in the *New York Times* condemning Sanger's complicity in uniting demands for contraception with negative eugenics—promoting the idea that the "unfit" should not reproduce.[25] Historian Linda Gordon wrote about these connections in her 1976 *Woman's Body, Woman's Rights: Birth Control in America*. It took Planned Parenthood forty-five years to admit Sanger's legacy at best was problematic and at worst helped produce some of the most damaging and violent ideas about reproductive control that remain powerful tools for nefarious counter-freedom movements to this day.

Historians could interpret Planned Parenthood's hesitance in addressing the troubling reputation of their founder as one of political expediency. Since at least the 1980s, Planned Parenthood had been weakened by its support for abortion access as health care. Demands to defund Planned Parenthood increased with each passing decade as "ending abortion" became a staple of Republican and political conservative agendas. While Planned Parenthood evaded discussions about Sanger's connections to eugenics to protect its image among Progressives, those on the right used this history to discredit the organization.[26] It is not my purpose to add fuel to the fire; I believe unequivocally in Planned Parenthood's current mission to bring reproductive health care to all those who need and want it. It is in the organization's best interest and in the best interest of reproductive justice movements to have a fair and nuanced conversation about the history of Planned Parenthood in the Southwest and to examine its complicated legacy within the Mexican-origin community. Given that Latinx people represent the fastest-growing demographic in the United States and health care is a crucial concern to our community, it is vital to understand the troubling relationship between Planned Parenthood and Mexican-origin people in the borderlands, namely that, as this book contends, Planned Parenthood influenced birth and population control advocates, policies, rhetoric, and logics on both sides of the border.

Third, writing a book about Mexican-origin women and their fight for reproductive freedom is itself an act of reproductive care to advance reproductive justice. After enduring the Trump administration's multilevel attacks against migrants, mostly from Mexico and Central America, the catastrophic loss of our constitutional right to abortion, and the ever-escalating fears about "white genocide," Latina reproduction is once again the focus of great fear and animosity.[27] Although I finished writing the book during the Biden administration the vestiges of Trump's America left deep, ghastly scars. As this book goes into production, the presidential election of 2024 where Trump is once again the GOP front-runner is in full swing. Tensions over further reproductive violence are at a fever pitch.

The El Paso border region received special focus when Trump was last president. It was the site of massive migration and migrant detention. Grotesque images emerged in 2019 of women, men, and children held behind barbed-wire fences under highway overpasses because detention centers were beyond capacity.[28] Then on August 3 of that same year, a young white male, determined to "kill Mexicans overrunning the country," drove hundreds of miles to shoot up a local Walmart along El Paso's main interstate. He killed twenty-three people and injured another twenty-three—reviving a painful history of extrajudicial and vigilante violence familiar to generations of Mexican-origin and Native peoples in the region.[29] In November 2020, El Paso became the epicenter of the Covid-19 pandemic, leaving thousands of mostly Mexican-origin people hospitalized and dying of a preventable disease. This too revived memories of epidemics past, harkening back to the spread of tuberculosis, typhus, and other diseases once linked to the Mexican-origin community via racialist public health quarantines in the early twentieth century. These devastating events brutally connect people and place to a deeply painful past, bringing together Mexican-origin, Chicana/o/x people and the US-Mexico borderlands in the symbiotic embrace that Anzaldúa once called "una herida abierta," an open wound that never fully heals, a wound that bleeds (re)producing cultures of violence, resistance, love, and pain.

Fighting for Control traced the contours and inflection points of a systemic and structural gendered racism focused squarely on Mexican descent women's reproduction. It is also about how Mexican-origin women lived through it, fought back, and used contraception for their own emancipation while lifting each other and their communities along the way. As Vicki Ruiz contends, "The exploration of identities, the conservation and creation of cultural practices and traditions, and the reconstruction of historical narratives are not without political intent."[30] This book is very much part of a longer reproductive justice and care political project. I seek to do more than provide a diagnosis of the systems' attempts at killing, maiming, destroying, and controlling Mexican-origin women, but one that centers collective existence, persistence, and transformation in the face of unrelenting aggression and violence.

This book is in no way a complete or all-encompassing report on the reproductive lives of Mexican-origin women in the borderlands. There remains so much more history to understand and honor. Instead, *Fighting for Control* is a window into how some Mexican-origin women used Planned Parenthood clinics for their own needs, how they grappled with the heavy population control rhetoric of the family planning movement and lived to tell about it, how they managed to create spaces for reproductive agency and liberation, and how that spirit continues to foster struggles for justice among us today.

Acknowledgments

Tracing the emotional genealogy of a project is an important way of putting the work and its author into perspective. Writing a book is a long process punctuated by more than research trips and fellowships. Knowing who picked you up as you tripped over each thought, writing the names of those who nourished you as you meandered through the dreadful and delightful parts of the journey is a needed reminder that no major intellectual endeavor is done alone.

These next few pages are my clumsy attempt at capturing the magnitude of my gratitude for everyone who walked alongside me, fed me—both figuratively and literally—and lifted me up as I made my way to the finish line.

This book received generous support from the University of Iowa, the Ford Foundation, the American Council of Learned Societies, and the American Association of University Women. These funding sources facilitated travel to archives across the country and provided financial support so I could write. Many archives gave generously of their time and care, namely the Sophia Smith Collection at Smith College and the Schlesinger Library at Radcliffe Institute for Advanced Study. One archive remains at the center of this study and deserves admiration for sustaining me for over a decade of research. Thank you to Claudia Rivers, Abbie Weiser, and the staff of the C. L. Sonnichsen Special Collections Department at the University of Texas at El Paso. Claudia and Abbie were essential for the completion of this book. Mil gracias.

Now to my mentors who deserve mountains of flowers: Ernesto Chávez, my dissertation chair and dear friend, never doubted me. Even after my first and second pregnancies, even after moving away and then coming back, he stood firm by me and my research. This kind of mentorship, care, and encouragement is rare in the academy. He remains unconditionally in my corner and for that I am so thankful. When we first discussed my dissertation topic, he exclaimed: "What do I know about birth control?" As it turns out, he knew tons about revolutionary struggles against the long history of anti-Mexican racism in the borderlands. My book would not be what it is without his wisdom and expertise. Carole Joffe checked in with me at every turn, reading various iterations of the book, framing its edges, listening to me with great attentiveness as I tried to figure out my arguments. In the process, she became a marvelous friend. Alexandra Minna Stern's genuine interest in my research remains a model for me with my students. She is a relentless champion of my work, and I am forever in her debt. The support of Nicole Guidotti-Hernández and her deep engagement with my research has been incredibly generative. For reading and rereading some truly disastrous early drafts of conference papers that became chapters in this book and always knowing how to engage them thoughtfully and with great care, Monica Perales should receive a medal. She also never minced words with me about the profession from the beginning, influencing how I understood my place in the academy in important ways. Maria Cotera took a chance on me as I vied for time to finish this book during the last two years. Her careful reading of my chapters helped clarify histories that still seem too fresh to count as history. Marisela R. Chávez shared critical aspects of her research that have made this study stronger. Leslie Reagan answered a message from me as I tried to make sense of reproduction in the borderlands in graduate school and continued to foster my thinking about reproductive health in the borderlands so many years later. Jacki Rand was my first faculty mentor at the University of Iowa, offering an honest, plain rendering of this place and still managing to read terrible drafts of my book proposal with serious insights for how to make it better. Miroslava Chávez-García's keen eyes gazed on too many "final" drafts of this book; she deserves her own acknowledgment chapter. Her dedication to the craft of writing good, sound history will stay with me for years to come. And to Vicki Ruiz, Chicana feminist mentor extraordinaire! I would not be here without the histories she produced, without the precious archival materials she generously shared, and without her modeling what reproductive care looks like in the academy.

To the mentors who have welcomed me with open arms into their hearts and homes (this goes for many of those above and below as well—I have had my fair share of delicious meals with so many of you!). My dear colleagues in the Department of Gender, Women's and Sexuality Studies, History, and Latina/o/x Studies, and beyond at University of Iowa, who have supported me by taking on so much so that I could complete this book, my special admiration and gratitude to Meena Khandelwal, Brady G'sell, Naomi Greyser, Leslie Schwalm, E Cram, Christopher-Rasheem McMillan, Ani Dutta, Teresa Magnum, Corey Creekmur, Lisa Heineman, Eric Vázquez, Elizabeth Rodriguez Fielder, Rene Rocha, José Fernandez, Jorge Guerra, Ari Ariel, Yasmine Ramadan, Mariola Espinosa, Landon Storrs, Viridiana Hernández Fernández, Robert Rouphail, Louise Seamster, and Victor Ray.

There are wonderful students who mentored me as well. My most heartfelt appreciation to Ruth Kahssai, Isabela Flores, Ally McKeone, and Alexia Sanchez. So much gratitude to Ana Fernanda Fraga, who scoured Mexico City archives so that I could finish writing chapter 6! A very special and warm note of thanks and love to Erika Zierke, who put in so much time on this project (and others) until the bitter end.

I am a proud member of a wonderful crew of scholars of the history of reproduction and reproductive justice. I am grateful for the community we've built together over the years and the encouragement each of you has shown me throughout this process. Many thanks to Natalie Lira, Lauren McIvor Thompson, Elizabeth O'Brien, Cynthia Greenlee, Jennifer Holland, Cassia Roth, Rachell Sánchez Rivera, Brianna Theobald, Karissa Haugeberg, Rebecca Kluchin, Mytheli Sreenivas, Leslie Reagan, Lynn Thomas, and Rickie Solinger. I look forward to continuing our research together and expanding this vibrant field.

To the care theorists, who in the past several years have invigorated how I write and think about the power and politics of care. Without you, I could not have imagined reproductive care as a mode of critical analysis and radical transformation.

Much love to my NEH "Philosophives," Janet Jakobsen, Preeti Sharma, Janel Anderson, and Stephanie Santos, for critically engaging my nascent ideas about care as liberatory practice. To Asha Bhandary, Joan Tronto, and Daniel Engster for welcoming me into this exciting intellectual world.

The University of North Carolina Press (UNCP) with the excellent direction of my editor Andreina Fernandez delivered this manuscript into the hands of the most capable and diligent reviewers. UNCP has been an excellent steward of this project; Andreina's patience, generosity, and precision are unparalleled.

To the beautiful, brilliant women whose scholarship and collective love of celebration, joy, and unwavering sense of justice move me to tears as I write your names. I love you, Alicia Romero, Natalie Fixmer-Oraiz, Ashley Howard, Asha Bhandary, Celeste Menchaca, Laura Gutierrez, Citlali Sosa, and Natalie Lira. You inspired me to think deeply about the lives of the women in this book, to try to recuperate their experiences and state plainly why their lives must matter to us now. You have also been the best writing partners. Alicia endured writing parts of the dissertation with me and then helped me think thorough critical chapters of the book during the pandemic all while doing her own incredible work in New Mexico. Natalie Fixmer-Oraiz and I have produced a collaborative writing practice that is unmatched. I remain in awe of her brilliance and her generous, radiant heart. Ashley and I have laughed, talked research and fashion, and cried (mostly me) in between and during our Pomodoro sessions. What an honor to have finished our tenure babies together— and found matching jumpsuits to celebrate! SWV dance and sing-along here we come, Dr. Howard! Asha taught me that it is possible to run for miles and talk theory. Without her expertise in care theory, major aspects of this book would have remained murky and underdeveloped. To the "mujeres of the borderlands writing group," Celeste, Laura, and Citlali, we have known each other since graduate school and have cheered each other on during our weekly writing Zoom sessions and have built new and vibrant avenues for borderlands history together. Natalie Lira and I have gone through the dissertation-to-book process nearly at the same time, and when I thought I could not do more, she nudged me onward. Every woman in this group has endured some form of glorious accomplishment and sustained difficulty in the past few years. We've sat at each other's kitchen tables or gabbed on the phone trying to make sense of our intellectual pursuits and domestic obligations. We've done our best to lift each other up throughout. Let's carry this reproductive care forward.

There are many circles of love in my life, extended kinship groups built over decades, mostly because when my parents came to the United States, we had no extended family in California. Wherever I've moved, my friend group has grown. My friends are my family. Mike (MK) Bess has spun so much yarn with me over the years, talking borderlands history blog, sci-fi novels, politics, and even the future of artificial intelligence. Not only have you indulged my many quirks, but you read more versions of different chapters than I can count. My pandemic "bestie beastie" text thread composed of Simon Balto and Ashley Howard remains strong even in the aftermath and has become a place of daily solace. My music group, Ari, Natalie, John, and Guillermo, allows me to sing my guts out every Wednesday night because lord knows we all need moments of expressive, bodily joy!

To the blessed humans who have remained my friends since we met in grade school and as bartenders and nannies and roommates, working, laughing, dancing, crying, having babies, and getting married over the course of the past forty years. Neena Dagnino, Helen Dinh, Danielle and Kristin Franzino, John Becker and Ember Kelley, Susana Gallardo, Francesca Alonso, and Shaun Lewis, I love you all so much. Thank you for keeping me grounded, never letting me forget who I am and where I came from.

It is imperative to honor those who are no longer with us. My memories of them have guided my every word. My father, Jesus Maria Murillo (1930–2011), died as I began to form my initial thoughts about this project. His incandescent demand for justice forms the inner core of my consciousness. *Gracias padre mio por todo.* Thank you to Johanna Lopez-Velador and Makeda Scott, brilliant *mujeres* taken from this world too soon. Your convictions and forthrightness grounded in radical reproductive justice are ever-present in this book. To the woman who helped raise me, Phyllis Soto (1931–2022), you are forever missed. A proud Chicana activist in 1960s' and 1970s' San Jose, she helped my mother with my brother and me when we were little growing up on the Eastside. She showered me with so much love and affection, all the while modeling for me the very essence of Chicana community-building. She was the very best *abuelita* when mine were so far away. To Bertha Gonzalez Chávez (1930–2018), who taught me much about the world of women and reproductive care when I, as a young mother, first interviewed her for my dissertation. I had no idea what I was doing when I asked her about her life coming of age in Mexico and the United States in the 1940s and 1950s. She guided me through her experiences with Scheherazade's narrative skill, all the while welcoming my curiosity with unabashed honesty.

To the incredible women who I had the joy of interviewing for this project, especially Amelia "Amy" Castillo, Senator Leticia Van de Putte, and Bertha Gonzalez Chávez. What an honor it was to tell your stories of political insurgency and community love. May we continue to nourish the visions and dreams you fought for and follow your footsteps into the future.

Thank you to the Goddess on High for my miracle of a family: Granny Sue and Tio Marko for being my El Paso touchstones. To Margarita Villa and Monique Clark for being such good, loving sisters holding my hand all those times I thought I should move on and do something else. To Mathew Phipps Hines, my brother from another mother, for making me laugh and smile daily—like it's his job—and for his unconditional care. To my brother, Tio Berny, and the beautiful Betty, for nurturing me and loving my children and family with such abandon. To my *mam* for helping me raise my babies so that I could follow my heart. She did so with so much love and tenderness. *Gracias, madre mia.* To Guillermo, my rock of a husband, whose uncompromising love has fueled my soul and passion for my research since the day we met. I love you. And of course, to my two children, Leo Lucia and Isamaria, who I conceived and tended to while I wrote this book. You are twin stars in my universe. You've shown me what reproductive care means every day since you were born. This book is for you.

Notes

Prologue

1. For San Jose as borderlands, see Pitti, *The Devil in Silicon Valley*.

2. Geiger and Davis, "A Growing Number of American Teenagers—Particularly Girls—Are Facing Depression." These statistics are pre-pandemic. The numbers have become worse.

3. Tapia, *American Pietas*, chap. 4.

4. In March 2023, Colorado Rep. Lauren Boebert praised high birth rates among (white) rural youths as she spoke to an audience about becoming a grandmother at thirty-six. See Kurtz, "Boebert Praises High Rural Teen Birth Rates"; for an extended analysis about the rise in anxieties over teen pregnancy in the late 1990s and early 2000s, see Fixmer-Oraiz, *Homeland Maternity*, chap. 4.

Introduction

1. In celebration of *Roe v. Wade's* fortieth anniversary, Linda Kerber argued for greater focus on local histories about women's reproduction and the movement for reproductive rights. She states, "Here is where our students—undergraduate and graduate—can make a real difference by their research. Working with advisers and archivists, they can frame questions, and they can seek to reconstruct a history that is in grave danger of being lost. The answers they find can contribute to the accumulation of necessary knowledge . . ." Kerber, "The 40th Anniversary of *Roe v. Wade*. For more on reproductive justice history literature, see Gutiérrez, *Fertile Matters*; Espino, "Women Sterilized as They Give Birth"; Schoen, *Choice and Coercion*; Briggs, *Reproducing Empire*; McQuade, "Troubling Reproduction"; Melcher, *Pregnancy, Motherhood and Choice*; Stern, "Sterilized in the Name of Public Health"; Lira, *Laboratory of Deficiency*; Theobald, *Reproduction on the Reservation*.

2. Due to financial mismanagement, Planned Parenthood of El Paso closed its doors in 2009, two years before the Texas state legislature cut off funding to Planned Parenthood facilities in the state. For nine years, El Paso was the largest city in the country without a Planned Parenthood clinic. In 2018, Planned Parenthood of Greater Texas, with support from two unidentified donors, reopened a clinic in the Sun City that remains in operation today. See Moore's "The Return of Planned Parenthood to El Paso."

3. There were clinics in other cities in Texas as well as in Arizona before the El Paso clinic opened, but none in cities on the US-Mexico border. For more on borderland birth control clinics, see Melcher, *Pregnancy, Motherhood, and Choice*; McQuade, "Troubling Reproduction"; Anderson, *Sixty Years of Choice*.

4. Prentiss, *Debating God's Economy*, 2–3.

5. Tentler, *Catholics and Contraception*, 73; Tobin, *The American Religious Debate over Birth Control*, chap. 5.

6. Tentler, *Catholics and Contraception*, 72.

7. The organization affiliated with Planned Parenthood in 1946 during a state meeting in Dallas. "Meeting Minutes September 1946," Planned Parenthood of El Paso records, MS 286, Box 1.

8. Reagan, "Crossing the Border for Abortions"; Gutierrez-Romine, *From Back Alley to the Border*; Murillo, "Espanta Cigüeñas." Because of public pressure in the city, and perhaps, because of their own conservative views on abortion, Planned Parenthood of El Paso never offered abortion services, before or after *Roe v. Wade*.

9. Morgan and Roberts, "Reproductive Governance in Latin America."

10. For a succinct analysis of Mexico's population policy, see Laveaga, "'Let's Become Fewer.'"

11. For extensive histories of population control, see Connelly, *Fatal Misconception*, chap. 6; Merchant, *Building the Population Bomb*.

12. Drucker, "The Diaphragm in the City."

13. Schoen, *Choice and Coercion*.

14. Goetting, "Draft of Speech," box 11, folder 4.

15. Chávez, "A Glass Half Empty."

16. Gutiérrez, *Fertile Matters*, 5–6.

17. For an extended discussion of anti-Blackness and anti-Indigenous thinking through the medicalization of reproduction in Mexico, see O'Brien, *Surgery and Salvation*.

18. Gómez, *Manifest Destinies*, 83.

19. For more on gendered racial formation, see Kitch, *The Specter of Sex*; Kandaswamy, "Gendering Racial Formation."

20. Garcia, *Desert Immigrants*, 127.

21. Omi and Winant, *Racial Formation in the United States*.

22. Perales, *Smeltertown*, 30.

23. Robert Miles's definition of racism as not only an ideology but also a practice is important here. Miles, *Racism after "Race Relations*," 60–61.

24. Connelly, *Fatal Misconception*, 7.

25. Anthropologist Iris López contends that in Puerto Rico the discourse of overpopulation as dangerous and a barrier to modernity became part of the United States political position toward the island after it became a colony of the United States in 1898. López, *Matters of Choice*, 5–6, 9–10.

26. I discuss the idea of "border rule" in further detail in "The Politics of US-Mexico Border Rule and Reproductive (In)Justice" in *The Nursing Clio Reader* (forthcoming, 2025), but I borrow the term *border rule* from scholar-activist Harsha Walia in *Border and Rule*.

27. This framework is, of course, indebted to Michel Foucault's theorization of biopolitics and governmentality. See Foucault, *The History of Sexuality* and *Security, Territory, Population*; also see Mytheli Sreenivas's analysis of populations and biopolitics in *Reproductive Politics and the Making of Modern India*, 14–19; and

Alexandra Minna Stern's theorization of biopower in the borderlands in "Building, Boundaries and Blood," 52–53.

28. Pascoe, *What Comes Naturally*, 121–22.

29. For a multiracial history of the borderlands, see Lim, *Porous Borders*.

30. Silliman et al., "Women of Color and Their Struggle for Reproductive Justice," 13–14.

31. Jennifer Morgan's framing of race and population governance in the colonial period has been helpful for my analysis here. Morgan, *Reckoning with Slavery*.

32. "South El Paso Birth Control Clinic Given Endorsement of Club Women," *El Paso Herald-Post* (El Paso, Texas), February 6, 1937.

33. See my article for a similar argument: Murillo, "Birth Control, Border Control."

34. Further studies are needed to understand why Texas never adopted compulsory sterilization laws like other states did, particularly in the 1920s and 1930s. In 1948, Clarence Gamble, along with the Human Betterment League, attempted to bring sterilization laws to Texas, even furnishing model legislation, but their plan never found enough supporters. Planned Parenthood of El Paso consistently declined the sterilization services offered by Gamble. Clarence Gamble papers, 1920–1970s, H MS c23, box 42, folder 687, Center for the History of Medicine, Francis A. Countway Library of Medicine.

35. Chávez, "A Glass Half Empty"; Stern, "Sterilized in the Name of Public Health," 1128–38; Gutiérrez, *Fertile Matters*; Espino, "Women Sterilized as They Give Birth."

36. Ginsburg and Rapp, "Introduction," 3, and Colen, "'Like a Mother to Them,'" *Conceiving the New World Order*; Chávez, "A Glass Half Empty."

37. Although there were other racialized populations in El Paso, including Black, Asian, and Native groups, their population numbers were much smaller compared to the Mexican-origin community. Given the proximity to Mexico, Mexican-origin people would remain the main demographic threat to Anglo rule in the region. See McQuade, "Troubling Reproduction"; Lira, *Laboratory of Deficiency*; Sinclair, "Birth City."

38. Clarke, *Disciplining Reproduction*, 7.

39. Stern, "Sterilized in the Name of Public Health," 1128–38; Gutiérrez, *Fertile Matters*; Espino, "Women Sterilized as They Give Birth"; Lira, *Laboratory of Deficiency*.

40. Goetting, "Draft of Speech."

41. Goetting, "Draft of Speech."

42. Beth Krier, "A Crusader for Birth Control in Mexico," *Los Angeles Times*, May 22, 1987.

43. Kennedy, *Birth Control in America*; James Reed, *From Private Vice to Public Virtue*; Gordon, *The Moral Property of Women*; McCann, *Birth Control Politics in the United States*; Kline, *Building a Better Race*; Schoen, *Choice and Coercion*; Hartman, *Reproductive Rights and Wrongs*; Connelly, *Fatal Misconception*; Tone, *Controlling Reproduction*.

44. Guidotti-Hernández, "Embodied Forms of State Domination: Gender and the Camp Grant Massacre," 91.

45. Held, "The Ethics of Care as Moral Theory," *The Ethics of Care*, 2.

46. There is a long history of labor organizing in the borderlands. Chicana factory workers led one of the most well-documented labor strikes in 1972. Their actions helped usher in massive labor and care organizing that extends to the present day. La Mujer Obrera, a women worker collective in El Paso, is a direct result of the two-year Farah strike. Ruiz, *From Out of the Shadows*, 127–30; Marquez, "Organizing Mexican-American Women in the Garment Industry," 68.

47. Ross, "African-American Women and Abortion."

48. Gutiérrez, "'We Will No Longer Be Silent or Invisible': Latinas Organizing for Reproductive Justice," in Silliman et al., eds., *Undivided Rights*, 221.

49. For groundbreaking scholarship on the history of Mexican-origin women and Puerto Rican women's sterilization abuses, see the scholarship of Virginia Espino, Elena Gutiérrez, Alexandra Minna Stern, Laura Briggs, Jennifer Nelson, Lena McQuade, Iris Lopez, and Natalie Lira.

50. Hartman, "Venus in Two Acts," 3.

51. Ruiz, *From Out of the Shadows*, 35.

52. For key examples of Chicana histories by Chicana historians, see Ruiz, *From Out of the Shadows*; Castañeda, *Three Decades of Engendering History*; Pérez, *The Decolonial Imaginary*; González, *Refusing the Favor*; Espinoza, Cotera, and Blackwell, eds., *Chicana Movidas*; Chávez-García, *Negotiating Conquest*; Perales, *Smeltertown*; Lira, *Laboratory of Deficiency*; Menchaca, "Borderland Visualities"; Gutierrez, *A Constant Threat*; Riddell, "Californio Local Liberalisms."

53. For more on the histories of Puerto Rican women and cohesive family planning campaigns, see Lopez, *Matters of Choice*; Ramirez de Arellano and Seipp, *Colonialism, Catholicism, and Contraception*; Briggs, *Reproducing Empire*.

54. Nelson, *More Than Medicine*.

55. Blackwell, *¡Chicana Power! Contested Histories of Feminism in the Chicano Movement*, 62–63.

56. Ruiz and Tiano, eds., *Women on the U.S.-Mexico Border*, 2–3.

57. Emma Pérez's "Letter to Gloria Anzaldúa" engages with critiques of Anzaldúa's use of Mexican writer and philosopher José Vasconcelos's articulations of *mestizaje*. While Vasconcelos believed the superiority of the white European race would ultimately triumph over the so-called Black and Indigenous races in this "raza cosmica," Anzaldúa certainly was not a proponent of this ideology. Instead, her "mestiza consciousness" described a transformative move to a new multiracial, pluriversal consciousness. RJ scholars are proposing a similar move as RJ frameworks are deployed across disciplines. Pérez, *Queering the Border*.

58. Loretta et al., eds., *Radical Reproductive Justice*, 11.

59. Kennedy, *Birth Control in America*; Reed, *From Private Vice to Public Virtue*; Gordon, *The Moral Property of Women*; McCann, *Birth Control Politics in the United States*; Chesler, *Woman of Valor*; Baker, *Margaret Sanger*.

60. Tone, *Devices and Desires*; Tone, *Controlling Reproduction*; Watkins, *On the Pill*; Asbell, *The Pill*.

61. Holz, *The Birth Control Clinic in a Marketplace World*; Hajo, *Birth Control on Main Street*; Ramírez de Arellano and Seipp, *Colonialism, Catholicism, and Contraception*; Tobin, *The American Religious Debate over Birth Control*; Tentler, *Catholics and Contraception*; Davis, *Sacred Work*; Leon, *An Image of God*.

62. Mohr, *Abortion in America*; Petchesky, *Abortion and Woman's Choice*; Luker, *Abortion and the Politics of Motherhood*; Reagan, *When Abortion Was A Crime*; Joffe, *Doctors of Conscience*; Schoen, *Abortion after Roe*; Nelson, *Women of Color and the Reproductive Rights Movement*; Silliman et al., *Undivided Rights*.

Chapter 1

1. Year: *1880*; Census Place: *Upper Lake, Lake, California*; Roll: *66*; Page: *70C*; Enumeration District: *052*.

2. Obituary: Calvin Smith Babbitt, *El Paso Herald Post*, June 25, 1909.

3. Ruiz, "Dead Ends or Gold Mines?," 42; Romo, *Ringside Seat to a Revolution*.

4. Obituary: Calvin Smith Babbitt, *El Paso Herald Post*, June 25, 1909; Babbitt, *The Remedy*, 66.

5. Stern, "Buildings, Boundaries, and Blood," 58–59.

6. Babbitt, *The Remedy*, 3.

7. Jordan, *The Blood of the Nation*, 21–22.

8. Ross and Jordan were both at Stanford at the turn of the century.

9. Lovett, *Conceiving the Future*, 7.

10. Ross as quoted by Lovett, *Conceiving the Future*, 86.

11. Babbitt, *The Remedy*, 45–46.

12. Babbitt, *The Remedy*, 13–14, 45–46.

13. Babbitt was living in California when its state senators championed both the Page Act in 1875 and then the Chinese Exclusion Act in 1882.

14. Babbitt, *The Remedy*, 45; Luibhéid, *Denied Entry*, 34–35.

15. Rodríguez-Muñiz, *Figures of the Future*, 31–32.

16. Babbitt, *The Remedy*, 53.

17. Rodríguez-Muñiz, *Figures of the Future*, 31.

18. "Questions Pertaining to Mexican Immigration," Harry H. Laughlin Papers Manuscript Collection L1, C-4-1:7 Box, "John C. Box—Texas Representative—Immigration Committee, Correspondence," Special Collections, Truman State University.

19. Morgan, *Reckoning with Slavery*, 89; Ian Hacking's "Making Up People," cited in *Reckoning with Slavery*, 93.

20. Morgan, *Reckoning with Slavery*, 89, 93.

21. Gutiérrez, *Fertile Matters*, 9.

22. The idea for examining gendered racialization projects—projects I believe helped define population concerns throughout the colonial, national, and modern periods—derives from Omi and Winant's theory of racial formation and Natalia Molina's extension of relational forms of race-making. Omi and Winant, *Racial Formation in the United States*; Molina, HoSang, and Gutiérrez, *Relational Formations of Race*, 7.

23. Chávez, *The U.S. War with Mexico*, 3.

24. Menchaca, *The Mexican American Experience in Texas*, 31.

25. Menchaca, *Recovering History, Constructing Race*, 17.

26. Rodríguez-Muñiz, *Figures of the Future*, xv.

27. DeLay, "Blood Talk," 232.

28. DeLay, "Blood Talk," 232.

29. Tjarks, "Comparative Demographic Analysis of Texas, 1777–1793," 299; Stephanson, *Manifest Destiny*, 37.

30. De León, *They Called Them Greasers*, 3.

31. Eisenhower, *So Far from God*, 12–13; Weber, *Foreigners in Their Native Land*, 88–89; Reséndez, *Changing National Identities at the Frontier*, 28–29; Chávez, *The U.S. War with Mexico*, 6.

32. Chávez, *The U.S. War with Mexico*, 6.

33. Reséndez, *Changing National Identities at the Frontier*, 26–27.

34. Chávez, *The U.S. War with Mexico*, 6; Reséndez, *Changing National Identities at the Frontier*, 42.

35. Reséndez, *Changing National Identities at the Frontier*, 29, 37–38.

36. Chávez, *The U.S. War with Mexico*, 6; Reséndez, *Changing National Identities at the Frontier*, 264. Although Reséndez contests this notion of "fixed identities" during this period, arguing instead for a more muddied version of "changing loyalties," his conclusions are in tension with the racial calculations and white supremacist visions constructed by men like John C. Calhoun and leaders of the Texas rebellion, such as Stephen F. Austin.

37. Weber, *Foreigners in Their Native Land*, 132.

38. Solomon Foot as quoted in Rodríguez, "The US–Mexico War and American Literary History," 11.

39. Calhoun, "Conquest of Mexico (Speech)."

40. Calhoun, "Conquest of Mexico (Speech)."

41. McWilliams, Meier, and García. *North from Mexico*, 71.

42. Vargas, *Crucible of Struggle*, 102.

43. Hernandez, *City of Inmates*, 10; for more on the legal history of Mexican American racial formation, see Gómez, *Manifest Destinies*.

44. Acuña, *Occupied America*, 55.

45. Gómez, *Manifest Destinies*, 5–6.

46. For a pioneering analysis of racial purity discourse in the colonial period, see Martínez, *Genealogical Fictions*.

47. With the constitutional end of abortion after the *Dobbs v. Jackson Women's Health Organization* (2022) Supreme Court decision, people who can get pregnant are also experiencing a similar stratification of rights based on what state they live in.

48. Jacobson, *Whiteness of a Different Color*, 43.

49. Jacobson, *Whiteness of a Different Color*, 7.

50. Martinez, *Saga of a Legendary Border City*, 10–11.

51. Timmons, *El Paso*, 105.

52. Martinez, *Saga of a Legendary Border City*, 13.

53. Timmons, *El Paso*, 105–6.

54. Timmons, *El Paso*, 105.

55. Timmons, *El Paso*, 105–7.

56. Lim, *Porous Borders*, 21.

57. Garcia, *Desert Immigrants*, 24; Martinez, *Saga of a Legendary Border City*, 23. El Paso del Norte was renamed Ciudad Juárez in honor of Benito Juárez.

58. Garcia, *Desert Immigrants*, 13–15.

59. White, *Out of the Desert*, 52.

60. Lim, *Porous Borders*, 2; Garcia, *Desert Immigrants*, 13.

61. Garcia, *Desert Immigrants*, 18.

62. Peffer, *Forbidden Families*, 32.

63. Peffer, *Forbidden Families*, 43.

64. Luibhéid, *Denied Entry*, 37.

65. Jones, *Birthright Citizens*, 1.

66. Murillo, "Birth Control, Border Control"; Stern, *Eugenic Nation*, 16.

67. Ngai, *Impossible Subjects*, 5.

68. Stern, *Eugenic Nation*, 11.

69. Roberts, *Killing the Black Body*, 61–62; McCann, *Birth Control Politics in the United States*, 101–2.

70. Lovett, *Conceiving the Future*, 78.

71. Lovett, *Conceiving the Future*, 80.

72. For more on the history of white vigilante violence, see Carrigan and Webb, *Forgotten Dead*; Carrigan, *The Making of Lynching Culture*.

73. Muñoz Martinez, *The Injustice Never Leaves You*, 7, 10; see also Miguel Antonio Levario, *Militarizing the Border*.

74. Nicholas Villanueva Jr., *The Lynching of Mexicans in the Texas Borderlands*, 104.

75. Muñoz Martinez, *The Injustice Never Leaves You*, 6.

76. Muñoz Martinez, *The Injustice Never Leaves You*, 3.

77. Foley, *The White Scourge*, 40.

78. Stern, *Eugenic Nation*, 58.

79. Molina, *Fit to Be Citizens?*, 53.

80. Stern, *Eugenic Nation*, 59; McKiernan-González, *Fevered Measures*, chap. 5.

81. Stern, "Buildings Boundaries and Blood," 42, 45.

82. "Dr. Claude C. Pierce Correspondence," folder 4, box 43, Planned Parenthood Federation of America, Series #2: Birth Control Federation of America. Sophia Smith Collection, Smith College, Northampton, MA.

83. Gabbert, "El Paso, a Sight for Sore Eyes."

84. Ruiz, *From Out of the Shadows*, 13.

85. Martinez, *Saga of a Legendary Border City*, 45.

86. Martinez, *Saga of a Legendary Border City*, 45.

87. Martinez, *Chicanos of El Paso*, 6.

88. Martinez, *Chicanos of El Paso*, 6.

89. Sinclair, "White Plague, Mexican Menace."

90. "A Short History of South El Paso, Department of Planning City of El Paso, October 1967: Part III: The 1925 Kessler Report," 23–25, South El Paso, Chicano Vertical File. C.L. Sonnichesen Special Collections Department, University of Texas at El Paso.

91. Garcia, *Desert Immigrants*, 6.

92. Ngai, *Impossible Subjects*, 18–19.

93. Ruiz, *From Out of the Shadows*, 13.

94. Ngai, *Impossible Subjects*, 17; Hernández, *Migra!*

95. Ngai, *Impossible Subjects*, 27.

96. Nagi, *Impossible Subjects*, 27.

97. Ngai, *Impossible Subjects*, 25.

98. Hill, "Composition of the American Population by Race and Country of Origin," ; "American Population by Race," p. 1, box 83, Series VI, Subject Files, Sanger Papers, Sophia Smith Collection.

99. Hill, "Composition of the American Population by Race and Country of Origin," 7.

100. Molina, *How Race Is Made in America*, 74–75, 82–83.

101. For extensive histories about deportation, see Balderrama and Rodríguez, *Decade of Betrayal*; Enciso, *Que se quedean allá*.

102. "Mexican Problems Committee—Texas Rehabilitation Commission," Cleofás Calleros Papers, MS 231, box 5, folder 5.

103. "Mexican Problems Committee—Texas Rehabilitation Commission," Cleofás Calleros Papers, MS 231, box 5, folder 5.

104. Stern, *Eugenic Nation*, 17.

105. Grant, *The Conquest of a Continent*, xi; Lira, *Laboratory of Deficiency*, chap. 3; Lira and Stern, "Mexican Americans and Eugenic Sterilization."

106. Stern, *Eugenic Nation*, 111–12.

107. Stern, *Eugenic Nation*, 208.

108. McCann, *Birth Control Politics in the United States*, 99–100; for a brief discussion of rising immigration and border controls, see Overmyer-Velázquez, "Good Neighbors and White Mexicans."

109. Molina mentions Box's efforts to push for legislation through Congress that sought to expressly racialize Mexicans as part of "Amerind stocks that no longer exist." Molina, "'In a Race All Their Own.'"

110. "Letter from Laughlin to Box, January 29, 1930," Harry H. Laughlin Papers Manuscript Collection L1, box C-4-1:7, "John C. Box—Texas Representative—Immigration Committee, Correspondence," Special Collections, Truman State University.

111. Stern, "Buildings, Boundaries, and Blood," 77.

112. "Letter from Laughlin to Box, January 29, 1930" and "Letter from Laughlin to Box, February 5, 1930," Harry H. Laughlin Papers Manuscript Collection L1, box C-4-1:7, "John C. Box—Texas Representative—Immigration Committee, Correspondence," Special Collections, Truman State University.

113. "Letter from Laughlin to Box, February 5, 1930," and "Letter from Box to Laughlin, April 2, 1930," Harry H. Laughlin Papers Manuscript Collection L1,

box C-4-1:7, "John C. Box—Texas Representative—Immigration Committee, Correspondence," Special Collections, Truman State University.

114. Molina, "'In a Race All Their Own,'" 190.

115. Grant, *The Conquest of a Continent*, 324.

116. Grant, *The Conquest of a Continent*, 324, 327–28.

117. Perales, *Smeltertown*, 24.

118. "Letter to Charles Davenport from Harry Laughlin, August 22, 1929," Harry H. Laughlin Papers Manuscript Collection L1, box C-4-6:13, "Mexican Immigration," Special Collections, Truman State University.

119. For an incisive argument on the anxieties surrounding notions of a white nation imperiled, see Beltrán, *Cruelty as Citizenship*.

Chapter 2

1. "Clinic Needed Is Questioned," *El Paso Times*, February 25, 1937.

2. "Clinic Needed Is Questioned," *El Paso Times*, February 25, 1937.

3. For a national and international history of Planned Parenthood, see Gordon, *The Moral Property of Women*; Kennedy, *Birth Control in America*; McCann, *Birth Control Politics in the United States, 1916–1945*; and Connelly, *Fatal Misconception*.

4. Lira, *Laboratory of Deficiency*, 76.

5. Dame-Griff, "The Future Is Brown."

6. Perales, "'Who Has a Greater Job Than a Mother?'," 171.

7. Scholarship examining Filipina migration and the building of professions focused on care provide the foundations for how I am using economies of care. See Choy, *Empire of Care*; Tungohan, *Care Activism*; for an extensive study of Mexican-origin women as domestic workers, see Ruiz, "By the Day or the Week."

8. Ruiz, *From Out of the Shadows*, 166.

9. Lira, *Laboratory of Deficiency*, 76.

10. Rozek, "The Entry of Mexican Women into Urban Based Industries," 19; see also Gonzales, "Chicanas and Mexican Immigrant Families, 1920–1940."

11. Garcia, "The Catholic Church, Mexican Ethno-Catholicism, and Inculturation in El Paso," 39.

12. Garcia, "The Catholic Church, Mexican Ethno-Catholicism, and Inculturation in El Paso," 41.

13. Goetting, "My Association and Friendship with Margaret Sanger," in *Our Margaret Sanger by Many of Her Friends, Relatives and Colleagues*, vol. 1, edited by Erma Brown, Dorothy Brush, Masake Leward, and Ellen Watumull, 1st ed. (Copyright applied for 1959), unpublished manuscript, Sophia Smith Collection, 82; "Mrs. Sanger Meets at Luncheon with El Paso Doctors," *El Paso-Herald Post*, December 8, 1934. Sanger had visited El Paso in 1934, but no moves were made then to establish a clinic.

14. Goetting, *Our Margaret Sanger*, 84.

15. "Birth Control Money Sought: Will Raise Clinic Money through Membership in Organization," *El Paso Herald-Post*, February 26, 1937.

16. Sanger quoted in "Birth Control Lecture Heard by El Pasoans," *El Paso Times*, February 25, 1937.

17. Tobin, *The American Religious Debate over Birth Control*, 16.

18. "Goetting Scrapbook," box 5, folder 1. Betty Mary Smith Goetting papers, 1910–1979, MS 316, C. L. Sonnichsen Special Collections Department. The University of Texas at El Paso Library.

19. Pascoe, *Relations of Rescue*, 33.

20. Ladd-Taylor, *Mother-Work*, 4–5.

21. Ladd-Taylor, *Mother-Work*, 5.

22. Abrams, "Guardians of Virtue," 438.

23. Abrams, "Guardians of Virtue," 438–39.

24. Perales, "'Who Has a Greater Job Than a Mother?,'" 169.

25. Gabbert, "Defining the Boundaries of Care," 367.

26. Chávez Leyva. "'¿Que Son Los Niños?,'" 188.

27. Chávez Leyva, "'¿Que Son Los Niños?,'" 189.

28. Ruiz, *From Out of the Shadows*, 35.

29. Ruiz, *From Out of the Shadows*, 36 and 37.

30. Ruiz, *From Out of the Shadows*, 48.

31. Benita Roth's *Separate Roads to Feminism*, documenting the history and ideas of second wave feminists across race and class, is instructive in examining the divergent roads to feminist thought and activism that take place before the 1960s. In the 1920s and 1930s, Mexican-origin women and Anglo women in the borderlands had fundamentally different relationships to health and reproductive care, which dramatically alters their relationship to these issues into the future.

32. For a thoughtful analysis of the nascent birth control movement's connections to women's suffrage, see Prescott and Thompson, "A Right to Ourselves."

33. Nadkarni, *Eugenic Feminism*, 34–35.

34. Law scholar Mary Ziegler argues that after the 1930s, eugenic feminism fell out of favor among birth control advocates, including Sanger. This chapter critiques Ziegler's chronology. See Ziegler, "Eugenic Feminism."

35. Roberts, "Privatization and Punishment in the New Age of Reprogenetics," 1344; Colen, "'Like a Mother to Them,'" 78.

36. Colen, "'Like a Mother to Them,'" 80–81.

37. "David Smith Passes Away" Obituary, *El Paso Times*, May 6, 1939.

38. 1900 US Census, Jefferson Ward 2, Marion, Texas, Roll 1658, p. 9A, District 0091, FHL microfilm 1241658, Ancestry.com.

39. Kurt Eugene Goetting conversation with author, August 26, 2016.

40. Wilson and Van Velkinburgh, "Betty Mary Goetting Brought Birth Control to El Paso," 10–13.

41. "Social Personals," *El Paso Morning Times*, December 31, 1918; "Engagement Announcement of Miss Betty Mary Smith to Mr. Charles A. Goetting," *El Paso Herald Post*, June 7, 1919.

42. Standard Certificate of Death for Charles Augustus Goetting, Texas State Department of Health Bureau of Vital Statistics, El Paso, Texas, February 17, 1931.

43. Wilson and Van Velkinburgh, "Betty Mary Goetting Brought Birth Control to El Paso," 10–13; "Literature Department Will Meet," *El Paso Evening Post*, October 14, 1930.

44. "Betty Mary Goetting Obituary," *El Paso Herald-Post*, April 10, 1980; "Women's Organizations," *El Paso Herald Post*, November 8, 1929; "Mrs. Goetting to Present Book Review," *El Paso Herald-Post*, March 2, 1955.

45. Letter from Margaret Sanger to V.V.P., Betty Mary Goetting Papers, box 1.

46. McCann, *Birth Control Politics in the United States*; Kennedy, *Birth Control in America*, 24.

47. "Letter from Mary Ware Dennett to Goetting, May 6, 1919," Betty Mary Goetting Papers, box 1, folder 1.

48. Kennedy, *Birth Control in America*, 83.

49. "Letter from Birth Control Review to Betty Mary Goetting, May 1919," Betty Mary Goetting, MS 316, box 1, folder 3.

50. "Letter from Sanger to Betty Mary Goetting," Betty Mary Goetting, MS 316, box 1, folder 3.

51. "Letter from Sanger to Betty Mary Goetting," Betty Mary Goetting, MS 316, box 1, folder 3.

52. "Betty Mary Goetting Speeches," box 11, folder 4. Betty Mary Smith Goetting papers, 1910–1979, MS 316, C. L. Sonnichsen Special Collections Department.

53. Stern, *Eugenic Nation*, 59.

54. Nadkarni, *Eugenic Feminism*, 10.

55. For discussions of racial *Others*, including Mexicans, denied entry north from Ciudad Juárez to El Paso, see Gabbert, "El Paso, a Sight for Sore Eyes," 15–42; Menchaca, "'The Freedom of Jail'"; Lim, *Porous Borders*.

56. Reed, *From Private Vice to Public Virtue*, 114–15; McCann, *Birth Control Politics in the United States*, 119–20. According to McCann, eugenicists were reluctant to join Sanger—McCann explains that Charles Davenport "refused" to attend the 1925 ABCL convention—but Sanger, nonetheless, employed lesser-known eugenicists in her cause.

57. Nadkarni, *Eugenic Feminism*, 11.

58. Nadkarni, *Eugenic Feminism*, 24.

59. Gordon, *The Moral Property of Women*, 171.

60. McArthur and Smith, *Texas through Women's Eyes*, 90–91.

61. Anderson, *Sixty Years of Choice*, 12; McArthur and Smith, *Texas through Women's Eyes*, 90–91.

62. Anderson, *Sixty Years of Choice*, 20, 25.

63. Anderson, *Sixty Years of Choice*, 34.

64. McArthur and Smith, *Texas through Women's Eyes*, 91.

65. *1942 Directory of Planned Parenthood Services*, 7.

66. McArthur and Smith, *Texas through Women's Eyes*, 91; Anderson, *Sixty Years of Choice*, 32–33.

67. Reed, *From Private Vice to Public Virtue*, 211.

68. "Improving Human Stock Advocated by Sterilization: Teaching Birth Control Among Financially Dependent Also Favored," Luce's Press Clipping Bureau, New York, New York, Clipping from Dallas News, Texas, April 24, 1935. The Margaret Sanger Papers (microfilmed), Sophia Smith Collection.

69. "Improving Human Stock Advocated by Sterilization."

70. "Katie Ripley to Clarence Gamble, May 26, 1936," Clarence James Gamble, Papers, 1920–1970s, H MS C23, box 42, folder 680, Center for the History of Medicine, Francis A. Countway Library of Medicine, Harvard.

71. Melcher, *Pregnancy, Motherhood, and Choice*, 57.

72. Melcher, *Pregnancy, Motherhood, and Choice*, 65 and 66.

73. "First Birth Control Clinic to Be Started Here," *Arizona Daily Star*, November 16, 1934.

74. Melcher, *Pregnancy, Motherhood, and Choice*, 65.

75. Melcher, *Pregnancy, Motherhood, and Choice*, 68.

76. For an excellent analysis of the family planning movement in India and Japan, see Sreenivas, *Reproductive Politics and the Making of Modern India*; Takeuchi-Demirci, *Contraceptive Diplomacy*; Hodges, *Contraception, Colonialism, and Commerce*.

77. "Katie Ripley to Clarence Gamble, December 7, 1936."

78. Reed, *From Private Vice to Public Virtue*, 226.

79. "Clarence Gamble to Dr. George W. Cox, October 23, 1937," Clarence James Gamble, Papers, 1920–1970s, H MS C23, box 42, folder 682, Center for the History of Medicine. The amount $1,750 in 1937 is the equivalent of $38,000 in 2024.

80. "Margaret Sanger to Mary Betty Goetting, July 6, 1937," Margaret Sanger Papers, Collected Documents, Series III, Subseries 1. The Margaret Sanger Papers (microfilmed), Sophia Smith Collection.

81. "Clarence Gamble to Agnes Nelms, October 29, 1937," Clarence James Gamble, Papers, 1920–1970s, H MS C23, box 42, folder 682, Center for the History of Medicine.

82. "Clarence Gamble to Agnes Nelms, March 28, 1938," Clarence James Gamble, Papers, 1920–1970s, H MS C23, box 42, folder 682, Center for the History of Medicine.

83. Schoen, *Choice and Coercion*, 76 and 4.

84. "Clarence Gamble to Agnes Nelms, March 28, 1938," Clarence James Gamble, Papers, 1920–1970s, H MS C23, box 42, folder 682, Center for the History of Medicine; Briggs, *Reproducing Empire*.

85. "Martha Mumford to Clarence Gamble, 1939, Houston, Texas," Clarence James Gamble, Papers, 1920–1970s, H MS C23, box 42, folder 684, Center for the History of Medicine.

86. "Martha Mumford letter to Clarence Gamble, May 6, 1939," Clarence Gamble letter to Martha Mumford, May 18, 1939," Clarence James Gamble, Papers, 1920–1970s, H MS C23, box 42, folder 684, Center for the History of Medicine.

87. Anderson, *Sixty Years of Choice*, 8; Perales, *Smeltertown*, 237.

88. For a thorough analysis of Mexican American political participation in El Paso, see Garcia, *The Making of a Mexican American Mayor*.

89. "Clarence Gamble letter to Martha Mumford, May 18, 1939," Clarence James Gamble, Papers, 1920–1970s, H MS C23, box 42, folder 684, Center for the History of Medicine.

90. "Field Report: Mumford, May 14, 1939," Clarence James Gamble, Papers, 1920–1970s, H MS C23, box 42, folder 684, Center for the History of Medicine.

91. "Field Report: Mumford, May 14, 1939," Clarence James Gamble, Papers, 1920–1970s, H MS C23, box 42, folder 684, Center for the History of Medicine.

92. "Clarence Gamble to El Paso's Mothers' Health Center," Clarence James Gamble, Papers, 1920–1970s, H MS C23, box 42, folder 685, Center for the History of Medicine; "¡Muchos Niños! Pamphlet," "Clarence Gamble to El Paso's Mothers' Health Center," Clarence James Gamble, Papers, 1920–1970s, H MS C23, box 42, folder 685, Center for the History of Medicine; "Instrucciones as Los Pacientes," Clarence James Gamble, Papers, 1920–1970s, H MS C23, box 42, folder 685, Center for the History of Medicine. Translation of last document, figure 2.2: "[Birth Control] is also a benefit for children when you do not have them so close together and intervals between each birth. You have seen, for yourself, newborn babies die in homes that need food for already growing families, where the mother, herself, has no proper nutrients to eat. BIRTH CONTROL is not an operation. BIRTH CONTROL is not abortion. BIRTH CONTROL is just a method to avoid conception, postponing the birth of a child until you acquire the necessary means to welcome it. The BIRTH CONTROL METHOD only requires a bit of common sense, but in reality is simple to use and with patience and care anyone interested in learning to use it can. Using BIRTH CONTROL is ultimately moral, when the goal is to lengthen the time between births in order to assume the health of the mother and happiness in the home. The truly religious woman is bold and moral when she declares, 'I want to have only as many children as I can maintain and educate, but no more.' Be certain that BIRTH CONTROL does not impede women from having more children. It allows her to have them when she wants them. The use of this BIRTH CONTROL METHOD is STRICTLY VOLUNTARY."

93. Author unknown, "Progress Report on El Paso Clinic, circa 1942," Clarence James Gamble, Papers, 1920–1970s, H MS C23, box 42, folder 686, Center for the History of Medicine.

94. "Progress Report on El Paso Clinic, circa 1942."

95. "Progress Report on El Paso Clinic, circa 1942."

96. "Progress Report on El Paso Clinic, circa 1942."

97. "City-county" refers to the fact that in El Paso, the city and the county shared governance over public health institutions. They referred to themselves this way. "E.P. Health Officer Will Advocate Birth Control in City and County in Effort to Decrease Death Rate," *El Paso Herald-Post*, July 26, 1933.

98. Several studies exist that have attempted to trace the devastating history of infant mortality in El Paso; see Roberstad, "Infant Mortality in El Paso County"; Gabbert, "Defining the Boundaries of Care"; Sinclair, "Birth City."

99. Ladd-Taylor, *Mother-Work*, 87.

100. Melcher, *Pregnancy, Motherhood, and Choice*, 43–44.

101. "E.P. Health Officer Will Advocate Birth Control in City and County in Effort to Decrease Death Rate," *El Paso Herald-Post*, July 26, 1933.

102. "E.P. Health Officer Will Advocate Birth Control"; "El Pasoans Shun Birth Control: Want Babies: Only One Asks Information on Subject at County Health Office," *El Paso Herald-Post*, August 3, 1933.

103. "E.P. Health Officer Will Advocate Birth Control."

104. "El Pasoans Shun Birth Control."

105. "Health Officer Urges Birth Control but Will Not Give Out Information," *El Paso Times*, July 27, 1933.

106. "Catholics Protest Contraceptive Sale," *El Paso Herald-Post*, July 11, 1934.

107. "Catholics Protest Contraceptive Sale."

108. "Clinic Turned Down for Birth Control: Doctors Here Say Few Physicians May Get Together Later," *El Paso Herald-Post*, December 11, 1934.

109. "Cites Savings in Deaths," *El Paso-Herald Post*, December 10, 1936.

110. "Texas to Receive Large Health Fund," *El Paso-Herald Post*, February 18, 1936.

111. Garcia, "Mexican Americans and the Politics of Citizenship," 188.

112. Garcia, "Mexican Americans and the Politics of Citizenship"; Overmyer-Velázquez, "Good Neighbors and White Mexicans."

113. "Latins Fight City Ratings as Colored," *El Paso Times*, October 7, 1936.

114. Gabbert, "Defining the Boundaries of Care," chap. 9; Sinclair, "Birth City," chap. 2.

115. Garcia, "Mexican Americans and the Politics of Citizenship," 191–92.

116. "Latins Fight City Ratings as Colored."

117. "U.S. Drops 'Colored' Rating of Mexicans," *El Paso Times*, October 21, 1936.

118. "U.S. Drops 'Colored' Rating of Mexicans."

119. Mary Melcher notes that given her son's respiratory condition and the adage that the dry desert climate could help mitigate it, Sanger moved to Tucson, Arizona, that same year. Melcher, *Pregnancy, Motherhood, and Choice*, 57.

120. "Mrs. Sanger Meets at Luncheon with El Paso Doctors," *El Paso Herald-Post*, December 8, 1934.

121. "Mrs. Sanger Meets at Luncheon with El Paso Doctors."

122. "Protestants and Jews Attack Catholic Birth Control Stand," *El Paso Times*, December 16, 1935.

123. Goetting, *Our Margaret Sanger*, 83.

124. Goetting, *Our Margaret Sanger*, 83.

125. "Clinic Need Is Questioned," *El Paso Herald-Post*, February 25, 1937.

126. "Birth Control Lecture Heard by El Pasoans," *El Paso Times*, February 25, 1937.

127. "Birth Control Lecture Heard by El Pasoans."

128. Lira, *Laboratory of Deficiency*.

129. "Birth Control Lecture Heard by El Pasoans."

130. Stern, *Eugenic Nation*, 5.

131. Schoen, *Choice and Coercion*, 82.

132. For histories of sterilization, see Zipf, *Bad Girls at Samarcand*; Lawrence, "The Indian Health Service and the Sterilization of Native Women"; Roberts, *Killing the Black Body*; Lira, *Laboratory of Deficiency*; Espino, "Women Sterilized as They Give Birth"; Caitlin Dickerson, Seth Freed Wessler and Miriam Jordan, "Immigrants Say They Were Pressured into Unneeded Surgeries," *New York Times*, September 29, 2020.

133. Kline, *Building a Better Race*, chap. 2. For discussion of sterilizations and whiteness after World War II, see Kluchin, *Fit to Be Tied*.

134. Paul, "'Three Generations of Imbeciles Are Enough,'" 643; Hopkins, "Was There a 'Southern Eugenics?,'" 38.

135. Goetting, *Our Margaret Sanger*, 84.

136. Smith, "'All Good Things Start with the Women,'" 268.

137. Rev. Daniel J. Quigley, "Clinics or Asylums?" *El Paso Times*, March 2, 1937.

138. Rev. H. D. Buchanan, "Clamor for Birth Control Comes Now, as It Always Has, from the Well-to-Do," *El Paso Times*, February 22, 1937.

139. Buchanan, "Clamor for Birth Control Comes Now."

140. Many school districts across the Southwest engaged in tactics that essentially prohibited Mexican students from accessing and enjoying the same educational facilities and opportunities as their white counterparts. Aguirre, "Mendez v. Westminster School District."

141. Ruiz, *From Out of the Shadows*, 40; Garcia, *Desert Immigrants*, chap. 6.

142. Garcia, *Desert Immigrants*, 113.

143. Goetting, *Our Margaret Sanger*, 86, quote on 85.

144. Goetting, *Our Margaret Sanger*, 86.

145. "Thinking Out Loud: Fears Birth Control," *El Paso Herald-Post*, March 3, 1937.

146. "Thinking Out Loud."

147. Stern, "Buildings, Boundaries, and Blood," 68.

148. Gordon, *The Moral Property of Women*, 139; Davis, *Women, Race and Class*, chap. 9.

149. For more on the YWCA, see Guthrie, "The Young Women's Christian Association of El Paso."

150. "Birth Control Clinic on Southside Urged," *El Paso-Herald Post*, February 21, 1938.

151. Board Meeting Minutes, February 1937, box 11, MS 286, Planned Parenthood of El Paso, Texas, Papers, Special Collections, University of El Paso, Texas.

152. Board Meeting Minutes, March 1937, box 11, Planned Parenthood of El Paso Papers; "Birth Control Money Sought," *El Paso Herald-Post*, February 26, 1937.

153. "El Paso Birth Control Clinic under Sangers Plan Opens Tuesday," *El Paso Herald-Post*, April 24, 1937.

154. Board of Director Minutes, February, March, and April 1937, folder 1, box 11, Planned Parenthood of El Paso Papers.

155. Board of Director Meeting Minutes, March 1937.

155. "'Birth Control' in Name of Clinic," *El Paso Herald-Post*, December 5, 1939.

157. "El Paso Birth Control Clinic under Sangers Plan Opens Tuesday."

158. "Its Anniversary," *El Paso Evening Post*, February 2, 1928; "Juarez Custom Men Released by Court," *El Paso Herald*, February 15, 1929.

159. "Se Inauguro Hoy Nueva Clinica," *El Continental* (El Paso, Texas), April 27, 1937. Original: "La señora Emma Hensley está a cargo de la nueva clinica, habiendo llegado de la ciudad de México, donde hizo sus cursos de preparación y por lo tanta habla correctamente el español." According to the newspapers, Boretz, a native of New York, and his family were part of El Paso's high society. Morris Boretz served

on the boards of various clubs, such as the Kiwanis and the Progress Club, alongside important members of the community including Maurice Schwartz, whose wife Hedwig had been part of the original birth control committee. See "Club Names Hershberg," *El Paso Evening Post*, December 8, 1930; "Hostess to New Mexico Governor," *El Paso Times*, February 12, 1930; "Kiwanians Join," *El Paso Evening Post*, November 13, 1930; "Boretz Obituary," *El Paso Times*, December 8, 1987.

160. "250 El Paso Wives Get Family Planning Advice at E.P. Clinic," *El Paso Herald-Post*, July 26, 1937.

161. "Speeches circa 1940," Betty Mary Smith Goetting Papers, MS 316, box 11, folder 4.

162. "Sra. Maude Gillespie," *El Continental*, March 3, 1940, Betty Mary Smith Goetting Papers, MS 316, box 5.

163. "Sra. Maude Gillespie."

164. It is unclear to what degree the Church supported the work of Planned Parenthood.

165. "Organization Timeline," Planned Parenthood of El Paso records, MS 286, box 11.

166. *Directory of Planned Parenthood Clinic Services*, 12.

167. "Organization Timeline."

168. "Meeting Minutes December 1946," Planned Parenthood of El Paso records, MS286, box 1.

169. "Organization Timeline."

170. "Clinic Need Is Questioned."

171. Tobin, *The American Religious Debate over Birth Control*, 149.

172. Rabbi Edward L. Israel as quoted in Tobin, *The American Religious Debate over Birth Control*, 151.

173. "Mansfield Hits Drawing of E.P. Publication," *El Paso Herald-Post*, February 13, 1939.

174. "Mansfield Hits Drawing of E.P. Publication."

175. "March 1939 Minutes," box 11, Old Minutes, Planned Parenthood of El Paso Papers.

176. "Murders Show Necessity for Birth Control," *El Paso Herald-Post*, April 7, 1938.

177. "Copy of Letter Sent to Sanger from Tracht, March 20, 1953." Betty Mary Goetting Papers box 1, folder 5.

178. "Ruth L. Tracht Dies: Funeral Mass Set at Church," *El Paso Herald-Post*, June 16, 1981.

179. "Copy of Letter Sent to Ruth Tracht from Sanger, March 26, 1953." Betty Mary Goetting Papers, box 11, folder 22.

180. "Copy of Letter Sent to Ruth Tracht from Sanger, March 26, 1953."

Chapter 3

1. "Porque mi prima en contra de mi volutad, me habia llevado a El Paso, para que me pusieran el diafragma," Bertha González Chávez oral history, conducted by Lina Murillo, August 4, 2015. Translated by the author.

2. "Como todos los hombres, no se pueden esperar. ¡Uh! Ellos tienen su necesidad ya. Entonces, ya no me pude poner, pues, salí embarazada de mi cuarto hijo." Bertha González Chávez oral history.

3. Bertha González Chávez oral history.

4. "Contando mentiras, yo tenía 14 años, y dije que tenía 16. Y entré al hospital de aprendiz," Bertha González Chávez oral history.

5. "No eramos ricos, ni tan poco pobres," Bertha González Chávez oral history interview with Marisela Chávez, July 15, 1993.

6. "Y claro que queriamos algo mas que enfermeria, no queriamos enfermeria. Queriamos algo, de deveras profesion." Bertha González Chávez oral history interview with Marisela Chávez, July 15, 1993.

7. "Entrabas como aprendice enfermeria. Te daban un entrenamiento y una vez que y te daban lecciones, le daban a uno un titulo de enfermera practica. Entonces, ya podia trabajar uno. Claro, seguias aprendiendo, nunca se acaba el aprendizaje. Pero una ve que ya tenias el titulo de enfermera pratica, ya tenia mas reconocimiento. Y las clases eran no muy formales, pero formales suficientemente como para cuando ir a pasar el examen, se pasaba el examen escrito y aparte habia sinodales, o sea un grupo de doctores que hacen diferentes clases de preguntas y califican sobre aquello. Una vez que se decide si pasaste el examen, entonces te dan aquel titulo, que de veras no era nada, pero que se podia hacer algo. Ya cuando menos podias poner inyecciones, attender partos, todas esas cosas." Bertha González Chávez oral history interview with Marisela Chavez, July 15, 1993.

8. O'Brien, *Surgery and Salvation*, 187.

9. Murillo, "Espanta Cigüeñas," 801.

10. Bertha González Chávez oral history.

11. "Puro asolearme, desvelarme porque cuando la penicilina se ponia cada tres horas, dia y noche, hasta que se acababa la dosis. Entonces era dia y noche. O me iba a quedar a las casas porque habia veces que me tocaba un ranchito. Y luego ya me traian en troca en la mañana." Bertha González Chávez oral history interview with Marisela Chávez, July 15, 1993.

12. "Mucha gente no pagaba, no tenia dinero. O te abonaban. Pero era algo," and "Ahora si atendiamos una mujer en parto, pues eso cobraba uno mas, como 100 pesos, ya despues, ya eran 200. Ya sabiamos que cuando teniamos un parto, ese dia se compraba mas carne." Bertha González Chávez oral history interview with Marisela Chávez, July 15, 1993.

13. "Para mi era porque a mi me gustaba porque no es lo mismo la casa que salir." Bertha González Chávez oral history interview with Marisela Chávez, August 17, 1993.

14. See the scholarship of Vicki Ruiz, Deena Gonzalez, Emma Pérez, Monica Perales, Elizabeth Escobedo, Irene Ledesma, Natalie Lira, Miroslava Chávez-Garcia, Celeste Menchaca, Erika Perez, Maria Raquel Casas, Margie Brown-Coronel, and Antonia Castaneda.

15. In chapters 4 and 5, it will become clearer that the colonial nature of medical provision in the borderlands precluded Mexican-origin women from receiving sound reproductive health care for themselves, their children, and their families.

16. Lira, *Laboratory of Deficiency*. Lira's book through the prism of reproductive care, as a critical foundation for reproductive justice, allowed me to read deeper into the stories of women like Rosie Zavella. Perhaps we can see Pacific Colony as a forced community, where institutionalized youths might have engaged with each other as members of the same marginalized group—for instance, as a community of people deemed "feebleminded" by the state or as members of the same racial or ethnic group or people labeled as disposable. We can imagine ways that they cared for each other beyond the demands placed on them by doctors, nurses, therapists, psychologists, and others there to study and surveil them. Lira presents the lives of women like Zavella, whose distress over the death of her charge in the infirmary tells us much about reproductive care (Lira, 100). The death of Zavella's charge thwarted her ability to continue comforting, supporting, and uplifting the most marginalized members in her community. It left her without words and without recourse for reestablishing the binds of community care needed for future members—in and out of the institution. On the other hand, as Lira notes, Zavella also connected deeply with other institutionalized people as lovers, both women and men, during her time at the institution. As Lira writes, "these young women asserted their desires and tried to find pleasures and joy during their forced confinement" (Lira, 102). These kinds of reproductive care centered on tenderness, lovemaking, and intimacy in spaces devoted to brutally severing these human expressions reveal how Mexican-origin women in the direst of circumstances imagined possible liberatory futures as they enacted them in the present.

17. For an excellent analysis, see Wilson Gilmore, "Race and Globalization."

18. Morgan and Weinbaum, "Introduction: Reproductive Racial Capitalism,"1.

19. Morgan and Weinbaum, "Introduction: Reproductive Racial Capitalism," 2.

20. Melamed, "Racial Capitalism," 77.

21. Bhattacharya, *Social Reproduction Theory*, 2.

22. For a Global South articulation of pluriversal politics, see anthropologist Escobar, *Pluriversal Politics*.

23. Lugones, "Playfulness, 'World'-Traveling, and Loving Perceptions," 390.

24. Escobar, *Pluriversal Politics*, 39.

25. Sandoval, *Methodology of the Oppressed*, 44–46.

26. Pérez, *The Decolonial Imaginary*, 33.

27. Anzaldúa, *Light in the Darkness*, 35.

28. Chávez-García and Castillo-Muñoz, "Gender and Intimacy across the U.S.-Mexico Borderlands," 5, 6.

29. Pérez, *The Decolonial Imaginary*, 33.

30. Bhattacharya, *Social Reproduction Theory*, 18.

31. Sandoval, *Methodology of the Oppressed*, 68, 69.

32. Tronto, *Moral Boundaries*, 4.

33. Rozek, "The Entry of Mexican Women into Urban Based Industries," 19.

34. Mexican-origin women tap into what Chela Sandoval refers to as "oppositional consciousness" or what Anzaldúa named "a mestiza consciousness," birthed from "'world'-traveling," living, and resisting in the US-Mexico borderlands, that produces the will to care for their communities despite their marginality to

cultural and material capital and power. Sandoval, *Methodology of the Oppressed*, 70, 71.

35. Bhandary, *Freedom to Care*, 120.

36. Gordon, *The Moral Property of Women*, 7.

37. Jaffray, *Reproduction and Its Discontents in Mexico*, chap. 3; O'Brien, *Surgery and Salvation*, 45–46.

38. Jaffary, *Reproduction and its Discontents in Mexico*, 83.

39. Bates, "Protective Custody," ii.

40. Bates, "Protective Custody," 1–3.

41. Mohr, *Abortion in America*, 89.

42. Mohr, *Abortion in America*, 97.

43. Beisel and Kay, "Abortion, Race, and Gender in Nineteenth-Century America."

44. Storer as quoted by Reagan in *When Abortion Was a Crime*, 11.

45. Reagan, *When Abortion Was a Crime*, 13–14.

46. Jaffary, *Reproduction and Its Discontents*, 89.

47. Jaffary, *Reproduction and Its Discontents*, 90.

48. O'Brien, *Surgery and Salvation*, 111.

49. O'Brien, *Surgery and Salvation*, 109, 111.

50. Jaffary, *Reproduction and Its Discontents*, 90.

51. Jaffary, *Reproduction and Its Discontents*, 91.

52. Foucault, *The History of Sexuality*, 123.

53. Foucault, *The History of Sexuality*, 123.

54. Kaplan, "Manifest Domesticity," 582.

55. French, "Prostitutes and Guardian Angels," 533.

56. French, "Prostitutes and Guardian Angels," 533.

57. For historical discussion of sexuality, race, and bodily comportment in the borderlands, see Mitchell, *Coyote Nation*.

58. Sánchez, *Becoming Mexican American*, footnote 26, 302.

59. Mitchell, *West of Sex*, 9.

60. For additional histories of vice and moral panics in the borderlands around "white slavery" and sex work among immigrant women, see Menchaca, "'The Freedom of Jail,'" 27–41; Peña Delgado, "Border Control and Sexual Policing"; Gabbert, "Prostitution and Moral Reform in the Borderlands."

61. Both George Sanchez and Vicki Ruiz mention these encounters. Sanchez, *Becoming Mexican American*, footnote 26, 30; Ruiz, *From Out of the Shadows*, 62.

62. For sociological studies on the taxi-dancer phenomenon in the 1930s, see Cressey, *The Taxi-Dance Hall*; Fritz, "The Women Who Danced for a Living"; España-Maram, *Creating Masculinity in Los Angeles's Little Manila*.

63. "Vida de Elisa Morales y datos sobre prostitución, etc." and "Vida de Gloria Navas y datos sobre prostitución," Notes from interview with Elisa Morales and Gloria Navas by Luis Felipe Recinos, "Notes gathered for his book, Mexican immigration to the United States, and related material, 1926–1928," Manuel Gamio Collection, Banc MSS Z-R5. Bancroft Library, Berkeley Library. Translated by the author.

64. Ruiz, *From Out of the Shadows*, 62.

65. Apodaca, "The Chicana Woman," 85. Fritz described similar feelings and cultural ruptures between young Polish American women and their migrant parents. Fritz, "The Women Who Danced for a Living," 255.

66. Notes from interview with Elisa Morales by Luis Felipe Recinos, "Notes gathered for his book, Mexican immigration to the United States, and related material, 1926–1928," Manuel Gamio Collection, Banc MSS Z-R5. Bancroft Library, Berkeley Library. Translated by the author.

67. "Mi hermana tambien es muy distinta de lo que soy yo," Notes from interview with Elisa Morales by Luis Felipe Recinos, "Notes gathered for his book, Mexican immigration to the United States, and related material, 1926–1928."

68. "Se mostró un tanto indignada y me dijo que condicionces ningunas, que ella pagaba su renta, que ella era muy libre y que le simpatizaba, que me quedará a dormir con ella." Notes from the Gloria Navas interview by Luis Felipe Recinos, "Notes gathered for his book, Mexican immigration to the United States, and related material, 1926–1928."

69. Notes from the Gloria Navas interview by Luis Felipe Recinos, "Notes gathered for his book, Mexican immigration to the United States, and related material, 1926–1928."

70. Notes from the Gloria Navas interview by Luis Felipe Recinos, "Notes gathered for his book, Mexican immigration to the United States, and related material, 1926–1928."

71. Notes from the Gloria Navas interview by Luis Felipe Recinos, "Notes gathered for his book, Mexican immigration to the United States, and related material, 1926–1928." According to the inflation calculator, this would be roughly $383 to $460 per week.

72. "Hace algunos años que trabajé en el Teatro, cantaba coplas y bailaba bailes españoles y el jarabe tapatío, he recorrido casi todo California trabajando en los tatros mexicanos y asi me gano la vida." And she also stated that "También he trabajado hasta de mesera para ganarme la vida, pero resulta que trabajaba 12 horas diarias y me pagaban muy poquito y no me gustaba ese trabajo." Notes from the Gloria Navas interview by Luis Felipe Recinos, "Notes gathered for his book, Mexican immigration to the United States, and related material, 1926–1928."

73. González, "Chicanas and Mexican Immigrant Families," 62; Sanchez, *Becoming Mexican American*, 19; Salazar Parreñas, "'White Trash' Meets the 'Little Brown Monkeys'"; Fritz, "The Women Who Danced for a Living."

74. "Yo soy absolutamente libre," Notes from the Gloria Navas interview by Luis Felipe Recinos, "Notes gathered for his book, Mexican immigration to the United States, and related material, 1926–1928."

75. "Muchas creen que Gustavito es mi querido porque vivimos en la misma casa y que nos queremos muchos y cuando he traido a Los Angeles a mis muchachitos él me los lleva a pásear, pero, aunque nada tendria de particular eso, no es cierto, Gustavito me quiere mucho porque yo lo he cuidad, cuando él no ha tenido ni amigos ni dinero entonces yo he sido para él más que una hermana, and he has been the same for me. Ni a él ni a mi nos importa que hablen de nostrosos." Notes from the Gloria Navas interview by Luis Felipe Recinos, "Notes

gathered for his book, Mexican immigration to the United States, and related material, 1926–1928."

76. "Mi religión es la católica, pero no voy a la Iglesia más que en tiempo de cuaresma, entonces hasta comulgo confieso y le digo al sacerdote todos mis pecados; pero yo sé que no le hago mal a nadie, que no robo, que vivo de mi trabajo y que cuando me voy con algún muchacho no es por interés, sino que es por mi propio gusto y no lo hago a escondidas de nadie, pues no tengo quien me mande ni deseo tener, es mejor ser libre y hacer lo que más le guste a uno." Notes from the Gloria Navas interview by Luis Felipe Recinos, "Notes gathered for his book, Mexican immigration to the United States, and related material, 1926–1928."

77. ". . . al llegar a casa se lavaria con unos polvos que le daba un doctor americano." Notes from interview with Elisa Morales by Luis Felipe Recinos, "Notes gathered for his book, Mexican immigration to the United States, and related material, 1926–1928."

78. "Yo le he mandado varias amigas y se les ha vendido una cadenita de oro con unas bolitas en los extremos y que ellas se ponen esas cadenita en la matriz asi no tienen hijos." Notes from the Gloria Navas interview by Luis Felipe Recinos," Notes gathered for his book, Mexican immigration to the United States, and related material, 1926–1928."

79. Fritz, "The Women Who Danced for a Living," 256.

80. Notes from interview with Elisa Morales by Luis Felipe Recinos, "Notes gathered for his book, Mexican immigration to the United States, and related material, 1926–1928."

81. Chávez-García, *States of Delinquency*, 6; Stern, *Eugenic Nation*, 23.

82. Lira, *Laboratory of Deficiency*, 85.

83. Gutiérrez, "'We Will No Longer Be Silent or Invisible," 222.

84. "Open Birth Control Clinic," *El Paso Times*, April 25, 1937.

85. "Open Birth Control Clinic."

86. "Nurse Directs Birth Control Clinic," *El Paso Times*, October 9, 1938.

87. "Women with Seven Babies Thankful for Birth Control," *El Paso Herald-Post*, February 23, 1938.

88. "Women with Seven Babies Thankful for Birth Control."

89. "Women with Seven Babies Thankful for Birth Control."

90. "250 El Paso Wives Get Family Planning Advice at E.P. Clinic," *El Paso Herald-Post*, July 26, 1937.

91. "El Paso Mothers' Health Center: Quarterly Report, July 27, 1937," Goetting Papers.

92. "El Paso Mothers' Health Center: Quarterly Report, July 27, 1937."

93. "El Paso Mothers' Health Center: Quarterly Report, July 27, 1937."

94. For an excellent history of Smeltertown, see Perales, *Smeltertown*.

95. "Directions for Patients/Instrucciones a los Pacientes," Goetting Papers.

96. "Mother Kisses Hand of Doctor Instructing in Birth Control," *El Paso Times*, August 11, 1937.

97. "El Paso Mothers' Health Center: Quarterly Report, July 27, 1937."

98. Schoen, *Choice and Coercion*.

99. "Every Child a Wanted Child," February 23, 1938, El Paso Vertical File, Border Heritage Center, Main Branch, El Paso Public Library, El Paso, Texas.

100. Annual Report, 1938–1939, El Paso Mothers' Health Center, Planned Parenthood of El Paso Papers.

101. "1170 Patients at Birth Clinic in 12 Months" *El Paso Herald-Post*, February 22, 1939.

102. "Board of Meeting Minutes, March 1941," Planned Parenthood of El Paso Papers, Box 11 old minutes.

103. Planned Parenthood of El Paso Board Meeting Minutes from February 1945 to December 1954 contain data about new and returning patients. After compiling the numbers and accounting for missing figures for at least five months in the span of nine years where data was not made available, I calculate an average of "new patients." Planned Parenthood of El Paso, box 1.

104. Planned Parenthood of El Paso Board Meeting Minutes from February 1945 to December 1954 contain data about new and returning patients. After compiling the numbers and accounting for missing figures for at least five months in the span of nine years where data was not made available, I calculate an average of "new patients."

105. Martinez, *Saga of a Legendary City: Ciudad Juárez*, "Appendix," 253–54.

106. Escobedo, *From Coverall to Zootsuits*, 32–33.

107. Drucker, *Contraception*, 25.

108. López, *Matters of Choice*, 38.

109. O'Brien, *Surgery and Salvation*, 192.

110. O'Brien, *Surgery and Salvation*, 190.

111. O'Brien, *Surgery and Salvation*, 190.

112. "Bueno, algunas veces las hacian pero no nomas para hacer el ligamento. Lo que pasaba, es que por ejemplo, las tenian que operar," Bertha Chávez González, Interview with Lina Murillo.

113. Anzaldúa, *Borderlands/La Frontera*, 101.

Chapter 4

1. For a history of contraceptive devices, see Tone, *Devices and Desires.*

2. "United States Food Reserves Save Vast Areas of the World from Disastrous Famine," *El Paso Times*, January 24, 1953.

3. Briggs, "Chapter 4: Demon Mothers in the Social Laboratory," in *Reproducing Empire*; Gutiérrez, *Fertile Matters*, 15–16; Critchlow, *Intended Consequences*, 22, 28.

4. "Planned Parenthood Center Plans Annual Drive," *El Paso Herald-Post*, January 28, 1950.

5. For an international histories of family planning, see López, "Gambling on the Protestants"; Takeuchi-Demirci, *Contraceptive Diplomacy*; Ahluwalia, *Reproductive Restraints*; Sreenivas, *Reproductive Politics and the Making of Modern India*; Anagnost, "A Surfeit of Bodies"; Connelly, *Fatal Misconception*; Briggs, *Reproducing Empire.*

6. In 1952, Goetting reported on the national board meeting of the Planned Parenthood of America, of which Goetting was a member, in New York that "among the distinguished guests were Dr. Amino, president of PP in Japan and Dr. Singh of India . . . Two nurses are in India now setting up clinics similar to ours." In "Meeting Minutes August 1952," Planned Parenthood of El Paso records, box 1.

7. Connelly, *Fatal Misconception*, 155.

8. Robertson, *The Malthusian Moment*, 52–53.

9. Merchant, *Building the Population Bomb*, 12–13.

10. Vogt, *Road to Survival*, 4–5 and 15.

11. Vogt, *Road to Survival*, 4.

12. Vogt, *Road to Survival*, 17.

13. Rodríguez-Muñiz, *Figures of the Future*, 32.

14. Desrochers, Pierre, and Christine Hoffbauer, "The Post War Intellectual Roots of the Population Bomb," 46.

15. Connelly, *Fatal Misconception*, 130; Critchlow, *Intended Consequences*, 5.

16. Connelly, *Fatal Misconception*, 130.

17. Sreenivas, *Reproductive Politics and the Making of Modern India*, 109–10.

18. Connelly, *Fatal Misconception*, 168.

19. Connelly, *Fatal Misconception*, 168.

20. "India's Program Gives Big Lift to Planned Parenthood," *El Paso Herald-Post*, February 4, 1953.

21. "India's Program Gives Big Lift to Planned Parenthood."

22. "Letter from Margaret Sanger to Betty Mary Goetting, April 10, 1952," the Margaret Sanger Papers (microfilmed), Sophia Smith Collection.

23. Ruiz, *From Out of the Shadows*, 49.

24. Dolores Briones interview by the author, July 13, 2015.

25. Ruiz, *From Out of the Shadows*, 50.

26. Blackwell, *¡Chicana Power!*, 27.

27. Tentler, *Catholics and Contraception*, 2.

28. Bridges, *The Poverty of Privacy Rights*, 5.

29. "Resignation Letter from Elizabeth Patterson to Mrs. Driver (PPEP Board Member), April 12, 1959," Planned Parenthood of El Paso Collection, MS 286, box 1.

30. "Meeting Minutes September 6, 1939," Planned Parenthood of El Paso records, box 11.

31. "Meeting Minutes June 1958," Planned Parenthood of El Paso records, box 1; Newark Maternity Hospital was built in 1937—the same year PPEP opened its first clinic—at the intersection of East Fifth Street and Hill Street in South El Paso. "New E.P. Clinic to Be Started in Near Future," *El Paso Times*, January 6, 1937.

32. "Meeting Minutes March 1959," Planned Parenthood of El Paso records, box 1.

33. "Meeting Minutes October 1958," Planned Parenthood of El Paso records, box 1.

34. "Meeting Minutes March 1959," Planned Parenthood of El Paso records, box 1.

35. "Meeting Minutes March 1959," and "Meeting Minutes July 1959," Planned Parenthood of El Paso records, box 1.

36. Dolores Briones interview.

37. Gutiérrez, "We Will No Longer Be Silent or Invisible," 221.

38. Ruiz, *From Out of the Shadows*, xiv.

39. Blackwell, *¡Chicana Power!*, 27.

40. The data available for these years was annualized from the following documents. Not all months were available; therefore, averages were taken for each year based on the numbers that existed in board meeting minutes. "Meeting Minutes from February 1945–January 1946," Planned Parenthood of El Paso records, 1907–2000s, box 1, MS 286, C. L. Sonnichsen Special Collection Department. "Meeting Minutes February 1946–January 1947," Planned Parenthood of El Paso records, 1907–2000s, box 1, MS 286. "Meeting minutes for January 8, 1947," Planned Parenthood of El Paso records, 1907–2000s, box 1, MS 286; "Meeting minutes for December 31, 1947," Planned Parenthood of El Paso records, 1907–2000s, box 1, MS 286; "Meeting minutes for January 1, 1949," Planned Parenthood of El Paso records, 1907–2000s, box 1, MS 286; "Meeting Minutes from April 1949–December 1949," Planned Parenthood of El Paso records, 1907–2000s, box 1, MS 286. "Meeting Minutes from February 1950–December 1950," Planned Parenthood of El Paso records, 1907–2000s, box 1, MS 286.

41. "El Paso Mothers' Health Center: Quarterly Report, July 27, 1937," Goetting Papers.

42. "Meeting Minutes September 1, 1965," Planned Parenthood of El Paso records, 1907–2000s, box 2, MS 286; Tentler, *Catholics and Contraception*, 134.

43. "Agenda: Medical Meeting, July 1960," Planned Parenthood of El Paso records, 1907–2000s, box 1, MS 286.

44. "Agenda: Medical Meeting, July 1960," Planned Parenthood of El Paso records, 1907–2000s, box 1, MS 286.

45. Copper Owens, *Medical Bondage*, 3.

46. For further discussions of racialized and classed obstetric violence, see O'Brien's *Surgery and Salvation*, chap. 6.

47. Underman, *Feeling Medicine*, 25–26.

48. Puelles, "¿Quiénes cuidan nuestras vulvas y vaginas?"; Davis, "Obstetric Racism."

49. "Agenda: Medical Meeting, July 1960," Planned Parenthood of El Paso records, 1907–2000s, box 1, MS 286.

50. "Meeting Minutes March 1961," Planned Parenthood of El Paso records, 1907–2000s, box 2, MS 286.

51. "Meeting Minutes March 1961," Planned Parenthood of El Paso records, 1907–2000s, box 2, MS 286.

52. "Agenda: Medical Meeting, July 1960," Planned Parenthood of El Paso records, 1907–2000s, box 1, MS 286; Holz, *The Birth Control Clinic in a Marketplace World*, 103.

53. "Meeting Minutes February 1960–January 1961," Planned Parenthood of El Paso records, 1907–2000s, box 1, MS 286. All numbers are available for this year.

54. "Meeting Minutes February 1961–January 1962," Planned Parenthood of El Paso records, 1907–2000s, box 1, MS 286. The data is not complete for 1961, with

the months of February and November missing from the data set; however, the numbers available were annualized to give an approximation of the number of new and returning patients to the clinic. The number of supplies were also annualized as only nine months were available with this information.

55. "Meeting Minutes August 1961," Planned Parenthood of El Paso records, 1907–2000s, box 1, MS 286,.

56. Steven M. Spencer, "New Case-History Facts on Birth Control Pills," *Saturday Evening Post*, June 30, 1962; "Meeting Minutes July 1962," Planned Parenthood of El Paso records, 1907–2000s, box 1, MS 286.

57. "Meeting Minutes March 1962," Planned Parenthood of El Paso records, 1907–2000s, box 1, MS 286.

58. "Meeting Minutes August 1962," Planned Parenthood of El Paso records, 1907–2000s, box 1, MS 286.

59. Emily S. Mann and Grzanka, "Agency-Without-Choice."

60. Laveaga, *Jungle Laboratories*, 66.

61. Laveaga, *Jungle Laboratories*, 67.

62. Laveaga, *Jungle Laboratories*, 69.

63. For early experiments of the Pill, see Ramírez de Arellano and Seipp, *Colonialism, Catholicism, and Contraception*; Watkins, *On the Pill*; Briggs, *Reproducing Empire*.

64. Watkins, *On the Pill*, 19; Gordon, *The Moral Property of Women*, 181–82; Ramírez de Arellano and Seipp, *Colonialism, Catholicism, and Contraception*, 128.

65. Mary Calderone as quoted in Holz, *The Birth Control Clinic in the Marketplace World*, 102.

66. "Mary Calderone remarks November 1960," Planned Parenthood of El Paso records, 1907–2000s, box 1, MS 286.

67. "Meeting Minutes May 1962," Planned Parenthood of El Paso records, 1907–2000s, box 1, MS 286.

68. "Meeting Minutes October 1962," Planned Parenthood of El Paso records, 1907–2000s, box 1, MS 286.

69. "Meeting Minutes July 1962," Planned Parenthood of El Paso records, 1907–2000s, box 1, MS 286.

70. "Meeting Minutes January 1962," Planned Parenthood of El Paso records, 1907–2000s, box 1, MS 286.

71. "Meeting Minutes December 1962," Planned Parenthood of El Paso records, 1907–2000s, box 1, MS 286.

72. "Inside Washington—A Weekly Sizeup," *El Paso Herald-Post* (El Paso, Texas), June 3, 1961.

73. "Meeting Minutes February 1963," Planned Parenthood of El Paso records, 1907–2000s, box 1, MS 286.

74. "Meeting Minutes February 1963."

75. "Meeting Minutes February 1963."

76. It was rare for clinic records to provide explanations for why some patients stopped returning to the clinic or ended their use of birth control. Meeting minutes from September 1958, before the Pill was introduced, gave this brief explanation:

"She found that 42 families had moved to other addresses; 37 had left town or failed to say where they had gone; 31 interviewed of which only 3 were not planning returned visits to the clinic and 7 were pregnant, 5 of which were planned pregnancies." In "Meeting Minutes September 3, 1958," Planned Parenthood of El Paso Records, 1907–2000s, box 1, MSC 286.

77. Briggs, *Reproducing Empire*, 132.

78. "Planned Parenthood of El Paso Medical Advisory Committee May 1963," Planned Parenthood of El Paso records, 1907–2000s, box 1, MS 286.

79. "Meeting Minutes October 1963," Planned Parenthood of El Paso records, 1907–2000s, box 1, MS 286.

80. "Meeting Minutes November 1963," Planned Parenthood of El Paso records, 1907–2000s, box 1, MS 286.

81. "Meeting Minutes December 1963," Planned Parenthood of El Paso records, 1907–2000s, box 1, MS 286.

82. "Meeting Minutes April 1964," Planned Parenthood of El Paso records, 1907–2000s, box 2, MS 286.

83. "Meeting Minutes April 1964."

84. Birth control campaigns were critical to empire-building in Puerto Rico—a colony of the United States—as early as the 1930s; see Ramírez de Arellano and Seipp, *Colonialism, Catholicism, and Contraception*, and Briggs, *Reproducing Empire*.

85. Gordon, *The Moral Property of Women*, 289.

86. "Meeting Minutes April 1964"; Laveaga, *Jungle Laboratories*, 52.

87. "Usted Puede Espaciar su Familia Clinca para Señoras," Advertisement for Planned Parenthood, *El Continental*, May 26, 1964.

88. "Meeting Minutes July 1964," Planned Parenthood of El Paso records, 1907–2000s, box 2, MS 286.

89. "Meeting Minutes September 1964," Planned Parenthood of El Paso records, 1907–2000s, box 2, MS 286; "Meeting Minutes December 1964," Planned Parenthood of El Paso records, 1907–2000s, box 2, MS 286.

90. "Meeting Minutes May 1960," Planned Parenthood of El Paso records, 1907–2000s, box 1, MS 286.

91. "Meeting Minutes December 1964."

92. "Meeting Minutes November 1964," Planned Parenthood of El Paso records, 1907–2000s, box 2, MS 286.

93. "Meeting Minutes December 1964."

94. Foner, *Women and the American Labor Movement*, 417–18.

95. Rozek, "The Entry of Mexican Women," 27.

96. Ruiz, *From Out of the Shadows*, 74 and chap. 6.

97. Ruiz, "By the Day or the Week," 64.

98. Mitchell, "Borderlands/La Familia," 188 and fn 9.

99. "Meeting Minutes December 1964."

100. "Meeting Minutes June 1965," Planned Parenthood of El Paso records, 1907–2000s, box 2, MS 286; Ramírez de Arellano and Seipp, *Colonialism, Catholicism, and Contraception*, 124–25.

101. Briggs, *Reproducing Empire*, 123.

102. Ramírez de Arellano and Seipp, *Colonialism, Catholicism, and Contraception*, 125.

103. Ramírez de Arellano and Seipp, *Colonialism, Catholicism, and Contraception*, 128.

104. Ramírez de Arellano and Seipp, *Colonialism, Catholicism, and Contraception*, 128–29.

105. Ramírez de Arellano and Seipp, *Colonialism, Catholicism, and Contraception*, 130.

106. "Meeting Minutes June 1964," Planned Parenthood of El Paso records, 1907–2000s, box 2, MS 286.

107. "Meeting Minutes June 1964."

108. "Meeting Minutes September 1964," Planned Parenthood of El Paso records, 1907–2000s, box 2, MS 286.

109. "Meeting Minutes December 1964."

110. "Planned Parenthood Center of El Paso Annual Report 1964," Planned Parenthood of El Paso records, 1907–2000s, box 2, MS 286.

111. "Planned Parenthood Minutes January 1965," Planned Parenthood of El Paso records, 1907–2000s, box 2, MS 286.

112. "Planned Parenthood Center of El Paso Annual Report 1964."

113. "Meeting Minutes April 1965," Planned Parenthood of El Paso records, 1907–2000s, box 2, MS 286.

114. "Knock on Every Door Project: Report July 1965," Planned Parenthood of El Paso records, 1907–2000s, box 2, MS 286.

115. "Meeting Minutes June 1, 1960" and "Meeting Minutes July 1961," Planned Parenthood of El Paso records, 1907–2000s, box 1, MS 286.

116. "Knock on Every Door Project: Report July 1965."

117. "Meeting Minutes August 1965," Planned Parenthood of El Paso records, 1907–2000s, box 2, MS 286.

118. "Knock on Every Door: Report for the Year 1965," Planned Parenthood of El Paso records, 1907–2000s, box 2, MS 286.

119. "Knock on Every Door: Report for the Year 1965."

120. "Knock on Every Door: Report for the Year 1965."

121. "Knock on Every Door: Report for the Year 1965."

122. "Knock on Every Door Project: Report July 1965."

123. Mitchell, "Borderlands/La Familia," 193.

124. Linda Gordon describes the proliferation of ineffective birth control options starting in the 1930s as some firms employed "door-to-door peddlers who made fraudulent claims." Gordon explains these options were most often touted among "women who were denied access to better information." Gordon, *The Moral Property of Women*, 224.

125. "Knock on Every Door Project: Report July 1965."

126. "Meeting Minutes January 1966," Planned Parenthood of El Paso records, 1907–2000s, box 2, MS 286.

127. Critchlow, *Intended Consequences*, 22, 28.

128. "Medical Advisory Committee Meeting February 1965," Planned Parenthood of El Paso records, 1907–2000s, box 2, MS 286.

129. Solinger, *Pregnancy and Power*, 176–77.

130. Guttmacher as quoted in Solinger, *Pregnancy and Power*, 177.

131. It is unclear to what degree coverture, which stipulates that by marriage, a man and woman are considered "one legal person," the man being the head of said person, was considered during this time. Before *Griswold v. Connecticut*, the Supreme Court case that legalized contraception for married couples in the summer of 1965, birth control clinics operated in a legal gray zone where board members and doctors set parameters for the distribution of birth control, specifically as states set different legal barriers.

132. "Meeting Minutes October 1965," Planned Parenthood of El Paso records, 1907–2000s, box 2, MS 286.

133. "Meeting Minutes November 1965," Planned Parenthood of El Paso records, 1907–2000s, box 2, MS 286.

134. Roberts, *Killing the Black Body*, 142–43.

135. "Meeting Minutes December 1966," Planned Parenthood of El Paso records, 1907–2000s, box 2, MS 286.

136. "Meeting Minutes December 1966."

137. "Meeting Minutes December 1966."

138. Espino also describes a similar "top-down" approach in Los Angeles as poor women of color were forcefully compelled to use birth control. Espino, "Women Sterilized as They Give Birth," 175–76.

139. "Statistical Analysis of a Sampling of 100 Interviews in South El Paso, 1966," Planned Parenthood of El Paso records, 1907–2000s, box 2, MS 286.

140. "Planned Parenthood Center of El Paso, May 1968 Report," Planned Parenthood of El Paso records, 1907–2000s, box 2, MS 286.

141. "Meeting Minutes June 1967," Planned Parenthood of El Paso records, 1907–2000s, box 2, MS 286.

142. "Meeting Minutes December 1967," Planned Parenthood of El Paso records, 1907–2000s, box 2, MS 286.

143. "Meeting Minutes March 1968," Planned Parenthood of El Paso records, 1907–2000s, box 2, MS 286.

144. "Clinical Evaluation of a New Application for Vaginal Contraceptive Foam, 1969," Betty Mary Goetting Papers, box 5, MS 316, 1.

145. "Clinical Evaluation of a New Application for Vaginal Contraceptive Foam, 1969," Betty Mary Goetting Papers, box 5, MS 316, 2.

146. "Clinical Evaluation of a New Application for Vaginal Contraceptive Foam, 1969," Betty Mary Goetting Papers, box 5, MS 316, 5.

147. Their data did not account for stillbirths and miscarriages and those children surviving their first birthday as high infant mortality had been a long-standing issue in South El Paso for decades. "Clinical Evaluation of a New Application for Vaginal Contraceptive Foam, 1969," Betty Mary Goetting Papers, box 5, MS 316, 5.

148. "Clinical Evaluation of a New Application for Vaginal Contraceptive Foam, 1969," Betty Mary Goetting Papers, box 5, MS 316, 5–7.

149. Hatcher and Trussell et al., *Contraceptive Technologies*, 769–70.

150. "Clinical Evaluation of a New Application for Vaginal Contraceptive Foam, 1969," Betty Mary Goetting Papers, box 5, MS 316, 10.

151. "Clinical Evaluation of a New Application for Vaginal Contraceptive Foam, 1969," Betty Mary Goetting Papers, box 5, MS 316.

152. "Clinical Evaluation of a New Application for Vaginal Contraceptive Foam, 1969," Betty Mary Goetting Papers, box 5, MS 316, 10.

153. Ramírez de Arrellano and Seipp, *Colonialism, Catholicism, and Contraception*, 131; Marks, *Sexual Chemistry*, 244–45.

154. Marks, *Sexual Chemistry*, 244–45.

155. "Meeting Minutes July 1968," Planned Parenthood of El Paso records, 1907–2000s, box 2, MS 286.

156. "Meeting Minutes October 1968," Planned Parenthood of El Paso records, 1907–2000s, box 2, MS 286.

157. "Meeting Minutes December 1968," Planned Parenthood of El Paso records, 1907–2000s, box 2, MS 286.

158. "Planned Parenthood Showing of 'Knock on Every Door' Slated," *El Paso Times*, February 1, 1970, El Paso, Texas.

159. Ramírez de Arellano and Seipp, *Colonialism, Catholicism, and Contraception*, 131.

160. Briggs, *Reproducing Empire*, 124.

161. "Planned Parenthood Showing of 'Knock on Every Door' Slated."

162. "Planned Parenthood Showing of 'Knock on Every Door' Slated."

163. Ross, "African-American Women and Abortion," 141.

164. "Planned Parenthood Showing of 'Knock on Every Door' Slated."

165. Watkins, *On the Pill*, 74.

166. Peggy Pascoe as quoted in Ruiz, *From Out of the Shadows*, 47.

167. "Meeting Minutes August 1960," Planned Parenthood of El Paso records, 1907–2000s, box 2, MS 286.

168. "Meeting Minutes August 1960."

169. "Meeting Minutes April 1967," Planned Parenthood of El Paso records, 1907–2000s, box 2, MS 286.

170. Gutiérrez, *Fertile Matters*, 17–18.

171. The numbers represented in the totals for 1970 are approximations since the figures for the months of February, April, and May are missing, as well as the month of November for the data on Pap smears. Using the average of the data collected for the existing months, I have calculated the approximate figures discussed previously. "Meeting Minutes March 1970," "Meeting Minutes April 1970," "Meeting Minutes July 1970," "Meeting Minutes August 1970," "Meeting Minutes September 1970," "Meeting Minutes October 1970," "Meeting Minutes November 1970," "Meeting Minutes December 1970," and "Meeting Minutes January 1971," Planned Parenthood of El Paso records, 1907–2000s, box 3, MS 286.

172. Lira, *Laboratory of Deficiency*; Gutiérrez, *Fertile Matters*; Stern, "Sterilization Abuse in State Prisons; Briggs, *Reproducing Empire*, 107.

Chapter 5

1. The Isley Brothers, "Fight the Power, Part I" track #1 on *The Heat Is On*, 1975.

2. "Resolution by Luz Gutierrez from Crystal City, Texas for the 1977 IWY conference," Martha Cotera Papers, box 9, folder 10. Gutierrez wrote this in anticipation of the second IWY conference held in Houston, Texas in 1977, organized by President Gerald Ford and supported by several large women's organizations in the United States. The first International Women's Year conference, convened by the United Nations, was held in Mexico City, Mexico, in 1975. It focused on greater access to education for women, creating equality of opportunities between women and men, and expanding discussions about family planning and population policies. See "International Women's Year: Population and the Conference in Mexico," *Population and Development Review* 2, no. 2 (1975): 346–50.

3. The year before Luz Gutierrez wrote her resolution, ten women stepped forward to file a class action lawsuit against Los Angeles-USC Medical Center claiming they had been sterilized without their consent or under duress. For more on the history of *Madrigal v. Quilligan* case and the history of sterilization abuse, see Espino, "Women Sterilized as They Give Birth."

4. Although historian Sandra I. Enríquez has written a brief history of the Father Rahm Clinic, she uses sources and voices of many of the men who shaped the institution. This chapter uses oral histories and collections from the founding women members of the clinic. See Enríquez, "A Totality of Our Well-Being."

5. For more histories on racial formation and public health, see Molina, *Fit to Be Citizens?*; McKiernan-Gonzalez, *Fevered Measures*; and Stern, *Eugenic Nation*.

6. Duarte, "Centro de Salud Familiar La Fe," 28.

7. Duarte, "Centro de Salud Familiar La Fe," 4, 29.

8. Vidal, *Women: New Voice of La Raza*, 3.

9. Marisela R. Chávez, *Chicana Liberation*, 52.

10. Vidal, *Women: New Voice of La Raza*, 3–4. According to her colleagues at *The Militant* newspaper, Vidal was born in Argentina and arrived in the United States as a young person. She quickly joined the Socialist Workers Party in the 1960s and became an active participant in militant youth organizing of the 1960s and 1970s. See Studer, "Mirta Vidal: Lifelong Socialist."

11. Brianna Theobald, *Reproduction on the Reservation*, 147.

12. "Martha Cotera biography circa 1973," Martha Cotera Papers, box 2, folder 7.

13. "Martha Cotera biography circa 1973."

14. "The Mexican American: Quest for Equality," Martha Cotera Papers, box 15 "Civil Rights Chicano."

15. One of the first foundational texts on the study of Mexican-origin people is Sánchez, *Forgotten People*.

16. Rogers, "Poverty behind the Cactus Curtain."

17. Pycior, *LBJ and Mexican Americans*, 203.

18. "Mexican American Problems Aired at Cabinet-Level Conference," *El Paso Times*, October 28, 1967.

19. "Ximenes Continues EP Talks," *El Paso Times*, October 16, 1967.

20. "Welcome to El Paso," *El Paso Times*, October 27, 1967.

21. "Cabinet-Level Discussions Get Under Way in EP," *El Paso Times*, October 28, 1967.

22. "Welcome to El Paso."

23. Pycior, *LBJ and Mexican Americans*, 210.

24. "New Mexican-American Groups Demand 'Rights,'" *El Paso Times*, October 29, 1967.

25. "New Mexican-American Groups Demand 'Rights.'"

26. "New Mexican-American Groups Demand 'Rights.'"

27. "New Mexican-American Groups Demand 'Rights.'"

28. Frank Moreno Martínez, as quoted by Pycior, *LBJ and Mexican Americans*, 213.

29. Elroy Bode, "South El Paso and Hope," *Texas Observer*, October 27, 1967.

30. Marquez, *Power and Politics in a Chicano Barrio*, 80–98.

31. "Three Children Die in Fire," *El Paso Times*, January 5, 1967.

32. Loretta Overton, "Group Stages Protest Against Housing Conditions," *El Paso Herald-Post*, January 7, 1967.

33. A joint statement made by Thomason and Telles, as quoted in Marquez's *Power and Politics in a Chicano Barrio*, 67.

34. "South El Paso: An Analysis," Department of Planning of City of El Paso, July 1967, Department of Planning Collection (City of El Paso), MS 204, box 51, C.L. Sonnichsen Special Collections Department.

35. Anthropologist Margaret Clark wrote her dissertation after studying experiences of health care in the Mexican-origin community of Sal Si Puedes in San José, California, in the 1950s. She later wrote *Health in the Mexican-American Culture*.

36. Tim Sinclair, "Project MACHOS," *Texas Observer*, April 11, 1969.

37. "South El Paso: An Analysis."

38. Albert Pena, a Texas county commissioner, suggested that Mexicans in Texas lived behind a "cactus curtain" hiding from national attention the misery in which many lived. Rogers, "Poverty behind the Cactus Curtain."

39. Roth, *Separate Roads to Feminism*, 131.

40. "Letter from Amelia Castillo, November 4, 1972." Amelia Castillo Papers, MS637, box 4.

41. For some discussions of health care during the Chicana/o movement, see Gutiérrez in *Undivided Rights*, chaps. 12, 13, and 14; Blackwell, *¡Chicana Power!*; and Enríquez, "'A Totality of Our Well-Being.'" For more contemporary studies of sexuality and contraception, see Hurtado, *Voicing Chicana Feminisms*.

42. "Group 5: Series: 5: The Chicana Rights Project," Mexican American Legal Defense and Educational Fund (MALDEF) Records, Mo673, Dept. of Special Collections, Stanford University Libraries, Stanford, California. The Father Rahm Clinic predates these national efforts to address the legal reproductive rights of Chicanas by the Chicana Rights Project, which started in 1973.

43. For discussions of these contradictions, see Kluchin, *Fit to Be Tied*; and the feature documentary film *No Más Bebés*.

44. Ross, "Understanding Reproductive Justice," 14.

45. Kathy Flores, "Sociological Perspectives: Chicano Attitudes toward Birth Control," *Imágenes de la Chicana*. N.d. MS Comisión Femenil Mexicana Nacional Archives: Series IX: Publications box 56, folder 20 University of California, Santa Barbara; Loeb, "La Chicana."

46. Fernández, *The Young Lords*, 135.

47. Dionne Espinoza, "'Revolutionary Sisters'"; Nelson, *Women of Color and the Reproductive Rights Movement*; Nelson, *Body and Soul*, chap. 3; Fernández, *The Young Lords*, 267.

48. Gordon, *The Moral Property of Women*, 243.

49. Gordon, *The Moral Property of Women*, 245.

50. Connelly, *Fatal Misconception*, 188–89.

51. For connections between birth control, population control, and eugenics, see Connelly, *Fatal Misconception*; Gutiérrez, *Fertile Matters*; and Kluchin, *Fit to Be Tied*.

52. "Announcement by Amelia Castillo," box 1, folder 3, *Moviemiento Estudiantil Chicano de Atzlan (El Paso) Records, 1967–2000*, MS 254, C. L. Sonnichsen Special Collections Department.

53. "Announcement by Amelia Castillo."

54. "Mrs. Sanger Meets at Luncheon with El Paso Doctors," *El Paso Herald-Post*, December 8, 1934.

55. Oral history with Amelia Castillo, July 22, 2016.

56. Oral history with Amelia Castillo, July 22, 2016.

57. Oral history with Amelia Castillo, July 22, 2016.

58. Oral history with Amelia Castillo, July 22, 2016.

59. "HEW Grants $26,060 for UTEP Social Work," *El Paso Herald-Post*, September 10, 1969.

60. Oral history with Amelia Castillo, July 22, 2016.

61. Amelia Castillo interview, July 22, 2016.

62. "Talent Show Will Raise School Funds," *El Paso Times*, February 6, 1953.

63. "Here's How!" *El Paso Times*, January 17, 1954.

64. "EP Painters Union Donates Labor for Community Project," *El Paso Times*, February 14, 1954.

65. "Here's How!"

66. "Rev. Harold Rahm Works for All Men," *El Paso Herald-Post*, February 17, 1968.

67. Amelia Castillo interview, July 22, 2016.

68. Duarte, "Centro de Salud Familiar La Fe," 33.

69. Duarte, "Centro de Salud Familiar La Fe," 33.

70. Amelia Castillo and Mrs. Enedina Cordero pictured receiving a large check for $18,000 for Father Rahm Clinic. "Check Presentation," *El Paso Herald-Post*, March 22, 1972.

71. Amelia Castillo interview, July 22, 2016.

72. Amelia Castillo interview, July 22, 2016.

73. See Patricia Zavella's discussion of reproductive justice and the movement's fight for the "right to *health*, which is not guaranteed by human rights norms or

practices." Before activists formally articulated the concept of reproductive justice, Chicana and Chicano activists were demanding health and wellness as fundamental to their humanity. Zavella, *The Movement for Reproductive Justice*, 199.

74. Amelia Castillo interview, July 22, 2016.

75. Amelia Castillo interview, July 22, 2016.

76. "Speaking the Public Mind: Have Services," *El Paso Times*, December 20, 1974.

77. Gutiérrez, *Fertile Matters*, 16; In 1970, the Father Rahm Clinic received $12,000 from the Urban Coalition from a $72,000 grant made to the clinic by the US Department of Health, Education, and Welfare (HEW). "Father Rahm Clinic Gets Grant," *El Paso Herald-Post*, August 13, 1970.

78. Enríquez, "A Totality of Our Well-Being," 187.

79. Amelia Castillo interview, July 22, 2016.

80. "Planned Parenthood of El Paso Committees-1973," Planned Parenthood of El Paso Records, MS 286, box 3, folder 5. Little is known about Dr. José Cázares-Zavala's work and relationship to PPEP.

81. Vidal, *Women: New Voice of La Raza*, 13.

82. Vidal, *Women: New Voice of La Raza*, 13.

83. Oral history interview with Amelia Castillo, July 22, 2016.

84. Oral history interview with Amelia Castillo, July 22, 2016.

85. Oral history interview with Amelia Castillo, original: "Yo soy madre de seis [hijos], ni una vez esta Iglesia me a dado el dinero para una examinación, medicamento, nada," July 22, 2016.

86. Oral history interview with Amelia Castillo, July 22, 2016 ; Duarte, "Centro de Salud Familiar La Fe," 30. Duarte suggests, however, that the name was officially changed in January 1974; "Workshop for La Fe Scheduled," *El Paso Times*, May 4, 1974.

87. "Mayor Unveils El Paso's All-America City Plaque," *El Paso Herald-Post*, Thursday, February 19, 1970.

88. "El Paso Named All-America City," *El Paso Herald-Post*, Thursday, February 19, 1970.

89. Thomas Barry, "Look and the National Municipal League Salute All America Cities, 1969," *Look* (March 1970), 60.

90. "El Paso Named All-America City," 5.

91. "Look and the National Municipal League Salute All America Cities," 63.

92. Martinez, *Chicanos of El Paso*, 6.

93. Many thanks to the reviewers for bringing together this national context in reference to the *Look* magazine language. See Roosevelt, "Radio Address from Albany, New York."

94. Johnson, "Special Message to the Congress on the Problems of the American Indian," 7.

95. "Look and the National Municipal League Salute All America Cities," 63.

96. Peter Schrag, "The Forgotten American," *Harper's Magazine*, August 1969, 28.

97. Robertson, *The Malthusian Moment*, 5–7.

98. "Planned Parenthood Center of El Paso: Board Meeting, Februarys 5, 1969," Planned Parenthood of El Paso Records MS286, C. L. Sonnichsen Special Collections Department; "Planned Parenthood Center of El Paso: Board Meeting, October 1, 1969," Planned Parenthood of El Paso Records MS286, C. L. Sonnichsen Special Collections Department.

99. "Planned Parenthood Center of El Paso: Board of Directors Meeting, January 7, 1970," Planned Parenthood of El Paso Records MS286, C. L. Sonnichsen Special Collections Department.

100. "Planned Parenthood Center of El Paso: Board Meeting March 4, 1970," Planned Parenthood of El Paso Records MS286, C. L. Sonnichsen Special Collections Department.

101. "Lee Loevinger, 91, Kennedy-Era Anti-Trust Chief," *New York Times*, May 4, 2003.

102. "Compulsory Birth Control Forecast," *El Paso Times*, February 17, 1970. Betty Mary Smith Goetting Papers, box 8.

103. "Compulsory Birth Control Forecast."

104. "Planned Parenthood Center of El Paso: Board Meeting, April 1, 1970," Planned Parenthood of El Paso Records MS286, C. L. Sonnichsen Special Collections Department.

105. "Planned Parenthood Center of El Paso: Board Meeting, April 1, 1970."

106. "Planned Parenthood Center of El Paso: Board Meeting, April 1, 1970."

107. "Planned Parenthood Center of El Paso: Board Meeting, December 6, 1969," Planned Parenthood of El Paso Records MS286, C. L. Sonnichsen Special Collections Department.

108. Oral history interview Amelia Castillo, July 22, 2016.

109. Jane Pemberton, "Court Oks Health Center for Birth Control Program," *El Paso Herald-Post*, March 9, 1970.

110. "Court Oks Health Center for Birth Control Program."

111. "Court Oks Health Center for Birth Control Program."

112. "Pill Advocate Hissed by Women Militants," *El Paso Herald-Post*, February 25, 1970; "Birth Control Pill Still Called 'Boon' and 'Bane,'" February 26, 1970, *El Paso Herald-Post*.

113. "Parenthood Director Named," *El Paso Herald-Post*, November 21, 1961.

114. "Speaker Sees World Population Doubled," *El Paso Herald-Post*, January 17, 1956; "The Gadabout," *El Paso Herald-Post*, November 11, 1959; "Meeting Minutes September 1962," El Paso Planned Parenthood Records, MS 286.

115. "Speaker Sees World Population Doubled."

116. "Court Oks Health Center for Birth Control Program."

117. "Birth Control Program Okd for Health Center," *El Paso Times*, March 10, 1970.

118. "Birth Control Program Okd for Health Center."

119. "Court Oks Health Center For Birth Control Program."

120. "Birth Control Program Okd for Health Center."

121. "Court Oks Health Center For Birth Control Program."

122. Bridges, *The Poverty of Privacy Rights*.

123. See Tentler, *An American History*, for an in-depth discussion of Catholics and birth control in 1960s and 1970s.

124. Kaiser, *The Politics of Sex and Religion*, 5.

125. Kaiser, *The Politics of Sex and Religion*, 5.

126. "Birth Control Program Okd For Health Center."

127. Garcia, *The Making of the Mexican American Mayor*, 51–83.

128. "Problems of South El Paso Rate as Big Challenge to Whole City," *El Paso Times*, March 4, 1979.

129. Martinez, *The Chicanos of El Paso*, 6.

130. Chicano/a historians, such as Oscar Martínez, Mario García, Vicki Ruiz and Monica Pérales, have been writing about this for decades. For Mexican migration and El Paso's economy at the beginning of the twentieth century, see Garcia, *Desert Immigrants*; Ruiz, *From Out of the Shadows*; Perales, *Smeltertown*.

131. "Speaking the Public Mind: Agrees with Letter on Population Control," *El Paso Times*, March 5, 1979. El Paso, Texas.

132. "Thinking Out Loud: Favors Planned Parenthood," *El Paso Herald-Post*, April 6, 1970.

133. Carmichael, "Toward Black Liberation"; Michael Kaufman, "Stokely Carmichael, Rights Leader Who Coined 'Black Power' Dies at 57," *New York Times*, November 16, 1998.

134. Robertson, *The Malthusian Moment*, 178–79.

135. "MAYA Sets Protest Rally for Sunday," *El Paso Times*, March 21, 1970.

136. "Planned Parenthood Opposition Seen," *El Paso Times*, March 20, 1970.

137. "Birth Control Said Not for Closed Talks," *El Paso Herald-Post*, March 27, 1970; "Judge Raps Closed Meetings of City-County Health Unit," *El Paso Times*, March 28, 1970.

138. "Ask Ouster of Health Board," *El Paso Herald-Post*, April 6, 1970.

139. "Health Board Blocks Birth Control Plan," *El Paso Herald-Post*, April 23, 1970.

140. "Health Board Blocks Birth Control Plan."

141. "Health Board Blocks Birth Control Plan."

142. "Planned Parenthood Center of El Paso: Board Meeting March 4, 1970," Planned Parenthood of El Paso Records MS286, C. L. Sonnichsen Special Collections Department; "Planned Parenthood Center of El Paso: Board Meeting April 1, 1970."

143. "Organizers Explain Need for 'Pressure,'" *El Paso Herald-Post*, January 4, 1972.

144. "The Chicano Health Careers Institute, funded by Chicano Health Development, Inc. in the 1970s out of San Antonio, Texas."; for a borderlands documentation of Chicana and Chicano health, see the "Health" section of the Chicano Vertical Files, C. L. Sonnichsen Special Collections Department.

145. "Father Rahm Health Referral Service," *For Your Health: A Su Salud* 1, no. 2 (Department of Health, Education and Welfare, March 1972), Health, Chicano Vertical File, C. L. Sonnichsen Special Collections Department.

146. "Father Rahm Health Referral Service."

147. "Father Rahm Health Referral Service."

148. Enríquez, "A Totality of Our Well-Being," 185.

149. Duarte, "Centro de Salud Familiar La Fe," 56–57.

150. Hayes-Bautista, "Latino Health Policy, Forty Years Later," 145.

151. Hayes-Bautista, "Latino Health Policy, Forty Years Later," 146.

152. "Ribbon-Cutting Ceremony for New Clinic 1986," Martha Cotera Papers, box 15, "Crystal City Health Clinic."

153. Hayes-Bautista, "Latino Health Policy, Forty Years Later," 146.

154. "Chicano Health Careers Institute pamphlet," Chicano Health Policy Development, Chicano Vertical Files, Courtesy of Sonnichsen Special Collection Department, University of Texas at El Paso.

155. "Project Rehab Purchase Set of Tenement," *El Paso Times*, October 23, 1970.

Chapter 6

1. "Federación Mexicana de Asociaciónes y Empresas Privadas," translation: Mexican Federation of Private Associations and Companies.

2. Beth Krier, "A Crusader for Birth Control in Mexico," *Los Angeles Times*, May 22, 1987; Krier, "Family Planning Crusader Battles Mexico's Growth," *Chicago Sun-Times*, June 14, 1987.

3. "A Crusader for Birth Control in Mexico."

4. "A Crusader for Birth Control in Mexico"; Sophia Smith Collection of Women's History, Planned Parenthood Federation of America records group II (PPFA II), box 7, folder "Planned Parenthood Review 1985–1986," *Review* (Winter 1986): 44–46.

5. "A Crusader for Birth Control in Mexico."

6. "A Crusader for Birth Control in Mexico."

7. Bean, Edmonston, and Passel, *Undocumented Migration to the United States*, 2.

8. "A Crusader for Birth Control in Mexico."

9. "A Crusader for Birth Control in Mexico."

10. "Salinas: 'Let's Be More Open,'" *New York Times*, February 13, 1988, 27.

11. Minian, *Undocumented Lives*, 17.

12. Minian, *Undocumented Lives*, 18.

13. Minian, *Undocumented Lives*, 17.

14. Cravey, *Women and Work in Mexico's Maquiladoras*, 11.

15. Cravey, *Women and Work in Mexico's Maquiladoras*, 15.

16. *El Paso Times* Editorial Board, "Editorial: Federico De La Vega's Legacy along the Border," *El Paso Times*, December 12, 2015, https://www.elpasotimes.com/story /opinion/editorials/2015/12/23/editorial-federico-de-la-vegas-legacy-along-border /77857576/).

17. "Editorial: Federico De La Vega's Legacy along the Border."

18. Connelly, *Fatal Misconception*, 2.

19. For eugenic histories of Mexico, see Stepan, *"The Hour of Eugenics"*; Stern, "Eugenics beyond Borders"; Sánchez Rivera, "What Happened to Mexican Eugenics?"

20. Stern, "Eugenics beyond Borders," 170.

21. Vasconcelos, *The Cosmic Race*, 9.

22. Stern, "Responsible Mothers and Normal Children," 371.

23. Rodríguez-Muñiz, *Figures of the Future*, 32–33.

24. Stern, "Eugenics beyond Borders," 170.

25. Saade Granados, "¿Quiénes deben procrear?," 2.

26. Suárez y López-Guazo, "Evolucionismo y Eugenesia en México," 20; Stepan, *"The Hour of Eugenics,"* 56.

27. Blache Z. de Baralt, "El Feminismo Eugénico," *El Diario*, December 24, 1911. Original: "El [Caleb Saleeby] simpatiza francamente con el feminism militante y se declara sin ambajes partidiario del voto para la mujer."

28. Pérez, *The Decolonial Imaginary*, 32–33.

29. Cabrera, "Demographic Dynamics and Development," 107.

30. González Navarro, *Población y Sociedad en México, 1900–1970*, 120.

31. Ibáñez, "El machismo y feminismo en la literatura," 9; Cabrera, "Demographic Dynamics and Development," 107–8.

32. Ibáñez, "El machismo y feminismo en la literatura," 10.

33. Stepan, *"The hour of eugenics,"* 56–57.

34. Susan E. Klepp mentions revolutionary periods, such as the American and French revolutions, as critical moments for fertility control in the eighteenth century and cites Williams Leasure's work focused on the Mexican Revolution in 1910. However, demographers such as Gustavo Cabrera and Amado de Miguel show that while Mexican feminists considered family planning during Mexico's revolutionary period, fertility decline during that time is largely associated with the raging battles of the revolution and the Cristero War (1926–29), which ushered in waves of starvation, migration, and high infant mortality rates. Klepp, *Revolutionary Conceptions*, 12; Leasure, "Mexican Fertility and the Revolution of 1910–1920"; Cabrera, "Demographic Dynamics and Development"; De Miguel, *Ensayo Sobre La Poblacion de Mexico*.

35. Cabrera, "Demographic Dynamics and Development," 106–7.

36. Cabrera, "Demographic Dynamics and Development," 106–7.

37. Robert McCaa, "Missing Millions," 368.

38. Stern, "Responsible Mothers and Normal Children," 370; O'Brien, *Surgery and Salvation*, 188.

39. De Miguel, *Ensayo Sobre La Poblacion de Mexico*, 105.

40. González Navarro, *Población y Sociedad en México*, 120.

41. Cabrera, "Demographic Dynamics and Development," 108–9.

42. De Miguel, *Ensayo Sobre La Poblacion de Mexico*, 132.

43. "International Women's Year: Population and the Conference in Mexico."

44. Gutiérrez, *Fertile Matters*, 71.

45. McCaa, "The Peopling of Mexico," in *A Population History of North America*, 277.

46. Alexander, "Myth and Reality of the Mexican Miracle."

47. Feliciano, "Mexico's Demographic Transformation: From 1900 to 1990," 605.

48. Connelly, *Fatal Misconception*, 117.

49. Connelly, *Fatal Misconception*, 303–4.

50. "Says High Birthrate Highest," *El Paso Times*, May 23, 1963.

51. Gutiérrez, *Fertile Matters*, chap. 2.

52. Letter to Mrs. William C. Collins, President of PPEP from Bill Lynde, May 7, 1963, box 3, folder 14, Planned Parenthood of El Paso Records, MS 286, C. L. Sonnichsen Special Collections Department.

53. In other articles, I write extensively about the history of the transborder abortion network created in the El Paso–Ciudad Juárez borderlands. See Murillo, "Espanta Cigüeñas," and "A View from Northern Mexico."

54. "Says High Birthrate Highest," *El Paso Times*, May 23, 1963.

55. "Says High Birthrate Highest."

56. "Mexican Farmland Becoming Scarce," *El Paso Times*, August 2, 1968; "Birth Rate in 1967 Lowest," *El Paso Times*, August 2, 1968. These side-by-side news articles reveal this connection.

57. "Birth Rate in Texas Has Dropped to 30-Year Low," *El Paso Herald-Post*, August 1, 1967.

58. "Birth Rate in Texas Has Dropped to 30-Year Low."

59. W. J. Hooten, "Everyday Events: Fewer Whites," *El Paso Times*, June 6, 1967.

60. Stern, "From 'Race Suicide' to 'White Extinction.'"

61. Perrillo, "The Perils of Bilingualism," 86.

62. Pérez, *The Decolonial Imaginary*, 58.

63. Brown, "Hospital Provides Healing, Hope in Drug War's Epicenter."

64. Their public story in the early days is hazy as records reveal little of their lives before they rose to prominence in the 1960s.

65. Information retrieved from Ancestry.com via the Strauser family tree, https://www.ancestry.com/family-tree/person/tree/17062686/person/342040623874/facts; "Newlyweds," *El Paso Herald-Post*, December 5, 1959.

66. "De La Vega: Obituary," *El Paso Times*, June 22, 1983; "Federico De La Vega," *Nova Quarterly: The University of Texas at El Paso*, spring 1995, 13.

67. Aguilar, *El Norte Sin Algodones*, 105–7.

68. Gabriela Minjáres, "Deja Federico De La Vega un legado a la Ciudad," *El Diario*, December 17, 2015; Wright, "Feminicidio, narcoviolence, and gentrification in Ciudad Juárez," 837.

69. Aguilar, *El Norte Sin Algodones*, 105–7. Aguilar puts it this way: "Las maquiladoras nacieron fronterizas."

70. Cordes et al., "Mexico, Maquiladoras, and Occupational Medicine Training," 62.

71. Cordes et al., "Mexico, Maquiladoras, and Occupational Medicine Training," 63.

72. Ruiz, "Mexican Women and Multinationals: The Packing of the Border Industrialization Program," unpublished, Vicki Ruiz Collection, 11–12.

73. Ruiz, "Mexican Women and Multinationals," 11–12.

74. Bob Ybarra, "Mexico Relaxes Restrictions on U.S. Assembly Plants," *El Paso Herald-Post*, November 23, 1972.

75. Ruiz, "Mexican Women and Multinationals," 12.

76. Koerner, "Pregnancy Discrimination in Mexico," 235.

77. "Board of Directors Meeting Minutes December 1964," Planned Parenthood El Paso Papers, box 3.

78. Fernández-Kelly, *For We Are Sold*, 19.

79. Fernández-Kelly, *For We Are Sold*, 20; See also Aguilar, *El Norte Sin Algodones*.

80. Fernández-Kelly, *For We Are Sold*, 21.

81. FEMAP website, "Conócenos," https://www.femap.org.mx/fundadora. Translated by the author: "Como una asociación de carácter civil, privada, no lucrativa, fundada por la Sra. Guadalupe Arizpe de De la Vega, cuando se aprueba la primer política de población y cuando inicia la industria maquiladora en nuestra región, convirtiéndola en una institución pionera en el campo de la planificación familiar y el trabajo comunitario con promotoras voluntarias, centrando su trabajo especialmente en la salud materno-infantil."

82. Laveaga, "'Let's Become Fewer,'" 2; Sánchez Nateras, "Vámonos haciendo menos," 23.

83. In 1936, Artemio de la Vega established the first Cervecería Cuauhtémoc, from Monterrey, dealership to sell Carta Blanca beer in Ciudad Juárez. Carta Blanca is considered the "people's beer" in Mexico. Gabriela Minjáres, "Deja Federico De La Vega un legado a la Ciudad," *El Diario*, December 17, 2015.

84. "Meeting Minutes June 1959," Planned Parenthood of El Paso records, box 1.

85. Espinosa Tavares, "'They Are Coming in So Fast That If We Had Publicity about the Clinic We Would Be Swamped,'" 77.

86. Ziegler, *After Roe*, 117.

87. Nelson, *Women of Color and the Reproductive Rights Movement*, 2–3; Robertson, *The Malthusian Moment*, 179; Ziegler, *After Roe*, 114–16.

88. Gutiérrez, *Fertile Matters*, 1; Ziegler, *After Roe*, 117.

89. "Program: Thirty Sixth Annual Meeting of Planned Parenthood of El Paso," Planned Parenthood of El Paso records, MS 286, box 4, Meeting Programs.

90. "Program: Thirty Seventh Annual Meeting of Planned Parenthood of El Paso," Planned Parenthood of El Paso records, MS 286, box 4, Meeting Programs.

91. Murillo, "Espanta Cigüeñas"; Reagan, "Crossing the Border for Abortions."

92. "Program: Thirty Seventh Annual Meeting of Planned Parenthood of El Paso."

93. Bush, "Foreword," vii.

94. Bush, "Foreword," vii.

95. Bush, "Foreword," viii.

96. Connelly, *Fatal Misconception*, 304.

97. Gutiérrez, *Fertile Matters*, 15.

98. Critchlow, *Intended Consequences*, 77.

99. Brown, "Hospital Provides Healing, Hope in Drug War's Epicenter."

100. "Planned Parenthood Center of El Paso Meeting Programs: President's Report 1976," box 4, folder 17, Planned Parenthood of El Paso Records, MS 286, C. L. Sonnichsen Special Collections Department.

101. "Family Planning Takes—" *Omaha World-Herald*, September 29, 1984.

102. "Family Planning Takes—."

103. Generally unincorporated shanty towns around Ciudad Juárez with little to no infrastructure—such as running water, electricity, paved roads, and sewage systems.

104. "Family Planning Takes—."

105. "Family Planning Takes—."

106. Fernández-Kelly, *For We Are Sold*, 50.

107. Fernández-Kelly, *For We Are Sold*, 5 and 50–51.

108. Fernández-Kelly, *For We Are Sold*, 58–59.

109. Fernández-Kelly, *For We Are Sold*, 53.

110. Fernández-Kelly, *For We Are Sold*, 66.

111. Fernández-Kelly, *For We Are Sold*, 55.

112. Fernández-Kelly, *For We Are Sold*, 57.

113. Wright, "Feminicidio, narcoviolence, and gentrification in Ciudad Juárez," 837.

114. Fernández-Kelly, *For We Are Sold*, 66.

115. For an extensive examination of Hardin's anti-immigrant campaigns, see Chávez-García, "The Architects of Hate."

116. "Obituary: W.T. Rowald," *The Montclair Times*, July 16, 1998; "Letter from Thad Rowland to Elizabeth Beteta in Mexico City, July 9, 1986," box 23, Garrett Hardin papers. Uarch FacPap 14, Department of Special Collections, University Libraries, University of California, Santa Barbara. I would like to thank Miroslava Chávez-Garcia for sharing with me critical documents about Hardin's and Rowland's communications with the de la Vega family. Without her guidance, I would not have been able to make this important connection.

117. "Address of Participants in ACAPI Include a P.O. Box for Guadalupe and Francisco De La Vega in El Paso," box 23, Garrett Hardin papers. Uarch FacPap 14, Department of Special Collections, University Libraries, University of California, Santa Barbara.

118. "Notes from the Juarez Meeting," box 23, Garrett Hardin papers. Uarch Fac-Pap 14, Department of Special Collections, University Libraries, University of California, Santa Barbara.

119. "Letter from Hardin to Rowland July 1986," box 23, Garrett Hardin papers. Uarch FacPap 14, Department of Special Collections, University Libraries, University of California, Santa Barbara.

120. "Letter Rowland to Hardin, March 1987," box 23, Garrett Hardin papers. Uarch FacPap 14, Department of Special Collections, University Libraries, University of California, Santa Barbara.

121. "Notes about Their April 1987 Meeting in Dallas with Mark D'Arcangelo, Thad Rowland, Federico De La Vega, and Joe Hood," box 23, Garrett Hardin papers. Uarch FacPap 14, Department of Special Collections, University Libraries, University of California, Santa Barbara.

122. Discussion of the so-called Wattenberg Thesis, box 24, Garrett Hardin papers. Uarch FacPap 14, Department of Special Collections, University Libraries, University of California, Santa Barbara.

123. "Letter from Hardin to Rowland November 1986," box 23, Garrett Hardin papers. Uarch FacPap 14, Department of Special Collections, University Libraries, University of California, Santa Barbara.

124. "Notes from the Juarez Meeting."

125. PR Newswire, "FEMAP Foundation Receives $45,000 Grant."

126. Adair Margo is married to Dee Margo, former Republican mayor of El Paso, and was the chairman of the President's Committee on the Arts and Humanities under George W. Bush. She received the Presidential Citizens Medal from George W. Bush in 2008. "President and Mrs. Bush Attend Presentation of the 2008 National Medals of Arts and National Humanities Medals," Office of the Press Secretary, November 17, 2008.

127. Finley and Esposito, "Neoliberalism and the Non-Profit Industrial Complex," 5.

128. Van Der Tak, "Communicating Messages," 69.

129. Gutiérrez, *Fertile Matters*, 75.

130. "International Fertility Research Program: Annual Report."

131. Kessel, *A Public Health Odyssey*, 64.

132. Ravenholt, "Foreword," x; Critchlow, *Intended Consequences*, 178; Connelly, *Fatal Misconception*, 231.

133. Kessel, *A Public Health Odyssey*, 54–56.

134. Robert Reinhold, "Mexico's Birthrate Seems Sharply Off," *New York Times*, November 5, 1979.

135. "Mexico's Birthrate Seems Sharply Off."

136. Juan M. Vasquez, "Mexico—A 'Success' on Population," *Los Angeles Times*, September 15, 1984.

137. "Mexico—A 'Success' on Population"; also see J. Joseph Speidel, interview by Rebecca Sharpless, transcript of audio recording, October 10–11, 2002, Population and Reproductive Health Oral History Project, Sophia Smith Collection, p. 16.

138. Laveaga, "'Let's Become Fewer,'" 27.

139. "Family Planning Crusader Battles Mexico's Growth."

140. "Mexico a 'Success' on Population."

141. Wayne A. Cornelius, "When the Door Is Closed to Illegal Aliens, Who Pays," *New York Times*, June 1, 1977.

142. Espino, "Women Sterilized as They Give Birth," 165.

143. Gutiérrez, *Fertile Matter*, 38–39.

144. Connelly, *Fatal Misconception*, 246.

145. Guadalupe de La Vega as quoted in Krier's article "A Crusader for Birth Control in Mexico."

146. Ruiz, "Mexican Women and Multinationals," 19.

147. Devon Gerard Peña as quoted by Ruiz in "Mexican Women and Multinationals," 20.

148. Ruiz, "Mexican Women and Multinationals," 20.

149. "Mexico—A 'Success' on Population."

150. "Family Planning Takes—."

151. "Mexico—A 'Success' on Population."

152. "A Crusader for Birth Control in Mexico."

153. "Mexico—A 'Success' on Population."

154. O'Brien, "The Many Meanings of Aborto," 953.

155. Connelly, *Fatal Misconception*, 11; Solinger, *Pregnancy and Power*, 115.

156. Bustamante, "Proposition 187 and Operation Gatekeeper"; Nevins, *Operation Gatekeeper*.

157. Wright, "Feminicidio, Narcoviolence, and Gentrification in Ciudad Juárez," 833–34.

158. Hernández, "Dislocation And Globalization on the United States-Mexico Border."

159. Franz, "Mexican/Migrant Mothers and 'Anchor Babies.'"

160. Cisneros, "'Alien' Sexuality."

Epilogue

1. Rielly, Mollie. "Leticia Van De Putte, Texas Legislator, Slams Male Colleagues During Abortion Filibuster." *Huffpost*, June 23, 2013. https://www.huffpost.com/entry/leticia-van-de-putte_n_3500497.

2. Van de Putte interview in January 2021.

3. Navarro, *Latina Legislator*, 59.

4. Navarro, *Latina Legislator*, 64.

5. Navarro, *Latina Legislator*, 60.

6. Navarro, *Latina Legislator*, 68.

7. I argue that in the borderlands Judaism was also seen as a more progressive and modern religion that Catholicism, especially considering organizing among Protestant and Jewish women within the birth control movement in El Paso.

8. Gallardo, "'It's Not a Natural Order,'" 108.

9. Gutiérrez, "We Will No Longer Be Silent or Invisible," 221.

10. Held, *The Ethics of Care*, 10.

11. Held, *The Ethics of Care*, 10.

12. Zavella, *The Movement for Reproductive Justice*, 9.

13. Zavella, *The Movement for Reproductive Justice*, 7.

14. Pérez, *The Decolonial Imaginary*, 7.

15. Téllez, "Mi madre, Mi hija, y yo," 58. Also see Patricia Hill Collins's discussion of motherwork in "Shifting the Center."

16. Sandoval, "US Third-World Feminism," 15.

17. Espinoza, et al., eds. *Chicana Movidas*, 15.

18. Ruiz, *Las Obreras*, 2.

19. Gonzalez, "Gender on the Borderlands," 15.

20. Ross et al., *Radical Reproductive Justice*, 11.

21. Chávez, *Chicana Liberation*, 3.

22. Ruiz, *From Out of the Shadows*, xiii.

23. Bhandary, *Freedom to Care*, 8.

24. Making these connections would be impossible were it not for the scholarship of Chicana historians. For nearly fifty years, they have documented the lives and experiences of Mexican-origin women in the United States as acts of political resistance and care. From Martha Cotera's pioneering *Diosa y Hembra* (1976) and Vicki Ruiz's (1987) *Cannery Women, Cannery Lives* to more recent edited collections such as Espinoza, Cotera, and Blackwell's *Chicana Movidas*, Chicana scholars have provided the intellectual and historical grounding for *Fighting for Control*.

25. Alexis McGill Johnson, "I'm the Head of Planned Parenthood. We're Done Making Excuses for Our Founder," *New York Times*, April 17, 2021.

26. There are dubious tomes passed off as series academic works written by anti-abortionists discussing Sanger's connections to eugenics—for example, Angela Franks *Margaret Sanger's Eugenic Legacy* (2005) and Robert G. Marshall and Charles Donovan's *Blessed Are the Barren: The Social Policy of Planned Parenthood* (1991).

27. For the most recent scholarship on fears of Latina fertility, see Chávez, "Fear of White Replacement."

28. "Under the Bridge: Migrants Held in El Paso Tell of Dust, Cold and Hunger," *The Guardian*, March 31, 2019.

29. See Muñoz Martinez, *The Injustice Never Leaves You* and Levario, *Militarizing the Border*.

30. Ruiz, *From Out of the Shadows*, xiii.

Bibliography

Primary Sources

Amelia Mendez Castillo, MS637, C. L. Sonnichsen Special Collections Department. The University of Texas at El Paso Library.

Betty Mary Smith Goetting papers, 1910–1979, MS 316, C. L. Sonnichsen Special Collections Department. The University of Texas at El Paso Library.

Chicano Vertical File. Sonnichsen Special Collections Department. The University of Texas at El Paso.

Clarence Gamble papers, 1920–1970s (inclusive), 1920–1966 (bulk). H MS c23. Harvard Medical Library, Francis A. Countway Library of Medicine, Boston, MA.

Cleofás Calleros Papers, MS 231, Sonnichsen Special Collections Department. The University of Texas at El Paso Library.

El Paso Vertical File, Border Heritage Center, Main Branch, El Paso Public Library, El Paso, Texas.

Garrett Hardin papers. Uarch FacPap 14, Department of Special Collections, University Libraries, University of California, Santa Barbara.

Harry H. Laughlin Papers (MS L1), Special Collections and Museums, Pickler Memorial Library, Truman State University.

The Isley Brothers, "Fight the Power, Part I," track #1 on *The Heat Is On*, 1975.

Kathy Flores, "Sociological Perspectives: Chicano Attitudes toward Birth Control," *Imágenes de la Chicano*. N.d. MS Comisión Femenil Mexicana Nacional Archives: Series IX: Publications box 56, folder 20. University of California, Santa Barbara.

Manuel Gamio Collection, Banc MSS Z-R5. Bancroft Library, Berkeley Library.

Margaret Sanger Papers Microfilm Edition: Smith College Collections Series.

The Margaret Sanger Papers (unfilmed), Sophia Smith Collection, Smith College, Northampton, Mass.

Martha Cotera Papers, Nettie Lee Benson Latin American Collection, University of Texas Libraries, the University of Texas at Austin.

Planned Parenthood of El Paso records, 1907–2000s, MS 286, C. L. Sonnichsen Special Collections Department. The University of Texas at El Paso Library.

US Bureau of the Census. Year: 1900. [database online]. Provo, UT, USA: Ancestry .com Operations Inc, 2004.

Vicki L. Ruiz Papers, Unprocessed materials, University of California, Irvine.

Newspapers

Birth Control Review (New York, New York)
El Continental (El Paso, Texas)
El Paso Herald-Post (El Paso, Texas)
The El Paso Times (El Paso, Texas)
New York Times (New York, New York)
The Progressive (Madison, Wisconsin)

Oral Histories

Briones, Dolores. Interview by the author. July 13, 2015.
Castillo, Amelia. Interview by the author. July 22, 2016.
Chávez, Bertha González. Interview by the author. August 4, 2015.
Escobar, Bonnie. Interview by the author. July 7, 2015.
Holder, Anne. Interview by the author. July 8, 2016.
Goetting, Kurt Eugene. Interview by the author. August 26, 2016.

Secondary Sources

Abrams, Laura. "Guardians of Virtue: The Social Reformers and the 'Girl Problem,' 1890–1920," *Social Service Review* 74, no. 3 (September 2000): 436–52.
Acuña, Rodolfo. *Occupied America: A History of Chicanos.* 4th ed. New York: Longman, 2000.
Aguilar, Luis Aboites. *El Norte Sin Algodones, 1970–2010: Estancamiento, Incoformidad y El Violento Adios al Optimismo.* Ciudad de Mexico: El Colegio de Mexico, 2019.
Aguirre, Frederick P. "Mendez v. Westminster School District: How It Affected Brown v. Board of Education." *Journal of Hispanic Higher Education* 4, no. 4 (October 2005): 321–32.
Ahluwalia, Sanjam. *Reproductive Restraints: Birth Control in India, 1877–1947.* Urbana: University of Illinois Press, 2010.
Anagnost, Ana. "A Surfeit of Bodies: Population and the Rationality of the State in Post-Mao China." In *Conceiving the New World Order: The Global Politics of Reproduction,* edited by Faye D. Ginsburg and Rayna Rapp, 22–41. Berkeley: University of California Press, 1995.
Anderson, Maria H. *Sixty Years of Choice, 1936–1996.* Houston: Planned Parenthood of Houston and Southeast Texas, 2001.
Anzaldúa, Gloria. *Borderlands/La Frontera: The New Mestiza.* San Francisco: Aunt Lute Books, 1999.
———. *Light in the Darkness, Luz en lo Oscuro: Rewriting Identity, Spirituality, and Reality.* Durham, NC: Duke University Press, 2015.
Apodaca, Maria Linda. "The Chicana Woman: An Historical Materialist Perspective." *Latin American Perspectives* 4, no. 1/2 (1977): 70–89.
Asbell, Bernard. *The Pill: A Biography of the Drug That Changed the World.* New York: Random House, 1995.

Babbitt, C. S. *The Remedy for the Decadence of the Latin Race*. El Paso, TX: El Paso Printing Company, 1909.

Baker, Jean H. *Margaret Sanger: A Life of Passion*. New York: Hill and Wang, 2011.

Balderrama, Francisco, and Raymond Rodríguez. *Decade of Betrayal: Repatriation in the 1930s*. Albuquerque: University of New Mexico Press, 2006.

Bates, Anna Louise. "Protective Custody: A Feminist Interpretation of Anthony Comstock's Life and Laws." Order No. 9122996. State University of New York at Binghamton, 1991. http://login.proxy.lib.uiowa.edu/login?url=https://www.proquest.com/dissertations-theses/protective-custody-feminist-interpretation/docview/303971837/se-2.

Bean, Frank D., Barry Edmonston, and Jeffrey S. Passel, eds. *Undocumented Migration to the United States: IRCA and the Experience of the 1980s*. Vol. 7. Washington, DC: Urban Institute, 1990.

Beisel, Nicola, and Tamara Kay, "Abortion, Race, and Gender in Nineteenth-Century America." *American Sociological Review* 69, no. 4 (2004): 498–518.

Beltrán, Cristina. *Cruelty as Citizenship: How Migrant Suffering Sustains White Democracy*. Minneapolis: University of Minnesota Press, 2020.

Bhandary, Asha. *Freedom to Care: Liberalism, Dependency Care, and Culture*. New York: Routledge, 2019.

Bhattacharya, Tithi, ed. *Social Reproduction Theory: Remapping Class, Centering Oppression*. London: Pluto Press, 2017.

Blackwell, Maylei. *¡Chicana Power!: Contested Histories of Feminism in the Chicano Movement*. Austin: University of Texas Press, 2011.

Bridges, Khiara. *The Poverty of Privacy Rights*. Stanford, CA: Stanford Law Books, 2017.

Briggs, Laura. *Reproducing Empire: Sex, Race, Science and U.S. Imperialism in Puerto Rico*. Berkeley: University of California Press, 2002.

Brown, Allie. "Hospital Provides Healing, Hope in Drug War's Epicenter." CNN. September 9, 2010. http://www.cnn.com/2010/WORLD/americas/09/09/cnnheroes.delavega.juarez.hospital/.

Bush, George H. W. Foreword to *World Population Crisis: The United States Response*, by Phyllis Tilson Piotrow. New York: Praeger, 1973: vii–ix.

Bustamante, Jorge A. "Proposition 187 and Operation Gatekeeper: Cases for the Sociology of International Migrations and Human Rights." *Migraciones internacionales* 1, no. 1 (2001): 7–34.

Cabrera, Gustavo. "Demographic Dynamics and Development: The Role of Population Policy in Mexico." *Population and Development Review* (1994), Vol. 20 Supplement: The New Politics of Population: Conflict and Consensus in Family Planning: 105–20.

Calhoun, John C. "Conquest of Mexico (Speech)." 1848. Teaching American History. https://teachingamericanhistory.org/document/conquest-of-mexico/.

Carmichael, Stokely. "Toward Black Liberation." *The Massachusetts Review* 7, no. 4 (1966): 639–51.

Carrigan, William D. *The Making of Lynching Culture: Violence and Vigilantism in Central Texas, 1836–1916*. Urbana: University of Illinois Press, 2006.

Carrigan, William D., and Clive Webb. *Forgotten Dead: Mob Violence against Mexicans in the United States, 1848–1928*. Oxford: Oxford University Press, 2013.

Castañeda, Antonia I. *Three Decades of Engendering History: Selected Works of Antonia I. Castañeda*. Vol. 9. Denton: University of North Texas Press, 2014.

Chávez, Ernesto. *The U.S. War with Mexico: A Brief History with Documents*. Boston: Bedford/St. Martin's 2008.

Chávez, Leo R. "Fear of White Replacement: Latina Fertility, White Demographic Decline, and Immigration Reform." In *A Field Guide to White Supremacy*, edited by Kathleen Belew and Ramón Gutiérrez, 177–202. Oakland: University of California Press, 2021.

———. "A Glass Half Empty: Latina Reproduction and Public Discourse." *Human Organization* 63, no. 2 (2004): 173–88.

Chávez, Marisela R. *Chicana Liberation: Women and Mexican American Politics in Los Angeles, 1945–1981*. Urbana: University of Illinois Press, 2024.

Chávez-García, Miroslava. *Negotiating Conquest: Gender and Power in California, 1770s to 1880s*. Tucson: University of Arizona Press, 2004.

———. *States of Delinquency: Race and Science in the Making of California's Juvenile Justice System*. Berkeley: University of California Press, 2012.

Chávez-García, Miroslava, and Verónica Castillo-Muñoz. "The Architects of Hate: Garrett Hardin and Cordelia S. May's Fight for Immigration Restriction and Eugenics in the Name of the Environment." *Journal of American Ethnic History* 43, no. 1 (2023): 88–117.

———. "Gender and Intimacy across the U.S.-Mexico Borderlands." *Pacific Historical Review* 89, no. 1 (2020): 4–15.

Chávez Leyva, Yolanda. "'¿Que Son Los Niños?': Mexican Children along the United States-Mexico Border, 1880–1930." PhD diss., University of Arizona, 1999.

Chesler, Ellen. *Woman of Valor: Margaret Sanger and the Birth Control Movement in America*. New York: Simon and Schuster, 1992.

Choy, Catherine Ceniza. *Empire of Care: Nursing and Migration in Filipino American History*. Durham, NC: Duke University Press, 2003.

Cisneros, Natalie. "'Alien' Sexuality: Race, Maternity, and Citizenship." *Hypatia* 28, no. 2 (2013): 290–306. http://www.jstor.org/stable/24542122.

Clark, Margaret. *Health in the Mexican-American Culture: A Community Study*. Berkeley: University of California Press, 1959.

Clarke, Adele. *Disciplining Reproduction: Modernity, American Life Sciences*. Berkeley: University of California Press, 1998.

Colen, Shellee. "'Like a Mother to Them': Stratified Reproduction and West Indian Childcare Workers and Employers in New York." In *Conceiving the New World Order: The Global Politics of Reproduction*, edited by Faye D. Ginsburg and Rayna Rapp. Berkeley: University of California Press, 1995: 380–96.

Collins, Patricia Hill. "Shifting the Center: Race, Class, and Feminist Theorizing about Motherhood." In *Mothering*, edited by Evelyn Nakano Glenn, Grace Chang, and Linda Rennie Forcey, 45–65. New York: Routledge, 2016.

Connelly, Matthew. *Fatal Misconception: The Struggle to Control World Population.* Cambridge, MA: Belknap Press of Harvard University Press, 2008.

Copper Owens, Deirdre. *Medical Bondage: Race, Gender, and the Origins of American Gynecology.* Athens: University of Georgia Press, 2018.

Cordes, D. H., et al. "Mexico, Maquiladoras, and Occupational Medicine Training." *Asia-Pacific Journal of Public Health* 3 (1989): 61–67.

Cotera, Martha. *Diosa y Hemba: The History and Heritage of Chicanas in the US.* Austin: Information Systems Development, 1976.

Cravey, Altha J. *Women and Work in Mexico's Maquiladoras.* Lanham, MD: Rowman & Littlefield, 1998.

Cressey, Paul. G. *The Taxi-Dance Hall: A Sociological Study in Commercialized Recreation and City Life.* Chicago: University of Chicago Press, 2008.

Critchlow, Donald. *Intended Consequences: Birth Control, Abortion, and the Federal Government in Modern America.* Oxford: Oxford University Press, 1999.

Dame-Griff, E. Cassandra. "The Future Is Brown . . . and Fat: Population Control, Latina/o/x 'Health' and Protecting the Future Nation-State," *Fat Studies* 9, no. 3 (2019): 220–33. https://doi.org/10.1080/21604851.2019.1643183.

Davis, Angela Y. *Women, Race and Class.* New York: Vintage Books, 1983.

Davis, Dána-Ain. "Obstetric Racism: The Racial Politics of Pregnancy, Labor, and Birthing," *Medical Anthropology* 38, no. 7 (2019): 560–73. https://doi.org/10.1080/01459740.2018.1549389.

Davis, Tom. *Sacred Work: Planned Parenthood and Its Clergy Alliances.* New Brunswick, NJ: Rutgers University Press, 2005.

DeLay, Brian. "Blood Talk: Violence and Belonging in the Navajo–New Mexican Borderland." In *Contested Spaces of Early America*, edited by Juliana Barr and Edward Countryman, 229–58. Philadelphia: University of Pennsylvania Press, 2014.

De León, Arnoldo. *They Called Them Greasers: Anglo Attitudes toward Mexicans in Texas, 1821–1900.* Austin: University of Texas Press, 1983.

de Miguel, Amado. *Ensayo Sobre La Poblacion de Mexico.* Madrid: Centro de Investigaciones Sociologicas, 1983.

Desrochers, Pierre, and Christine Hoffbauer. "The Post War Intellectual Roots of the Population Bomb. Fairfield Osborn's 'Our Plundered Planet' and William Vogt's 'Road to Survival' in Restrospect." *The Electric Journal of Sustainable Development* 1, no. 3 (2009): 73.

Directory of Planned Parenthood Clinic Services. New York: Planned Parenthood Federation of America, March 1947.

Drucker, Donna. *Contraception: A Concise History.* Cambridge, MA: MIT Press, 2020.

———. "The Diaphragm in the City: Contraceptive Research at the Birth Control Clinical Research Bureau, 1925–1939." *Icon* 26, no. 2 (2021): 11–32. https://www.jstor.org/stable/27120653.

Duarte, Pete T. "Centro de Salud Familiar La Fe: From Struggling Volunteerism to Regulated Bureaucracy." Master's thesis, University of Texas at El Paso, 1993.

Eisenhower, John S. D. *So Far from God: The U.S. War with Mexico, 1846–1848*. New York: Anchor Books, 1990.

Enciso, Fernando Saúl Alanís. *Que se quedean allá: El Gobierno de Mexico y la repatrición de Mexicanos en Estados Unidos*. Tijuana: El Colegio de la Frontera Norte, 2007.

Enríquez, Sandra I. "A Totality of Our Well-Being: The Creation and Evolution of Centro de Salud Familiar La Fe in South El Paso." In *Civil Rights in Black and Brown: Histories of Resistance and Struggle in Texas*, edited by Max Krochmal and J. Todd Moye. Austin: University of Texas Press, 2021: 177–98.

Escobar, Arturo. *Pluriversal Politics: The Real and the Possible*. Durham, NC: Duke University Press, 2020.

Escobedo, Elizabeth Rachel. *From Coveralls to Zoot Suits: The Lives of Mexican American Women on the World War II Home Front*. Chapel Hill: University of North Carolina Press, 2013.

España-Maram, Linda. *Creating Masculinity in Los Angeles's Little Manila: Working-Class Filipinos and Popular Culture, 1920s–1950s*. New York: Columbia University Press, 2006.

Espino, Virginia Rose. "Women Sterilized as They Give Birth: Population Control, Eugenics, and Social Protest in the Twentieth-Century United States." PhD diss., Arizona State University, 2007.

Espinosa Tavares, Martha Liliana. "'They Are Coming in So Fast That If We Had Publicity about the Clinic We Would Be Swamped': Edris Rice-Wray, the First Family Planning Clinic in Mexico (1959), and the Intervention of US-Based Private Foundations." *Journal of Women's History* 34, no. 2 (2022): 76–96. https://10.1353/jowh.2022.0014.

Espinoza, Dionne. "'Revolutionary Sisters': Women's Solidarity and Collective Identification among Chicana Brown Berets in East Los Angeles, 1967–1970." *Aztlán* 26, no. 1 (2001): 15–58.

Espinoza, Dionne, María Eugenia Cotera, and Maylei Blackwell, eds., "Introduction: Movements, Movimientos, and Movidas." *Chicana Movidas: New Narratives of Activism and Feminism in the Movement Era*, 1–30. Austin: University of Texas Press, 2018.

Feliciano, Zadia M. "Mexico's Demographic Transformation: From 1900 to 1990." *A Population History of North America* (2000): 601–30.

Fernández, Johanna. *The Young Lords: A Radical History*. Chapel Hill: University of North Carolina Press, 2019.

Fernández-Kelly, María Patricia. *For We Are Sold, I and My People: Women and Industry in Mexico's Frontier*. Albany: State University of New York Press, 1983.

Finley, Laura F., and Luigi Esposito. "Neoliberalism and the Non-Profit Industrial Complex: The Limits of a Market Approach to Service Delivery." *Peace Studies Journal* 5, no. 3 (2012): 4–26.

Fixmer-Oraiz, Natalie. *Homeland Maternity: US Security Culture and the New Reproductive Regime*. Urbana: University of Illinois Press, 2019.

Franks, Angela. *Margaret Sanger's Eugenic Legacy: The Control of Female Fertility*. McFarland, 2005.

Franz, Margaret E. "Mexican/Migrant Mothers and 'Anchor Babies' in Anti-Immigration Discourses: Meanings of Citizenship and Illegality in the United States." Master's thesis, Georgia State University, 2013.

French, William. "Prostitutes and Guardian Angels: Women, Work, and the Family in Porfirian Mexico." *Hispanic American Historical Review* 72, no. 4 (1992): 529–53.

Fritz, Angela I. "The Women Who Danced for a Living: Exploring Taxi Dancers' Childhood in Chicago's Polish American Communities, 1920–1926." *Journal of the History of Sexuality* 23, no. 2 (2014): 247–72.

Foley, Neil. *The White Scourge: Mexicans, Blacks, and Poor Whites in Texas Cotton Culture.* Berkeley: University of California Press, 1997.

Foner, Philip S. *Women and the American Labor Movement: From the First Trade Unions to the Present.* Chicago: Haymarket, 2018.

Foucault, Michel. *The History of Sexuality: An Introduction.* Vol. 1. New York: Vintage Books, 1990.

———. *Security, Territory, Population: Lectures at the Collège de France, 1977–1978.* London: Palgrave Macmillan, 2009.

Gabbert, Ann R., "Defining the Boundaries of Care: Local Responses to Global Concerns in El Paso Public Health Policy, 1881–1941." PhD diss., University of Texas at El Paso, 2006.

———. "El Paso, a Sight for Sore Eyes: Medical and Legal Aspects of Syrian Immigration, 1906–1907." *The Historian* 65, no. 1 (2002).

———. "Prostitution and Moral Reform in the Borderlands: El Paso, 1890–1920." *Journal of the History of Sexuality* 12, no. 4 (2003): 575–604.

Gallardo, Susana L. "'It's Not a Natural Order:' Religion and the Emergence of Chicana Feminism in the Cursillo Movement in San Jose." In *Chicana Movidas: New Narratives of Activism and Feminism in the Movement Era*, edited by Dione Espinoza, María Eugenia Cotera, and Maylei Blackwell. Austin: University of Texas Press, 2018: 91–109.

Garcia, Mario. "The Catholic Church, Mexican Ethno-Catholicism, and Inculturation in El Paso: 1900–1930." *Catholic Southwest* 22, (2011): 39–47.

———. *Desert Immigrants: The Mexicans of El Paso, 1880–1920.* New Haven, CT: Yale University Press, 1981.

———. *The Making of a Mexican American Mayor: Raymond L. Telles of El Paso.* El Paso, TX: Texas Western Press, 1998.

———. "Mexican Americans and the Politics of Citizenship: The Case of El Paso 1936." *New Mexico Historical Review* 59, no. 2 (1984): 188–204.

Geiger, A. W., and Leslie Davis, "A Growing Number of American Teenagers—Particularly Girls—Are Facing Depression," July 12, 2019. https://www.pewresearch.org/short-reads/2019/07/12/a-growing-number-of-american-teenagers-particularly-girls-are-facing-depression/.

Ginsburg, Faye, and Rayna Rapp, eds. "Introduction: Conceiving the New World Order." In *Conceiving the New World Order: The Global Politics of Reproduction.* Berkeley: University of California Press, 1995: 1–17.

Gómez, Laura. *Manifest Destinies: The Making of the Mexican American Race.* New York: New York University Press, 2007.

Gonzales, Rosalinda. "Chicanas and Mexican Immigrant Families, 1920–1940: Women's Subordination and Family Exploitation." In *Decades of Discontent: The Women's Movement, 1920–1940*, edited by Lois Scharf and Joan Jensen. Westport: Greenwood Press, 1983: 59–84.

González, Deena. "Gender on the Borderlands: Re-Textualizing the Classics." *Frontiers: A Journal of Women Studies*, 24, no. 2/3 (2003): 15–29.

———. *Refusing the Favor: The Spanish-Mexican Women of Santa Fe, 1820–1880*. Oxford: Oxford University Press, 1999.

González Navarro, Moisés. *Población y Sociedad en México, 1900–1970*. Part I. Ciudad de Mexico: Universidad Nacional Autónoma de México, 1974.

Gordon, Linda. *The Moral Property of Women: A History of Birth Control Politics in America*. Urbana: University of Illinois Press, 2002.

Grant, Madison. *The Conquest of a Continent; or, The Expansion of Races in America*. New York: Charles Scribner's Sons, 1933.

Guidotti-Hernández, Nicole M. "Embodied Forms of State Domination: Gender and the Camp Grant Massacre," *Social Text* 29, no. 3 (2010): 91–117.

Guthrie, Julia Ann. "The Young Women's Christian Association of El Paso." Master's thesis, University of Texas at El Paso, 1952. http://login.proxy.lib .uiowa.edu/login?url=https://www.proquest.com/dissertations-theses/young -womens-christian-association-el-paso/docview/301980802/se-2.

Gutiérrez, Elena. *Fertile Matters: The Politics of Mexican-Origin Women's Reproduction*. Austin: University of Texas Press, 2008.

———. "'We Will No Longer Be Silent or Invisible." In *Undivided Rights: Women of Color Organizing for Reproductive Justice*, Loretta Ross, Elena Gutiérrez, Marlene Gerber, and Jael Silliman, eds. Chicago: Haymarket Books, 2004.

Gutiérrez, Laura D. *A Constant Threat: Deportation and Return Migration to Northern Mexico, 1918–1965*. PhD diss., University of California, San Diego, 2016.

Gutierrez-Romine, Alicia. *From Back Alley to the Border: Criminal Abortion in California, 1920–1969*. Lincoln: University of Nebraska Press, 2020.

Hajo, Cathy Moran. *Birth Control on Main Street: Organizing Clinics in the United States, 1916–1939*. Urbana: University of Illinois Press, 2010.

Hartman, Betsy. *Reproductive Rights and Wrongs: The Global Politics of Population Control*. Boston: South End Press, 1995.

Hartman, Saidiya. "Venus in Two Acts." *Small Axe: A Caribbean Journal of Criticism* 12, no. 2 (2008): 1–14.

Hatcher, Robert A., and James Trussell et al. *Contraceptive Technologies*. New York: Ardent Media, 1998.

Hayes-Bautista, David. "Latino Health Policy, Forty Years Later." *Aztlan* (2010): 145–48.

Held, Virginia. *The Ethics of Care: Personal, Political, and Global*. Oxford: Oxford University Press, 2006.

Hernández, Francisca James. "Dislocation and Globalization on the United States-Mexico Border: The Case of Garment Workers in El Paso, Texas."

In *Feminismos en la antropología: nuevas propuestas críticas*, Liliana Suárez, Emma Martín, Rosalva Aída Hernández, eds. Donostia-San Sebastián: Ankulegi, 2008.

Hernandez, Kelly Lytle. *City of Inmates: Conquest, Rebellion, and the Rise of Human Caging in Los Angeles*. Chapel Hill: University of North Carolina Press, 2017.

———. *Migra!: A History of the U.S. Border Patrol*. Berkeley: University of California Press, 2010.

Hill, Joseph A. "Composition of the American Population by Race and Country of Origin." *Annals of the American Academy of Political and Social Science*. Philadelphia: Pennsylvania, 1936.

Hodges, Sarah. *Contraception, Colonialism, and Commerce: Birth Control in South India, 1920–1940*. Hampshire: Ashgate, 2008.

Holz, Rose. *The Birth Control Clinic in a Marketplace World*. Rochester, NY: University of Rochester, 2014.

Hopkins, Ramona L. "Was There a 'Southern Eugenics?': A Comparative Case Study of Eugenics in Texas and Virginia, 1900–1940." Master's thesis, University of Houston, 2009.

Hurtado, Aída. *Voicing Chicana Feminisms: Young Women Speak Out on Sexuality and Identity*. New York: New York University Press, 2003.

Ibáñez, José Antonio. "El machismo y feminismo en la literatura de Rosario Castellanos, Ángeles Mastretta y Héctor Zagal." Master's thesis, Universidad La Salle Preparatoria, 2013.

"International Fertility Research Program: Annual Report, September 30, 1978–September 29, 1979." Research Triangle Park, North Carolina, 1979.

"International Women's Year: Population and the Conference in Mexico." *Population and Development Review* 2, no. 2 (1975): 346–50.

Jacobson, Matthew Frye. *Whiteness of a Different Color: European Immigrants and the Alchemy of Race*. Cambridge, MA: Harvard University Press, 1998.

Jaffray, Nora. *Reproduction and Its Discontents in Mexico: Childbirth and Contraception from 1750 to 1905*. Chapel Hill: University of North Carolina Press, 2016.

Joffe, Carole. *Doctors of Conscience: The Struggle to Provide Abortion before and after* Roe v. Wade. Boston: Beacon Press, 1995.

Johnson, Lyndon B. "Special Message to the Congress on the Problems of the American Indian: 'The Forgotten American.'" March 6, 1968. The American Presidency Project. https://www.presidency.ucsb.edu/node/237467.

Jones, Martha S. *Birthright Citizens: A History of Race and Rights in Antebellum America*. Cambridge: Cambridge University Press, 2018.

Jordan, David Starr. *The Blood of the Nation: A Study of the Decay of the Races through the Survival of the Unfit*. Boston: American Unitarian Association, 1902.

Kaiser, Robert Blair. *The Politics of Sex and Religion: A Case History in the Development of Doctrine, 1962–1984*. Kansas City, MO: Leavin Press, 1985.

Kandaswamy, Priya. "Gendering Racial Formation." *Racial Formation in the Twenty-First Century* (2012): 23–43.

Kaplan, Amy. "Manifest Domesticity." *American Literature* 70, no. 3 (1998): 581–606.

Kennedy, David. *Birth Control in America: The Career of Margaret Sanger.* New Haven, CT: Yale University Press, 1970.

Kerber, Linda. "The 40th Anniversary of *Roe v. Wade*: A Teachable Moment." *Perspectives on History: The Newsmagazine of the American Historical Association* 50, no. 7 (October 2012). https://www.historians.org/publications -and-directories/perspectives-on-history/october-2012/the-40th-anniversary -of-roe-v-wade.

Kessel, Elton. *A Public Health Odyssey: My Life in Service and Research.* South Harwich: ARTSHIPpublishing, 2006.

Kitch, Sally L. *The Specter of Sex: Gendered Foundations of Racial Formation in the United States.* Albany: State University of New York Press, 2009.

Klepp, Susan E. *Revolutionary Conceptions: Women Fertility, and Family Limitation in America, 1760–1820.* Chapel Hill: University of North Carolina Press, 2009.

Kline, Wendy. *Building a Better Race: Gender, Sexuality, and Eugenics from the Turn of the Century to the Baby Boom.* Berkeley: University of California Press, 2001.

Kluchin, Rebecca. *Fit to Be Tied: Sterilization and Reproductive Rights in America, 1950–1980.* New Brunswick, NJ: Rutgers University, 2009.

Koerner, Reka S. "Pregnancy Discrimination in Mexico: Has Mexico Complied with the North American Agreement on Labor Cooperation." *Texas Forum on Civil Liberties and Civil Rights* 4 (1998): 235–64.

Kurtz, Judy, "Boebert Praises High Rural Teen Birth Rates, Announces She's Going to Be a '36-Year-Old Grandmother,'" March 11, 2023. https://www.wfla .com/news/national/boebert-praises-high-rural-teen-birth-rates-announces -shes-going-to-be-a-36-year-old-grandmother/.

Ladd-Taylor, Molly. *Mother-Work: Women, Child Welfare, and the State, 1890–1930.* Urbana: University of Illinois Press, 1994.

Laveaga, Gabriela Soto. *Jungle Laboratories: Mexican Peasant, National Projects, and the Making of the Pill.* Durham, NC: Duke University Press, 2009.

———. "'Let's Become Fewer': Soap Operas, Contraception, and Nationalizing the Mexican Family in an Overpopulated World." *Sexuality Research & Social Policy* 4 (2007): 19–33.

Lawrence, Jane. "The Indian Health Service and the Sterilization of Native Women." *The American Indian Quarterly* 4, no. 3 (Summer 2000): 400–419.

Leasure, J. William. "Mexican Fertility and the Revolution of 1910–1920." *Population Review* 8 (1988): 47–75.

Leon, Sharon M. *An Image of God: The Catholic Struggle with Eugenics.* Chicago: University of Chicago Press, 2013.

Levario, Miguel Antonio. *Militarizing the Border: When Mexicans Became the Enemy.* College Station: Texas A&M University Press, 2012.

Lim, Julian. *Porous Borders: Multiracial Migrations and the Law in the US-Mexico Borderlands.* Chapel Hill: University of North Carolina Press, 2017.

Lira, Natalie. *Laboratory of Deficiency: Sterilization and Confinement in California, 1900–1950s.* Vol. 6. Berkeley: University of California Press, 2021.

Lira, Natalie, and Alexandra Minna Stern. "Mexican Americans and Eugenic Sterilization: Resisting Reproductive Injustice in California, 1920–1950." *Aztlán: A Journal of Chicano Studies* 39, no. 2 (2014): 9–34.

Loeb, Catherine. "La Chicana: A Bibliographic Survey." *Frontiers: A Journal of Women Studies* 5, no. 2 (1980): 59–74.

Lopez, Iris. *Matters of Choice: Puerto Rican Women's Struggle for Reproductive Freedom*. New Brunswick, NJ: Rutgers University Press, 2008.

López, Raúl Necochea. "Gambling on the Protestants: The Pathfinder Fund and Birth Control in Peru, 1958–1965." *Bulletin of the History of Medicine* 88, no. 2 (2014): 344–71.

Lovett, Lisa. *Conceiving the Future: Pronatalism, Reproduction, and the Family in the United States*. Chapel Hill: University of North Carolina Press, 2007.

Lugones, Maria. "Playfulness, 'World'-Traveling, and Loving Perceptions." In *Making Face, Making Soul: Haciendo Caras: Creative and Critical Perspectives by Women of Color*, edited by Gloria Anzaldua. San Francisco: Aunt Lute Foundation Book, 1990: 390–402.

Luibhéid, Eithne. *Denied Entry: Controlling Sexuality at the Border*. Minneapolis: University of Minnesota Press, 2002.

Luker, Kristin. *Abortion and the Politics of Motherhood*. Berkeley, University of California Press, 1984.

Mann, Emily S., and Patrick R. Grzanka. "Agency-Without-Choice: The Visual Rhetorics of Long-Acting Reversible Contraception Promotion." *Symbolic Interaction* 41, no. 3 (2018): 334–356. https://doi.org/10.1002/symb.349.

Marks, Lara V. *Sexual Chemistry: A History of the Contraceptive Pill*. New Haven, CT: Yale University Press, 2001.

Marquez, Benjamin. "Organizing Mexican-American Women in the Garment Industry: La Mujer Obrera." *Women & Politics* 15, no. 1 (1995): 65–87.

———. *Power and Politics in a Chicano Barrio: A Study of Mobilization Efforts and Community Power in El Paso*. Lanham: University Press of America, 1985.

Marshall, Robert G., and Charles A. Donovan. *Blessed Are The Barren: The Social Policy of Planned Parenthood*. San Francisco: Ignatius Press, 1991.

Martínez, María Elena. *Genealogical Fictions: Limpieza de Sangre, Religion, and Gender in Colonial Mexico*. Palo Alto, CA: Stanford University Press, 2011.

Martinez, Oscar. *Chicanos of El Paso: An Assessment of Progress*. El Paso, TX: Texas Western Press, 1980.

———. *Saga of a Legendary Border City: Ciudad Juarez*. Tucson: University of Arizona Press, 2018.

McArthur, Judith N., and Harold L. Smith. *Texas through Women's Eyes: The Twentieth Century Experience*. Austin: University of Texas Press, 2010.

McCaa, Robert. "Missing Millions: The Demographic Costs of the Mexican Revolution." *Mexican Studies* 19, no. 2 (2003): 367–400.

———. "The Peopling of Mexico." In *A Population History of North America*, edited by Michael R. Haines and Richard H. Steckel, 277. Cambridge: Cambridge University Press, 2001.

McCann, Carole. *Birth Control Politics in the United States, 1916–1945*. Ithaca, NY: Cornell University Press, 1994.

McKiernan-Gonzalez, John. *Fevered Measures: Public Health and Race at the Texas-Mexico Border, 1848–1942*. Durham, NC: Duke University Press, 2012.

McQuade, Lena. "Troubling Reproduction: Sexuality, Race and Colonialism in New Mexico, 1919–1945." PhD diss., University of New Mexico, 2008.

McWilliams, Carey, Matt S. Meier, and Alma M. García. "'The Freedom of Jail': Women, Detention, and the Expansion of Immigration Governance along the US–Mexico Border, 1903–1917." *Journal of American Ethnic History* 39, no. 4 (2020): 27–41.

———. *North from Mexico: The Spanish-Speaking People of the United States*. London: Bloomsbury Academic, 2016.

Melamed, Jodi. "Racial Capitalism." *Critical Ethnic Studies* 1, no. 1 (Spring 2015): 76–85.

Melcher, Mary. *Pregnancy, Motherhood and Choice in Twentieth-Century Arizona*. Tucson: University of Arizona Press, 2012.

Menchaca, Martha. *The Mexican American Experience in Texas: Citizenship, Segregation, and the Struggle for Equality*. Austin: University of Texas Press, 2022.

———. *Recovering History, Constructing Race: The Indian, Black, and White Roots of Mexican Americans*. Austin: University of Texas Press, 2001.

Merchant, Emily Klancher. *Building the Population Bomb*. Oxford: Oxford University Press, 2021.

Miles, Robert. *Racism after "Race Relations."* London: Routledge, 1993.

Minian, Ana Raquel. *Undocumented Lives: The Untold Story of Mexican Migration*. Cambridge, MA: Harvard University Press, 2018.

Mitchell, Pablo. "Borderlands/La Familia: Mexicans, Homes, and Colonialism in the Early Twentieth Century Southwest." In *On the Borders of Love and Power: Families and Kinship in the Intercultural American Southwest*, edited by David Wallace Adams and Crista DeLuzio, 185–207. Berkeley: University of California Press, 2012.

———. *Coyote Nation: Sexuality, Race, and Conquest in Modernizing New Mexico, 1880–1920*. Chicago: University of Chicago Press, 2008.

———. *West of Sex: Making Mexican America, 1900–1930*. Chicago: University of Chicago Press, 2012.

Mohr, James. *Abortion in America: The Origins and Evolution of National Policy, 1800–1900*. Oxford: Oxford University Press, 1979.

Molina, Natalia. *Fit to Be Citizens?: Public Health and Race in Los Angeles, 1879–1939*. Vol. 20. Berkeley: University of California Press, 2006.

———. *How Race Is Made In America: Immigration, Citizenship, and the Historical Power of Racial Scripts*. Berkeley and Los Angeles: University of California Press, 2014.

———. "'In a Race All Their Own': The Quest to Make Mexicans Ineligible for U.S. Citizenship." *Pacific Historical Review* 79, no. 2 (May 2010): 188.

Molina, Natalia, Daniel Martinez HoSang, and Ramón Gutiérrez, eds. *Relational Formations of Race: Theory, Method, and Practice*. Berkeley: University of California, 2019.

Moore, Robert. "The Return of Planned Parenthood to El Paso." *Texas Monthly*, October 3, 2018. https://www.texasmonthly.com/news-politics/return-planned -parenthood-el-paso/.

Morgan, Jennifer. *Reckoning with Slavery: Gender, Kinship, and Capitalism in the Early Black Atlantic*. Durham, NC: Duke University Press, 2021.

Morgan, Jennifer, and Alys Eve Weinbaum. "Introduction: Reproductive Racial Capitalism." *History of the Present* 14, no. 1 (2024): 1–19.

Morgan, Lynn M., and Elizabeth F. S. Roberts. "Reproductive Governance in Latin America." *Anthropology & Medicine* 19, no. 2 (2012): 243.

Muñoz Martinez, Monica. *The Injustice Never Leaves You: Anti-Mexican Violence in Texas*. Cambridge, MA: Harvard University Press, 2018.

Murillo, Lina-Maria. "A View from Northern Mexico: Abortion before *Roe v. Wade*." *Bulletin of the History of Medicine* (forthcoming 2023).

——. "Birth Control, Border Control: The Movement for Contraception in El Paso, Texas, 1936–1940." *Pacific Historical Review* 90, no. 3 (2021): 314–44.

——. "Espanta Cigüeñas: Race and Abortion in the US-Mexico Borderlands: Winner of the 2023 Catharine Stimpson Prize for Outstanding Feminist Scholarship." *Signs: Journal of Women in Culture and Society* 48, no. 4 (2023): 795–823.

Nadkarni, Asha. *Eugenic Feminism: Reproductive Nationalism in the United States and India*. Minneapolis: University of Minnesota Press.

Navarro, Sharron A. *Latina Legislator: Leticia Van de Putte and the Road to Leadership*. No. 13. College Station: Texas A&M University Press, 2008.

Nelson, Alondra. *Body and Soul: The Black Panther Party and the Fight against Medical Discrimination*. Minneapolis: University of Minnesota Press, 2011.

Nelson, Jennifer. *More Than Medicine: A History of the Feminist Women's Health Movement*. New York University Press, 2015.

——. *Women of Color and the Reproductive Rights Movement*. New York: New York University Press, 2003.

Nevins, Joseph. *Operation Gatekeeper: The Rise of the "illegal alien" and the Remaking of the US–Mexico boundary*. New York: Routledge, 2001.

Ngai, Mae M. *Impossible Subjects: Illegal Aliens and the Making of Modern America*. Princeton, NJ: Princeton University Press, 2014.

1942 Directory of Planned Parenthood Services: Conception Control, Fertility Promotion (Sterility Clinics). New York: Planned Parenthood Federation of America, 1942.

O'Brien, Elizabeth. "The Many Meanings of Aborto: Pregnancy Termination and the Instability of a Medical Category over Time." *Women's History Review* 30, no. 6 (2021): 952–70.

——. *Surgery and Salvation: The Roots of Reproductive Injustice in Mexico, 1770–1940*. Chapel Hill: University of North Carolina Press, 2023.

Omi, Michael, and Howard Winant. *Racial Formation in the United States: From the 1960s to the 1990s*. New York: Routledge, 1994.

Overmyer-Velázquez, Mark. "Good Neighbors and White Mexicans: Constructing Race and Nation on the Mexico-U.S. Border." *Journal of American Ethnic History* 33, no. 1 (2013): 5–34.

Pascoe, Peggy. *Relations of Rescue: The Search for Female Moral Authority in the American West, 1874–1939*. Oxford: Oxford University Press, 1990.

———. *What Comes Naturally: Miscegenation Law and the Making of Race in America*. Oxford: Oxford University Press, 2009.

Paul, Julius. "'Three Generations of Imbeciles Are Enough': State Eugenic Sterilization Laws in American Thought and Practice." Washington, DC: Walter Reed Army Institute of Research, 1965. http://readingroom.law.gsu.edu/cgi /viewcontent.cgi?article=1097&context=buckvbell.

Peffer, George Anthony. "Forbidden Families: Emigration Experiences of Chinese Women under the Page Law, 1875–1882." *Journal of American Ethnic History* 6, no. 1 (Fall 1986): 28–46.

Peña Delgado, Grace. "Border Control and Sexual Policing: White Slavery and Prostitution along the U.S.-Mexico Borderlands, 1903–1910." *Western Historical Quarterly* 43, no. 2 (2012): 157–78.

Perales, Monica. *Smeltertown: Making and Remembering a Southwest Border Community*. Chapel Hill: University of North Carolina Press, 2010.

———. "'Who Has a Greater Job Than a Mother?' Defining Mexican Motherhood on the U.S.-Mexico Border in the Early Twentieth Century." In *On the Borders of Love and Power: Families and Kinship in the Intercultural Southwest*, edited by David Wallace Adams and Crista DeLuzio. Berkeley: University of California Press: 163–84.

Pérez, Emma. *The Decolonial Imaginary: Writing Chicanas into History*. Bloomington: Indiana University Press, 1999.

Perrillo, Jonna. "The Perils of Bilingualism: Anglo Anxiety and Spanish Instruction in the Borderlands." *Journal of American History* 108, no. 1 (2021): 86. https://doi.org/10.1093/jahist/jaab064.

Petchesky, Rosalind Pollack. *Abortion and Woman's Choice: The State, Sexuality, and Reproductive Freedom*. Boston: Northeastern University Press, 1990.

Piotrow, Phyllis Tilson. *World Population Crisis: The United States Response*. New York: Praeger, 1973.

Pitti, Stephen. *The Devil in Silicon Valley: Race, Mexican Americans, and Northern California*. Princeton, NJ: Princeton University Press, 2003.

Prentiss, Craig R. *Debating God's Economy: Social Justice in America on the Eve of Vatican II*. University Park, PA: Penn State University Press, 2010.

Prescott, H., and Lauren MacIvor Thompson. "A Right to Ourselves: Women's Suffrage and the Birth Control Movement." *The Journal of the Gilded Age and Progressive Era* 19, no. 4 (2020): 542–58. https://doi.org/10.1017 /S1537781420000304.

PR Newswire. "FEMAP Foundation Receives $45,000 Grant for Hospital de la Familia's Neonatal Wing Expansion; Cooper Industries Supports Group With

Three- Year Commitment." March 22, 2000. https://www.proquest.com
/docview/449376323?sourcetype=Wire%20Feeds.

Puelles, Liset C. "¿Quiénes cuidan nuestras vulvas y vaginas?" https://orcid.org
/0000-0002-3459-5554.

Pycior, Julie Leininger. *LBJ and Mexican Americans: The Paradox of Power.*
Austin: University of Texas Press, 1997.

Ramírez de Arellano, Annette B., and Conrad Seipp. *Colonialism, Catholicism, and
Contraception: A History of Birth Control in Puerto Rico.* Chapel Hill: University
of North Carolina Press, 1983.

Ravenholt, Reimer. Foreword to *A Public Health Odyssey: My Life in Service and
Research*, by Elton Kessel, vii–xii. South Harwich: ARTSHIPpublishing, 2006.

Reagan, Leslie J. "Crossing the Border for Abortions: California Activists, Mexican
Clinics, and the Creation of a Feminist Health Agency in the 1960s." *Feminist
Studies* 26, no. 2, (2000): 323–48.

Reed, James. *From Private Vice to Public Virtue: The Birth Control Movement and
American Society since 1830.* New York: Basic Books, 1978.

Reséndez, Andrés. *Changing National Identities at the Frontier: Texas and New
Mexico, 1800–1850.* Cambridge: Cambridge University Press, 2004.

Riddell, Citlali Lucia. "Californio Local Liberalisms: The Lasting Impact of
Mexican Ideologies in California, 1848–1890." PhD diss., UCLA, 2020.

Roberstad, Janice L. "Infant Mortality in El Paso County: Ethnic and Socioeconomic
Correlates." Order No. EP01224, University of Texas at El Paso, 1975. https://
www.proquest.com/dissertations-theses/infant-mortality-el-paso-county-ethnic
/docview/302795579/se-2.

Roberts, Dorothy. *Killing the Black Body: Race, Reproduction, and the Meaning of
Liberty.* New York: Vintage, 2014.

———. "Privatization and Punishment in the New Age of Reprogenetics," *Emory
Law Journal* (2005): 1344.

Robertson, Thomas. *The Malthusian Moment: Global Population and the Birth of
American Environmentalism.* New Brunswick, NJ: Rutgers University Press, 2012.

Rodríguez, Jaime Javier, "The US–Mexico War and American Literary History."
Oxford Research Encyclopedia of Literature. Oxford: Oxford University Press,
2019.

Rodríguez-Muñiz, Michael. *Figures of the Future: Latino Civil Rights and the Politics
of Demographic Change.* Princeton, NJ: Princeton University Press, 2021.

Rogers, John. "Poverty behind the Cactus Curtain." *The Progressive*, March 30,
no. 3 (1966): 23–25.

Romo, David Dorado. *Ringside Seat to a Revolution: An Underground Cultural
History of El Paso and Juárez: 1893–1923.* El Paso, TX: Cinco Puntos Press, 2014.

Roosevelt, Franklin D. "Radio Address from Albany, New York: 'The "Forgotten
Man" Speech.'" April 7, 1932. The American Presidency Project. https://www
.presidency.ucsb.edu/node/288092.

Ross, Loretta. "African-American Women and Abortion: 1800–1970." In *Theorizing
Black Feminisms: The Visionary Pragmatism of Black Women*, edited by Stanlie M.
James and Abena P. A. Busia, 141–42. London: Routledge, 1993.

———. "Understanding Reproductive Justice: Transforming the Pro-Choice Movement." *Off Our Backs* 36, no. 4 (2006): 14–19.

Ross, Loretta, Lynn Roberts, Erika Derkas, Whitney Peoples, and Pamela Bridgewater Toure, eds. *Radical Reproductive Justice: Foundations, Theory, Practice, and Critique.* New York: Feminist Press, 2017.

Roth, Benita. *Separate Roads to Feminism: Black, Chicana, and White Feminist Movements in America's Second Wave.* Cambridge University Press, 2004.

Rozek, Barbara. "The Entry of Mexican Women into Urban Based Industries." In *Women and Texas History*, edited by Fane Downs and Nancy Barker, 15–33. Austin: Texas State Historical Association, 1993.

Ruiz, Vicki L. "By the Day or the Week: Mexicana Domestic Workers in El Paso." In *Women on the US-Mexico Border: Responses to Change*, 61–76. New York: Routledge, 2020.

———. *Cannery Women, Cannery lives: Mexican Women, Unionization, and the California Food Processing Industry, 1930–1950.* Albuquerque: University of New Mexico Press, 1987.

———. "Dead Ends or Gold Mines?: Using Missionary Records in Mexican-American Women's History." *Frontiers: A Journal of Women Studies* 12, no. 1 (1991).

———. *From Out of the Shadows: Mexican Women in the Twentieth-Century America.* Oxford: Oxford University Press, 2008.

———. *Las Obreras: Chicana Politics of Work and Family.* Los Angeles: UCLA Chicano Studies Research Center Publications, 2000.

Saade Granados, Marta. "¿Quiénes deben procrear? Los médicos eugenistas bajo el signo social (México, 1931–1940)." *Cuicuilco* 11, no. 31 (2004): 1–36.

Salazar Parreñas, Rachel. "'White Trash' Meets the 'Little Brown Monkeys': The Taxi Dance Hall as a Site of Interracial and Gender Alliances between White Working Class Women and Filipino Immigrant Men in the 1920s and 30s." *Amerasian Journal* 24, no. 2 (1998): 115–34.

Sánchez, George J. *Becoming Mexican American: Ethnicity, Culture, and Identity in Chicano Los Angeles, 1900–1945.* New York: Oxford University Press, 1993.

———. *Forgotten People: A Study of New Mexicans.* Albuquerque: University of New Mexico Press, 1940.

Sánchez Nateras, Gerardo. "Vámonos haciendo menos: políticas de población y discurso visual de la planificación familiar en México durante el sexenio de Luis Echeverría (1970–1976)." Tesis de licenciatura, Universidad Nacional Autónoma de México, 2012.

Sánchez Rivera, Rachell. "What Happened to Mexican Eugenics?: Racism and the Reproduction of the Nation." PhD diss., Cambridge University, 2019.

Sandoval, Chela. *Methodology of the Oppressed.* Minneapolis: University of Minnesota Press, 2000.

———. "US Third World Feminism: The Theory and Method of Oppositional Consciousness in the Postmodern World." *Genders*, no. 10 (1991): 1–24.

Sanger, Margaret. *Woman and the New Race.* New York: Bretano's, 1920.

Schoen, Johanna. *Abortion after Roe: Abortion after Legalization.* Chapel Hill: University of North Carolina Press, 2015.

———. *Choice and Coercion: Birth Control, Sterilization, and Abortion in Public Health and Welfare*. Chapel Hill: University of North Carolina Press, 2005.

Silliman, Jael, Marlene Gerber Fried, Loretta Ross, and Elena Gutiérrez. "Introduction: Women of Color and Their Struggle for Reproductive Justice." In *Undivided Rights: Women of Color Organizing for Reproductive Justice*, 7–30. Chicago: Haymarket Books, 2004.

Sinclair, Heather. "Birth City: Race and Violence in the History of Childbirth and Midwifery in El Paso-Ciudad Juárez Borderlands, 1907–2013." PhD diss., University of Texas at El Paso, 2016.

———. "White Plague, Mexican Menace: Migration, Gendered Contagion in El Paso, Texas, 1880–1930." *Pacific Historical Review* 85, no. 4 (November 2016): 475–505.

Smith, Harold L. "'All Good Things Start with the Women': The Origin of the Texas Birth Control Movement, 1933–1945." *Southwestern Historical Quarterly* 114, no. 3 (January 2011): 253–85.

Solinger, Rickie. *Pregnancy and Power: A History of Reproductive Politics in the United States*. New York: New York University Press, 2019.

Sreenivas, Mytheli. *Reproductive Politics and the Making of Modern India*. Seattle: University of Washington Press, 2021.

Stepan, Nancy Leys. *"The Hour of Eugenics": Race, Gender, and Nation in Latin America*. Ithaca, NY: Cornell University Press, 1991.

Stephanson, Anders. *Manifest Destiny: American Expansionism and the Empire of Right*. New York: Hill and Wang, 1995.

Stern, Alexandra Minna. "Buildings, Boundaries, and Blood: Medicalization and Nation-Building on the U.S.-Mexico Border, 1910–1930." *The Hispanic American Historical Review* 79, no. 1 (February 1999): 41–81.

———. *Eugenic Nation: Faults and Frontiers of Better Breeding in Modern America*. Berkeley: University of California Press, 2005.

———. "Eugenics beyond Borders: Science and Medicalization in Mexico and the U.S.-West, 1900–1950." PhD diss., University of Chicago, 1999.

———. "From 'Race Suicide' to 'White Extinction': White Nationalism, Nativism, and Eugenics over the Past Century." *Journal of American History* 109, no. 2 (2022): 348–61.

———. "Responsible Mothers and Normal Children: Eugenics, Nationalism, and Welfare in Post-Revolutionary Mexico, 1920–1940." *Journal of Historical Sociology* 12, no. 4 (1999): 369–98.

———. "Sterilized in the Name of Public Health," *American Journal of Public Health* 95, no. 7 (July 2005).

Studer, John. "Mirta Vidal, Lifelong Socialist." *The Militant* 68, no. 3 (2004). https://www.themilitant.com/2004/6803/680353.html.

Suárez y López-Guazo, Laura. "Evolucionismo y Eugenesia en México." *Boletín Mexicano Historia Filosofía de la Medicina* 12, no. 1 (2009): 19–23.

Tajima-Pena, Renee, Virginia Espino, Maria Hurtado, Consuelo Hermosillo, Antonia Hernández, Bernard Rosenfield, Claudio Rocha, et al., dirs. 2015. *No Más Bebés = No More Babies*. Moon Canyon Films.

Takeuchi-Demirci, Aiko. *Contraceptive Diplomacy: Reproductive Politics and Imperial Ambitions in the United States and Japan*. Stanford, CA: Stanford University Press, 2018.

Tapia, Ruby. *American Pietas: Visions of Race, Death, and the Maternal*. Minneapolis: University of Minnesota Press, 2011.

Téllez, Michelle. "Mi madre, Mi hija, y yo," In *Latina/Chicana Mothering*, edited by Dorsía Smith Silva. Toronto: Demeter Press, 2011: 57–70.

Tentler, Leslie Woodcock. *An American History: Catholics and Contraception*. Ithaca: Cornell University Press, 2004.

Theobald, Brianna. *Reproduction on the Reservation: Pregnancy, Childbirth, and Colonialism in the Long Twentieth Century*. Chapel Hill: University of North Carolina Press, 2019.

Timmons, W. H. *El Paso: A Borderlands History*. El Paso, TX: Texas Western Press, 1990.

Tjarks, Alicia V. "Comparative Demographic Analysis of Texas, 1777–1793." *The Southwestern Historical Quarterly* 77, no. 3 (1974): 291–338.

Tobin, Kathleen. *The American Religious Debate over Birth Control, 1907–1937*. Jefferson, NC: McFarland and Company, 2001.

Tone, Andrea, ed. *Controlling Reproduction: An American History*. Wilmington, DE: Scholarly Resources, 1997.

——. *Devices and Desires: A History of Contraceptives in America*. New York: Hill and Wang, 2001.

Tronto, Joan. *Moral Boundaries: A Political Argument for an Ethic of Care*. New York: Routledge Press, 1993.

Tungohan, Ethel. *Care Activism: Migrant Domestic Workers Movement-Building and Communities of Care*. Urbana: University of Illinois Press, 2023.

Underman, Kelly. *Feeling Medicine: How the Pelvic Exam Shapes Medical Training*. New York: New York University Press, 2020.

Van Der Tak, Jean. "Communicating Population "Messages". *European Demographic Information Bulletin* 9 (1978): 69–73.

Vargas, Zaragosa. *Crucible of Struggle: A History of Mexican Americans From Colonial Times to the Present Era*. New York: University of Oxford Press, 2017.

Vasconcelos, José. *The Cosmic Race: La Raza Cósmica*. Baltimore: John Hopkins Press, 1979.

Vidal, Mirta. *Women: New Voice of La Raza*. New York: Pathfinder Press, 1971.

Villanueva, Nicholas, Jr. *The Lynching of Mexicans in the Texas Borderlands*. Albuquerque: University of New Mexico Press, 2017.

Vogt, William. *Road to Survival*. New York: William Sloane Associates, 1948.

Walia, Harsha. *Border and Rule: Global Migration, Capitalism, and the Rise of Racist Nationalism*. Chicago: Haymarket Books, 2021.

Watkins, Elizabeth Siegel. *On the Pill: A Social History of Oral Contraceptives, 1950–1970*. Baltimore: Johns Hopkins University Press, 1998.

Weber, David. *Foreigners in Their Native Land: The Historical Roots of the Mexican Americans*. Albuquerque: University of New Mexico Press, 1973.

White, Owen. *Out of the Desert: The Historical Romance of El Paso*. El Paso, TX: The McMath Publishers, 1923.

Wilson, Kim, and Jane Van Velkinburgh, "Betty Mary Goetting Brought Birth Control to El Paso." In *Borderlands* 28, edited by Heather Coons, 10–13. El Paso: El Paso Community College, 2010.

Wilson Gilmore, Ruth. "Race and Globalization." In *Geographies of Global Change: Remapping the World*, 2nd ed., edited by Peter J. Taylor, R. J. Johnston, and Michael Watts, 261–74. Hoboken, NJ: Wiley-Blackwell, 2002.

Wright, Melissa W. "Feminicidio, Narcoviolence, and Gentrification in Ciudad Juárez: The Feminist Fight," *Environment and Planning D: Society and Space* 31 (2013): 830–45.

Zamora, Bernice. "Love, a Mother's." In *Palabra: A Sampling of Contemporary Latino Writers*, Benjamin Alire Sáenz and Rosemary Catacalos, eds. San Francisco State University: The Poetry Center and American Poetry Archives, 1993.

Zavella, Patricia. *The Movement for Reproductive Justice: Empowering Women of Color through Social Activism*. New York: New York University Press, 2020.

Ziegler, Mary. *After Roe: The Lost History of the Abortion Debate*. Cambridge, MA: Harvard University Press, 2015.

———. "Eugenic Feminism: Mental Hygiene, the Women's Movement, and the Campaign for Eugenic Legal Reform, 1900–1935." *Harvard Journal of Law and Gender* 31, no. 1 (Winter 2008): 211–36.

Zipf, Karin L. *Bad Girls at Samarcand: Sexuality and Sterilization in a Southern Juvenile Reformatory*. Baton Rouge: Louisiana State University Press, 2016.

Index

Box, John Calvin, 46
Bracero Program, 28, 140, 199, 210
Bridges, Khiara, 186
Briggs, Laura, 152
Buchanan, H. D., 75–76
Buck v. Bell, 83
Bush, George H. W., 214–15

Cabrera, Gustavo, 203, 287n34
Calderon, Mary, 135–36
Calhoun, John C., 32
California: immigration to, 231; population control measures in, 64; Southern California Population Crisis Committee, 196–97; sterilization programs in, 74, 227, 280n3
Calleros, Cleofás, 43–45, 71–72
Carmichael, Stokely, 189
Carpenter, Gray, 150–51
Carter, Jimmy, 227
Casti Connubii. See Catholic Church
Castillo, Amelia, 4–5, 8, 16, 19, 166, 170–72, *174*, 183, 186, 192
Castillo-Muñoz, Verónica, 97
Catholic Church: confrontation of Sanger and, 72–78; cultural indifference towards contraception, 229–30; description of birth control movement leaders in, 69; disputes with other religious groups over birth control, 73; Federación Mexicana de Asociaciónes y Empresas Privadas (FEMAP) and, 197–98; objection to El Paso distributing contraceptive information, 184–90; pickets of pharmacies by, 71; poverty and, 185–86; resistance to birth control efforts, 6–7, 53, 70–72, 187; Sanger's antagonism of, 53–54; stereotypes of Mexican-origin women, 235
Cázares-Zavala, José, 175–76
Centro de Salud Familiar La Fe. *See* Father Rahm Clinic
Chaves, Dennis, 72
Chávez, Alberto, 89

Chávez, Ernesto, 31
Chávez, Leo R., 10
Chávez, Marisela, 92, 160, 241
Chávez Garcia, Miroslava, 97
"Chicana *movidas*," 240
Chicana/o movement: abortion and, 213; bridging activism and, 241; calls for self-determination in, 160–62, 167, 176, 191, 194; Chicana feminist theory, 96–97; Chicano health organizations, 193; Father Rahm Clinic and, 7–8, 158–59; Health Action Committee and, 193; health care and, 157–59; interventions in reproductive care movement, 233–35, 240, 242, 245; marginalization of Mexican origin people, 162–65, 187–90, 194; racial formation of Mexican-origin people in Southwest and, 236; reproductive health and, 19, 165–69; reproductive justice and, 160–62, 237–38, 241; youth-led protests and, 164, 189–90
Chicana Rights Project, 167
"Chicano Attitudes toward Birth Control" (Flores), 168
Chicano Health Career Institute, 193
Chinese Exclusion Act, 37, 42
Chinese women, 37
Cisneros, Natalie, 231
Ciudad Juárez, Mexico: abortion in, 8, 214–16, 230; concerns over birth rates in, 205–7; *feminicidio* in, 231; maquiladora system in, 200, 209–10; population control in, 205–8; railroad in, 36; de la Vega and, 8. *See also* El Paso, Texas; Federación Mexicana de Asociaciónes y Empresas Privadas (FEMAP); Mexico; Vega, Guadalupe Arizpe de la
Clark, Adele, 14
Clinica de la Raza, 193
clinics. *See names of specific clinics*
Clinton administration, 230–31
CNN, 208

Planned Parenthood of El Paso (PPEP) (*continued*)
Campaign and, 211; IUDs and, 146–47; city-county health clinics and, 179, 182–91; and "Knock on Every Door" campaign, 153–54; and "Knock on Every Door" pamphlet, *149*; Mexican-origin women as employees of, 116, 243; name change of, 7, 81; 1942 communiqué with Gamble, 67–69; pamphlets and flyers of, *68*; patient statistics of, 117, 131, 134, 136, 145–46, 156, 192; population control and, 122–23, 127, 166, 181–84, 214; research sources of, 18–19; top-down approach of, 147–48, 153; Twenty-Five Month Club Enovid Program and, 147–48; de la Vega and, 212, 215–16. *See also* Mothers' Health Center

Pokorny, John, 206–7
Polk, James K., 32
Ponce de León, Juan María, 35
The Population Bomb (Ehrlich), 156
population control: abortion, 213–16; birth control campaigns, 4–5; Bush and, 214–15; Ciudad Juárez and, 205–8; Cold War and, 122–23; demographic transition theory, 219; in Mexico, 9, 201–5, 225–28; new voices in movement for, 219–20, 224–25; Nixon administration and, 175; the Pill and, 184–85; Planned Parenthood of El Paso (PPEP) and, 181–84; PPEP and, 122, 127; PPFA and, 124–25; public health and immigration controls, 39–45; reproductive care vs, 165–69; reproductive coercion, 14–15; and *Roe v. Wade*, 213–16; and Southern California Population Crisis Committee, 196–97; sterilization, 14–16, 45, 62–63, 74–75, 94, 118, 167, 227, 253n34, 280n3; US public policy discourse about, 138; de la Vega and,

198, 207–8; Vogt and, 124–25. *See also* birth control; birth control advocates; sterilization programs
population control ideology, 12–13, 19, 25–27, 51–52, 61, 78, 123, 167–69, 188, 199, 236. *See also* eugenics; reproductive care; white supremacy
Population Council, 146
Porth, Francis, 154
Portillo, Jose Lopez, 226
poverty: and birth control campaigns, 52, 75–76, 83, 188; Catholic Church and, 185–86; Goetting and, 6; infant mortality and, 70; in Mexican-origin community, 67; national dialogue on, 180–81; school segregation and, 76; in South El Paso, 164–65; and War on Poverty programs, 143, 162, 164–65, 183
Powell, Alex, 71–72
Prather, Bess N., 64
Preciado, Aurora, 117
Project Bravo, 175, 183–84
Protestant clergy, 73, 82
Puerto Rico, 140–42, 252n25

Quenon, J. Max, 179
Quigley, Daniel, 75

race suicide, 27, 54–55, 207
racial capitalism: birth control advocates, 84–85; family planning movements, 5; reproductive care, 95
racism: Anglos' racial fears, 48; Chinese Exclusion Act, 37; in clinical trials, 150; disease and, 159; in El Paso-Ciudad Juárez borderlands, 24; in El Paso mass shooting (2019), 245; in eugenic fertility controls, 62–63; Great Depression and, 43–44; Jim Crow, 71–72; *Knock on Every Door* (film) and, 152–53; and migration to United States, 37; and overcrowding in South El Paso, 41–42; pain tolerance of women of color and, 132;

racial degeneration, 25–27; racialization of Mexicans in United States, 11, 236; racial tropes of Mexican women, 20; and reproductive care, 98; and reproductive control, 6, 10–12, 84–85; settler colonialism and, 30–34; US Census Bureau and, 71; US citizenship and, 34–35; violence against Mexicans, 38–39

Radical Reproductive Justice (Ross et al.), 20

Rahm, Harold, 8, 172–73. *See also* Father Rahm Clinic

Ramírez de Arellano, Annette, 141–42, 152

Rau, Dhanvanthi Rama, 126

Reagan, Ronald, 197

Recinos, Luis Felipe, 104–8

religion: conversion, 56; in favor of birth control, 82–85. *See also* Catholic Church

The Remedy for the Decadence of the Latin Race (Babbitt), 25–26

reproductive care: in borderlands, 117–21; in community clinics, 192–94; in early 20th century borderlands, 104–9, 120; genealogy of, 93–100; in Oakland, CA, 193; in postdepression-era borderlands, 109–16, 120; social work as, 170–72; theories of, 241–42

reproductive control: absence of rights as issue, 10; choice and coercion in, 10–11; crime reduction and, 83, *84*; eugenic feminism and, 56–62; Mexican feminists and, 203; Mothers' Health Center and, 79; population quality and, 45–46; racism and, 10–11; stratified reproduction and, 57; women leaders of, 4–5. *See also* eugenics

reproductive justice (RJ), 16–18, 20, 93–94, 99, 160–62, 237–38, 241–42; Native women and, 161; in Texas, 243

research sources, 18–19, 238–39

R. E. Thomason (hospital), 159, 164, 172–73, 175–76

Riley, H. John, 224

Ripley, Katie, 62–63, 66

Road to Survival (Vogt), 125

Roberts, Elizabeth, 230

Robledo, Irene, 154–55

Rock, John, 135, 137

Rodriguez, Maria de los Angeles, 229

Rodríguez-Muñiz, Michael, 29

Roe v. Wade, 213–16, 242, 251n1

Rogers, Will, 53

Rosales, Ismael, 164

Rosales, Leticia, 164

Rosales, Orlando, 164

Rose Gregory Houchen House, 55–56

Rosenfield, Allan, *197*

Ross, Edward Alsworth, 27

Ross, Loretta, 17, 153, 168, 238

Roth, Benita, 260n31

Rowland, Thaddeus William, Jr., 220, *221–22*, 223

Ruiz, Vicki, 18, 40, 56, 105, 127–28, 131, 228–29, 240, 245

Russia, 35

Saleeby, Caleb, 202–3

Salmon, Evangelina Martinez, 216–17, 229

Sánchez, George J., 104

Sandoval, Chela, 96–98, 128, 240, 268n34

Sanger, Margaret: California population control measures and, 64; Catholic Church and, 7, 53–54, 72–78; Comstock Act and, 60; eugenic feminism and, 56–62; first exchange with Goetting and, 60; Gamble and, 63; impetus for activism of, 208; IPPF and, 126; "La Brújula del Hogar" (pamphlet), 202–3; Mothers' Health Center and, 6; photo of, *86*; population control ideology and, 51–52, 124; PPFA's condemnation of, 243–44;

of cultural capital, 224; connection to Goetting, 199; establishment of FEMAP, 200–201; family lineage of, 209; family planning and overpopulation, 198–99; field workers and, 217; first clinic opened by, 215–16; IFRP and, 225; labor and, 9, 210–12; photo of, *197*, 218; population control and, 207–9, 231–32; PPEP and, 212, 215–16; presentation to Southern California Population Crisis Committee, 196–97, 226, 228; race and, 24; reproductive health care and, 4–5; rise of, 8; transnational capital and, 16

Vega Mathews, Federico de la, 200, 208, 223

Velarde, Al, 184

Vidal, Mirta, 160

Vivavaidya, Mechai, *197*

Vogt, William, 124–27, 156

Walker, Francis Amasa, 38

Watts Rebellion, 164

Weddington, Sarah Ragle, 213

Weinbaum, Alys Eve, 95

White, Frank T., 35–36

white supremacy: Babbitt and, 25–27; demographobia and, 29–30; family planning movements and, 5; fertility rates and, 27; immigration and, 27–28, 42; maternalism and, 55–56; population control ideology and, 13; reproductive care and, 95; segregationist strategies in United States, 32–33; violence and, 38–39; white birth rates and, 48, 207

white women: archives and, 239; birth control activism and, 48–49, 87–88; eugenic feminism and, 56–62; maternalism and, 54–56; opposition to birth control movement, 50; as patients of Planned Parenthood of El Paso (PPEP), 134; reproductive fragility of, 132. *See also* birth control advocates

Winant, Howard, 11

World Population Crisis: The United States Response (Piotrow), 214

World Population Emergency Campaign (WPEC), 169

Wright, Melissa, 231

Wright, Harold H., 82

Young Women's Christian Association (YWCA), 78–79

Zavella, Patricia, 238

Zavella, Rosie, 268n16